Eventful Archaeologies

THE INSTITUTE FOR EUROPEAN AND MEDITERRANEAN ARCHAEOLOGY
DISTINGUISHED MONOGRAPH SERIES

Peter F. Biehl, Sarunas Milisauskas, and Stephen L. Dyson, editors

The Magdalenian Household: Unraveling Domesticity
Ezra Zubrow, Françoise Audouze, and James Enloe, editors

Eventful Archaeologies: New Approaches to Social Transformation in the Archaeological Record
Douglas J. Bolender, editor

EVENTFUL ARCHAEOLOGIES:

New Approaches to Social Transformation in the Archaeological Record

IEMA PROCEEDINGS, VOLUME 1

EDITED BY

Douglas J. Bolender

STATE UNIVERSITY OF
NEW YORK PRESS

Logo and cover/interior art credit: A vessel with wagon motifs from Bronocice Poland, 3400 BC. Courtesy of Sarunas Milisauskas and Janusz Kruk, 1982, Die Wagendarstellung auf einem Trichterbecher aus Bronocice, Polen, *Archäologisches Korrespondenzblatt* 12:141–144.

Published by
State University of New York Press, Albany

For information, contact
State University of New York Press, Albany, NY
www.sunypress.edu

Production, Eileen Meehan
Marketing, Michael Campochiaro

Library of Congress Cataloging-in-Publication Data

Eventful archaeologies : new approaches to social transformation in the archaeological record / Douglas J. Bolender, [editor].
      p. cm.—(The Institute for European and Mediterranean Archaeology
                  Distinguished Monograph Series)
      Includes bibliographical references and index.
      ISBN 978-1-4384-3423-0 (hardcover : alk. paper)
      ISBN 978-1-4384-3422-3 (pbk. : alk. paper)
            1. Social archaeology.
            2. Ethnoarchaeology.
            I. Bolender, Douglas J.
            CC72.4E86   2010
            930.1—dc22

                        2010005362

            10 9 8 7 6 5 4 3 2 1

This volume is dedicated to the memory of Samuel B. Paley, fine scholar and colleague, whose vision of intersecting and interacting worlds of archaeology helped lay the foundations for the Institute for European and Mediterranean Archaeology.

Contents

Preface   IX

Introduction   *Douglas J. Bolender*
Toward an Eventful Archaeology   3

Part I
Eventful Prehistories

Chapter One   *Ezra B. W. Zubrow*
Cascading Prehistoric Events: Fractalizing Prehistoric Research   17

Chapter Two   *Françoise Audouze and Boris Valentin*
A Paleohistorical Approach to Upper Paleolithic Structural Changes 29

Chapter Three   *Dušan Borić*
Becoming, Phenomenal Change, Event: Past and
Archaeological Re-presentations   48

Chapter Four   *Alasdair Whittle, Alex Bayliss, and Frances Healy*
Event and Short-Term Process: Times for the Early Neolithic of
Southern Britain   68

CHAPTER FIVE   *Pedro Díaz-del-Río*

The Neolithic Argonauts of the Western Mediterranean and
Other Underdetermined Hypotheses of Colonial Encounters   88

CHAPTER SIX   *Bettina Arnold*

Eventful Archaeology, the Heuneburg Mudbrick Wall,
and the Early Iron Age of Southwest Germany   100

PART II
EVENTFUL HISTORIES AND BEYOND

CHAPTER SEVEN   *John Bintliff*

The Annales, Events, and the Fate of Cities   117

CHAPTER EIGHT   *Timothy Taylor*

Modeling the "Amazon" Phenomenon: Colonization
Events and Gender Performances   132

CHAPTER NINE   *Louise Revell*

The Allure of the Event in Roman Provincial Archaeology   151

CHAPTER TEN   *Penelope M. Allison*

The AD 79 Eruption of Mt. Vesuvius: A Significant or Insignificant Event?   166

CHAPTER ELEVEN   *John P. Grattan*

Testing Eventful Archaeologies: Eventful Archaeology and
Volcanic "Disasters"   179

CHAPTER TWELVE   *Oscar Aldred and Gavin Lucas*

Events, Temporalities, and Landscapes in Iceland   189

CHAPTER THIRTEEN   *Christopher N. Matthews*

Freedom as a Negotiated History, or an Alternative Sort of Event:
The Transformation of Home, Work, and Self in Early New York   199

EPILOGUE

CHAPTER FOURTEEN   *Graeme Barker*

Archaeology and the Human Career: Revolutions, Transformations, Events   219

INDEX   237

Preface

Toward an Eventful Archaeology

At first glance Pompeii and Iceland would seem to be worlds apart. On the one side are the sunny shores of the Bay of Naples. On the other, one encounters settlements in the cold, rainy north. One lies at the center of what is regarded as 'Western Civilization', the other at its outer margins. However, the archaeological worlds of the two widely separated cultures have important points in common. They represent two of the epochal peoples in the Western narrative, the Vikings and the Romans. Both are places, where volcanoes have made decisive interventions in historical times. Finally, they are part of exploring cultures, where written texts are abundant and cannot help to shape the narrative, no matter how much the archaeologist may try to escape that reality.

It can be argued that historians of the written word create 'events' in history out of a confusing mass of inscribed textual material. Readers accept those 'events' or else create different 'events' as they peruse the written page. The initial archaeological investigator creates a material text and material events through field research and through the presentation of the results of field research. Both historians and archaeologists are 'authors' dealing with material produced by human beings. Both create 'events' that are often more significant to them than to the people who experienced them.

As the first *IEMA* conference and its proceedings clearly show, a key dilemma arises immediately because the contemporary archaeologist and especially those of anthropological orientation want to see themselves more as social scientists than as humanists. Patterns and processes, if not laws, are what they seek, and events become secondary, even distracting. The more abstract, the more scientific the discourse sounds.

This book offers a fresh consideration of 'events' and archaeology, and we would argue that the interpretative landscape needs to have a too strong emphasis on 'process' modified by a greater concern for the specific and the contingent. The world of the 'post-depositional' that behavioral archaeologists talked about years ago is central to archaeological thinking, but it is more the 'destroyer' than the 'creator' of events in the archaeological record. Human action is always played out against a background of natural processes, which only rarely, as in the case of the eruption of Vesuvius in AD 79, can be described as 'events'. The behavior of human beings is obviously shaped by the complex of encoded processes that in the past anthropologists called 'culture'. These ethnographers recreated such patterns through field observation. The archaeologist must recreate them through the careful and systematic reading shaped by social science models, but also conscious of defining episodes, or what is here designated as 'events'. Scholars can define events in a variety of ways as we can see in this book. Social science oriented archaeologists feel nervous with the contingency implied in the 'event', but the spectacular 'event' in the past sustains an expensive, if esoteric professional world. Archaeologists may feel somewhat ambivalent about the event filled world of the burial, but the public loves it. Bloody events were presumably behind the abandonment of a villa treasure. We archaeologists want to look at the end of Roman Britain as a process. Public imagination is sustained by gold and silver.

Events not only bring together a whole range of cultural process and material goods in limited moments in time, but they remind us of punctuality and contingency in history. Moreover, they are everywhere, shaping the archaeological record, but also the archaeologists themselves, and the traditions in which she/he works.

The issues raised by this conference and its papers are important. The social science consensus in many archaeological subfields is breaking down. One does not want a future dominated by the often sterile particularism, so often characteristic of anthropological as well as classical archaeology or the abstract theoretical chatter of so much of the post-modern intellectual world. Archaeology at the core is about the real and the particular, and the event, as manifested in the material remains, is an important reality focus.

***

THE IEMA DISTINGUISHED MONOGRAPH SERIES

This book is the first volume of the newly founded *Distinguished Monographs Series* of the Institute for European and Mediterranean Archaeology (IEMA) at the University at Buffalo, State University of New York. The Institute was founded in 2007 with the support of the College of Arts and Sciences as part of its UB2020 strategic strength 'Culture and Text'. We thank the Dean of the College of Arts Sciences, Bruce McCombe, for his continuing support and vision, and acknowledge all the time and energy the first *IEMA* director J. Theodore Peña and the *IEMA* governing board members Bradley Ault, Tina Thurston, Samuel Paley, Vance Watrous and Ezra Zubrow have invested to get the institute off the ground. The new *IEMA Distinguished Monographs Series* is published by SUNY Press and we thank its executive director Gary Dunham for his tremendous support in getting the series started. We are also grateful to the SUNY Press editorial team, especially to Amanda Lanne, and Eileen Meehan for the design of the logo of the distinguished monograph series and the design, production and printing of the book. Presently, the publication series consists of the proceedings of our yearly postdoctoral conference on Theories and Methods in European and Mediterranean Archaeology and a separate monographs series for synthetic works that have a topical focus and include archaeological data description and interpretation. All books in our series will be peer-reviewed and are available via our publisher SUNY Press (www.sunypress.com).

And special thanks are owed to our first *IEMA* postdoctoral scholar Douglas Bolender for organizing the conference and editing the first volume of the series. We also thank Graeme Barker of the University of Cambridge for his inaugural lecture for the opening of our institute and for contributing his seminal lecture to this volume. We would also express our deep gratitude to our colleagues and the department of anthropology and classics and visual studies for their support and encouragement. And finally, we want to acknowledge the work of our graduate students of the University at Buffalo. They animate the institute with their new and original ideas in European and Mediterranean Archaeology.

Peter F. Biehl, Sarunas Milisauskas,
and Stephen L. Dyson
IEMA Publication Series Editors

Introduction

Toward an Eventful Archaeology

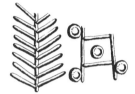

Douglas J. Bolender

Throughout the twentieth century, archaeology has had an uneasy relationship with history. These divisions have been particularly salient in the United States where history has been allied with the humanities, archaeology with the social sciences. At times, archaeologists have explicitly rejected a role for history within the social sciences (e.g., Binford 1962). The result has been a methodological and theoretical divide between historical and prehistoric archaeologies and the restriction of historical archaeology as a temporally and regionally specific subdiscipline (Paynter 2000). European archaeology has enjoyed a closer relationship with history but historical archaeologies—such as medieval, modern, and classical—often form their own distinct studies, separate from one another and the broad sweep of European prehistory. In both the United States and Europe, historical archaeologies often have been subordinated to research agendas dictated by history (Champion 1990).

Attempts to place historical and archaeological methods and sources on an equal footing have often looked to the *Annales* historians for inspiration. Fernand Braudel (1995) explicitly linked the program of *Annales* historians with the social sciences and Lévi-Strauss's (2000) structural anthropology. Archaeologists have found common ground in the *Annales* emphasis on long-term processes, everyday life, and material culture (Bintliff 1991; Hodder 1987; Knapp 1992; Thurston 1997). Traditionally, *Annales* historians have viewed the temporality of the event with suspicion and as an unreliable basis for a grounded social history and associated it with nineteenth-century political history and the arbitrariness of narrative form (cf. White 1973, 1987). This discomfort with the potentially accidental basis of the event, its historical contingency, and to some degree the role of personal agency in shaping society, has been largely echoed throughout the archaeological literature. With the rise of postprocessual perspectives, archaeologists have more openly embraced questions of agency, locality, and relativistic cultural trajectories. Nonetheless, the social significance of the event—and the connection between agency and historical process—remains largely undeveloped territory within archaeology.

Recently, in Beck et al. (2007), we suggested the eventful sociology proposed by William Sewell (2005) as a framework for archaeological analysis. Sewell brings two important formulations to the notion of the event: first, a specific construction of social structure that gives material evidence an equal footing with ideas; and second, identification of the event with episodes that result in a significant reordering of social structures. It is Sewell's grounding of social structures and social transformation in the material that makes it amenable to the architectural record.

Sewell positions the concept of social structure at the core his theory of the event. Sewell's perspective can be traced to Anthony Giddens's (1979, 1984) theory of structuration and his emphasis on the dual and processual nature of social structure. This duality in structure is recursively constituted through rules and resources. For Giddens, resources do not denote actual things or people, but instead the capacity to command real things and people. Thus, structure is comprised of virtual rules and resources that are enacted in social practice and has no enduring material aspect. Instead, it derives its continuity through the operation of memory and knowledge (Giddens 1984:377). Sewell believes that this conception of social structure is problematic: If rules and resources are both virtual, how can structures be simultaneously constituted of rules and resources? And what distinguishes one from the other? Instead, Sewell reformulates Giddens's duality of structure as interplay between mental schemas and material resources. Sewell's schemas, like Giddens's rules, are virtual and can be applied in a broad range of situations. However, resources are actual and, in any instance of social action, are fixed to specificities of time and place (Sewell 2005:133). Sewell retains the recursive quality of Giddens's theory of structuration suggesting that it is the mutual implication of virtual schemas and actual resources that constitute social structures. Structures are as much a product of social practice as they are things that define practices.

Sewell considers five qualities of social structures that inevitably lead to structural change: (1) structures are multiple and (2) intersecting; (3) schemas are transposable; and (4) resources carry multiple social meanings, and (5) are unpredictable (Sewell 2005:140–143). At any given moment, social agents enact a multiplicity of structures and these structures intersect and overlap. In fact, it is the materiality of resources which provide much of the continuity to social practice. However, the intersection of structures implies that a specific resource may be socially constituted through multiple schemas or different social agents depending on the structures that he or she enacts in a particular context. While the viability of particular structures is limited by the ability of agents to reliably enact them, the multiplicity of potential structures resists the stasis of social institutions associated with structuralist approaches. This multiplicity of structures is juxtaposed with the unpredictability of the material world: a bad harvest, a late spring, an odds-defying victory at war, an epidemic, or a dynastic line that fails to produce an heir.

It is within this formulation of social structure that Sewell situates the event. Following the lead of Marshall Sahlins (e.g., 1981, 1985, 1991, 1995), he distinguishes the event as "sequences of occurrences that result in transformations of structures" (Sewell 2005:227) from happenings, which simply reproduce existing social structures without significant change. For a sequence of occurrences to take on the significance of an event it must cascade across multiple structural domains and result in durable ruptures between resources and schemas that threaten the integrity of the structural network; for example, the difference between a worker calling in sick and a sustained strike or a single bad harvest versus a multiyear drought. Structural disjunctions occur when the schemas once used to mobilize an array of resources lose their capacity to reliably order the world. The social disarray engendered during episodes of disjunction cannot be tolerated for significant periods of time and the failure of previously reliable structures opens the opportunity for novel articulations of schemas and resources that may not have been possible in the previous order.

Thus, Sewell's social event occurs in three stages: (1) a series of context-dependent occurrences produce (2) a cascade of disarticulations between previously reliable resources and schemas, finally resulting in (3) the opportunity—and necessity—for novel rearticulations of social structure. While structural disjunction sets the stage for novel practices, the event itself is bound to those innovations that effectively resolve the discontinuities between schemas and resources. The success of these specific cultural innovations is indicated in their replication and institutionalization in social practice. It is this aspect of Sewell's event that most distinguishes it from the capricious event of traditional history and establishes it within the framework of the social sciences. Events are historically contingent and produce novelty but in their resolution they are constrained by the social efficacy of the rearticulations they produce. This emphasis on the transformative significance of the event is not a rejection of the traditional *Annales* attention to the *longue durée*. The slow accumulation of innovation and change inherent in the multiplicity of structures potentially enacted in any given circumstance can stress the articulations of schemas and resources and set the stage of an event. According to Sewell, it is in these eventful ruptures that those discontinuities are manifest and subject to reformulation. The event becomes the mechanism for structural change. Are historical transformations always eventful? Sewell seems to suggest that they are. Changes in practices accumulate, stressing existing structural patterns, but the structures themselves endure until they are transformed through the process of rupture and rearticulation. The relationship between specific events and other temporalities of change are an open, and empirical, question. Using Sewell's scheme, all social transformations are eventful—as defined by a transformation of structural relationships between material resources and organizing schema—but these eventful transformations may not always occur within the temporally restrictive cascade of ruptures that constitute a particular historical event. These accumulated changes may have implications for the next big rupture but retain a social reality beyond that event and may not be simply latent potentials waiting the next event to come along.

It is Sewell's emphasis on the materiality of resources, and their recursive constitution of structure in conjunction with schemas, that opens his eventful history to archaeological interrogation. The disjunction and rearticulation of structures through the course of an event imply novel constellations of resources—the kind of patterned shifts that should be visible in the archaeological record as material resources take on new meanings or positions in structural rearticulation. Sewell's eventful perspective provides a historical approach to social transformation that allows archaeologists to work independently or in complement to historical sources and sets the archaeological record on an equal footing with history.

Why Sewell, events, and archaeology? I think the answer to this is remarkably simple. First, if we take the idea of the event seriously—and I think we must if we take the idea of agency seriously—then events are an inevitable and necessary aspect of social reproduction and transformation. Simply put, they are part of the archaeological record we are attempting to understand. Sewell lays out a conception of the event that potentially is amenable to an archaeological or material context and presents a fairly comprehensive program of the event and its relation to historical process. And, most importantly, I think it is possible, using his framework, to avoid limiting an eventful analysis to moments of historically recorded events. Many of the contributors to this volume look beyond Sewell and develop other, and important, ways of thinking about social and transformative events in the archaeological record.

HISTORICAL EVENTS VERSUS EVENTFUL ARCHAEOLOGY

While Sewell's approach was developed explicitly to address the stochastic and temporally short unfolding of historical events, this volume distinguishes between an archaeology of events—the specific transformative historical moments—and an eventful approach to the archaeological record. Sewell (2005:124) points to this distinction in his own discussion of structure as a noun that always implies the transitive verb of structuring. Something structures something else, therefore structures are inherently relational. I would suggest a similar difference between the event and an eventful analysis. Events always occur in the past tense and are an artifact of a historical analysis; we draw the boundaries of what constitutes an event versus what does not (this is not to say that the distinction is unreal or arbitrary). Alternatively, an eventful perspective is primarily concerned with the dynamics of social reproduction and change rather than the identification of transformative events in the archaeological record.

The spatial scale, temporality, and durability of an event are determined by our analytical scope. Marriages, births, and deaths are all eventful occurrences for individuals (by Sewell's standards as moments that entail significant rearrangements of schemas/resources). From the perspective of affected individuals, households, or other localized social institutions these occurrences may indeed be events resulting in fundamental reorganizations of social practices and experience. From a broader perspective these occurrences may simply represent the temporal expression of highly durable social structures and practices: individual transformations that reproduce enduring social patterns. Sewell reserves the term *event* for major structural transformations but this is an arbitrary distinction, one based in the "whole society" as the historical subject. Sewell's distinction, arbitrary as it may be, has the value of not overly diluting the significance of a social event but there is no reason that an eventful perspective cannot be extended to these localized transformations.

I think that we must understand these ongoing processes of social reproduction as eventful in order to fully grasp the nature of the significant alterations in these practices that constitute an "event." This is especially important in the archaeological context where we often extrapolate from a relatively small number of examples to society in general. It is important that we do not contrast the event with stasis but rather see an event as a meaningfully bounded temporal and spatial alteration in social practices. This difference between the event and the eventful is aptly described by de Certeau in his description of the rupture between the historian in the archive and the historian as contemporary agent:

> [F]or the moment they detach themselves from the monumental studies that will place them among their peers, and walking out into the street, they ask, "What in God's name is this business? What about the bizarre relation I am keeping with current society and, through the intermediary of my technical activities, with death?" (Certeau 1988:56)

De Certeau illustrates a fundamental schism that separates the historian and the historical operation from the reality of social process; the problem of historical retrospection. There is another aspect of de Certeau's historiography that I find useful in conceptualizing an eventful archaeology. He suggests that the process of history is best revealed at the boundaries, the edges of social practice, where we see rupture, lack of continuity, contradiction, and rebellion. This strategy also is found in many of Foucault's (e.g., 1973, 1994, 1995) works in which he situates his historical analyses on the social peripheries where the masks of ideological conformity break down and that which is assumed and naturalized is exposed as constructed and political. These are the places where we can see beyond the façade of monolithic social structure and into the inner workings of structures and practices that do not always conform to those broader outlines. Can we take this idea of social process exposed in the boundaries and apply it to the historical event?

The event represents the social boundary *par excellence*, one that is generalizable to any circumstance, because change always exposes the failure of a strict social reproduction. This is the most basic social boundary, and in creating a rupture in society not only does it change society but it always leaves a hole in history where we, too, can peer in and see the workings beneath the naturalized appearance of social process; to understand social change we must be able to see the diversity of practices, the lack of conformity, that characterize the complexity of real life and historical process.

Another concern is the arbitrary (or totalizing) designation of an eventful episode—that we characterize an entire historical moment as being eventful or (by default) not. We create, and rift from context, the temporal and social boundaries that fall within its purview. As with any subject that we isolate from context, we must take care to define and delimit not just what is included within the eventful umbrella but also what is left out, and ideally, point to the connections and relationships between the two. This was a part—often neglected—of the *Annaliste* project: the integration of temporalities. But temporalities cannot be integrated in or of themselves; they must be populated with people and occurrences.

As Bintliff notes (this volume) one of the principal strengths of the *Annales* approach is that it does not predetermine the relevant temporality for any particular historical analysis. While an eventful perspective resists the tendency to divide time into discrete blocks or periods there is a risk in beginning an analysis with a particular event, especially in the archaeological record where the identification of a transformative event is more likely to be one of the products of interpretation than the beginning point. Beginning with events in the archaeological record leads to the unavoidable problem of predetermining the field of analysis—and the possible chasing of chimera (Grattan this volume). At any rate, the cataloguing of historical events is a hollow exercise as an end in or of itself.

An eventful analysis must deal with other temporalities as sudden or radical social transformations can only be identified and understood within the broader context of social trajectories and continuities. So, while an event may characterize a particular temporality of social change, an eventful analysis must comprise multiple temporal scales. Social transformations are never monolithic, excepting the exceedingly rare circumstances in which particular cultures disappear, utterly collapse, or are somehow completely subsumed within other social traditions. In almost all cases of eventful change only some subset of social practices and institutions (*structures*) will completely disappear, only some truly novel structures will appear. The effects of structural rupture and novel rearticulation may certainly cascade through many social domains and practices coloring structures with the affects of the event but these kinds of changes may be part of other temporalities and modes of social transformation as well. To identify and understand eventful transformations one must also identify and understand continuities. As Revell points out (this volume), "[T]he challenge then becomes that rather than a return to single narrative of events with uniform outcomes, we need to allow for a more complex interweaving of event and change." This includes recognition that the salience of past events is determined in large part by our analytical and interpretative focus. Particular moments in history may be more or less eventful depending on our emphasis on, for example, political, religious, or gender-oriented analyses and narratives.

The tendency to separate history into events and process is perhaps misplaced, as we always draw the temporal and social subjective boundaries of the event in an arbitrary manner—one aspect of society may indeed experience ruptures that constitute an eventful episode but this does not mean that all of society is eventful in that moment. While at first glance this appears to undermine the significance of the event and an eventful perspective I believe that this actually strengthens it: the whole point of the event is to separate analytically the concatenation of changing structures from a singular social structure or historical subject, both synchronically and diachronically.

AN EVENTFUL ANALYSIS AS A RELATIONAL ANALYSIS

The temporal resolution of the event creates an inherent problem in archaeological contexts. While the archaeological record is ripe with the occurrences of a day or an isolated moment it is nearly impossible, in any archaeological context, historical or prehistorical, to order these occurrences into the sequential resolution that Sewell (1996) employs in his analysis of the taking of the Bastille or the events that Sahlins (1981) describes around Captain Cook's transformation in the Hawai'ian islands. The question of the temporal resolution of the event is a very real one in the archaeological record. Whittle et al. (this volume) explore the potential of advances in radiocarbon databases and statistical processing to narrow archaeological time frames, but we are still a long way from the short-term temporalities of the traditional historical event.

Archaeology is unlikely to ever attain the temporal resolution required to expose the unfolding sequences of actions that make up an event. This is implicit in the nature of events; by definition, ruptures in the articulation between resource and schema do not result in enduring material residues, although the disruptions themselves may be evident. In this sense, an eventful archaeology will never be an archaeology of the inside of events themselves. Instead events are visible in the transformations they produce, the transition from one set of practices, and concordant material residues, and another. Instead an eventful perspective resituates the problem of temporal resolution as a question of identifying structural relationships and their transformation. Massive social transformations may be evident without a detailed analysis of existing social relationships before and after an event. The introduction of new social structures is probably a good example of these kinds of social transformations, for example, the first appearance of state institutions or religious conversions. In these cases novelty may serve as sufficient to mark change but in many cases events will not involve the introduction of entirely new social practices or institutions but rather transformations of existing relationships. A successful eventful archaeology must employ a large number of cultural domains of activity and practices in the archaeological record and understand their changing articulations.

As many contributors to this volume note, an eventful approach requires that we are as sensitive to what does not change as what does. Events can only be understood in the context of continuities. Likewise, Matthews (this volume) draws our attention to the inverse of events, "non-events," in which structure overwhelms agency in contexts where change is evident in the historical record or even in the experience of people and yet this apparent change, or radical rupture, masks underlying continuities. These "non-events" may still be highly eventful in the sense that new schemas may be introduced—in Matthew's example the notion of "freedom" and its connection to new notions of individuality, respectability, and the organization of labor relations—while perpetuating fundamental inequalities within society. In other words, instances in which structural innovations produce and reinforce social continuities.

The Temporality of the Event from a Material Perspective

Sewell provides a framework for archaeologists to enter the event as a material process. He is not the first to emphasize the role of the material in creating and stabilizing the social (e.g., Bourdieu 1977; Gieryn 2000, 2002; Lefebvre 1991; Soja 1989). Archaeology has always had a prominent place for space as a constitutive force in the social—the prominence of sites, monumentality, settlement pattern analysis, catchment analysis, phenomenological approaches, labor, etc.—if at times an underdeveloped analysis of how exactly these spatial and material practices constitute the social. Addressing the materiality of social events has implications for the temporality of events.

There is a tendency found in Giddens, Sahlins, and, despite his explicitly material conception of social structure, Sewell to reduce the material to the product of the mental. The material and spatial often are portrayed as the backdrop upon which the actions of historical agency unfolds instead of as a fully constitutive aspect of social production and reproduction and therefore of history itself. Giddens does stress a regionalism to social structure and practice but this largely replicates formal processual conceptions of space and time as abstract axes upon which social phenomena (material and virtual) are mapped and clustered (categorized in temporal-spatial assemblages) (Giddens 1984). Materiality is not merely the form of an object or idea, it is constitutive of it. This is a serious problem for any archaeologically or materially oriented analysis of history and leads to the question of what a material or archaeological perspective on the event really looks like.

Following Soja (1989) and others, an eventful perspective can forefront the degree to which the material constrains the virtual. The fixed spatial and temporal materiality of objects, social agents, and social interaction (*place*) in fact provides both context and constraints on social practice and transformation without relying on notions of superstructure (ideology) or an overly cognitive notion of culture to maintain social structures and practices. The spatial-material context of social practice greatly reduces the range of practical options for social agents. Aldred and Lucas (this volume) in their analysis of medieval Icelandic landscapes call attention to this continued material resilience of past practices, and their role in shaping future practices.

Shifting the focus from the material forming the background for eventful action to the material constituting eventful action has significant implications for the temporality of events themselves. If we take the materiality of eventful transformations seriously we must also question the designation of these narrow temporal periods with the domain of the event. In his analysis of the taking of the Bastille, Sewell (1996) implies a number of structural ruptures and rearticulations of schema and resource that occur in the short days spanning the period between the outbreak of violence and its political resolution. To what degree are these new relations of ideas and things real at the end of this sequence of events?

The reshuffling of ideas is fluid and rapid but they can just as rapidly fall apart. The fragile political resolution of the Bastille could easily have been reversed or repressed in coming weeks or years demoting the significance of that event in historical memory and consequence. To the degree that an event results in a transformation of structures it must be realized in new patterns of practice (new structures, including the material aspects of these structures) and not simply in the implication of these structures. One of the benefits of Sewell's conception of a dual virtual-actual social structure is that it relieves memory and habit from shouldering the burden of cultural reproduction through a shared reliance on the spatial and material. The transformation of structures becomes real as it results in new articulations of material and spatial practice, not simply new ways of thinking. One consequence for the event is that while the ruptures and rearticulations that characterize an event may occur over a relatively short time period (traditional *Annales l'histoire événementielle*) they are not actual until these new ideas have become manifest in social practice, including the creation and allocation of existing or new actual resources. New ways of doing things require time and space to come into being. The consequences of new potential structures become more real as they permeate the world and more and more aspects of social production become tied to them.

Gavin Lucas (2008) has recently highlighted the issue of the reversibility of an archaeological event as a significant quality affecting its representation in the archaeological record. With some caveats, I think that we can provisionally apply this test to the significance of events in history. Those that result in embedded structures are less reversible. In other words, events are transformative only to the extent that they result in real changes in structured practice. The rupture, as Sewell says, is a moment of potential but it is not the change. The change is found in the practices that replace previous structures and that follow the event itself. From a material perspective this results in an inevitable blurring of the short-term with processes taking place over a longer time scale (in *Annales* terms, still much shorter than *la longue durée*: a conflation of *l'histoire événementielle* and *la moyenne durée*). The upshot of this blurring is that when we think about an event as including the actual practice of new social structures in time and space the gap between the temporality of the event and that of the archaeological record may not be quite so insurmountable.

ALTERNATIVE HISTORIES

An eventful archaeology has the potential to open alternative perspectives on what constitute transformative events. When we take on a concept such as the event that is grounded in historical scholarship we run the inevitable risk of conceptualizing events based on the textually based priorities of traditional history and social analysis. An eventful archaeology should not be a watered-down version of traditional history.

Contributions to this volume explore the possibility of an eventful approach to deep historical time periods, those without textual sources and in time periods with limited chronological resolution (see Audouze and Valentin, Diaz-del-Rio, Boric, Whittle, Bayliss, and Healy, and Arnold). These contexts present very real hurdles for eventful approaches. At the same time the use of historical texts creates its own problems. The potential of historical texts to reveal actor's motivations and a high degree of temporal resolution in the unfolding of events and social process in general can easily result in the privileging of the mental over the material (the role of schema over resource, in Sewell's terminology).

There are two principal ways in which an eventful archaeology can challenge the priorities of textually based history and social sciences. One is simply to challenge the salience of certain events in historical narratives. The second is to challenge priorities of historical process that are rooted in contemporary social theory that rarely give equal weight to the material aspects of social life. In the broadest sense, an eventful archaeology has the potential to challenge a social and historical theoretical perspective based in the modern, Western nation-state.

Historical narratives, especially those of "historical events" can also obscure the eventfulness of the past. The allure of the event, in Revell's turn of phrase, goes beyond the problem of historical representation to include biases in analysis. In this sense, an eventful archaeology can challenge event-oriented historical narratives. Revell (this volume) questions the importance of Roman narratives about the provinces to actual provincial social practice and events. This extends to our interpretation of archaeological contexts in historically known cultures in the absence of specific historical narratives. Ancient historical sources are far from complete and it is easy to interpolate from limited and one-sided histories and make connections between purported historical circumstances or events and social transformations. These far from complete accounts can draw us into making associations with what ancient historians found salient or worth recording and reinforce a tendency to place historically narrated events in the forefront of our own historical imaginations. Alternatively, Taylor's discussion (this volume) of Amazons reveals how the appearance of timelessness in historical narrative subverts the eventfulness of the Amazonian phenomenon.

Allison (this volume) explores perhaps the most iconic of archaeological events, the destruction of Pompeii and Herculaneum by the eruption of Mt. Vesuvius in AD 79. She contends that the dramatic nature of their destruction and preservation has tended to obscure the contingent, particular, and eventful histories of these places as they have instead been reconstructed as generic examples of "Roman life." Does the archaeological focus on the moment of Pompeii's destruction, so catastrophically eventful for the residents of the lost cities, mask the continuities in the broader region? Similarly, Grattan (this volume) focuses attention on the spurious association between natural disasters, catastrophes, and social transformation. While we should not ignore the potential impacts of environmental change—especially in our contemporary world—or natural disaster as a social stress or catalyst for change—events should not be reduced to the environment or external forces. Grattan rightly cautions against looking to the environmental record for correlations with social phenomena as a source of explanation or causality.

THE QUESTION OF DIFFERING HISTORICAL TEMPORALITIES THROUGHOUT HUMAN HISTORY

Many modern scholars have suggested that there is something unique in the modern world that makes it different from past or contemporary non-Western societies. At the heart of this difference is some specific Western social institution (e.g., capitalism, world systems, the nation-state) which is seen as so deeply ingrained throughout the spectrum of social struc-tures that it alters the way that modern society functions in ways that make it incomparable to other societies (e.g., Giddens 1984; Polanyi 1957; Wallerstein 1974). This notion of a uniquely modern social world and historical operation is found in many of the nineteenth-century social histories that lay at the foundation of twentieth-century sociology and social history. To what degree are these sentiments empirical (all of these scholars rather explicitly deny any real knowledge of the premodern world, so upon what comparative basis do they make this claim)?

For Marx and Engels (1998), the capitalist world is not just different in terms of structures but in terms of historical operation: change is necessary, constant, and faster than in other social modes. It is a less certain world of constant disruption, of structural instability (here to support the underlying superstructure of capitalism—although in their teleology capitalism is ultimately unstable as well). States may even orchestrate disruptive events to advance political or economic agendas (Klein 2007).

The state and the bureaucratic technologies of centralization, integration, and com-munication that extend the spatial (and therefore societal) reach of events have implications for an archaeology of the event in premodern (or non-state) settings. Events are situated in space and inherently have sites of localized action. The degree and extent to which these localized occurrences impact social structures has a great deal to do with social integra-tion. The state—or any politically integrative institution—has the capacity to translate local occurrences into social events that have effects far beyond the locality in which they unfold.

How should we expect events to be different in terms of scale, temporality, and types of social structures affected? I see little reason why pre-state societies should not be eventful or have events but we should be sensitive to potential differences in the operation of historical events in different social settings. The modern world is a highly integrated world with a multiplicity of structures and dependencies entangling every aspect of human life across the globe. Does this really change the mode and temporality of historical process—not just the structures and societies that constitute a moment in history, but the operation of history itself?

If we push an eventful perspective back far enough into human history we raise the question of when history becomes eventful. Or really when and what is the origin of human history? Audouze and Valentin (this volume) do exactly that in asking if it is possible to do an eventful archaeology of the Upper Paleolithic and if so, what would it look like? In this, they see a prominent place for the environment as a link between localized and weakly integrated groups. This draws attention to the connection between microhistory and event. An eventful perspective has inherent similarities to microhistory (Boric this volume) but where microhistory may be representative of broader historical trends, the event is seen as playing a transformative role in history.

References

Beck Jr., R. A., D. J. Bolender, J. A. Brown, and T. K. Earle 2007 Eventful Archaeology: The Place of Space in Structural Transformation. *Current Anthropology* 48(6):833–860.

Binford, L. 1962 Archaeology as Anthropology. *American Antiquity* 28:217–215.

Bintliff, J. (editor) 1991 *The Annales School and Archaeology*. Leicester University Press, Leicester.

Bourdieu, P. 1977 *Outline of a Theory of Practice*. Cambridge Studies in Social Anthropology; 16. Cambridge University Press, Cambridge; New York.

Braudel, F. 1995 History and the Social Sciences: The Longue Durée. In *Histories: French Constructions of the Past*, edited by Jacques Revel and Lynn Hunt, pp. 115–145. Translated by Sarah Matthews. The New Press Postwar French Thought Series, Ramona Naddaff, general editor. The New Press, New York.

Certeau, M. 1988 *The Writing of History*. European Perspectives. Columbia University Press, New York.

Champion, T. C. 1990 Medieval Archaeology and the Tyranny of the Historical Record. In *From the Baltic to the Black Sea, Studies in Medieval Archaeology*, edited by David Austin and Leslie Alcock, pp. 79–95. Unwin Hyman, London.

Foucault, M. 1973 *Madness and Civilization: A History of Insanity in the Age of Reason*. Vintage Books, New York.

Foucault, M. 1994 *The Birth of the Clinic: An Archaeology of Medical Perception*. Vintage Books, New York.

Foucault, M. 1995 *Discipline and Punish: The Birth of the Prison*. Vintage Books, New York.

Giddens, A. 1979 *Central Problems in Social Theory: Action, Structure, and Contradiction in Social Analysis*. Macmillan, London.

Giddens, A. 1984 *The Constitution of Society: Outline of the Theory of Structuration*. University of California Press, Berkeley.

Gieryn, T. F. 2000 A Space for Place in Sociology. *Annual Review of Sociology* 26:463–496.

Gieryn, T. F. 2002 What Buildings Do. *Theory and Society* 31(1):35–74.

Hodder, I. 1987 *Archaeology as Long-Term History*. New Directions in Archaeology. Cambridge University Press, Cambridge [Cambridgeshire]; New York.

Klein, N. 2007 *The Shock Doctrine: The Rise of Disaster Capitalism*. 1st ed. Metropolitan Books/ Henry Holt, New York.

Knapp, A. B. (editor) 1992 *Archaeology, Annales, and Ethnohistory*. Cambridge University Press, Cambridge.

Lefebvre, H. 1991 *The Production of Space*. Blackwell, Oxford, UK.

Lévi-Strauss, C. 2000 *Structural Anthropology*. Basic Books, New York.

Lucas, G. 2008 Time and the Archaeological Event. *Cambridge Archaeological Journal* 18(1):59–65.

Marx, K., and F. Engels 1998 *The Communist Manifesto*. Penguin, New York.

Paynter, R. 2000 Historical and Anthropological Archaeology: Forging Alliances. *Journal of Archaeological Research* 8(1):1–37.

Polanyi, K. 1957 The Economy as Instituted Process. In *Trade and Market in the Early Empires*, edited by Karl Polanyi, C. Arensberg, and H. Pearson, pp. 243–270. Free Press, New York.

Sahlins, M. 1981 *Historical Metaphors and Mythical Realities: Early History of the Sandwich Islands Kingdom*. University of Michigan Press, Ann Arbor.

Sahlins, M. 1985 *Islands of History*. University of Chicago Press, Chicago.

Sahlins, M. 1991 The Return of the Event, Again: With Reflections on the Beginnings of the Great Fijian War of 1843 to 1845 between the Kingdoms of Bau and Rewa. In *Clio in Oceania: Toward a Historical Anthropology*, edited by Aletta Biersack, pp. 37–100. Smithsonian Institution Press, Washington, DC.

Sahlins, M. 1995 *How "Natives" Think: About Captain Cook, for Example*. University of Chicago Press, Chicago.

Sewell, W. H. Jr. 1996 Historical Events as Structural Transformations: Inventing Revolution at the Bastille. *Theory and Society* 25:841–881.

Sewell, W. H. Jr. 2005 *Logics of History: Social Theory and Social Transformation*. Chicago Studies in Practices of Meaning. University of Chicago Press, Chicago.

Soja, E. W. 1989 *Postmodern Geographies: The Reassertion of Space in Critical Social Theory*. Verso, New York.

Thurston, T. L. 1997 Historians, Prehistorians, and the Tyranny of the Historical Record. *Journal of Archaeological Method and Theory* 4(3/4):239–263.

Wallerstein, I. 1974 *The Modern World System I*. Academic Press, San Diego.

White, H. V. 1973 *Metahistory: The Historical Imagination in Nineteenth-Century Europe*. Johns Hopkins University Press, Baltimore.

White, H. V. 1987 *The Content of the Form: Narrative Discourse and Historical Representation*. John Hopkins University Press, Baltimore.

PART I

Eventful Prehistories

Chapter One

Cascading Prehistoric Events

Fractalizing Prehistoric Research

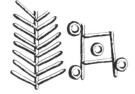

Ezra B. W. Zubrow

Abstract *Given that there is "Event Archaeology," this paper is definitional. It asks and answers several questions regarding the nature of prehistoric events. They are: what is a prehistoric event; how does one find events in the prehistoric record; how are prehistoric events represented in space and time; and what are the stages in the use of prehistoric events in archaeology. It focuses attention on grid- and vector-based representations as well as the importance of patchiness and three alternative representations of time. Answering the question "What types of event categories are there?" four types are suggested: "event standardized," "event aversive," "event contagious," and "event neutral" behavior. The utility for archaeologists of "event plots" showing different event systems and termination dates is explored. Prehistoric individuals and cultures created events. Archaeologists recreate them. And that is the way it should be.*

INTRODUCTION

Archaeology has always been concerned with time and space. We situate prehistoric events in particular times and at particular places. We do so using a recipe of archaeological adventure sautéed with descriptions of cultures, settlements, material artifacts and spiced with reconstructions and the use of numerous scientific techniques. Narratives and events contrast. There is a certain empowering quality about people in narratives for they are agents who do things out of love, fear, and desire. In events, the people are not agents of change rather they are just one group of phenomena upon whom general processes act.

For events in both space and time, one needs to distinguish clearly between the physical realities of those events in which we, and other organisms, change, exist, move, and subsist and the cultural constructions of past events in space and time by both the participants and the much later analysts.

Some Introductory Issues: An "event archaeology" should be concerned with both non-culturally and culturally constructed "events." For both types there has to be a successful methodology that allows one to find and represent events in the prehistoric record. Furthermore, did prehistoric populations perceive either non-culturally or culturally constructed events during the times of their occurrence? In other words, there are "emic," "analytic," and "reflexive" facets to prehistoric "events." Finally, one needs to consider how "event archaeology" or the "archaeology of events" develops in the field of archaeology.

How Does One Find Events in the Prehistoric Record?

There are several important aspects to finding and representing prehistoric events. One is a clear definition of "an event." Second is how one represents the time and space. Third is the level of resolution of analysis. Fourth is the clarity of the representing the boundaries of the event in time and space. Fifth is the cultural or noncultural construction of the past.

What Is an Event?

The definition of an event begins as an occurrence. This occurrence must be at least theoretically determinable both in time and space. As my mathematical friend, Velimer Jurdejevic (2009 Personal Communication), is fond of saying, "An event is a point in time and space." It may occur with or without human agents. An event may exist as one of a number of events in a chain of occurrences. However, it may also exist in isolation. It may be part of a set of causal relationships in that previous events may cause or impact future events. (Figure 1). Events both define and are temporal markers. They mark points of time in the sense of a task beginning or finishing.

Thus, that old conundrum of the sound of a tree falling in a forest is instructive. The event of the English oak falling about 10 miles north of Hastings on October 12, AD 1066, is marked by the sound of the fall. Human agents may hear it or not. If they hear it, and since it is two days before the battle, they may be Normans or members of the local culture and if so may interpret its fall very differently. Humans are the cultural constructors—the perceivers. Similarly, they may be causative or not. They may have caused the fall with an axe or indirectly by changing the conditions of the soil by nearby grazing and agriculture. Or they may have nothing to do with it all as in the case of a lightning strike or simply old age. In short, as they may or may not be the perceivers they may or may not be the agents.

One knows that time and space are absolutely inseparable from events. They constrain individual activities, the environment, and the ability of individuals or populations to impact their environment. Both individuals and populations have limited spatial and temporal reaches.

This physical limit has been called a prism (Lenntorp 1978). It impacts human behavior for prisms are physicalist, concrete, and observable realisms. They are not concerned

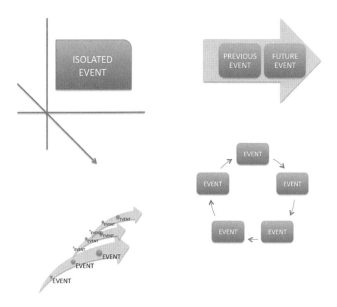

FIGURE 1 Types of Prehistoric Events.

with individual experiences or intentions. Space and time have a limited capacity to accommodate events because no two physical objects can occupy the same place at the same time. Furthermore, it means there is indivisibility of human beings and of the entities that make up the environment. Temporally, nothing is eternal. All entities including humans have a limited life span. All have a history or a biography whose discovery is part of the archaeological task. For humans—all behavior is time-demanding and is finite. Although one may participate in more than one event or task (multitasking) at a time, this is a limited ability.

REPRESENTING EVENTS IN SPACE

In modern spatial analysis one represents phenomena within an event space. The critical factors in representation are the concepts of the spatial, temporal, and attribute data layers. A good heuristic to imagine these phenomena are a set of layers similar to a birthday cake or an archaeological site. Each layer may be thought of as being described in three relational databases. There is a spatial database that locates the phenomenon in spatial coordinates, an attribute or subject database that describes the phenomenon with as many variables, pictures, sounds, etc. as is necessary, and a temporal database that locates the phenomena in time in terms of past, present, and future. An event is thus described by the contents of the three databases i.e., space x = 15, y = 12; attribute—building a house; and time = 150 BC.

For representing space in prehistoric events, archaeologists essentially use two types of spatial representation—grid-based systems and vector-based systems. Each has its advantages for particular types of events and processes.

Grid-Based Event Representation

Grid-based representations are advantageous for optimization and patchiness. For example, consider an event such as the construction of Hadrian's Wall or the Great Wall of China. If one wants to determine if someone optimized the construction for defense, there is an advantage to using the grid representation of space. The rationale is that one may apply all the power of matrix algebra to the optimization process. On these matrices, one may do discriminant, factor, and cluster analyses or find their eigenvalues. One may optimize across space and across the data layers. Of course, there is a large classic archaeological and anthropological literature about whether or not societies will optimize or suffice their foraging strategies, other types of subsistence strategies, reproduction, storage facilities, migration, and even kinship.

"Patchiness" is not as well known by archaeologists. For the person concerned with the spatial characteristics of events, the grid approach is useful for determining the degree of "patchiness." Patchiness has both disadvantages and advantages. One thinks of areas where precipitation events are "patchy." For example, in the Hay Hollow Valley of northeastern Arizona, the rain comes over the mesa across the valley and falls on one small area, leaving the rest to continue being a dry southwestern gully. Or, one considers the snowbelt just south of Buffalo where lake effect snows are twice the depth of areas a kilometer farther north. As a result of these events one farmer has sufficient moisture, the next does not. One hunter is able to move through the forest, the next is mired in the snow.

Tjeerd H. van Andel's Third Stage Project (van Andel and Davies 2003) is a real prehistoric example of the importance of "patchiness." He showed that summer temperatures during the third stage of the last glaciation were much colder than expected. Thus, prehistoric hunters and gatherers really had a relatively small window of places they could live permanently and of these most were coastal. Furthermore, the representation of the botanical environment of a great continuous primeval forest was not accurate. Instead, it was a quilt of patches that provided numerous refuge environments. Thus, human events such as killing animals, cooking, and sleeping were located either on the coast or in the refuges. The vast majority of the land was uninhabited.

Archaeologists who are interested in events might want to determine how "patchy" the events are. They could be concerned with the patchiness of the exploitation of both cultural and environmental resources. The degree of aggregation of events over space may change the trajectory of a culture over time. It is of obvious evolutionary importance. All other things being equal, the more patchy the events the greater the potential for a successful "biological" or "cultural evolutionary" selection. Patchiness is a type of variability. Unlike the gradual differences of a cline, patchiness has abrupt changes that result from large differences in adjacent small areas.[1]

---

[1]One should make several distinctions. First, the differences between "crowding" and "patchiness" are that "crowding" is experienced by the individual and is density dependent. Thus, it is dependent on the total number of events present. On the other hand, "patchiness" is group phenomena only dependent on the spatial pattern. It is not dependent of the total number of events nor does the individual experience it. The two need not necessarily correspond with one another.

An event pattern may have two different aspects that are usually labeled "intensity" and "grain." Intensity is a measure of the extent density varies from place to place—high intensity means large differences in density.

Vector-Based Event Representation

On the other hand, for numerous types of events that concern migratory, traveling, nomadic, and pastoral problems there are great advantages to using the node and vector systems of representing space. The greatest advantage is that it allows one to create mathematical networks and analyze the resulting networks more efficiently. One may solve common network problems on any theme containing lines that connect.

A standard archaeological problem is to determine whether or not a society is being adaptive by finding efficient routes. It may be a one-way trip (out of Africa hypothesis), multiple trips (out of Africa again and again), multiple trips from multiple destinations (out of Africa, Asia, and the Middle East), or a circular trip (out of Africa and back into Africa), or trips that must visit several locations on the route. The scale my be continental or far more local, such as moving to and from local salt deposits. The locations may need to be reached in a particular order. The reason being the need to obtain resources or enroll labor that is only available at a particular location before it makes any economic sense to move on to the next location. Or, one may solve for the problem by asking what is the optimal visiting sequence given an individual's constraints.

Another set of network problems is also particularly relevant. These may be seen as a variant on allocation problems. The issue is determine which resource or facility is closest and to determine the best way to get to the resource or facility given particular constraints.

Third, one may use a network to define a service area around a site. A service network identifies the accessible routes within a specified travel time or distance via the route network. Service areas identify the region that encompasses the accessible routes. Once you have a service network or service area, you can evaluate the true accessibility of the site. What may appear accessible need not be so, and vice versa.

REPRESENTING EVENTS IN TIME

Archaeologists are lucky. Their basic event question is simple. It is the existential one. Did it occur? The answer is based upon contextualizing identifiable objects. One does not mean "necessarily identifiable" in the sense of regarding cultural identification but "identifiable" as existing. In other words, one need not know the cultural identification for instance, Maya or Etruscan, of the "creation of a tomb" to know that the event, the burying of a person in a tomb, took place.

Temporally, one is concerned with when an event begins and when it ends. These boundaries clarify when the states change. For example, consider the following three states. First, one notes there is an Upper Paleolithic-Mesolithic campsite such as Verberie—one set of events represented by a floor; it is then abandoned—another set of events represented by a cultural and stratigraphic gap. It is then re-occupied at a later time by similar people—and

---

Grain refers to the spacing of the clumps—i.e., large areas of high density widely spaced would be fine grained. For example, cultural and environmental events each may be crowded or non-crowded, patchy or non-patchy, crowded and non-crowded in various combinations.

another set of events represented by a new floor higher in the stratigraphic record (Audouze 1991, 1999).

As one can see, the basis for tracing these changes is the concept of object identity. This identity, distinct from an object's properties, values, or structure, is that unique characteristic that distinguishes one object from another. Whether it is a floor, or a stratigraphic gap, or an artifact, it has an identity. And based on a small set of primitives relating to the identity states of objects one may derive a complete set of identity-based change operations. These operations are basic to understanding how events change. This approach highlights the minimum elements necessary for reasoning about change; namely, object identity, an ordering of "identity states," and co-occurrence of identities (Hornsby and Egenhofer 2000). The co-occurrence of identities is especially important to archaeologists. The degree to which objects co-occur—in other words, the distance that "like is near like" in space and/ or time determines the degree of association and relative chronological position.

Modeling time is analogous to space in that there are a variety of ways to model it. Does one wish to see time as continuous or discontinuous; infinitely divisible or only divisible up to a point; and are there points in time or only durations? Some archaeologists provide a beginning and an ending date for an event—assuming that it continues throughout the time span. "The bridge construction was between AD 100 and AD 120. However, is this every year, every month, every day? Is it, on the other hand, an intermittent event?

Others may provide a beginning date and duration. For example, the period of the "second temple" began with its construction in 516 BC and lasted some 570 years. Even others may provide an average time or a midpoint time to represent phenomena. The Mesolithic dates to 9300 BC. What is meant is that the Mesolithic begins earlier at the beginning of the Holocene perhaps 11000 BC and ends with the beginning of the Neolithic around 7700 BC. However, neither of the end dates is stated and is just assumed.

Each system has its strengths and weaknesses and each will provide different results when dating prehistoric events (See Figure 2).

What about regular events? For example in a Neolithic village, men go to the fields every third day. Or, every fall the reindeer hunters at Verberie followed the herd migration.

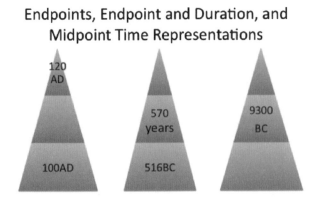

Endpoints, Endpoint and Duration, and Midpoint Time Representations

FIGURE 2 Three Different Time Representations.

One might use a probability framework for examining the temporal aspects of spatial activity. Given that the movement to a specific activity location is related to the frequency and regularity with which an individual chooses to participate in a specific activity. Then, the possible probability forms that an individual (or for that matter a population) will make a given trip at a particular time are illustrated in Figure 3. If the person is traveling to regularly scheduled events, such as attending a religious ceremony or going to a clan meeting, the probability distribution would correspond to Figure 3a. There is only a specific time that the event is offered and it is quite limited. One either matches that time or there is no reason for going. Thus, the probability distribution corresponds to a regular set of spikes. There is high probability of going when the event occurs and less probability of going when the event is not occurring. This is "event standardized" behavior.

The second distribution is the type of trips necessary to obtain resources that are consumed regularly. The resources are always available. However, from the point of view of the individual, there is a gradual increase in probability for taking the trip prior to the trip but immediately afterward there is very little reason and thus very little probability to take the trip. In fact, the probability will not start to grow until resources from the previous trip are partially consumed. One may call this "event aversive behavior." This is shown in Figure 3b.

The third type of distribution is shown in Figure 3c. It shows that there is a sudden high probability for the trip. However, once the trip is undertaken there is a relatively high probability that the person or individual will take it again and even again. The probability slowly diminishes. Then, after a period of low probability, there is a sudden high probability for the trip. This type of activity is clustered in time. Demographers have shown this is frequently the case with migrants. In fact, they have defined what is called the hyper migrant. A migrant who migrates five times is very likely to migrate a sixth. This is "event contagious behavior."

Finally, one has trips to events that occur randomly in time. Participation in such a trip or corresponding event does not effect the probability of participating again. One might call this "event neutral behavior," and it is shown in Figure 3d.

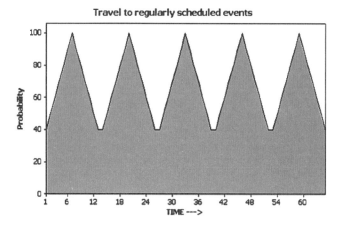

FIGURE 3A Event Standardized Behavior.

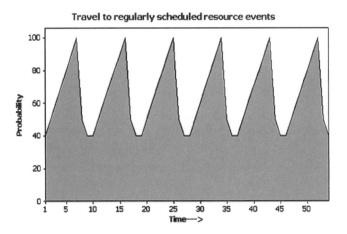

FIGURE 3B Event Aversive Behavior.

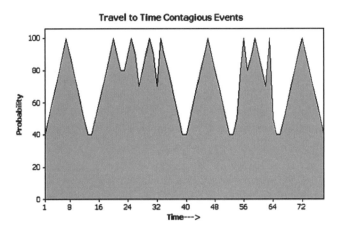

FIGURE 3C Event Contagious Behavior.

Another way to conceive of prehistoric events is to consider the events as part of system that is changing over space and time. People's activities are events that either succeed or fail over time. The individual events either contribute to or do not contribute to the success of the system. One may then look at the events in terms of their success or failure rates. If they fail, the culture then repairs the system so that the next set of events is successful. One may model whether the failure repair times occur at a rate that is decreasing, increasing, or constant over time. One should be able to estimate such quantities as failure rate or the mean number of failures over time. Using "event plots" one may compare systems and determine whether the times between successive successes or failures is increasing, decreasing, or remaining constant. Event plots consist of horizontal lines representing the lifetime of each system, data points representing the

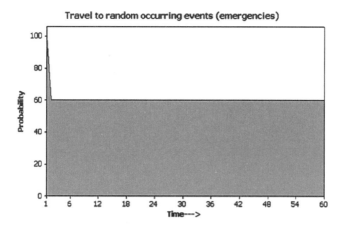

FIGURE 3D Event Neutral Behavior.

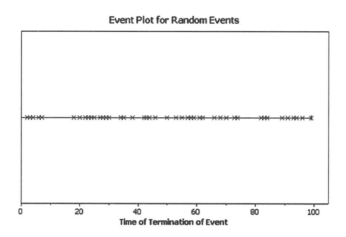

FIGURE 4A Random Events.

failure and retirement of each system, and frequency values representing the frequency of success or failure at each time. Figure 4a shows an event plot for randomly terminating events; Figure 4b shows an event plot for a generally decreasing number of event terminations with increasing lengths of time to termination; Figure 4c shows an event plot for alternating events whose termination times are similar to a sine wave—first long and then short and then long again; and finally Figure 4d shows a comparison of four types of event systems. There are a decreasing number of event terminations over increasing time, timed events, a strengthening number of terminations, and an increasing number of event terminations over decreasing time.

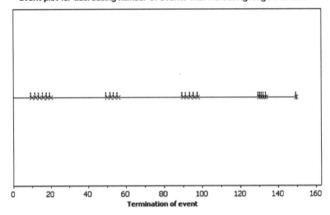

FIGURE 4B Decreasing Number of Events.

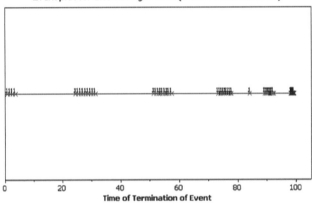

FIGURE 4C Alternating Events.

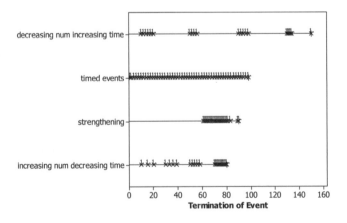

FIGURE 4D A Comparison of Event Systems.

How Has the Use of Prehistoric Events Evolved in the Field of Archaeology?

The use of the prehistoric event has changed over the last century of archaeological research. There is a pattern that is useful in understanding where the field was, how the field is developing, and where the field will be moving. There seems to be a series of stages or developments. They are the following:

Stage 1. Event location—namely, the location of the event in space and time

Stage 2. Event content—namely, describing what is the content of the event

Stage 3. Event delineation—namely, delineating the boundaries of the location of the event in space and time, as well as delineating the boundaries of the event's content through attributes

Stage 4. Event verification—namely, the use of analytical, numerical, or statistical methods to independently verify the existence of a particular event and at a particular time

Stage 5. Event correction—namely, the redefinition of an event on the basis of discrepancies in stages 3 and 4

Stage 6. Event simulation—namely, the use of experimental archaeology and/or ethnographic analogy to understand the processes of event content and then using predictive and non-predictive modeling to help define the event processes

Stage 7. Event systems—namely, examining the interrelationships among series of events to understand whether they are isolates, chains, or entire systems of interacting events

Stage 8. Event cognition—namely, recognizing that events are cognitively conceived differently depending upon who are the perceivers and who are the actors

Conclusions

This paper has examined the nature of prehistoric events. Several questions were asked. They are: What is a prehistoric event? How does one find events in the prehistoric record? How are prehistoric events represented in space and time? and, What are the stages in the use of prehistoric events in archaeology? It focused attention on grid and vector-based representations as well as the importance of optimization, patchiness, crowding, intensity, and grain, as well as three alternative representations of time. Four types of event categories were suggested—"event standardized," "event aversive," "event contagious," and "event neutral behavior." The utility of "event plots" showing different event systems and termination dates was explored, while a stage system for the use of prehistoric events in archaeology was suggested.

Finally, returning to the introduction, a word of warning. As events are parts of the world both in the realms of scientific analysis and realistic novels, they may be more or less descriptive, more or less accurate, and more or less suggestive. One of the problems facing all people concerned with events in archaeology is very similar. If the events described in the novels and analyzed in the sciences are constructed with off-the-shelf components that are only slightly customized, then the novels will not be very novel or the science very innovative.

References

Audouze, F. 1991 Subsistence Strategies and Economy in the Magdalenian of the Paris Basin, France Late Glacial in North-West Europe: Human Adaptation and Environmental Change at the End of the Pleistocene. Pp. 63–67. Council for British Archaeology Series: CBA Research Report: no 77, London.

Audouze, F. 1999 New Advances in French Prehistory. *Antiquity* 73(279):167–175.

Hornsby, K., and M. Egenhofer 2000 Identity-Based Change: A Foundation for Spatio-Temporal Knowledge Representation. *International Journal of Geographical Information Science* 14(3): 207–224.

Jurdejevic, V. 2009 Personal Communication November 25, 2009, Toronto, Ontario.

Lenntorp, B. 1978 A Time Geographic Simulation Model of Individual Activity Programmes. In *Timing Space and Spacing Time II: Human Activity and time Geography*, edited by D. N. P. T. Carlstein, and N. J. Thrift, pp. 162–180. Edward Arnold, London.

van Andel, T. H., and W. Davies (editors) 2003 Neanderthals and Modern Humans in the European Landscape during the Last Glaciation: Archaeological Results of the Stage 3 Project. McDonald Institute for Archaeological Research, Cambridge. Distributed by Oxbow Books, Oxford.

Chapter Two

A Paleohistorical Approach to Upper Paleolithic Structural Changes

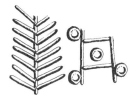

Françoise Audouze and Boris Valentin

Abstract *Are there events of transformative significance other than climatic or environmental events for predators such as hunter-gatherers? Can prehistorians perceive them? Can they perceive the pace of changes and the multiple scales in time and space at which the mutations occur? In comparison with historians, prehistorians have easier access to the successive structures defining different cultures or traditions than they do to events. Most events taking place at a historical time scale are out of their reach and they can only see traces—mostly indirect—of some of them, but they can identify processes of change induced by the events.*

We present in this paper a new approach - la Paléohistoire - dedicated to identifying these processes that lead to structural changes. It focuses on an intermediate scale of time, "temps intermédiaire," which extends between the prehistoric "longues époques" analogous to the Braudelian historical "longue durée" but measured in millennia, and the "temps très bref" of days, weeks, months. This "temps indermédiaire" is the time during which events and mutations occur, that transforms a tradition (i.e., a material) culture into another one as well as its socioeconomic organization. Using recent results in lithic and bone technology for identifying chaîne opératoire schemes, norms of production, goals and achievements, faunal analyses informing on hunting techniques, evidence of procurement strategies and long-distance exchanges, it becomes possible to reconstruct the string of mutations leading from a tradition to the next one, as well as to identify ruptures in continuity and to infer the resulting social transformations. Examples are drawn from the West European Tardiglacial.

Résumé *L'élégante formulation de W. Sewell pour formaliser les relations entre évènements historiques et changements structurels offre un cadre stimulant pour* *problématiser les changements sociaux et culturels durant le Paléolithique. Y a-t-il des évènements significatifs autres que climatiques ou environnementaux lorsqu'il s'agit de prédateurs tels que les chasseurs-cueilleurs? Les paléolithiciens peuvent-ils les percevoir? Peuvent-ils percevoir à quels rythmes ces changements se produisent et à quelles échelles temporelles et spatiales ces mutations interviennent? En comparaison des historiens, les paléolithiciens accèdent plus facilement aux structures qui définissent les différentes traditions culturelles qu'aux évènements. La plupart des évènements qui se déroulent à l'échelle historique leur échappent. Alors qu'on peut soupçonner que des évènements particuliers ont conduit à des changements brutaux, le manque de précision des dates C14 ne permet pas de le démontrer ni de préciser leur temporalité. Seuls peuvent être perçus quelques micro-évènements (tels que le changement de route de migration d'un troupeau de renne et son impact sur le cycle annuel de déplacement d'un groupe de chasseurs-cueilleurs au niveau d'un site ou d'une micro-région). On est parfois aussi en mesure de saisir les conséquences à plus ou moins long terme d'un évènement qui, lui-même, n'a pas laissé de traces (aboutissant par exemple à la disparition d'un circuit d'échange à longue distance).*

Nous présentons ici une nouvelle approche qui plaide pour une Paléohistoire portant sur une échelle de "temps intermédiaire" qui se place entre les "longues époques" préhistoriques analogues à la Longue Durée de F. Braudel mais mesurées en millénaires et le "temps très bref" qui se compte en jours, semaines, ou mois. Le temps intermédiaire est l'échelle de temps durant laquelle se produisent les évènements et les mutations qui transforment une culture ou tradition matérielle en une autre tradition matérielle, et, avec elle, son organisation socio-économique. Il est aujourd'hui possible de reconstituer les processus de changement et l'enchaînement de mutations qui mènent d'une tradition matérielle à une autre, d'identifier les moments de rupture au sein de la continuité et d'en inférer quelques transformations sociales corrélatives. On s'appuie pour cela sur des résultats récents portant sur la technologie des industries lithique et osseuse qui permettent d'identifier la finalité, les normes et les réalisations concrètes des productions d'outils et d'armes, également sur des analyses faunistiques qui montrent les changements dans les stratégies de chasse, et sur les données témoignant d'échanges à longue distance. Des exemples portant sur le Tardiglaciaire du Bassin Parisien, de la Suisse occidentale et de la vallée du Rhin moyen illustrent cette démarche.

Sewell's formulation of historical events brings provocative questions into play when applied to Paleolithic and its bands of hunter-gatherers (Beck et al. 2007). A first one is: Can we identify historical events during Paleolithic times? A second one is: Are there other events than environmental events for groups of predators such as the hunter-gatherers? Like all historians, French historians have theorized about historical events. For the microhistorian Arlette Farges (2002), not only is "an event…socially constructed, but it is a focal point between past and future and only exists if it includes a vision of the future for the people who create it or suffer it. It takes place in the large sphere of emotions because it has to be perceived and characterized in order to exist."

A FEW EXAMPLES OF PALEOLITHIC EVENTS

UNUSUAL BURIALS

Given these prerequisites, can we find traces of events in the Upper Paleolithic archeological record? Yes, but most of the time we do not know what they mean and if they are related to a structural change or not, and at which scale? To which social context are the very unusually rich children burials related? For example, at Sungir south of Moscow, a boy aged 12 to 13 and a girl aged 7 to 9 were buried head-to-head in a double burial. They were buried 26,400 years ago with a considerable wealth of ornaments including around 5,000 mammoth ivory beads each plus 250 perforated polar fox teeth and a 2 m long spear made from a mammoth tusk for the boy and miniature daggers and darts for the girl (Kuzmin et al. 2004). These children were treated both as adults judging from the weapons and ornaments but as children given the size of the ornaments. Another example is the three-to-seven-year-old epipalaeolithic child buried at the Madeleine shelter (Dordogne) dated between 10,200 and 9,600 years cal BC. He/she wore a multitude of ornaments including 1314 *Dentalium* shells coming from the Atlantic beaches and 243 other shells, some of them coming from the Mediterranean coast, others from Atlantic beaches. The small size of dentalia specimens suggest beadwork specially made for children (Vanhaeren et al. 2004). These perforated shells were too worn for such a short life of five or six years (Taborin 1993:326) and implied long distance exchanges. Should we see in these examples temporary occurrences of transmitted social inequality? Whatever the case may be, we can suppose that such burials correspond to funerals of importance, that is, impressive events in the course of everyday life.

INDIRECT TRACES OF CHANGE

If we follow Paul Veynes (1996), who writes about the everyday nature and banality of the past, and Arlette Farges (2002), who considers that historical events or rather series of events are created by series of human and social moves of low intensity, we could say that most events or traces of events were low-intensity events concerning a limited number of people, whether a mobile group or a regional band. However, events in cave art (whatever their signification) or disruption of long distance exchanges may probably be linked to higher-intensity events, because they impacted on larger regions.

A few painted cave figures were scratched—not covered, which is a common situation—but erased, smeared, or scratched by later painters. Such a situation is found at Grotte Cosquer where a red painted hand was deliberately covered by deep scratches (Clottes, Courtin, Varell 2005). At Grotte Chauvet as well, we find several reindeer figures scratched or smeared with black paint (Clottes et al., 2001, Figure 93, 123, 205). In these places of relation with a supernatural world, destroying a figure may have represented the partial destruction of a myth or of a belief and was certainly an emotional act of some consequence for individuals or for a group. We may see in such an iconoclastic behavior the trace of what could be a mutation in the symbolic system.

The presence of Mediterranean shells in the main late Magdalenian settlements of the Rhine valley and of southwestern Germany proves that they were part of a long-distance exchange network. Their absence in the ensuing Azilian levels demonstrates the disruption of this long-distance network, but we ignore what direct event triggered its disruption and the way it affected intermediaries along the line, even if we suppose that climatic change is indirectly responsible at a coarse-grain time scale (Floss 1994:321–341, 2000). This last example had a large impact at a supraregional scale, but is embedded in an unknown "cascade of events."

Other events only acquire their sense within a "conjuncture." A change in the migration route of game is a response to a known or ignored prior event. It necessarily alters the regular course of the nomadic life of hunter-gatherers and leads to a reorganization of the residential mobility system. We may have such an example with the upper and last level at the Magdalenian site of Pincevent in the Paris Basin. While all the earlier levels consist of camps related to the fall migration of reindeer, the last camp takes place from fall to early spring and hunting has shifted from the reindeer herd interception and mass killing to a hunting strategy of ambush and encounter primarily for killing horses and a few reindeer individuals (Bignon, Enloe, Bemilli 2006).

ENVIRONMENTAL EVENTS

When looking for Sewell's historical events in prehistory, environmental events are the most obvious. Volcanic eruptions are typical abrupt events that induce considerable change for groups living in the vicinity and beyond. The eruption of the Phlegrean Fields volcano in Southern Italy made South Italy a human desert for several centuries around 37,000 bp (calendar years). It apparently played a role in the transition from Middle Paleolithic to Upper Paleolithic in Italy, and maybe at a larger geographical scale. Around 10,950 cal BC, the Laacher See catastrophic eruption led to the formation of a lake in the Neuwied Basin and to a short-term temporary desertification of the microregion, with likely dramatic consequences at larger scale in Northern Europa (Riede 2008). Apart from these short-term events, climatic and environmental changes are the strongest factors in socioeconomic and cultural changes during the Paleolithic, whether slow or abrupt. Environment specialists and prehistorians are presently focusing on abrupt environmental changes (AEC) sometimes spanning only decades that may have given rise to rapid changes in prehistoric ways of life and cultures (Figure 1).

The role of climatic changes is quite visible at a coarse-grained time scale. For example, in the El Kowm Basin, the Umm El Tlel tell created by local sources and human occupations in a Syrian semi-desert area has yielded a 22 m high stratigraphy of discontinuous occupations spanning from Middle Acheulean until PPNB Neolithic (Boëda and Rasse 2006). The levels correspond to at least 150 archaeological levels among which 70 living floors a few cm thick could be individually indentified. Eric Boëda observes that it was occupied by different groups that arrived at a time of climatic change and left when a new change occurred. In every new sedimentary layer related to particular climatic conditions, one observes a cultural tradition different from the previous one and expressed by a different technical tradition in lithic production. If several successive groups are present in a sedimentary facies, they all belong to the same technical tradition: one sedimentary facies, one tradition, even if the sedimentary facies occurs at different periods of time within the

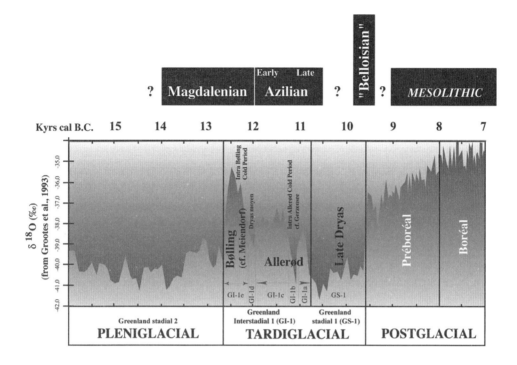

FIGURE 1 Tentative correlation between the climatic chronology (from the GRIP core, Greenland) and the main technical traditions of the Paris Basin at the end of the Pleistocene and the beginning of the Holocene.

Middle Paleolithic. The same phenomenon occurs in the Upper Paleolithic levels. But the dependence on climate at Umm El Tlel is not as deterministic as it may look: man is present in all the sedimentary facies, whatever the corresponding climate. And the variations in the mode of occupation (seasonal hunting camp, workshops, camps of longer duration, etc.) are independent from climatic types or periods (Boëda and Rasse 2006, Boëda, Al Sakhel, and Muhese 2007).

PROBLEMS FOR CORRELATING CULTURAL CHANGES TO CLIMATIC EVENTS

Nevertheless, correlating climatic changes and cultural traditions at a fine time scale is far from achieved even if there have been tremendous improvements in the precise dating of climatic events in the last 20 years—Global Change obliges. We now know that Abrupt Environmental Changes can occur in less than a generation span. Methodologically, two pitfalls remain to overcome: one is the ^{14}C imprecision and its plateaus that set many Late Paleolithic sites floating in dates brackets that can extend up to 500 years, such as the 13th millennium BP plateau in which most of the late Magdalenian open air settlements of the Paris Basin are located (Figure 1). Before 25,000 uncal BP, the situation is much more delicate: in the present state of knowledge, 4000 years separate the calibrated ^{14}C dates of Grotte Chauvet depending on the calibration curve used. There may also be a dating discrepancy between contemporary sites due to the material dated (i.e., bones samples versus charcoal).

On the climatic side, the Greenland ice cores have yielded information of unprecedented precision on dating and on temperatures (GISP2 2006). While the results obtained from the several Greenland drilled cores are consistent with one another for the Holocene, the farther we go back in time, the more their dates separate (Maievski and Bender 1995). Hardly a few years during the last five millennia, these dating differences increase with time, exceeding 150 years for the period between 12,000 and 15,000. The imprecision is increased by the curves smoothing. As a result, an abrupt climatic change such as the beginning of the Youngest Dryas that occurred in less than 20 years—maybe less than 10 years—is floating between 12,850 and 12,640 in calendar years BP. Another factor of imprecision comes from the thermal diffusion that smoothes the temperature differences over time. These problems may be solved as new counts and filtering methods improve the results and new cores are drilled in the Greenland and Antarctic ice such as the WAIS Divide ice core. These new results, which bring fast climatic changes on the scene, oblige the prehistorians to revise their perception of slow cultural changes but do not yet give them the means to transfer this new perception to facts, as long as new improvements in the dating methods are not achieved.

TEMPORALITIES AND STRUCTURES

The temporalities of climatic events vary and can be very different from human temporalities. In addition, Paleolithic man's temporality can only be approached through its settlements. Most of the time we do not know the temporality of stratified sites. Successive archaeological levels give us successive fixed images corresponding to varied durations. It is only at a very coarse-grained time scale that we can perceive an evolution. Historical events are totally eliminated from these images. Even environmental changes can be eliminated by erosion. Moreover, we don't know what kind of relation prehistoric groups had with their history. Indeed, we ignore it, but we are entitled to assume that Upper Paleolithic populations had means to keep in memory the experience gained in the past by historicizing it, whether in the oral tradition or in art or both. The return to Umm El Tlel of populations whose ancestors or people sharing the same technological tradition/culture had lived there could be an indication of a kind of historicization or at least of building a medium-term cultural memory.

Stratified archaeological sites give us a discontinuous succession of seemingly stable states. As a consequence, it is much easier to recover a global cultural structure at a given time from the record of archaeological levels than the "cascades of events" that leads to the reorganization of these structural systems. French prehistorians are getting more and more concerned with this problem. But presently many of them have no choice other than refining the time slices, eliminating pseudo-interstratification of successive cultural traditions (Bordes 2003), and finding new discrete technological characteristics, because the periods on which they work are only known at a very long-term scale (among others, Bon 2002; Klaric 2003). Providing secure and well-dated data remains a prerequisite for identifying the dynamics of change during many phases of the Upper Paleolithic.

Going in the direction of an eventful archaeology, one of us has proposed to develop for the Tardiglacial—the most well-dated period of the Upper Paleolithic—a Paleohistorical approach. It seeks to set up Prehistory in a historical framework by looking for the sequential dynamic transformations that lead from one technical tradition to the next and from one cultural tradition to the next, and by finding out operative explanations (Valentin 2006, 2008). This approach falls in *Les Annales* framework. In this, it is different from the descriptive chronologies built by previous prehistorians, some of them presenting these tabulated data under the same term of paleohistory.

It refers to *Les Annales* school to underline the intended total scope, and to Braudel's temporal scale because of its plasticity. This characteristic was criticized by several archaeologists of the eighties and nineties (for example, Fletcher 1992:38–39). Nevertheless such a flexible definition of the intermediate time permits adapting the temporal multidimensionality to specific problematics and data. Les *Annales* methods attracted the attention of English-speaking archaeologists nearly two decades ago (Bintliff ed. 1991a; Knapp ed. 1992a). While the theoretical discussions were thoughtful and well argued (Bintliff 1991b; Knapp 1992b; Sheratt 1992), applications turned out to be rather disappointing. Apart from a few very innovative long-term diachronic analyses including historical periods (Bintliff 1991b; Barker 1995), prehistoric data were lacking quantity and diversity (for example Duke 1992) compared to the wealth of data of all sorts used by the French Historians of *Les Annales* school. New theoretical debates quickly removed *Les Annales* concepts from the archaeologists' agenda. Sewell's work bridging social theory and history brings us back in an innovative way to *Les Annales* comprehensive conception of History.

La Paléohistoire: A History without Events and without Historical Figures but not without Actors

The goal of the *Paléohistoire* approach (Valentin 2008) is to understand how chains of changes transform prehistoric traditions/cultures, and to identify the pace of mutations. It refers to "a problem-history" *sensu* François Furet (1975) rather than to a narrative history. It is an inductive approach building upon a progressive construction of interrelated facts. It is based upon recent developments of technology applied mostly to lithic productions but also to bone artifacts, tools, weaponry, subsistence, settlement, even artistic creations. Techniques are, in Marx's sense, "forces of production," economically determined and determining, and this makes them an access to the social organization of subsistence activities (Valentin 2008:60). At the same time, they are the concretization of a system of values, representative not only of "manières de faire" (ways of doing) but also of "manières de voir" (ways of seeing), that participates in differentiating cultural traditions (Pelegrin 1995).

Building upon Braudel's temporalities (1969), B.V. has set up a ternary division of time adapted to the Prehistoric period (Figure 2). It is composed of a very short term (*temps très bref*) from minutes to months—to a certain extent shorter than Braudel's *temps court*— a very long term (*longues époques),* to a certain extent longer than *la longue durée* since it is spanning from centuries up to millennia longer than *la longue durée* since it is spanning from centuries to millennia. In between, the medium term or rather the intermediate periods (*temps intermédiaire* or *périodes intermédiaires*) includes the historians' *temps court*, the *longue durée*, and the well-known Braudel's *conjoncture*, and spans from seasons to centuries. The very long term is the time of prehistorians' approximative chronologies. Le *temps très*

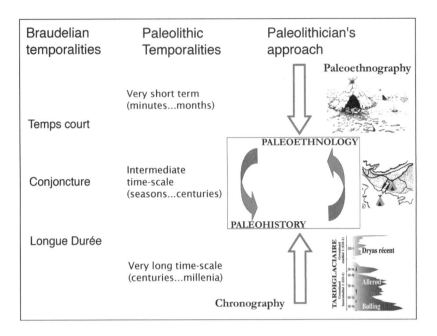

FIGURE 2 Paleolithicians's temporality and approach.

bref is the time of living floors, of seasonal occupations that can be analyzed from an anthropological point of view. It is the time scale at which it is possible to recognize the economic and sometimes the social value of technological choices. In between, the intermediate periods are the time scale at which prehistorians can perceive structural changes and combine the paleohistorical perspective with a paleoethnological approach. It is the time scale of a site occupation or of the period of time between two occupations at the same site (Valentin 2008:30–33). It is the time during which often inconspicuous technological and economical changes occur that may have decisive consequences and later can be identified as identity markers in comparison with earlier or later ones. They are difficult to document but given the nature of prehistoric data, they are the best reflection of the chain of natural and anthropic events that lead to a reorganization and recombination of the structural components of prehistoric cultural traditions. They are a key to explaining change.

TOOLS FOR BUILDING A *PALÉOHISTOIRE* OF THE TARDIGLACIAL PERIOD

The data to achieve a *Paléohistoire* derive primarily from lithics analyses, including the *chaîne opératoire* method. Let us here bring a few precisions about the *chaîne opératoire* methodology to avoid the numerous misunderstanding found in recent foreign papers. The *chaîne opératoire* is nothing more, but nothing less, than an analytical grid for analyzing any kind of production and for integrating in one comprehensive analysis categories of data of different nature: material, ideal, symbolic, linguistic, etc. French prehistorians have used it first for identifying core reduction sequences based upon flint blocks refitting, knapping experiments, and mental refitting. In an enlarged scope they also look for identifying intentionality (integrating desired tools in the process), knapping mental schemes and norms, levels of competence and apprenticeship, and productivity. While leading to schemes and norms representative of cultures, the *chaîne opératoire* method can also identify individuals or groups of individuals (Pigeot 1987; Ploux 1989).

But the *chaîne opératoire* can integrate quite different data such as specific technical knowledge and know-how, technical actions, symbols and rituals, speeches, gendered division of labor, command and control of actions, temporal and spatial continuity and discontinuities. It can be used to analyze material productions such as Paleolithic or Neolithic flint knapping, as well as the production, distribution, and use sequence of a particular type of pottery in relation to a gender division of labor in Morocco (Balfet 1994) or a fishing operation in Togo, including the net, the actions, the division of labor between chiefs and fishers, between men and women, the rituals, the vernacular denominations of tools, actions, and phases, and the anthropologist's description of actions and partition of phases (Martinelli 1994). It has even been used for sequencing speeches and gestures in Greek rhetoric discourses.

Lithics are the most numerous category of remains during prehistory and are present even if taphonomic processes have destroyed faunal and vegetal remains. Using them gives access to the largest number of sites. The *chaîne opératoire* method is not only applied here to reconstruct the tools production sequences, schemes, and norms, but also to identify the intentionality of the productions, and the range of variants and variations within and among levels, sites, or regions. It is used to find out about the signification of the various solutions observed in terms of adequacy to subsistence and transformation tasks and in terms of productivity (Audouze et al. 1986). Once, the various *chaînes opératoires* are identified for a series of assemblages, it becomes possible first to recognize discrete technical changes in the lithic productions and tools, then to chronologically order levels and sites according to these significant changes in the production and use of tools; then to build scenarios that are, at the time, the best informed hypotheses on structural changes and changing time scale, and to build hypotheses on their correlation with environmental changes.

The following example is drawn from sites located in the Paris Basin between the 14th millennium BP and the beginning of the Holocene and considers change in material culture, in settlement pattern and social organization, and change in the cognitive and symbolic realm. It is based upon several decades of research on the Tardiglacial in the Paris Basin, from the late Magdalenian to the late Azilian (extending over the 14th and 12th millennium BP) in a context of increasing mobility correlated to drastic environmental changes.

The Magdalenian and the Azilian Knapping Schemes

The late Magdalenian is characterized by two knapping schemes: a laminar scheme devised for producing long calibrated/modular blades that are used as such or retouched as tools—often rejuvenated and even transformed during long uses—a lamellar scheme devised for producing bladelets that are used as such or transformed in backed bladelets used as barbs hafted along hunting projectiles. The blades extraction is performed with a soft organic hammer that can be replaced by a soft stone hammer for the bladelets extraction. The volumetric constraints require a very careful selection or preparation of the flint nodule to shape it in an adapted oblong volume, and a constant maintenance of the core.

The next cultural tradition, Azilian, presents a different scheme. The soft stone hammer replaces the organic soft hammer at every stage of the reduction process. In a first chronological phase (i.e., early Azilian), the preparation stage of the flint nodules is reduced and adapted natural volumes are preferred, but the goal is still to obtain quite long blades. In a later phase, long blades are no longer felt necessary, short blades and flakes of every dimension are used to manufacture projectile points and short-life tools. There is no search for good quality flint. The whole knapping process is more or less careless. During the latest *identified* phase, strict laminar debitage even disappears, the goal being to produce only flakes, sometimes elongated. Such a drastic change from a curated sophisticated knapping process to a more expedient process expresses two technical logics and requires us to look for the chain of events in order to understand its rationale.

A Clue Brought by a Key Level

A transition level was recognized in the lower level of Hangest III.1 (Somme) in the north of the Paris Basin (Fagnart 1997). It led to seriating a series of archaeological Magdalenian and Azilian levels and to proposing a tentative scenario of evolution from Late Magdalenian to Azilian (Valentin 2008). This scenario sheds light on features that characterize Azilian and are already present in an unobstrusive way in the Late Magdalenian (Figure 3).

Until the early Alleröd, long blades still were part of the knapping objectives as in the Magdalenian, but already, from the late Magdalenian of Cepoy/Marsangy tradition short blades were also an objective and the use of a soft stone hammer predominates because it

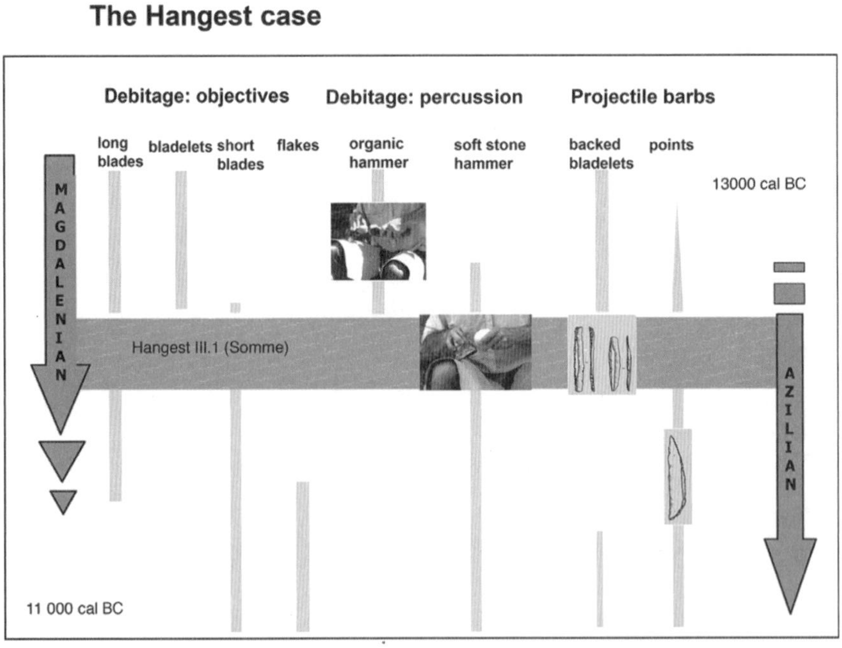

FIGURE 3 The place of a transitional lower level in Hangest III.1 (Somme) in a scenario of evolution from Late Magdalenian to Azilian in the Paris Basin.

is the appropriate hammer to use for getting short straight blades. The backed bladelets, that often have a slightly arched profile and that were so numerous in the late Magdalenian (up to 60% of the assemblages) decrease in number and are replaced by shouldered backed points first, then arched backed bipoints, then arched backed monopoints. Another innovation is found in the early Azilian: a flat retouch on blades; it is followed by the appearance of backed knives in the late Azilian, for example in Hangest Upper level.

A Rationale for these Changes

The *chaîne opératoire* (Pelegrin 2000; Valentin 2008:160 *sqq.*), the microwear and functional analyses, give us an access to the rationale of these technical changes and to the seeming loss of technical skill . We can relate this new need of straight flint blades retouched into points with a straight profile to a change in weaponry. The way backed points are inserted in the bone points is different from the way backed bladelets are inserted (Figure 4). The latter are inserted with mastic in the lateral grooves of bone points that require a long time to manufacture but can be recycled. Backed points are inserted at the apex of wooden points, easy to replace but also easily lost, particularly when hunters were used to hunting solitary game instead of herds, as it was proven by recent archeozoological studies (Bignon and Bodu 2006). The new requirements for the projectile flint points lead to a complete reorganization of the knapping activities since long blades get less and less useful in a context where the duration of tool use becomes shorter. The soft stone hammer, which was only used at the end of production sequences for short blades or by young apprentices during the Magdalenian, prevails over the soft organic hammer and smaller cores become suitable. This simplification

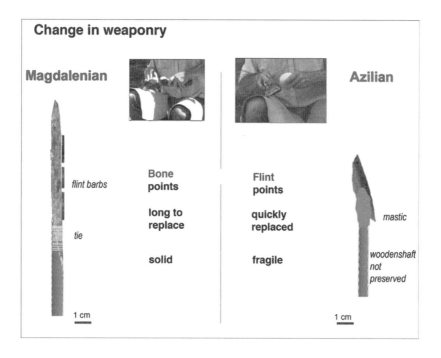

FIGURE 4 Main changes in weaponry between Magdalenian and Azilian.

of the knapping process allows the knapper to get rid of several constraints attached to the organic hammer percussion: spending time for finding good quality flint (which is costly in a context of increasing mobility), going through a long knapping apprenticeship, etc. Drawing upon Bleed design theory (1986) as adapted by J. Pelegrin (2000) and O'Farell (2004), this scenario establishes a relation between the simplification of the debitage (i.e., the knapping process) and the search for a fast replacement of projectile inserts. The difference in rate of losses and in time spent for repair results in a difference in maintenance opportunities between Magdalenian and Azilian. In addition, this scenario draws its inspiration from the Optimal Foraging Theory, especially from *considerations* on the way hunter-gatherers adapt their tool kit according to their mobility (Torrence 1983; Perlès 1992).

From Technique to Climatic and Environmental Changes

In turn, we can relate this change in weaponry with changes in hunting strategies as a consequence of changing game. At le Closeau (Early Azilian), the horse, deer, and boar faunal assemblage replaces the reindeer and horse faunal assemblage found in the Late Magdalenian sites (Bignon and Bodu 2006). And in the upper and last Magdalenian level at Pincevent, the reindeer migration does not take place any more (Bodu et al. 2006). Looking at these changes from a coarser-grained time scale, this scenario fits into the larger frame of environmental changes that see the warming of the climate during the Bölling/Alleröd temperate episode and the replacement of the tundra landscape by a mosaic of wooded areas and grassland areas. At the archaeological time scale, hunting strategies that had remained pretty much the same since the beginning of Upper Paleolithic (Fontana 2000) were drastically transformed in less than a millennium and probably much faster in reality.

Resilience or Different Temporalities?

Some of the characteristics of level Hangest III.1 remind us that such sequencings of changes are not unilinear. The resilience of some elements opposes a resistance to change. For example, backed bladelets appear in number in Hangest III.1 level while they were disappearing from the likely older levels of the Magdalenian sites of Cepoy and Marsangy, where backed points are already numerous (Schmider et al. 1992; Valentin 2008:123 *sqq.*). This kind of arhythmic development of weaponry cannot presently find an explanation because we don't know enough about the local environmental context and the precise chronological position of these sites. They also reappear at the end of the Azilian as lateral barbs in association with the backpoint.

Another example of resilience or an evidence of a different time scale for the evolution of portable art comes from the Alleröd level III of Pincevent: in an asserted late Azilian context, it yielded a limestone tablet with an engraved horse of Magdalenian style in spite of the general ban on figurative engravings or paintings that occurs after the end of the Magdalenian.

Other dimensions of prehistoric life evolve on longer time scales. The open-air settlement of le Closeau, west of Paris, includes four Azilian levels from the early stage to the final stage (Bodu 1998). The early Azilian settlement (around 12,400/12,000 BP) is composed of two large domestic units, one of which, surrounded by a circle of stones, finds its best comparisons with the late Magdalenian settlements units of Etiolles W11 or Gönnersdorf III. Small satellite flint workshops are linked to these two units as in the Magdalenian sites of Pincevent or Etiolles. The domestic hearth still occupies a central place and role even if the basin shape does not exist anymore, replaced by a flat hearth. Clearly, the major shift in settlement pattern appears later. It is characterized by a splitting of the settlement units in separate concentrations of artifacts. Analyses of spatial distribution are necessary to disclose specialized activities areas in the 13 undifferentiated large and dense concentrations of artifacts in the middle Azilian level of Le Closeau (around 11,200 BP). The only traces of fire are located on the verge of these concentrations. The late Azilian level at the end of Alleröd (around 10,800 BP) presents an even more de-structured space with many small concentrations of a monotonous content where an expedient flint knapping of poor quality yields mostly laminar flakes and the few tools are short scrapers along with mediocre backed monopoints. The late Azilian "manière de voir" has considerably diverged from the Magdalenian one where settlement organization is concerned.

This spatial de-structuration goes on in the last occupation at Le Closeau that belongs to the Belloisian tradition at the end of the Younger Dryas, While the knapping system comes back to long blades and highly skilled knapping, this typical Belloisian settlement exhibits large artifacts beds/concentrations representing repeated occupations. Due to the lack of faunal remains, only the flint workshop is visible in the concentration of refuse, the scarcity of tools, and the absence of the first-choice laminar products (Bodu P. 2000).

This change in settlement pattern co-evolves with a change in mobility pattern and a change of social interactions (Valentin 2008:79 *sqq.*). It is better exemplified in the Middle Rhine valley or in the site of Lake Neuchâtel than in the Paris Basin. The mobility pattern during the late Magdalenian is related to a reccurring cycle in which the origins of raw materials vary from one season to the next, and exhibit a radiating distribution, suggesting people coming from different origins (Floss 2000:90; Leesch 1997:199; Cattin 2002:254). During Azilian/Federmesser, in the Middle Rhine area, the moves are more erratic with local raw material in small winter occupations and more diversified raw materials in a few larger summer camps. While the higher percentage of materials come from short or long distances during the Magdalenian, intermediate distances are the most numerous in the following period, indicating a change in long-distance procurement and social network. It finds a parallel with the interruption of long-distance exchange of exotic shells. Movements seem to be restricted to adjacent regions, at a shorter spatial scale (Whallon 2006:263). At the same time, in the Paris Basin, there is an intensification of the residential mobility and of the local procurement of raw materials.

FROM PALEOHISTORY TO MACROHISTORY

Analyses on the short and medium term permits us to observe recurrences of phenomena. Another potentially fruitful approach is a macrohistory dedicated to the identification of technical cycles recurring during the Paleolithic. An example can be the recurrence of long modular blades that require a careful core preparation and a high knapping skill. They appear in a first cycle in the Late Gravettian in the Southwest, then in the classical Magdalenian, then in the Belloisian and the Long Blade industries. Some clues indicate that, as in the Magdalenian, these curated tools could sometimes be related to planned economies partly based on seasonal massive hunting (Valentin 2008:274). In the Belloisian, other dynamics could have played; the most recent hypothesis is an increase in value of prestigious hunting knives in a context of brutal climatic transition and correlated economical stress (Valentin, 2008:chapter 5).

DISCUSSION

Prehistory is undeniably not the best period for looking for historical events *stricto sensu*. Poor sampling and imprecise dates made the task of identifying "cascades of events" difficult if not impossible, but it is possible to shed light on structural changes at a coarse-grained scale of time compatible with the available measuring of time.

The *Paléohistoire* is not a new theory but it is an approach or a method that sets up a conceptual framework for integrating short-term characteristics and processes at the intermediate time scale or conjuncture scale. It is a bottom-up method that proceeds from the particular to the general, based on progressive inferences from the technical realm to other dimensions of society. The resulting scenarios are grounded in solid empirical archeological data and are valid only if they strictly conform to these data. This approach brings two essential contributions to the understanding of change. At the short-term scale, it gives significance to minute features in tool manufacturing that were considered neither important nor even observed before. It realizes this by relying on the *chaîne opératoire* to extract from knapping processes their goals and their more or less satisfactory materialization in products. It is not only the relation between the final morphology of tools and the production sequence that is investigated but also and above all the part played by the function and the functioning of tools or weapon parts in the conception and organization of the production sequence. The importance or nonimportance of axis symmetry, of a curving of the profile or of the back delineation of a flint point, of achieving these features by retouching or by predetermining the knapping operations are examples of these features.

At the intermediate time scale, it integrates in diachrony synchronic data of a paleoanthropological nature by seriating these features according to sites or archaeological levels in which they are present. It thus gives clues to understand how technical changes occur and what is the rationale behind these morphological or processing changes. It enlightens transitional mechanisms in which previous elements are recombined in order to successfully deal with innovative features.

Once the technical changes are identified and located in time, it becomes possible to expand the analysis and look for change in hunting strategies in relation to climatic change and for change in other dimensions such as raw material procurement patterns, settlement pattern, mobility, ornaments, art, long distance exchange, etc.

Because it relies on culturally significant features within a given technical scheme, it allows revision of the geographic extension of "Cultures" by looking to the spatial distribution of shared technical traditions. An example is the demonstration of the common identity of the Azilian and Federmesser technical tradition beyond regional variations.

As in Braudel's tiered division of time, the choice of the time scales is adapted to the data to analyze. One may hope that, once good excavations of well-preserved multilayered Paleolithic sites provide a larger body of well-analyzed data, once the dating methods bring us a finer and more reliable set of absolute dates, both for climatic events and Paleolithic occupations, the span of the prehistorian's conjuncture can be reduced to a span of time from half a century to a few centuries rather than millennia.

The even coarser-grained chronology of periods anterior to the Tardiglacial reduces the feasibility of this approach. However, if cycles are identified for the Tardiglacial and Holocene periods, it may become possible to identify similar cycles in the past and to relate them to the same type of climatic and/or economical events.

The same constraints limit our capacity to apprehend the pace of propagation of changes in time and space and what makes neighbors or non-neighbors adopt new ideas and "*manières de faire*" and "*manières de voir.*"

Another limit comes from the need for detailed and complete observations and analyses of large assemblages—a highly time-consuming task. Selecting too small a region for the analysis may result in missing supraregional variations and concluding a unilinear sequence. Expanding the area under scrutiny offers the opportunity to observe multilinear and multitemporal change.

Coming back to historical events, we are obliged to acknowledge that for the time being the only historical events (in Sewell's meaning) that can be clearly perceived in the Paleolithic remain major climatic events that oblige prehistoric populations to reorganize their food procurement strategy and thus to completely reorganize the socioeconomic system.

ACKNOWLEDGMENTS

The authors thank James R. Sackett and Douglas J. Bolender for improving the language and style of this paper. The imperfections remain ours.

References cited

Aujoulat, N. 2004 *Lascaux: le geste, l'espace et le temps.* Le Seuil, Paris.

Aujoulat, N. 2005 *Movement, Space, and Time.* Harry N. Abrams, Boston.

Beck, R. A., D. J. Bolender, J. A. Brown, and T. K. Earle 2007 Eventful Archaeology, *Current Anthropology* 48:833–860.

Bleed P. 1986 The Optimal Design of Hunting Weapons: Maintainability or Reliability. *American Antiquity* 51:737–747.

Boëda E., and M. Rasse 2006 De la lecture verticale à la lecture spatiale des enregistrements, archéologiques: réflexions géographiques tirées de l'exemple d'Umm El Tlel (Syrie centrale), *M@ppemonde* n°83. http://mappemonde.mgm.fr/num11/articles/art06301.html.

Boëda E., H. Al Sakhel, and S. Muhesen 2007 *Mission archéologique Umm El Tlel, / El Meirah, Bassin d'El Kowm, Syrie.* Unpublished Scientific Report (Ministère des AffairesEtrangères).

Bignon, O., and P. Bodu 2006 Stratégie cynégétique et mode de vie à l'Azilien ancien dans le Bassin parisien: les apports de l'exploitation des chevaux du Closeau (niveau inférieur; Rueil-Malmaison, Hauts-de-Seine), *L'Anthropologie* 110 (3):401–417.

Bignon, O., J. G. Enloe, and C. Bemilli 2006 Étude archéozoologique de l'unité T125: originalité de la chasse des rennes et des chevaux in Un dernier hiver à Pincevent. Les Magdaléniens du niveau IV-0. In *Gallia Préhistoire* 48, edited by P. Bodu, M. Julien, B. Valentin., G. Debout, pp. 19–35.

Bintliff, J. (editor) 1991a *The Annales School and Archaeology*. Leicester University Press, Leicester, London.

Bintliff, J. (editor) 1991b The Contribution of an Annalist/Structural History Approach to Archaeology. In *The Annales School and Archaeology*, edited by J. Bintliff J., pp. 1–33. Leicester University Press, Leicester, London.

Bodu, P. 1998 Magdalenians-Early Azilians in the Centre of the Paris Basin: a Filiation? The Example of Le Closeau (Rueil-Malmaison, France). In *The Organization of Lithic Technology in Late Glacial and Early Postglacial of Europe*, edited by S. Miliken, pp. 131–147. BAR International Series 700. British Archaeological Reports, Oxford.

Bodu, P. 2000 Les faciès tardiglaciaires à grandes lames rectilignes et les ensembles à pointes de Malaurie dans le sud du Bassin parisien: quelques réflexions à partir de l'exemple du Closeau (Hauts de Seine). In *Épipaléolithique et Mésolithique, Actes de la Table Ronde de Lausanne, 21–23 novembre 1997 (Cahiers d'Archéologie Romande n 18)*, edited by P. Crotti, pp. 89–182. Lausanne.

Bodu, P., M. Julien, B. Valentin, and G. Debout (editors) 2006 Un dernier hiver à Pincevent. Les Magdaléniens du niveau IV0, *Gallia Préhistoire* 48:1–160.

Bon, F. 2002 *L'Aurignacien entre Mer et Océan. Réflexion sur l'unité des phases anciennes de l'Aurignacien dans le sud de la France*. Mémoire de la Société Préhistorique Française, XXIX, Société Préhistorique Française, Paris, 253 pp.

Bordes, J.-G. 2003. Lithic Taphonomy of the Châtelperronian/Aurignacian Interstratifications in Roc de Combe and Le Piage (Lot, France). In *The Chronology of the Aurignacian and of the Transitional Technocomplexes. Dating, Stratigraphies, CulturalDating, Stratigraphies, Cultural Implications*, edited by Joao Zilhão and Francesco d'Errico, pp. 223–244. Instituto Português de Arqueologia, Lisbon.

Braudel, F. 1969 *Ecrits sur l'histoire*. Flammarion, Paris.

Cattin, M.-I. 2002 *Hauterive-Champréveyres, 13: Un campement magdalénien au bord du lac de Neuchâtel: exploitation du silex (secteur 1)* (Archéologie neuchâteloise, 26). Service et Musée cantonal d'archéologie, Neuchâtel.

Clottes, J., M.-A. Garcia, B. Gély, J.-M. Geneste, M. Girard et al. 2001 *La Grotte Chauvet—l'art des origines*. Éditions du Seuil, Paris.

Clottes, J., J. Courtin, and L. Vanrell 2005 *Cosquer redécouvert*. Art Rupestre, Éditions du Seuil, Paris.

Descola, Ph. 1994 Pourquoi les Indiens d'Amazonie n'ont pas domestiqué le pécari? Généalogie des objets et anthropologie de l'objectivation. In *De la préhistoire aux missiles balistiques. L'intelligence sociale des techniques*, edited by Bruno Latour and Pierre Lemonnier, pp. 329–344. Éditions La Découverte, Paris.

Duke, Ph. 1992 Braudel and North American Archaeology: An Example from the Northern Plains. In *Archaeology, Annales and Ethnohistory,* edited by Arthur Bernard Knapp, pp. 99–111. New Directions in Archaeology. Cambridge University Press, Cambridge.

Fagnart, J.-P. 1997 *La fin des temps glaciaires dans le Nord de la France. Approche archéologique et environnementale des occupations humaines du Tardiglaciaire, Éditions de la Société préhistorique française* (Mémoire de la Société préhistorique française, XXIV), Paris.

Farge A. 2002 Penser et définir l'événement en histoire. Approche des situations et des acteurs sociaux, Terrain, n° 38: 69-78. http://terrain.revues.org/document1929.html.

Fletcher, L. 1992 Time Perspectivism, Annales, and the Potential of Archaeology. In *Archaeology, Annales, and Ethnohistory*, edited by A. B. Knapp, pp. 35–49. Cambridge University Press, Cambridge.

Floss, H. 1994 *Rohmaterialversorgung im Paläolithikum des Mittelrheingebietes* (Römisch-Germanisches Zentralmuseum, Forschungsinstitut für Vor- und Frühgeschichte. Monographie 21). Dr. Rudolf Habelt Verlag, Bonn.

Floss, H. 2000 La fin du Paléolithique en Rhénanie (Magdaléniens, groupes à Federmesser, Ahrensbourgien).L'évolution du choix des matières premières lithiques, reflet d'un profond changement du climat et du comportement humain. In *L'Europe centrale et septentrionale au Tardiglaciaire*, actes de la Table-ronde internationale de Nemours, 14–16 mai 1997, edited by B. Valentin, P. Bodu, and M. Christensen. Éditions de l'A.P.R.A.I.F., Nemours.

Fontana, L. 2000 La chasse au renne au Paléolithique supérieur dans le sud-ouest de la France: nouvelles hypothèses de travail, *Paleo* 12(décembre 2000):141–164.

Furet, F. 1975 De l'histoire-récit à l'histoire-problème, *Diogène* 89 (janvier-mars 1975):106–123.

Gamble 1999 *The Palaeolithic Societies of Europe* (Cambridge World Archaeology series), Cambridge University Press, Cambridge.

GISP2 2006 http://www.gisp2.sr.unh.edu/.

Knapp, A. B. 1992a *Archaeology, Annales and Ethnohistory*. Cambridge University Press, Cambridge.

Knapp, A. B. 1992b Archaeology and Annales: Time, Space and Change. In *Archaeology, Annales and Ethnohistory*, edited by A. Bernard Knapp, pp. 135–142. Cambridge University Press, Cambridge.

Klaric, L. 2003 *L'unité technique des industries à burins du Raysse dans leur contexte diachronique. Réflexions sur la diversité culturelle au Gravettien à partir des données de La Picardie, d'Arcy-sur-Cure, de Brassempoy et du Cique de la Patrie.* Thèse de doctorat en Préhistoire, Université de Paris I, Paris.

Kuzmin, Y.V., G. S. Burr, A. J. T. Jull, and L. D. Sulerzhitsky 2004 AMS ^{14}C Age of the Upper Palaeolithic Skeletons from Sungir Site, Central Russian Plain. *Nuclear Instruments and Methods in Physics Research B* 223–224:731–734.

Leesch, D. 1997 *Hauterive Champréveyres, 10. Un campement magdalénien au bord du lac de Neuchâtel: cadre chronologique et culturel, mobilier et structures, analyse spatiale (secteur 1).* (Archéologie neuchâteloise, 19). Musée cantonal d'Archéologie. Neuchâtel.

Maievski, P., and M. Bender 1995 The GISP2 Ice Core Record—Paleoclimate Highlights, http://www.ncdc.noaa.gov/paleo/icecore/greenland/summit/document/gispinfo.htm#DatingGISP2.

Martinelli, B. 1991 Une chaîne opératoire halieutique au Togo. Réflexions sur la method. In *Observer l'action technique. Des chaînes opératoires, pour quoi faire?*, edited by H. Balfet, pp. 65–86. Éditions du CNRS, Paris.

Minc, L. D. 1986 Scarcity and Survival: The Role of Oral Tradition in Mediating Subsistance Crises. *Journal of Anthropological Archaeology* 5:39–113.

O'Farell, M. 2004 Les pointes de la Gravette de Corbiac (Dordogne) et considerations sur la chasse au Paléolithique supérieur ancient. In *Approches fonctionnelles en Préhistoire, Actes du XXV ème Congrès de la Société Préhistorique Française, Nanterre, 24–26 Novembre 2000*, edited by Pierre Bodu, Claude Constantin, pp. 121–138. Éditions Errance, Paris.

Pelegrin, J. 1995 *Technologie lithique : Le Chatelperronien de Roc-de-Combes (Lot) et de la Côte (Dordogne)*, Éditions du CNRS, Paris.

Pelegrin, J. 2000 Les techniques de débitage laminaire au Tardiglaciaire : critères de diagnose et quelques réflexions. In *L'Europe centrale et septentrionale au Tardiglaciaire, actes de la Table-ronde internationale de Nemours, 14–16 mai 1997,* edited by Boris Valentin, Pierre Bodu, and M. Christensen. Éditions de l'A.P.R.A.I.F., Nemours.

Perlès, C. 1992 In Search of Lithic Strategies: a Cognitive Approach to Prehistoric Chipped Stone Assemblages, In *Representations in Archaeology*, edited by C. Peebles, J-C. Gardin, pp. 223–247. Indiana University Press, Bloomington.

Pigeot, N. 1987 *Magdaléniens d'Étiolles. Economie de débitage et organisation sociale (l'unité d'habitation U5)* (supplément à Gallia Préhistoire XV). CNRS, Paris.

Plisson, H. 2005 Examen tracéologique des pointes aziliennes du Bois-Ragot. In *La Grotte du Bois-Ragot à Gouex (Vienne), Magdalénien et Azilien. Essais sur les hommes et leur environnement,* edited by A. Chollet, V. Dujardin, pp. 183–189. Mémoire de Société Préhistorique Française, XXXVIII. Éditions de la Société Préhistorique Française, Paris.

Ploux, S. 1989 *Approche archéologique de la variabilité des comportements techniques individuals. Les tailleurs de l'unité 27-M89 de Pincevent*, these de doctorat, Université de Paris X, 2 vol.

Riede, F. 2008 The Laacher See-Eruption (12,920 BP) and Material Culture Change at the End of the Allerød in Northern Europe, *Journal of Archaeological Science* 25:591–599.

Sheratt, A. 1992 What Can Archaeologists Learn from Annalistes? In *Archaeology, Annales and Ethno-history*, edited by A. Bernard Knapp, pp. 135–142. Cambridge University Press, Cambridge.

Skibo, J. M., and M. B. Schiffer 2008 *People and Things. A Behavioral Approach to Material Culture.* Springer, New York.

Taborin, Y. 1993 La Parue en coquillage au Paléolithique. XXIXème supplément à Gallia Préhistoire. Éditions du CNRS, Paris.

Torrence, R. 1983 Time Budgeting and Hunter-Gatherer Technology. In *Hunter-Gatherer Economy in Prehistory: an European Perspective*, edited by G. Bailey, pp. 135–142. Cambridge University Press, Cambridge.

Valentin, B. 2005 La fabrication des armatures et des outils en silex des couches aziliennes 3 et 4. In *La grotte du Bois-Ragot à Gouex (Vienne). Magdalénien et azilien, Essai sur les homes et leur environnement,* edited by A. Chollet and V. Dujardin, pp. 89–182. Mémoire de la Société Préhistorique Française XXXVIII. Éditions de la Société Préhistorique Française, Paris.

Valentin, B. 2006 *De l'Oise à la Vienne en passant par le Jourdain, Jalons pour une paléohistoire des derniers chasseurs.* Rapport d'HDR (Habilitation à la Direction de Recherche), Université de Paris I , Paris.

Valentin, B. 2008 *Jalons pour une paléohistoire des derniers chasseurs.* Publications de la Sorbonne, Paris.

Vanhaeren, M. 2002 *Les fonctions de la parure au Paléolithique supérieur: de l'individu à l'unité culturelle.* thèse de doctorat. Université de Bordeaux-I, Bordeaux.

Vanhaeren, M., F. d'Errico, I. Billy, and F. Grousset 2004 Tracing the Source of Upper Palaeolithic Shell Beads by Strontium Isotope Dating. *Journal of Archaeological Science* Volume 31(10):1481–1488.

Veynes, P. 1996 L'interprétation et l'interprète. A propos des choses de la religion. In *Enquête, Anthropologie, Histoire, Sociologie.* Enquête, n° 3: "Interpréter, surinterpréter": 241–272, http://enquete.revues.org/document623.html.

Whallon, R. 2006 Social Networks and Information: Non-"Utilitarian" Mobility among Hunter-Gatherers, *Journal of Anthropological Archaeology* 25(2):259–270.

CHAPTER THREE

Becoming, Phenomenal Change, Event

Past and Archaeological Re-presentations

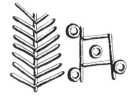

Dušan Borić

Abstract *First, the paper examines the usefulness of Braudel's tripartite division of history and subsequent discussions about the approaches of the* Annales *school of historical analyses within the field of phenomenological philosophy provided by Paul Ricoeur. This critique argues that the event should be seen as the main site of historical analyses since the notion of event, of different qualities and duration, conflates the* longue durée *levels identified by Braudel: geohistory happens on the human scale and in relation to trends and specific events while economies or empires of the second level equally depend on determining events. Implications for archaeology are examined.*

Second, the paper discusses the microhistorical "politics of event." Event is seen as the "principle of individuation" that emerges out of the perpetual process of becoming. Can archaeology tell a story of potentialities, of failed projects of history, of "non-events"? And, are microhistorical, individual narratives and events "slender clues" of much larger phenomena, or are different scales of historical analyses incommensurable? These questions are illustrated by an example of determining events of structured abandonment of built and mortuary features in a series of collective re-presentations within the context of changing cultural repertoires affecting Mesolithic foragers in the Danube Gorges of the Balkans from 6300 to 5900 cal BC.

> For when something occurs, it may be said that that which previously remained only a potential or a virtuality now emerges and becomes actual, though only in place of something else that could have arisen here at this time, but did not. This double "difference"—between what is here now but previously was not—and between what emerged and what did not, in all of its complexity and fatality and in all of its pregnant virtuality or potentiality is what I will call "the event." The event is a principle of individuation. (Kwinter 2001:48–49).

Introduction

It has recently been suggested that William Sewell's work (e.g., 2005) and his concept of the event in historical narratives can be a useful way also for archaeologists to think through their case studies and to come up with a novel perspective on the question of "structural change" in history (Beck et al. 2007). Yet, I feel that the Sewell's definition of event is very particular. Events are, according to Sewell, "rapid transformations of structure." I would like to suggest in this paper that it is important to keep the definition of the notion of event open, recognizing that it could be of different durations, to include both brief happenings that are not necessarily seen to have changed structures *and* changes that occur on longer time scales, including lifecycles of institutions, and even those events on the scale of geohistory. The reasons for these are both methodological and ontological/ethical for the disciplines of archaeology and history.

In this paper, I would like to examine the notion of event and theories of phenomenal change from the perspective of Deleuze and Guattari's (1987) discussion on *becoming* (following Bergson). In the world of seemingly stable phenomena, connecting events to becoming should be seen as a way of breaking out from the confines of "flattened" and spatialized time in an attempt to take temporal duration seriously (cf. Kwinter 2001).

In what follows, first I discuss the trajectory with regard to the use of the notion of event in the *Annales* school and a subsequent critique of certain of its elements provided from the perspective of phenomenological philosophy, with an important guidance offered by the philosopher Paul Ricoeur. Then, I discuss a possibility to use the notion of representation as a substitute for the use of notion of mentality in our discussions about the past reality and whether the notion of representation better serves the project of representing an eventful past. This then leads one to emphasize the microhistorical level of analyses as well as interdependence of different scales of inquiry. Here the notion of event is also related to the unfolding of individual projects, that is, to agents of social change, by illustrating these theoretical points with two examples that come from the Mesolithic-Neolithic Balkans. Further, I show how the "return of the event" and the individual as singularity has both methodological and ontological consequences in our attempts to represent the past. Finally, resurfacing from strictly methodological and epistemological concerns about the fate of the event in archaeological narratives, the transformative power of the event is related to the notion of becoming in the theorization of the relationship between the temporal flux and structural change. Hence, the paper unfolds from a contraintuitive perspective, different from the suggestion given in the title.

Events of Different Durations

Archaeologists deal with time and temporal scales in a routine way. The corollary negative effect that has been created is "spatialized" time, divided up in discrete blocks (periods, phases, subphases) where "transitions and origins have been the currency of theoretical debates" (Hodder 1999:130). On the methodological side of our concerns, these largely unsatisfactory conceptualizations of time in archaeological narratives require more explicit conceptualizations of "time" and an identification of its constitutive elements. One of the approaches adopted in archaeology, through influences coming from the French historian Fernand Braudel, points out the possibility of distinguishing and dealing with different temporal levels on their own merits while at the same time comprehending their interdependence. The notion of the "event" as a "singularity" (Kwinter 2001:26) or a "temporal building block" (Carr 1986:43) should play the key role in such an enterprise. This concept should make a particular archaeological sequence "rich" in interdependent temporal links, as a mode of analysis that prefers the "thick description" of social life (Geertz 1973) to the uniform *topos* of culture change.

In the discipline of archaeology, some of the initial interest with regard to a more explicit theoretization of time came from Hodder's (1987) project of archaeology as long-term history. Hodder problematized issues about continuity and change, structure and event in the archaeological analyses of material record via temporal scales proposed by Braudel in his work *The Mediterranean and the Mediterranean World in the Age of Philip II* (1972). Braudel's thesis about the plurality of social times has received a fair share of interest among the archaeologists in the last two decades of the twentieth century. This historian's scheme of three different temporal levels on which historical processes can be studied—very long-term structures of geohistory, social structures consisting of economic, political trends, and civilizations, and the level of traditional chronicle history of brief events—has a particular resonance for archaeologists, primarily in relation to the first level of long-term processes where archaeology traditionally finds itself at home (cf. Bailey 1981, 1983, 1987, 2007). Although archaeology may possibly best contribute to the analyses of the past at this first level, Hodder significantly emphasizes that we need to be aware that "it is the shorter-term changes which reproduce and create the longer term" (1987:5). Even more radically, Paul Ricoeur (1984:206ff.) in the first part of his trilogy *Time and Narrative*, under his analysis of historical intentionality in relation to the "fate of event," identifies the concept of event as the main site of historical analysis. This is related to Ricoeur's use of the notion of emplotment and the theory of plot derived from Aristotle. It suffices here to say that historical events in Ricoeur's view resemble the epistemological character and configuration of events and causalities in literary texts. According to this author, event is characterized by "singularity, contingency, deviation" (Ricoeur 1984:207) and henceforth, "due to the fact that they are narrated, events are singular *and* typical, contingent *and* expected, deviant *and* dependent on paradigms" (Ricoeur 1984:208; original emphasis). Ricoeur is determined to show that both the first and the second levels as identified by Braudel are conflated with the notion of event (for example, geohistory happens on the human scale and in relation to trends and specific events, while economies or empires of the second level equally depend on determining events). Yet, there is a difference in the quality of event at these two levels, since these determining events are distinguished from the notion of the "nervous" and "explosive" character of events as the "ephemera of brief happenings" (Hodder 1987:2) on the third level; thus, "the notion of event…lose[s] its usual qualities of brevity and suddenness in order to measure up to the discordances and ruptures that punctuate the life of economic, social, and ideological structures of an individual society" (Ricoeur 1984:230). The conclusion of Ricoeur's analyses in *Time and Narrative* has it that the Mediterranean in Braudel's work can be seen as a quasi-character, where the death of Philip II relates to the decline of the Mediterranean itself.

Braudel's emphasis on historically long time spans and the temporal pluralization that allows, in his words, "dissecting of history in various planes" (Braudel 1972:21) is important inasmuch as one emphasizes the "principle of unity" of the three levels. Yet, the problem with Braudel's analyses is that these different scales instead of communicating with each other rather just pile and "stuck up" these different levels (Ricoeur 2004:193). Braudel, as part of the *Annales* school and as a disciple of its founders Marc Bloch and Lucien Febvre, also expressed a certain "horror of the event." It certainly was a reaction to obsessive emphasis of the previous generations of historians on political events. In the last third of the twentieth century, however, one witnesses the "return of the event" in French historiography through the works of historians such as Jacques Le Goff and Pierre Nora (1974). As an echo of this return of the event in humanistic and social sciences, one also finds archaeological accounts identifying singular events and particular individuals as important sites of our analyses (e.g., Meskell 1996, 1998; Hodder 1999).

Productively joining together different temporal scales identified by Braudel, one achieves a synthesis of heterogeneous elements and, furthermore, points to a possibility of overcoming, in Jacques Le Goff's words, "the false dilemma of structure versus conjuncture and, even more important, structure versus event" (Le Goff 1980:235, cited by Ricoeur 1984:218). The notion of event must be kept as the basic building block of our *representations* of the past. And it is exactly this notion of representation that may interestingly relate to our theoretical musings about the importance of the event.

Re-presentation Instead of Mentality

Here we continue to reflect on the significance and the problematic of the concepts suggested by the *Annales* school, which served as an important inspiration for archaeologists in their theoretization of time, temporal durations, or in understanding and depicting the past through archaeological narratives. The hope is that many of the previously identified concepts by this particular historiographic school can be useful starting points in developing theoretically and ethically nuanced notions in attempts to deal with the time past. In the early phases of the establishment of the *Annales* school the sociological notion of "primitive mentality" was inherited from Lucien Lévy-Bruhl (1966; 1978), in the tradition of Émile Durkheim. The notion of mentality figured as the preferred site of analyses within this historiographic tradition and has for so long been one of the trademarks of the *Annales* school. However, more recently, some authors have emphasized certain problems with the notion of mentality (*mentalité*). For example, in his work *Demystifying mentalities*, Geoffrey Lloyd (1990) provides a very anthropological critique of the notion of mentality, suggesting that it is methodologically *useless* and ethically *harmful*: "[I]t is construction of the observer projected on the worldview of the actors in question" (Ricoeur 2004:199). Lloyd suggests the notion of the "style of inquiry" that is less judgmental and more true to our attempts of rescuing the "victims of history" (cf. Ricoeur 1988) from their anonymity while giving them their voice.

Ricoeur sees the use of the notion of mentality as "a lazy mode of explanation" (Ricoeur 2004:199). Going beyond the critique and deconstruction of the notion of mentality, he suggests that the notion of representation can better be used to express the idea of identities being connected to a particular social bond.

> [T]he notion of mentality seems to operate in a heavy-handed fashion, like the quasi-immobile structures of the long time span, or of cyclic conjunctures, the event being reduced to a function that indicates a break. Therefore, over against the unilateral, undifferentiated, massive idea of mentality, that of representation expresses better the plurivocity, the differentiation, and the multiple temporalization of social phenomena. (Ricoeur 2004:227)

Here, Ricoeur proposes "a mimetic relation between the operation of representing as the moment of doing history [by historians], and the represented object as the moment of making history" (Ricoeur 2004:229). This suggestion could be seen as reminiscent of Clifford Geertz's (1973) idea of self-understanding as being immanent to a culture.

Thus, from the side of concerns with methodology of narrating about the past, to speak of representations (in plural) of the past is to individuate the past in going beyond the notion of the event that indicates a structural change, transition, an arbitrary decision of decisive turns only (*contra* Sewell). It underlines the fundamental role of events as points of individuation and crossroads of possibilities. At the same time, this approach assures historians or archaeologists that they can rely on the *resistance* of a particular type of past reality that is in this way being represented. In other words, the material culture rhetoric of a particular material configuration, for instance, in the use of narrative theory in relation to a stratigraphic sequence (see Hodder 1993; 1995), could be productively seen as indicative of an individual's or community's self-representation, objectification, and/or resistance.

On the other hand, in terms of the ethics of archaeological practice, this emphasis on the notion of representation may help liberate history and the *representation* of the past from the historical determinism of totalizing history and "retrospective illusion of fatality" (Aron 1961:183). Ricoeur insists on the semantics of the word *re*-presentation in order to give voice to the social agents in the past.

Also, there is an inevitable dialectic relationship between a collective representation and a particular event that are mutually constitutive. In describing the milieu of layered historicity that led to the death of Captain Cook in Hawaii, here is how Marshall Sahlins conceptualizes the relationship between a particular event and its collective representation:

> Death of Cook: death of Lono. The event was absolutely unique, and it was repeated every year. For the event (any event) unfolds simultaneously on two levels: as individual action and as collective *representation*; or better, as the *relation* between certain life histories and a history that is over and above these, the existence of societies. To paraphrase Clifford Geertz, the event is unique actualization of a general phenomenon [1961:153–54]. Hence on the one hand, historical contingency and the particularities of individual action; and on the other hand, those recurrent dimensions of the event in which we recognize some cultural order. The paradox for an historical "science" is that the contingent circumstances, such as the accidents of biography or geography—are necessary conditions. (Sahlins 1985:108–109; first emphasis aided)

Such emphasis on particularities of individual actions leads us to the discussion of microhistory seen as a scale on which uncertainty and indeterminacy reign.

MICROHISTORY AND VARIATION IN SCALE

The methodological turn that brought back the event into historiography also, to a large extent, relates to the project of doing microhistory, which has been advocated by a number of French and Italian historians in the first place, and also taken up more recently in discussions by some archaeologists (e.g., Meskell, Hodder, Tringham, etc.). One of the very influential works of this historiographic school (although not even close as much in archaeology as in social anthropology) is Carlo Ginzburg's the *Cheese and the Worms: The Cosmos of a Sixteenth century Miller* (1980) where on the basis of written testimonies of sixteenth-century inquisition trials against what was seen as a miller's heretic theological views, one gets a complex picture of both exceptionality and paradigmatic nature of this particular individual in his time. While the advocates of microhistory point to the singularity by looking at the historical reality through the magnifying glass, the emphasis is rather placed on the notion of a *variation in scale*, seeing different concatenations at different scales.

There is a very diverse group of authors emphasizing the importance of the microhistorical scale, and of the event as the cornerstone of history. But, the notion of event also resurrects from the least expected corners of the theoretical spectrum. For example, although frequently (and one may add unjustly) accused for "terrorist antihistorism" (cf. Ricoeur 2004:195), here is what Lévi-Strauss thinks of history and the unpredictable character of the event, in an interview given in 1988:

> My respect for history and the taste I have for it originate in the feeling it gives me that no construction in the human mind can replace the unpredictable way in which things really happen. The event in its contingency seems to me an irreducible given. (Lévi-Strauss and Eribon 1991:125)

Lévi-Strauss continues:

> I have never claimed that you can reduce the whole human experience to mathematical models. The idea that structural analysis can account for everything in social life seems outrageous—it has never occurred to me. On the contrary, it seems to me that social life and the empirical reality surrounding it, when seen on human scale, unfold mostly at random (which is why I defer to history, with its utter unpredictability). I think that in this vast empirical stew, if you'll pardon the expression, where disorder reigns, are scattered small islands of organization. (Lévi-Strauss and Eribon 1991:102)

Importantly, the microhistory that relies on individuals and singular events is the scale that can best be characterized by *uncertainty*. While not denying the importance to process of heuristic schematization and abstraction when it comes to social and historical realities, one should not lose sight of singularities as instances that "do not fit." To quote one of the champions of generalizations, Max Weber, on this question: "It is absolutely necessary, in order to bring out the characteristic differences, to speak in terms of ideal types, thus in a certain sense doing violence to historical reality." (Weber 1992:233, note 68)

In this context of the discussion of the level of uncertainty on which individual projects unfold, one could ask a critical question: "How representative is a concatenation circumscribed in this way? What can it teach us that should be generalizable?" (Revel 1996: xxx). I will try to give some answers to this question by discussing a particular case study and by showing that the scale of microhistory can provide significant clues about much larger phenomena. In the following, I will turn to two contexts at two neighboring and contemporaneous sites in order to show how one could connect different scales and what particular events in relation to particular individuals may tell us about how these individual instances may reflect larger phenomena of social change. In doing so, I emphasize both their paradigmatic value for identifying larger trends as well as the inherent deviation of a series of events characteristic of individual projects.

INDIVIDUAL AND CULTURAL REPRESENTATIONS OF MESOLITHIC-NEOLITHIC TRANSFORMATIONS IN THE DANUBE GORGES OF THE BALKANS

The example that should illustrate previously developed theoretical points about the individuated character of the notions of event and representation relates to the period of forager-farmer transformations that started taking place in Europe around 6300 cal BC when the first Early Neolithic communities appear across southeastern Europe. One aspect of this phenomenon of "structural change" that I would in particular consider relates to instances of interactions between first farmers and local foragers and the mechanism of social change that constituted these interactions.

The case study I am focusing on is situated in the region of the Danube Gorges of the north-central Balkans. A number of Mesolithic-Neolithic sites in this region, found primarily on the banks of the River Danube, cover a long time span of the regional Mesolithic with the continuing existence into the Neolithic period. The eponymous site of Lepenski Vir is well known for its buildings with trapezoidal-shaped bases covered with limestone plaster. There were rectangular stone-lined hearths in the center of each building while ornamented boulder artworks, in a number of cases depicting human/fish hybrids, were found on the floor level, usually around the hearth (e.g., Borić 2005; Radovanović 1996; Srejović 1972). A particular type of existence was developing in this region over several millennia that connected the religious and ideological aspects of life with practical action of fishing on the River Danube. To illustrate a wider theoretical discussion on the importance of emphasizing the notion of event, not exclusively for explaining structural change but rather exposing it as the critical element in narratives about the past, I use examples of particular contexts from two neighboring sites in the region: Lepenski Vir and Vlasac.

LEPENSKI VIR

The most prominent feature at Lepenski Vir are buildings with trapezoidal bases that are exclusively confined to the phase of transformation (phase I–II) contemporaneous with the wider regional Early Neolithic. Aided by the new radiometric evidence, the duration of this phase can now be more precisely placed in the period from around 6200 to around 6000 or 5950 cal BC (Borić and Dimitrijević 2007, 2009; Borić et al. forthcoming). At the current chronological scale we see a significant change at around 5950/5900 cal BC with the introduction of the Neolithic way of life. This change is reflected in the introduction of domesticates but also in the changes affecting the mortuary domain with the appearance of crouched inhumations, among other archaeologically visible phenomena, as an indication of the arrival of the Neolithic cultural repertoire. Here, I will describe in particular several instances of structured deposition of animal remains in relation to particular burials. These instances seem to have been pregnant with specific ideological, symbolic, and/or religious messages. Furthermore, such examples, that is, recognition of particular events, can be seen as specific forms of individual and cultural representations.

One element frequently connected with the "special" (burial or other) contexts in Mesolithic Europe—from the Balkans to southern Scandinavia and Britain—relates to the deposition of red deer antlers with or without skull or antlers' symbolic use in shamanistic transformations, the practice that might also have been reified in preserved examples of red deer frontlets from Star Carr (cf. Conneler 2004; Borić 2007a). The region of the Danube Gorges with a long Mesolithic tradition is not an exception to this pattern and at a number of sites red deer antlers were associated with individual or group burials. On the other hand, similarly perpetuated over the long term, across southwest Asia the symbolism of aurochs, among other important animals, could be singled out as dominant in the visual depictions, structured depositions, and in form of bucrania found in buildings since the PPNA period (e.g., Cauvin 1998). In the period of Mesolithic-Neolithic transformations in the Danube Gorges and at the site of Lepenski Vir in particular, it seems that one encounters a meeting point of these two particular ways of expressing the symbolic power of particular animals, as the following examples indicate.

At Lepenski Vir, during phase I–II connected with trapezoidal buildings, one finds red deer antlers as elements of structured deposition placed on the floor upon the end of a life cycle of use of particular buildings, but also in association with burials (e.g., Borić 2003, 2007b; Borić and Dimitrijević 2005; Dimitrijević 2008). Such is the case with building 61/ XXIV where red deer antlers and a detached skull were found on the floor level along with disarticulated bones of several individuals marked as Burial 45a–c (Figure 1) (Burial 45b is dated by OxA-11701 to 6388–6077 cal BC at 95 percent confidence: Bonsall et al. 2008). A number of unspecified animal bones were found associated with the burial and this commingling of disarticulated human and animal bones could indicate a close connection and the existence of a continuum between human and animal realms, which is also indicated through depictions of boulder artworks (Borić 2005). Red deer antlers were also found in several other buildings (no. 22, 26, 28, 46, 57/XLIV) at the site, placed there upon the abandonment of these structures and often found in relation to articulated and disarticulated burials (e.g., burial pit with Burials 13–17).

Another instance that confirms this important link between burials and certain animals at Lepenski Vir relates to building 21, the last among trapezoidal buildings overlapped through horizontal displacement of each new floor while keeping a symmetry in the alignment of rectangular stone hearths of each overlapped building (see Stefanović and Borić 2008:Figure 15). The abandonment of the space of building 21 was marked by a burial interment made in a pit behind the rectangular hearth. The deceased was an adult male placed in an extended supine position parallel to the current of the River Danube, while the deceased's head was oriented to point in the downstream direction. This type of burial rite is typical of the Late Mesolithic period at a number of sites found along the river in the Danube Gorges and remains one of the rules for the burials found in association with trapezoidal buildings during the phase of transformation from around 6200–5900 cal BC. On

(a)

(b)

FIGURE 1 (a) Building 61/XXXIV; and (b) close-up of Burial 45b and red deer antlers, Lepenski Vir.

FIGURE 2 Burial 7/I and 7/II accompanied by an aurochs and red deer skulls, Building 21, Lepenski Vir.

the left shoulder of this primary articulation marked as Burial 7/I, a disarticulated human skull was found marked as 7/II (Figure 2). On the right shoulder of this individual an aurochs skull was found, while on the same side with the aurochs skull, underneath it, a red deer skull with antlers was also accompanying this burial. A sample from the red deer skull with antlers has been dated directly, giving a surprisingly late date but the one that can be comparable with the dates obtained for the two human individuals (red deer: 5840–5728; Burial 7/I: 6216–5884; Burial 7/II: 6080–5746—all cal BC at 95 percent of confidence, see Borić and Dimitrijević 2009; Borić et al. forthcoming). Such dating may indicate that this burial possibly overlaps with the beginning of phase III at Lepenski Vir, which marks the onset of the Middle Neolithic when most of the trapezoidal buildings might have already been abandoned and when crouched inhumations started dominating the mortuary record at the site.

An independent confirmation of such late dating are dietary signatures based on stable isotope analyses of the two individuals. While the disarticulated skull has the isotopic signature characteristic of the Mesolithic in the Danube Gorges, that is, the one where aquatic sources were considerably present in the diet, the isotopic signature of the articulated inhumation is considerably different, and it falls in the group of burials at this site where aquatic resources were no longer a dominant food source (see Borić et al. 2004). Finally, the very late dating of this burial can also be justified on the basis of the presence of the auroch skull. In no other chronologically earlier context were aurochs skulls found associated with any form of structured deposition at this or any other contemporaneous site in this region. On the other hand, there are instances of Middle Neolithic burials in the wider region of the Balkans associated with aurochs' skulls and horncores (see Borić 1999), confirming its exclusive connection to the Neolithic cultural repertoire. The described instance at Lepenski Vir may indicate the coexistence and merging of different burial rites, with people subscribing to both the "Mesolithic" potency of red deer and the "Neolithic" potency of aurochs.

It seems that in the last case one witnesses a profound cultural hybridization of two different cultural repertoires—one indigenous and the other new, associated with the spread of the Neolithic—found in a single burial at Lepenski Vir that encompassed heterogeneous, old, and new cultural elements: (1) attachment to the tradition of trapezoidal buildings; (2) the burial position of supine extended articulation parallel to the River Danube inherited from the Late Mesolithic and possibly related to beliefs about the totemic significance of migratory sturgeon species and their annual migration up and down the river; (3) an ornamented sandstone boulder placed on the top of the head of the deceased and visible on the floor level of building 21; (4) red deer skull with antlers as an important symbolic resource of Mesolithic communities in Europe; and, (5) the skull of aurochs as the symbolic representative of several millennia-long Neolithic "mentalities" or "representations" that are at this historical juncture appearing in the Danube Gorges and the central Balkans for the first time.

This pattern found in Burial 7/I is additionally confirmed in the case of another burial at Lepenski Vir. Burial 89, an extended supine inhumation parallel to the Danube, is dated to the same transformational phase (OxA-11702: 6210–5898 cal BC at 95 per cent confidence, see Bonsall et al. 2008). Here, an aurochs head with horncores was placed above the head of the deceased (Figure 3). Similar to the previously described instance, one finds the type of burial position that has its roots in the cultural repertoire of the local Mesolithic development, while the presence of aurochs in association with the deceased very likely indicates the importance of incoming Neolithic symbolic, ideological, and/or religious values, as an element of a wider cultural representation.

VLASAC

A related example comes from the neighboring site of Vlasac, the site in the immediate vicinity of the previously discussed Lepenski Vir and belonging to the same cultural phenomenon. New excavations at this site in 2006 brought to light an important discovery of a burial feature that suggests the continuous use of Vlasac from the Late/Terminal Mesolithic throughout the Early Neolithic, providing the first secure evidence about the contemporaneity of Vlasac and the phase of trapezoidal buildings at Lepenski Vir discussed previously (Borić 2006, 2007c, 2010b). Here one observes the same kind of burial rite as that seen at Lepenski Vir for the duration of the Late Mesolithic and the transformational phase at this site. In the discovered group burial "ossuary," for several centuries people buried their dead with the same pattern of laying down the body of the deceased parallel to the river and occasionally burning the bones of the old dead before interring a new body (Borić

FIGURE 3 Burial 89, Lepenski Vir, placed in extended position with aurochs skull placed over the head of the deceased.

et al. 2009). Similar to Lepenski Vir, the change here is visible at the micro scale primarily in relation to the individual adornment of the deceased. The burial rite remains the same in the phase of transformation (6200–5900 cal BC) and one also sees the continuing symbolic importance of the, so to speak, "Mesolithic" animal such as red deer being similarly placed as at Lepenski Vir in the act of structured deposition when abandoning this burial feature, on top of the last inhumation (Figure 4). The echo of wider changes is reflected in the type of bodily decoration. There is a major change during the mentioned period in the type of exotic, marine shell—"Neolithic" type of beads made of Spondylus species popular in later Neolithic times replace *Cyclope neritea*, a marine snail that previously dominated the aesthetic and social tastes in adornment during the long span of the Mesolithic period (Borić 2007b, 2007c). Beads made of Spondylus shells enter the world of this community at the time when the world of the Neolithic Balkans experiences the change that we at the long-term scale call the transition to farming.

Previous examples of cultural and individual representations, on the one hand, highlight the fact that a single burial could give away clues about larger-scale phenomena, thus collapsing the difference between micro and macro scales, showing the interdependence of different scales of inquiry and the fractal image of archaeological evidence at different scales. Here, one confronts the conflation of different scales that should not remain within separate domains. Previously separated for analytical reasons, these different scales now intersect, both in the way the social agents in the past represent their social worlds—those inherited

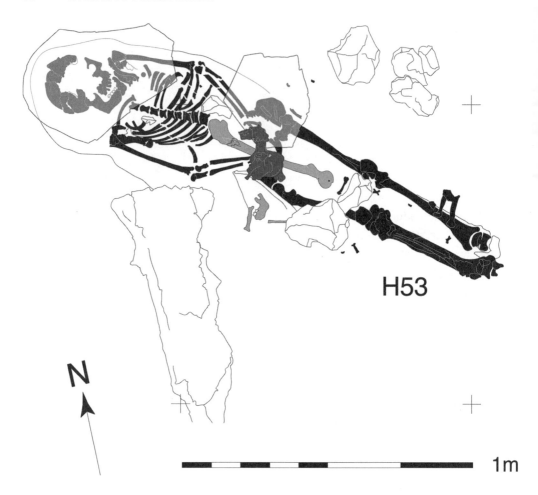

FIGURE 4 The last inhumation, Burial H53, in the group burial discovered at Vlasac in 2006. The burial is covered by stone plaques while the red deer skull with broken antlers was placed over the pelvis of the deceased symmetrically aligned with the skull of a child Burial H21.

from the past and those that are put to test by each new generation—and in our subsequent narrative configuring of these worlds through our representations, which are conjured from the evidence available to us. In the work of Jürgen Habermas one could find a very elegant understanding of the interdependence between different scales in the way individual and collective experiences tackle and eventually change pre-given structures, and here is a passage that succinctly summarizes Habermas's ideas:

> Habermas [suggests] the dialectical interdependence between a historically shaped understanding of the world and the experience and practice possible within its horizon. Innerworldly practice is indeed informed by general, pregiven structures of world-understanding; but these structures are in turn affected and changed by the cumulative results of experiencing and acting within the world. Social practice submits the background knowledge of the lifeworld to an "ongoing test" across the entire spectrum of validity claims that makes learning process possible—learning process that may well cast doubt on the adequacy of the world views informing social practice. (McCarthy 1987:ix)

Going beyond the concern with scales, described instances are at the same time not only a part of an emerging pattern of structural transformation taking place over several centuries of Mesolithic-Neolithic cultural, religious, social, ideological, economic, etc., changes, but are at the same time irreducibly singular events, that is, "unique actualizations of a general phenomenon" (Sahlins 1985:108; see above) that should be seen as active and engaging contributions to what we observe as the period of change. To make use of the previous discussion about the preferable use of the term *representation* to that of mentality, one could see the described instances of using heterogeneous forms of cultural representation in the context of structured deposition and burials as unique statements, or material narratives that are meaningfully constituted.

Recent methodological pedantry of insisting on the preferred use of the term *palimpsest* for the accumulative and aggregate nature of the archaeological record, instead of *event* (see Bailey 2007; Lucas 2008), while analytically elegant and useful for archaeological cases lacking in instances of structured deposition, misses an important epistemological and ethical point. This point relates to the need to preserve the sense of singularity of events, and I turn to this point next.

Preserving the Sense of Indeterminacy

Away from methodological phases of historical or archaeological operations, it is quite true that "singularity and brevity of the event go together with the major presupposition of the so-called event-oriented history, namely, that the individual is the ultimate bearer of historical change" (Ricoeur 2004:240). This emphasis on the individual seen in a number of recent archaeological accounts under the influence of third wave feminism (e.g., Hodder, Meskell, etc.) has also recently been criticized by some archaeologists, particularly in Britain, arguing that by the emphasis on individual in the past one imposes the individualism of the present-day culture onto the past agents. Yet, the importance of the individual, singular, event has to be differentiated from the individualism of the present-day for important methodological as well as ethical reasons. It relates to the question of seriously "reintroducing contingency into history:"

> People of the past once were, like us, subjects of initiative, of retrospection, and of prospection. The epistemological consequences of this consideration are substantial. Knowing that people of the past formulated expectations, predictions, desires, fears, and projects is to fracture historical determinism by retrospectively reintroducing contingency into history. (Ricoeur 2004:381–382)

Raymond Aron, speaking of contingency and necessity in historical causation, says the following: "We understand here by contingency both the possibility of conceiving the other event and the impossibility of deducing the event from the totality of the previous situation" (Aron 1961:222). His conception of history is seen as "the effort to resurrect, or more exactly the effort to put oneself back at the moment of the action in order to become the actor's contemporary" (Aron 1961:232). This is, then, also close to Collingwood's (1956) idea of "reenactment" of the past in the present.

We should remember that recent calls for the revival of grand narratives by neo-Darwinian archaeologists, such as Stephen Shennan, with regard to culture transmission and change are inevitably biased toward successful and victorious projects of human history seen as products of cultural selection homologous to natural selection. By such reasoning one neglects those individual and cultural projects that may seem as "dead ends" from a social evolutionary perspective of progressive development. The small scale of "uncertainty" and events that do not conform to larger structures are thus left to decay in historical forgetfulness. Here, one is obliged to strongly emphasize the importance of returning to the microhistory scale that, according to Raymond Aron (1961), is a way to "defatalize" the past, "to place oneself in the situation of the protagonists, who, themselves, had a future; to place oneself in the situation of uncertainty in which they found themselves when they were waiting for, fearing, hoping for, and in any case lacking knowledge of, what would come after" (Ricoeur 1998:124).

Close to this is Michel Foucault's (1972) plea for genealogy that, according to this author, is to "replace the unitary, necessary and invariant with the multiple, contingent, and arbitrary" (McCarthy 1987:xiv) since under historical event he sees the way "in terms of which we constitute ourselves as subjects and objects of knowledge" (McCarthy 1987:xiv).

BECOMING, PHENOMENAL CHANGE, AND EVENT

Going beyond the concerns for methodology/epistemology in our dealings with temporal duration and scales, or ethical concerns about preserving the sense of individuality of "victims of history" and their (un)successful projects reified in series of frequently incoherent and dissonant representations, in this final section of the paper I would like to go to the core of thinking about event and its problematization in the domain of theories of phenomenal change.

Sanford Kwinter, in his book *Architectures of Time: Toward a Theory of the Event in Modernist Culture* (2001), develops an exciting theory of phenomenal change by identifying event as the main site of what is proposed as a way to radicalize the theory of time (2001:11). While Kwinter quotes a wide spectrum of inspirations and develops his argument with regard to the modernist culture, his analysis strongly resonates with archaeologists as his discussion is closely connected to modernist architecture and the connection between temporal and material. In fact, it is exactly in materialities that Kwinter identifies particular thickness of temporal durations. In this way, his position is explicitly materialist in the sense of Epicurean atomism. His discussion is strongly influenced by the writings of Henri Bergson and also a particular discussion on "becoming" in Deleuze and Guattari's *A Thousand Plateaus* (1987:chapter 10). Kwinter is interested in exploring phenomenal change and " 'corruptive,' transformative effects of time in relation to the doctrine of essential and immutable forms" (2001:37). In developing a radical theory of time, Kwinter finds inspiration in the context of modernist culture in various representatives of Italian futurist movement, Nietzsche, and Foucault, but in particular in the work of Franz Kafka.

In Kafka's novel *The Metamorphosis* (1972), one follows a slow transformation or metamorphosis of the main character Gregor Samsa into a "monstrous vermin." Similar importance in this context can be attributed to anthropological philosophy of George Bataille's work on animality and the human fascination with "animal's glance" with "*the desire to destroy the self-consciousness* rather than to attain it" (Kwinter 2001:177; original emphasis). The uncanny world that Kafka so accurately constructs (and not only in *The Metamorphosis* [1972]) is conceptualized as an unstable world of (substratum) *becoming*. In this world, stages of change "begin as microscopic events that intervene in and mobilize an inert world of fixed relations by projecting into everything the aleatory flow of time…a time that destabilizes Forms, tearing them out of their fixed perches in Being and embedding them in the stochastic current of a (perpetual) *Verwandlung*, or Becoming" (Kwinter 2001:167).

In this radical theory of time and materials, what matters are movements of different speeds. Deleuze and Guattari (1987:261) call it *haecceity*—something that makes a thing that particular thing, its "thisness" or "whatness," in other words, "capacities to affect and be affected." For Deleuze, who developed his ideas about the event most explicitly in his work *The Logic of Sense* (1990), the event is a pure Outside, which also Kafka's works clearly reference (see above). The event is only possible through the movement and becoming, resisting the framework of past-present-future: "the event is always that which has just happened and that which is about to happen, but never that which is happening" (Deleuze 1990:63).

Conclusions

Three main ideas have been sketched in the previous discussion.

First, the importance of homological links along the axis individual:society event:structure was emphasized, seeing narratives as mediators between events and structures. In other words, it is the narrative that provides the coherence in connecting different levels as "synthesis of heterogeneous elements" (Ricoeur 1984). Event is understood as constitutive of different scales without a privileged site of inquiry between microhistory and large-scale phenomena, while it is the narrative that is seen as the "third time" that weaves such different scales together as historical/archaeological re-presentations of a particular past. Here one establishes a homology between the way social agents understood their world in the formation of their identity connected to a specific form of social bond (in other words: their culture or cultures) and our *re*-presentations of the past through interpretations.

Second, the event is emphasized as singularity/individuality, which relates both to methodological issues of heuristic importance when studying particular archaeological evidence as well as to the philosophy of history. The latter is in particular related to an obligation to preserve the sense of indeterminacy in history by stressing the notion of debt to the dead seen as "victims of history" (Ricoeur 1984, 2004). Archaeological interpretations can thus be seen as attempts at reenacting of the past lived action (*sensu* Collingwood 1956) that *really* happened (*sensu* Ranke: *als eigentlich war*) by emphasizing the truth element of the past as that which separates archaeological/historical narratives from fictional narratives. Such a perspective should prevent inflicting harm on the memory of past human beings when giving archaeological interpretations of a particular past while, at the same time, celebrating the sense of idiosyncrasy (cf. Borić 2010a).

Finally, it is suggested that events can hardly be disconnected from the continuity of becoming understood as a flow phenomenon of perpetual change. Such an understanding demands a radicalization in our perception of temporality and duration, seeing events as instances of evolving and ever-changing forms (morphogenesis). This is a move away from flattened time and a plea for apprehending materialities as temporal phenomena of different durations in the constitution of material temporalities.

In conclusion, I fear that by not comprehending the full complexity involved in the use of the notion of the event in our dealings with past traces, and in restricting the meaning of this notion only to "rapid transformations of structure," we may collapse our accounts to all too familiar stories of predetermined causalities and progress. We also may risk missing the opportunity to utilize the liberating power that the notion of event brings as the fundamental "temporal building block" in constructing archaeological/historical narratives.

ACKNOWLEDGMENTS

I would like to thank Douglas Bolender, Peter Biehl, and the Institute for European and Mediterranean Archaeology at the Department of Anthropology at the State University of New York at Buffalo for their invitation to participate in the conference "Toward an Eventful Archaeology" and for their generous hospitality.

References Cited

Aron, R. 1961 *Introduction to the Philosophy of History: An Essay on the Limits of Historical Objectivity*. Translated by G. J. Irwin. Beacon Press, Boston.

Bailey, G. 1981 Concepts, Time-Scales, and Explanations in Economic Prehistory. In *Economic Archaeology*, edited by A. Sheridan and G. Bailey, pp. 97–117. Oxford: British Archaeological Reports Series.

Bailey, G. 1983 Concepts of Time in Quaternary Prehistory. *Annual Review of Anthropology* 12:165–192.

Bailey, G. 1987 Breaking the Time Barrier. *Archaeological Review from Cambridge* 6:5–20.

Bailey, G. 2007 Time Perspectives, Palimpsests, and the Archaeology of Time. *Journal of Anthropological Archaeology* 26:198–223.

Beck, R. A. Jr., Douglas J. Bolender, James A. Brown, and Timothy K. Earle 2007 Eventful Archaeology: The Place of Space in Structural Transformation. *Current Anthropology* 48(6):833–860.

Bonsall, C. I. Radovanović, M. Roksandić, G. Cook, T. Higham, and C. Pickard 2008 Dating Burial Practices and Architecture at Lepenski Vir. In *The Iron Gates in Prehistory: New Perspectives*, edited by C. Bonsall, V. Boroneant, and I. Radovanović, pp. 175–204. BAR International Series 1893. British Archaeological Reports, Oxford.

Borić, D. 1999 Places that Created Time in the Danube Gorges and Beyond, c. 9000–5500 Cal BC. *Documenta Praehistorica* 26:47–70.

Borić, D. 2003 "Deep Time" Metaphor: Mnemonic and Apotropaic Practices at Lepenski Vir. *Journal of Social Archaeology* 3(1):41–75.

Borić, D. 2005 Body Metamorphosis and Animality: Volatile Bodies and Boulder Artworks from Lepenski Vir. *Cambridge Archaeological Journal* 15(1):35–69.

Borić, D. 2006 New Discoveries at the Mesolithic-Early Neolithic site of Vlasac: Preliminary Notes. *Mesolithic Miscellany* 18(1):7–14.

Borić, D. 2007a Images of Animality: Hybrid Bodies and Mimesis in Early Prehistoric Art. In *Material Beginnings: A Global Prehistory of Figurative Representation*, edited by C. Renfrew and I. Morley, pp. 89–105. The McDonald Institute for Archaeological Research, Cambridge.

Borić, D. 2007b The House between Grand Narratives and Microhistories: A House Society in the Balkans. In *The Durable House: House Society Models in Archaeology*, edited by Robin A. Beck Jr., pp. 97–129. Center for Archaeological Investigations, Occasional Paper No. 35, Carbondale.

Borić, D. 2007c Mesolithic-Neolithic Interactions in the Danube Gorges. In *Mesolithic-Neolithic Interactions in the Danube Basin*, edited by J. K. Kozlowski and M. Nowak, pp. 31–45. Archaeopress, Oxford.

Borić, D. 2010a Memory, Archaeology and the Historical Condition. In *Archaeology and Memory*, edited by D. Borić, pp. 1–34. Oxbow, Oxford.

Borić, D. 2010b Happy Forgetting? Remembering and Dismembering Dead Bodies at Vlasac. In *Archaeology and Memory*, edited by D. Boric, pp. 48–67. Oxbow, Oxford.

Borić, D., and V. Dimitrijević 2007 When did the 'Neolithic package' reach Lepenski Vir? Radiometric and faunal evidence. *Documenta Praehistorica* 34:53–72.

Borić, D., and V. Dimitrijević 2009 Apsolutna hronologija i stratigrafija Lepenskog Vira (Absolute Chronology and Stratigraphy of Lepenski Vir). *Starinar* LVII(2007):9–55.

Borić, D., G. Grupe, J. Peters, and Ž. Mikić 2004 Is the Mesolithic-Neolithic Subsistence Dichotomy Real? New Stable Isotope Evidence from the Danube Gorges. *European Journal of Archaeology* 7(3):221–248.

Borić, D., C. Alexander, and V. Dimitrijević (forthcoming) The Tempo of Mesolithic-Neolithic Transformation at Lepenski Vir: An Application of the Bayesian Statistical Modelling. To be submitted to *Antiquity*.

Borić, D., J. Raičević, and S. Stefanović 2009 Mesolithic cremations as elements of secondary mortuary rites at Vlasac (Serbia). *Documenta Praehistorica* 36:247–282

Braudel, F. 1972 *The Mediterranean and the Mediterranean World in the Age of Philip II*. Translated by S. Reynolds. Harper and Row, New York.

Carr, D. 1986 *Time, Narrative and History*. Indiana University Press, Bloomington, Indiana.

Cauvin, J. 2000 *The Birth of the Gods and the Origins of Agriculture*. Cambridge University Press, Cambridge.

Collingwood, R. G. 1953 *The Idea of History*. Edited by T. M. Knox. Clarendon Press, Oxford.

Conneller, C. 2004 Becoming Deer: Corporeal Transformations at Star Carr. *Archaeological Dialogues* 11(1):37–56.

Deleuze, G. 1990 *The Logic of Sense*. Athlone, London.

Deleuze, G., and F. Guattari 1987 *A Thousand Plateaus. Capitalism and Schizophrenia*. Translated by B. Massumi. University of Minnesota Press, Minneapolis.

Dimitrijević, V. 2008 Lepenski Vir Animal Bones: What Was Left in the Houses? In *The Iron Gates in Prehistory: New Perspectives,* edited by C. Bonsall, V. Boroneant, and I. Radovanović, pp. 117–130. BAR International Series 1893. British Archaeological Reports, Oxford

Foucault, M. 1972 *The Archaeology of Knowledge*. Translated by A. M. Sheridan Smith. Tavistock, London.

Geertz, C. 1961 *The Social History of an Indonesian Town*. MIT Press, Cambridge.

Geertz, C. 1973 *The Interpretation of Cultures. Selected Essays*. Basic Books, New York.

Ginzburg, C. 1980 *The Cheese and the Worms: The Cosmos of the Sixteenth Century Miller*. Translated by J. and A. Tedeschi. Johns Hopkins University Press, Baltimore.

Ginzburg, C. 1989 Clues: Roots of an Evidential Paradigm. In *Clues, Myths and the Historical Method*, edited by C. Ginzburg, pp. 96–125. The John Hopkins University Press, Baltimore.

Hodder, I. 1987 The Contribution of the Long Term. In *Archaeology as Long-Term History*, edited by Ian Hodder, pp. 1–8. Cambridge University Press, Cambridge.

Hodder, I. 1993 The Narrative and Rhetoric of Material Culture Sequences. *World Archaeology* 25(2):268–282.

Hodder, I. 1995 Material Culture in Time. In *Interpreting Archaeology. Finding meaning in the past*, edited by I. Hodder, M. Shanks, A. Alexandri, V. Buchli, J. Carman, J. Last, and G. Lucas, pp. 164–168. Routledge, London.

Hodder, I. 1999 *The Archaeological Process: An Introduction*. Blackwell Publishers, Oxford.

Kwinter, S. 2001 *Architectures of Time: Toward a Theory of the Event in Modernist Culture*. MIT Press, Cambridge.

Le Goff, J. 1980 *Time, Work, and Culture in the Middle Ages*. Translated by A. Goldhammer. University of Chicago Press, Chicago.

Le Goff, J., and Pierre Nora (editors) 1974 *Faire de l'histoire*. Paris: Gallimard.

Lévi-Strauss, C., and D. Eribon 1991 *Conversations with Claude Lévi-Strauss*. The University of Chicago Press, Chicago.

Lévy-Bruhl, L. 1966 *Primitive Mentality*. Translated by Lilian A. Clare. Beacon Press, Boston.

Lévy-Bruhl, L. 1978 *The Notebooks on Primitive Mentality*. Translated by P. Rivière. Harper Torchbooks, New York.

Lloyd, G., E. R. 1990 *Demystifying Mentalities*. Cambridge University Press, Cambridge.

Lucas, G. 2008 Time and Archaeological Event. *Cambridge Journal of Archaeology* 18(1) (Special Section: Time and Change in Archaeological Interpretation):59–65.

McCarthy, T. 1987 Introduction. In Jürgen Habermas, *The Philosophical Discourse of Modernity. Twelve Lectures*. Translated by Frederick Lawrence, pp. vii–xvii. Polity Press, Cambridge.

Meskell, L. 1996 The Somatization of Archaeology: Institutions, Discourses, Corporeality. *Norwegian Archaeological Review* 29(1):1–16.

Meskell, L. 1998. The Irresistible Body and the Seduction of Archaeology, In *Changing Bodies, Changing Meanings. Studies on the Human Body in Antiquity*, edited by D. Montserrat, pp. 139–161. Routledge, London.

Radovanović, I. 1996 *The Iron Gates Mesolithic*. International Monographs in Prehistory, Ann Arbor.

Revel, J. (editor) 1996 *Jeaux d'échelles: La Microanalyse à l'expérience*. EHESS-Gallimard-Seuil, Paris.

Ricoeur, P. 1984 *Time and Narrative, Volume I*. Translated by K. Blamey and D. Pellauer. University of Chicago Press, Chicago.

Ricoeur, P. 1988 *Time and Narrative, Volume 3*. Translated by K. Blamey and D. Pellauer. University of Chicago Press, Chicago.

Ricoeur, P. 1998 *Critique and Conviction. Conversations with François Azouvi and Marc de Launay*. Translated by K. Blamey. Polity Press, Cambridge.

Ricoeur, P. 2004 *Memory, History, Forgetting*. Translated by K. Blamey and D. Pellauer. University of Chicago Press. Chicago.

Sahlins, M. 1985 *Islands of History*. University of Chicago Press, Chicago.

Sewell, W. Jr. 2005 *Logics of History: Social Theory and Social Transformation*. Chicago Studies in Practices of Meaning. University of Chicago Press, Chicago.

Srejović, D. 1972 *Europe's First Monumental Sculpture: New Discoveries at Lepenski Vir*. Thames and Hudson, London.

Stefanović, S., and D. Borić 2008 The Newborn Infant Burials from Lepenski Vir: In Pursuit of Contextual Meanings. In *The Iron Gates in Prehistory: New Perspectives*, edited by C. Bonsall, V. Boroneant, and I. Radovanović, pp. 131–169. BAR International Series 1893. British Archaeological Reports, Oxford

Weber, M. 1992[1930] *The Protestant Ethic and the Spirit of Capitalism*. Translated by Talcott Parsons. Routledge, London.

CHAPTER FOUR

Event and Short-Term Process

Times for the Early Neolithic of Southern Britain

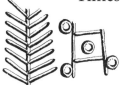

Alasdair Whittle, Alex Bayliss,
and Frances Healy

Abstract *Prehistory needs precise chronologies, and prehistorians should not be content without them. This paper draws attention to the resolution routinely achievable when radiocarbon dates are modelled in a Bayesian statistical framework: to the scales of lifetimes and generations. While events are thinkable, it is an eventful prehistory of concentrated horizons and short-term processes that we believe is within our grasp. Examples to illustrate these possibilities are taken from a major project on the radiocarbon dating of early Neolithic causewayed enclosures in southern Britain in the fourth millennium cal BC, concentrating on the sequence of events and processes which occurred within a small area of southern Britain (no more than 60 miles across) during the middle decades of the thirty-seventh century cal BC.*

EVENT AND SHORT-TERM PROCESS: POSSIBILITY AND PRECISION

What is an event? Human life is played out at many differing scales and tempos. We have little difficulty in our own lives in talking about events. We refer to great events and small events, generally reserving the term for things that we regard as both significant and concentrated in time. Neither aspect of the concept of the event is normally closely defined. We would have little difficulty in recognizing the Russian Revolution of 1917 as an event of major proportions. Before 1917, Russia was a Tsarist autocracy; after 1917, it became a quasi-democratic and then communist republic (Figes 1997). As such, the Russian Revolution should satisfy the rather narrower definition of event—as opposed to mere happenings and other occurrences—as marker of structural transformation proposed by William Sewell Jr. (2005). But the detail of time scales is not Sewell's strongest suit. One of his definitions appears to allow some flexibility:

> A historical event, then, is (1) a ramified sequence of occurrences that (2) is recognized as notable by contemporaries, and that (3) results in a durable transformation of structures. (Sewell 2005:228)

But how long is the ramified sequence allowed to run? In the Russian case, do we concentrate on the February Days of 1917, when open revolt and mutiny started in and around Petrograd/St Petersburg? Among other manifestations and immediately recognized perceptions of the overturning of the social order, a carnival atmosphere prevailed on the streets, down to new body postures and language, cross-dressing, and even open sexual intercourse (Figes 1997:319). At this stage, the Revolution was far from a durable transformation, so do we run the sequence on to the Provisional Government, and then the Bolshevik *coup d'état* in October 1917, or, given the threat of successful counter-revolution, to the end of the ensuing civil war in 1921 and the death of Lenin in 1924? Even in this limited analysis, Sewell's historical event is acted out over a number of years. There is, moreover, a compelling case for seeing the Russian Revolution as much more than the "compact eruption of 1917" (Figes 1997:xvii); a wider narrative can go back—among many other things—to the emancipation of the serfs in 1861, the assassination of Alexander II in 1881, the famine of 1891, the war with Japan in 1904–05, the revolts of 1905, the ill-fated and partial attempts at reform through the Duma, and finally the Great War. And to these events must be added a whole series of conditions, attitudes, and processes, including among others the despotism of the Tsar, the conservatism of the supporting elite, the lack of a developed bourgeoisie, limited industrialization, the failure of land reform and the shift of peasant population to the towns, and the fanaticism of the radical intelligentsia (Figes 1997:xviii and Parts 2–4).

Events have not had a good press in prehistory. Orlando Figes has referred to the longer timescale noted above in the case of the Russian Revolution in terms of the *longue durée* (1997:xviii). In actual fact, in Braudel's own terms, this is perhaps more a narrative of *conjonctures*, a history of social time, "another history, this time with slow but perceptible rhythms…the history of groups and groupings," leaving the *longue durée* as the near-unchanging conditions of deep geographical time, "a history of constant repetition, ever-recurring cycles" (Braudel 1975:20–21). In his famous characterization, *l'histoire événementielle* is cast merely as "surface disturbances, crests of foam that the tides of history carry on their strong backs"; "resounding events are often only momentary outbursts, surface manifestations of these larger movements and explicable only in terms of them" (Braudel 1975:21). Geoff Bailey (1981, 2007) has argued for the appropriateness of the *longue durée* as the perspective from which to approach prehistory, especially the timescales of the Palaeolithic, and this view has been supported for later prehistory by other advocates of *Annalistes* approaches (Bintliff 1991; Knapp 1992). In particular, he contrasts archaeology with "other disciplines that deal with quite different phenomena, scales of enquiry and methods of observation, and in general much shorter time spans" (Bailey 2007:213). To his view of the palimpsest nature of the archaeological record has been added another from the perspective of historical archaeology, according to which events are assemblages of things with differing times and histories (Lucas 2008:61–62; cf. Olivier 2001); even the event of digging a pit or grave can always be broken down into a series of shorter actions, and the "event" is always an aggregate, with recurrent material residuality (Lucas 2008:62).

To these reservations has been added a general acceptance that we cannot normally achieve much chronological precision in prehistory, except where dendrochronologies are available. Bailey has referred, in general terms, to "the lack of dating control" and to contemporaneity as "an arbitrary concept with no absolute measure" (2007:206), and Gavin Lucas to "lack of resolution," hinting strongly that this may not matter unless we want to "mimic history or ethnography" (2008:63). This is in effect, for later prehistory at least, to perpetuate the practice of informal inspection of radiocarbon dates (Bayliss et al. 2007a) and accept the consequent limitations of radiocarbon dating, with inbuilt uncertainty at two standard deviations of around 150–200 years (Bronk Ramsey 2008a:Figure 1).

Why does this matter for anyone concerned with European prehistory? Why not grasp the liberation of writing about "a different type of event and narrative of the past" (Lucas 2008:63). After all, Tim Ingold (1993) has already argued that chronology and history offer merely the sequence of events;

> In the mere succession of dates there are no events, because everything repeats; in the mere succession of events there is no time, as nothing does. (Ingold 1993:157)

A concept of temporality, especially allied to McTaggart's A-series, instead gathers in a sense of people's experience of the flow of time, looking both forward and back. Surely, it might be argued, if this is really our fundamental goal of understanding, this could be achieved within what we have called elsewhere "fuzzy" time frames (Whittle and Bayliss 2007). From a different perspective, John Robb (2007:287, 294) has advocated looking beyond the experience of the individual lifetime for longer-running process, at a scale of several centuries. Again, it might be argued, this could be achieved within coarse or relatively coarse chronological frames.

If, however, we want a prehistory with agents, if we want to investigate the chains of memory, connection, and desire that informed people's agency, if we want to go beyond a general sense of cultural order and recurrent practice, if we wish to unravel histories of encounter, contact, and change—in our case, in the Mesolithic-Neolithic transition of southern Britain and in the first centuries of the Neolithic in the fourth millennium cal BC—then sequence is crucial. Chronological order does not on its own bring the full sense of temporality as defined by Ingold (see above), but it offers the way to it, by providing relationships, durations, and tempo (Bayliss et al. 2008; Whittle et al. 2008). Sequence and tempo together may shed light on causality (A cannot cause B if A happened after B, and A is perhaps less likely to have directly caused B if A happened 300 years before B).

So from strong theoretical perspectives, prehistory needs chronological precision, and prehistorians should not be content without it. But is it really possible to obtain it, beyond the rare circumstances of routine dendrochronologies or tephrochronologies (which are extremely rare for the early Neolithic in southern Britain anyway),[1] and what sort of precision are we talking about?

---

[1] Restricted so far to the Post and Sweet Tracks, and their successors, in the Somerset Levels (Coles and Coles 1986; Hillam et al. 1990) and the floating sequence of the Haddenham long barrow, Cambridgeshire (Evans and Hodder 2006).

Events are certainly thinkable in prehistory. Events make up most of the archaeological record. Beyond the small events of, say, digging a pit, the planning and execution of communal enterprises from land clearance to monument construction can be thought of as significant events (Whittle 1988), since they brought numbers of people together, often changed the landscape, and sometimes endured in their altered settings for periods of time. There are also moments in the histories of monuments that can be thought of as events, such as the intense burning seen near the base of the ditch at the causewayed enclosure of Hembury, Devon (Liddell 1935:138), or various assaults on other causewayed enclosures such as Crickley Hill, Gloucestershire (Dixon 1988) and Hambledon Hill, Dorset (Healy 2004; Mercer and Healy 2008) and on the tor enclosure of Carn Brea, Cornwall (Mercer 1981). Whether these were all more than merely dramatic local episodes is a matter for discussion. Wider events are also certainly thinkable, including the initial adoption or introduction of domesticates and new material culture and practices. There was—in one year or another—the first cutting of turf or soil that initiated the construction of the first causewayed enclosure in southern Britain, and depending on the speed with which this was copied, imitated, or emulated, there is potentially an event or concentrated horizon (a ramified sequence, in Sewell's terms) of much wider significance. Determining the relative sequence of events is much harder: broadly speaking, archaeologically possible only with stratigraphic relationships. The relative tempo of events requires hard chronology—and both sequence and tempo need the kind of formal modeling proposed here. In another context, Tim Ingold (2007) has recently railed against the abstraction of discussions about "materiality" at the expense of materials, and since his list of other unwanted abstractions includes sociality, intentionality, and agency itself (Ingold 2007:2), we could perhaps use this to underline the importance of getting at and thinking about specific times before we get lost in the more abstruse philosophies of temporality, which abound in the current literature.

In this paper we repeat our advocacy of formal Bayesian modeling of radiocarbon dates as currently the best available approach to achieving the precision that our discipline needs (Bayliss and Bronk Ramsey 2004; Bayliss et al. 2007a; Bayliss and Whittle 2007; Bayliss et al. 2008; Whittle et al. 2008). We reassert the possibility of building chronological models with precision to the scale of lifetimes and even generations. Some events, though their character and significance may vary, may be closely dateable, but it is an eventful prehistory of concentrated horizons and short-term processes that we believe is within our reach. We conclude by noting for future discussion that our view of the long term may not be as simple, or as good, as we have been accustomed to think.

Beyond "Radiocarbon Dates": Toward Chronologies on a Human Scale

So, what has happened, fifty years after the onset of the first radiocarbon revolution, to bring this eventful (pre)history within the grasp of archaeologists everywhere? The answer is the development of methodology that allows the explicit, statistical modeling of calibrated radiocarbon dates together with other types of archaeological information. These

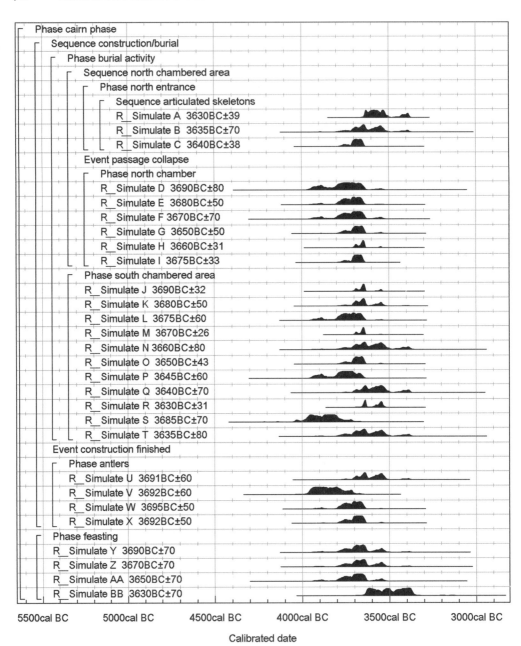

FIGURE 1 Calibrated probability distributions (Stuiver and Reimer 1993) of the simulated radiocarbon ages from a long barrow (the actual dates of these samples range from 3695 BC to 3630 BC).

contextual interpretations of all the data routinely allow much more precise chronologies to be suggested.

Consider, for example, the suite of radiocarbon dates from a fictitious long barrow shown in Figure 1. Visual inspection of this graph would lead most archaeologists to infer that activity on this site happened between *c.* 4000 cal BC and *c.* 3400 cal BC. A slightly more sophisticated variant of this approach, recognizing that radiocarbon dating is a probabilistic process and attempting to account for outliers, either by excluding low parts of probability distributions from the edges of the graph or by determining a time when most of the probability of most of the dates is concentrated, might suggest that activity on the site happened between *c.* 3800 cal BC and *c.* 3500 cal BC. Both of these interpretations would be *importantly wrong.* Because these are radiocarbon ages simulated from samples of known calendar age, we know that these samples actually date to between 3695 and 3630 BC. Without formal modeling, not only does it appear, incorrectly, that our site started earlier and carried on later than it did in reality, but we obtain a thoroughly misleading impression of the duration of activity on the site. It seems to have continued for 300 years or more, when in fact the dates only span a period of 65 years.[2]

The impact of using formal statistical modeling to consider all the chronological information we may have about a site, holistically, is shown in Figure 2. Here we have exactly the same assemblage of radiocarbon dates, but the stratigraphic sequence of dated contexts, the taphonomy of the dated samples, and the grouping of the samples because they come from a single coherent period of human activity are also included in the modeling of the site's chronology.[3] This model suggests that this construction of the monument was complete by *3710–3650 cal BC* (*95 percent probability; construction finished;* Figure 2), probably by *3700–3660 cal BC* (*68 percent probability*).[4] It went out of use in *3645–3610 cal BC* (*95 percent probability; end of cairn phase;* Figure 2), probably in the *3630s or 3620s cal BC* (*68 percent probability*). By comparing these dates, we can suggest that burial in the tomb continued for *15–90 years* (*95 percent probability; duration bodies;* Figure 3), probably for *30–70 years* (*68 percent probability*).

It should be noted at this point that we have now gone beyond the concept of the calibrated "radiocarbon date" (shown in outline in Figure 2). Our model produces *posterior density estimates* (shown in black in Figure 2, and given in italics when expressed as ranges in the text). These may relate one-to-one with radiocarbon dates; for example, the individual

---

[2]An audience of experienced British archaeologists, which met in Cardiff University in August 2006 to discuss results from the dating programme on causewayed enclosures, were asked to estimate the dates of construction and abandonment, and duration of use, from this simulation (Figure 1). The vast majority of the audience got the answers *importantly* wrong—81 percent estimated the start date inaccurately, all estimated the end date inaccurately, and 94 percent significantly overestimated the duration!

[3]Bayliss et al. (2007a) provide more detailed discussion of this simulation, and a more in-depth introduction to the practicalities of constructing Bayesian chronological models in archaeology. More basic introductions to chronological modeling are provided by Bayliss 2007; 2009. A user-friendly introduction to the principles of Bayesian statistics is provided by Lindley (1985), while Buck et al. (1996) introduce the approach from an archaeological viewpoint. Details of the mathematical methods involved can be found in a series of papers by Buck et al. (1991; 1992; 1994a; 1994b), Christen (1994), Christen and Litton (1995), Nicholls and Jones (2001), Steier and Rom (2000), and in the papers relating to the program OxCal by Bronk Ramsey (1995; 1998; 2000; 2001; 2008b).

[4]Throughout this paper the following format has been followed: dates "BC" are estimated or actual dates on the calendar scale and dates "cal BC" derive from calibrated radiocarbon ages (calibrated according to the probability method of Stuiver and Reimer 1993 and using data from Reimer et al. 2004). Dates "*cal BC*" in italics are posterior density estimates derived from Bayesian modeling.

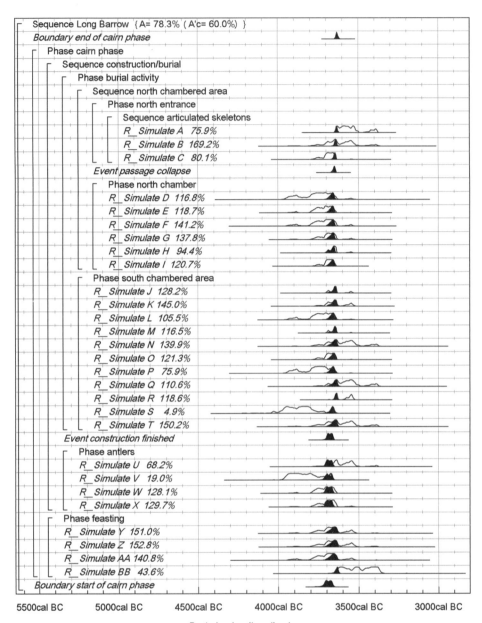

Sequence Long Barrow {A= 78.3% (A'c= 60.0%) }
Boundary end of cairn phase
Phase cairn phase
Sequence construction/burial
Phase burial activity
Sequence north chambered area
Phase north entrance
Sequence articulated skeletons
R_Simulate A 75.9%
R_Simulate B 169.2%
R_Simulate C 80.1%
Event passage collapse
Phase north chamber
R_Simulate D 116.8%
R_Simulate E 118.7%
R_Simulate F 141.2%
R_Simulate G 137.8%
R_Simulate H 94.4%
R_Simulate I 120.7%
Phase south chambered area
R_Simulate J 128.2%
R_Simulate K 145.0%
R_Simulate L 105.5%
R_Simulate M 116.5%
R_Simulate N 139.9%
R_Simulate O 121.3%
R_Simulate P 75.9%
R_Simulate Q 110.6%
R_Simulate R 118.6%
R_Simulate S 4.9%
R_Simulate T 150.2%
Event construction finished
Phase antlers
R_Simulate U 68.2%
R_Simulate V 19.0%
R_Simulate W 128.1%
R_Simulate X 129.7%
Phase feasting
R_Simulate Y 151.0%
R_Simulate Z 152.8%
R_Simulate AA 140.8%
R_Simulate BB 43.6%
Boundary start of cairn phase

5500cal BC   5000cal BC   4500cal BC   4000cal BC   3500cal BC   3000cal BC

Posterior density estimate

FIGURE 2 Probability distributions of simulated dates from a long barrow. Each distribution represents the relative probability that an event occurs at a particular time. For each of the dates two distributions have been plotted: one in outline, which is the result of simple radiocarbon calibration, and a solid one, based on the chronological model used; the "event" associated with, for example, "V," is the growth of the dated antler. Distributions other than those relating to particular samples correspond to aspects of the model. For example, the distribution "*construction finished*" is the estimated date when the barrow was built. The large square brackets down the lefthand side along with the OxCal keywords define the overall model exactly. The actual dates of these samples range from 3695 BC to 3630 BC.

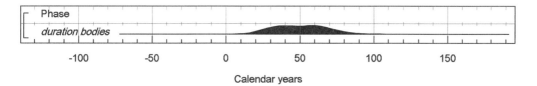

Calendar years

FIGURE 3 Probability distribution showing the number of calendar years during which bodies were interred in a long barrow according to the simulation shown in Figure 2 (these burials actually span 60 years).

who provided sample "B" died and was buried in *3655–3625 cal BC* (*95 percent probability*; B; Figure 2), probably in the *3640s or 3630s cal BC* (*68 percent probability*). But they may relate rather to some more significant event in the past. We are rarely, really, interested in the time when this twig or that antler ceased exchanging carbon with the atmosphere,[5] but we may be more interested in the time when a settlement was established or a new crop introduced. Bayesian modeling allows us to estimate the dates of these parameters formally. So, in Figure 2, after all the antlers used as tools in its construction had been shed, and before the first intact corpse was placed in the tomb, the monument's construction was complete (*construction finished*; Figure 2). This posterior density estimate does not derive from any one radiocarbon date, but rather all the radiocarbon dates and all the other, "prior" information included in the chronological model.

In this case, as we are using a group of radiocarbon ages simulated from samples of known calendar date, we know that our model is providing accurate outputs. In all cases, the posterior density estimates from this model include the actual ages of the relevant events (3690 BC, *construction finished*; 3630 BC, *end of cairn phase*; 3635 BC, *B*; 60 years, *duration bodies*). Such accuracy can be depended upon and is not an artifact of the shape of the calibration curve, although the calibration curve may have an effect on the maximum precision that can be obtained for a particular application (Bayliss et al. 2007a:Figures 10 and 11). Bayesian modeling of known-age data, particularly on samples of wood dated by dendrochronology, has also been shown to provide accurate chronologies (Galimberti et al. 2004; Hamilton et al. 2007; Tyers et al. 2009).

The simulation shown in Figures 1–3 is actually based on the sequence of archaeological events and radiocarbon dates from the Cotswold long cairn at Hazleton North, Gloucestershire (Saville 1990). The chronological models for this site are discussed in full by Meadows et al. (2007).

An illustration of the method in action is provided in Figure 4. This isolates the component of the preferred Hazleton model (Meadows et al. 2007:Figures 6–9) relating to the construction and primary use of the long barrow. It incorporates the radiocarbon dates and prior information contained within the box shown in Figure 5. It is apparent that the precision that we claim is achievable, not just in theory, but in practice.

---

[5]Although there are, of course, exceptions when a sample is of intrinsic interest (e.g., from a skeleton exhibiting evidence of a particular disease).

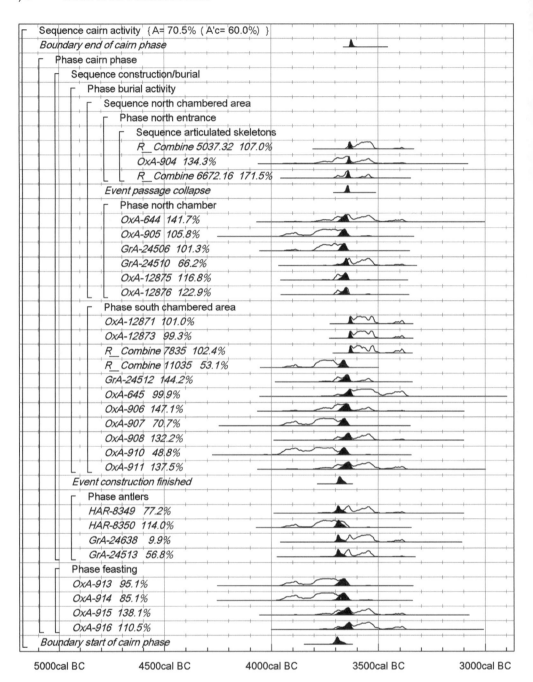

5000cal BC   4500cal BC   4000cal BC   3500cal BC   3000cal BC

Posterior density estimate

FIGURE 4 Probability distributions of radiocarbon dates from the construction and primary use of the Hazleton North long cairn. The format is identical to that of Figure 2. The large square brackets down the lefthand side along with the OxCal keywords define the overall model exactly.

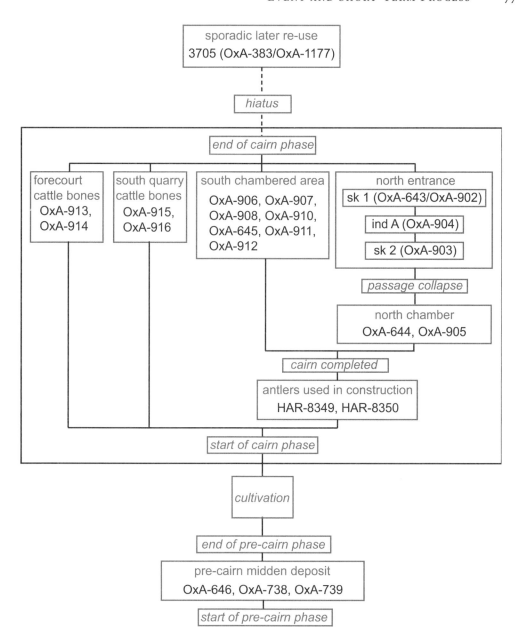

FIGURE 5 Summary of the "prior" information incorporated in the chronological model for Hazleton North long cairn (Meadows et al. 2007:Figures 6–9). The stratigraphic relationships between samples are shown with the earliest at the bottom (solid lines, relationships determined by excavation; dashed lines, relationships inferred on the basis of the radiocarbon results). The "prior" information incorporated into the model shown in Figure 4 is contained within the box.

Case Study: The Thirty-Seventh Century Cal bc
in Southern Britain

Applying this methodology, which has been adopted as routine best practice by English Heritage for more than a decade, we have been engaged over the last few years with two projects on the early Neolithic in southern Britain. Both build significantly on preexisting chronological schemes, even the best of which are based on informal, visual inspection of radiocarbon dates (e.g., Barclay 2007; Bradley 2007; Cleal 2004).

The first project was a study of five long barrows and long cairns in southern England (Bayliss and Whittle 2007). We used 167 radiocarbon dates to construct formal date estimates for the construction, use, and abandonment of Ascott-under-Wychwood, Oxfordshire (Bayliss et al. 2007b; Benson and Whittle 2007), Hazleton, Gloucestershire (Meadows et al. 2007), Fussell's Lodge, Wiltshire (Wysocki et al. 2007), West Kennet, Wiltshire (Bayliss et al. 2007c), and Wayland's Smithy, Oxfordshire (Whittle et al. 2007a). As already set out in detail elsewhere, from this sample we cannot show such barrow construction earlier than the thirty-eighth century cal bc, Ascott-under-Wychwood probably being the earliest of these monuments, though there are some possible candidates elsewhere in southern Britain for an earlier date. That is an important story, but one for another occasion (see Whittle et al. forthcoming; cf. Bayliss et al. 2008; Whittle 2007a); here the significant result is the presence of long barrows from at least the thirty-eighth century cal bc (Whittle et al. 2007b:Figure 4).

Most of these barrows were probably built quickly, in a generation or less,[6] though more extended sequences of construction can be modeled for both Fussell's Lodge and Wayland's Smithy I. At Fussell's Lodge, however, all three alternative models offered agree in their estimates for the date of mound construction, an event that in this case closed the use of the monument (Wysocki et al. 2007). These five barrows were built from the thirty-eighth (Ascott-under-Wychwood) to the early thirty-sixth (Wayland's Smithy I) centuries cal bc, with the subsequent construction of Wayland's Smithy II probably following in the thirty-fifth century cal bc.

All of these barrows were in use for comparatively short periods (Whittle et al. 2007b:Figure 6), in contrast to the interpretation of durability often given in the literature. The longest active primary use was at Ascott-under-Wychwood, probably the focus for deposition of human remains for three to five generations (Bayliss et al. 2007b). The primary use of West Kennet was probably contained within one generation (Bayliss et al. 2007c). The initiation of Wayland's Smithy I might relate to a massacre, and could span a decade or less (Whittle et al. 2007a). The endings of these monuments are discussed below in connection with causewayed enclosures.

Our second project, on the causewayed enclosures of southern Britain and Ireland, has been much more ambitious (Bayliss et al. 2008; Whittle et al. 2008; Whittle et al.

---

[6]For these studies, we have taken a generation as 25 years (Whittle et al. 2007b). Life tables such as published by Robb (2007) and Akins (1986), suggesting average lifespans of little more than 35–40 years, might suggest that our estimate is too generous, but it serves as a useful working figure.

forthcoming). We have used 871 radiocarbon dates (444 existing and 427 newly acquired) to build formal date estimates for the construction and primary use of just under 40 enclosures in southern Britain; we do not know the total number of these ditched arenas, the focus of often quite intense deposition and gatherings, but it is likely to exceed 80 or 90 sites (Oswald et al. 2001), so this means that we have dated a substantial sample in this study. We have also gathered up some 815 additional existing dates for other early Neolithic activity in southern Britain, in order to be able to put the appearance and development of causewayed enclosures into context, by comparison with parallel, independent models.

From this sample, no enclosure in southern Britain pre-dates the late thirty-eighth century cal BC (Bayliss et al. 2008). Causewayed enclosures appear to come in a rush from *c.* 3700 cal BC, such that the thirty-seventh century cal BC was a striking sequence of construction events, and it is open to debate whether the appearance of this horizon was event-like. Significantly, as already noted above, this event or concentrated horizon of novel construction follows the first appearance of long barrows, giving us important sequence. From our wider modeling of other early Neolithic activity, we can formally estimate a regionally varied start date for the appearance of Neolithic practices in southern Britain; this is from *c.* 4000 cal BC in southeast England, for example, but later elsewhere (Bayliss et al. 2008). Whether the Mesolithic-Neolithic transition in turn is to be thought of as an event, a ramified sequence of occurrences, a concentrated horizon of change, or a more extended transformation (as in the Russian case above) is again for extended discussion elsewhere (Whittle et al. forthcoming; cf. Whittle 2007a), but the important claim here is that it is only with such methodology that we can really begin to provide evidence to inform the debate on such questions.

If causewayed enclosures appear in a rush from *c.* 3700 cal BC, again counter to the expectations of the general literature, they were in use for varied spans of time. There were indeed very long-lived examples, such as Hambledon Hill (Healy 2004; Mercer and Healy 2008). This was in use for some three centuries, but the sequence of construction was episodic over this span. Other enclosures were in use for much shorter periods of time, such as Abingdon, Oxfordshire (Whittle et al. 2008:68). The two circuits at Abingdon were probably constructed within a decade or so of each other (Figure 6), and the primary use of the site probably lasted for little more than a generation (Figure 7). Once again, the application of the Bayesian approach to the interpretation of radiocarbon dates opens up the possibility of beginning to discern a sequence of varying construction events and durations of site use, within a broader historical framework for the phenomenon.

So far, we have given a very broad overview of what the Bayesian approach can offer in the study of the early Neolithic in southern Britain. In the second part of our case study here, we offer a brief, closer look at some developments in the latter part of the thirty-seventh century cal BC. Methodologically, even to be able to write such words for an archaeology virtually lacking dendrochronology is remarkable. Thematically, this particular example supports the view argued here that while events are relevant and potentially within our grasp, it is perhaps more often the trends within ramified and concentrated sequences of change that will be most accessible.

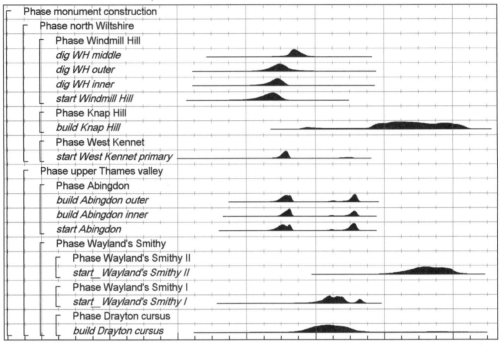

FIGURE 6 Probability distributions of construction dates for selected monuments in north Wiltshire and the upper Thames valley. Each distribution represents the relative probability that an event occurs at a particular time. The distributions have been taken from the models defined in Whittle et al. forthcoming:Figures 3.8–11 (Windmill Hill), Whittle et al. forthcoming:Figure 3.20 (Knap Hill), Bayliss et al. 2007c:Figures 4–7 (West Kennet), Whittle et al. forthcoming:Figures 8.18–21 (Abingdon), Whittle et al. 2007a:Figure 4 (Wayland's Smithy), and Barclay et al. 2003:Figure 8.3 recalculated using the updated calibration data of Reimer et al. 2004 (Drayton).

Our chosen example is concentrated on north Wiltshire, but draws also on south Wiltshire and the Cotswolds: thus, a study not only limited in time but over a distance of not more than 60 miles. The construction of the massive ceremonial arena of Windmill Hill, not far from the West Kennet long barrow, can now be dated to *3700–3640 cal BC* (*95 percent probability; start Windmill Hill*; Figure 6) (Whittle et al. 2008; Whittle et al. forthcoming:chapter 3). The primary use of Windmill Hill continued for *180–200 years* (*1 percent probability*) or *290–390 years* (*94 percent probability; end Windmill Hill*; Figure 7), into the second half of the thirty-fourth century cal BC (*3475–3460 cal BC; 1 percent probability*) or *3365–3295 cal BC* (*94 percent probability; end Windmill Hill*; Whittle et al. forthcoming:Figure 3.8). This extended initial enclosure phase now emerges, from our wider study of southern Britain and Ireland, as the exception rather than the rule. In the same part of north Wiltshire, the single circuit of Knap Hill causewayed enclosure is less precisely dated, but its construction can be estimated to belong probably to the thirty-fifth

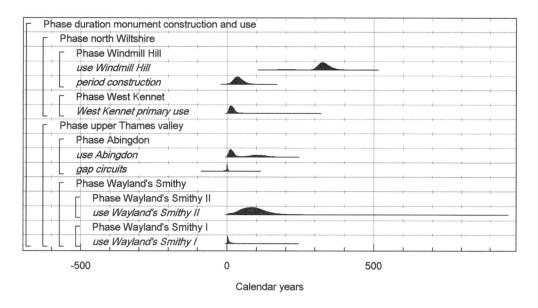

FIGURE 7 Probability distributions showing the number of calendar years for construction and use for selected monuments from north Wiltshire and the upper Thames valley. The distributions have been taken from the models detailed in Figure 6.

century cal BC (*3620–3585 cal BC* (*4 percent probability*); or *3530–3375 cal BC* (*91 percent probability; build Knap Hill*; Figure 6) and a short life can be inferred from the natural accumulation of silts poor in cultural material after this date.

Importantly, within a Bayesian framework, we can now suggest the order of construction of the three causewayed ditch circuits that make up the Windmill Hill enclosure (it is *69 percent probable* that the inner ditch was dug first, and *88 percent probable* that the middle ditch was dug last), and suggest that the circuits were built over a period of *5–75 years* (*95 percent probability; period construction*; Figure 7) (Whittle et al. 2008; Whittle et al. forthcoming:chapter 3).

We can also relate the histories of the long barrows discussed above to this sequence. West Kennet long barrow is within sight of the Windmill Hill enclosure. Its construction falls after that of the inner and outer circuits at Windmill Hill (*90 percent* and *72 percent probable* respectively) and before that of the middle circuit (*83 percent probable*) (Figure 6) (Whittle et al. 2008; Whittle et al. forthcoming; Bayliss et al. 2007c). The people whose remains were deposited at West Kennet may have been alive at the time that the community chose to construct the middle circuit of Windmill Hill. They had surely experienced the inner and outer circuits, and the older individuals among them could have participated in the digging of these earthworks.

Is this just a local sequence, of local events? The sample of long barrows whose chronologies we have formally modeled is very small, but it is striking that of the other four noted above, three also ended in the later thirty-seventh century cal BC (Figure 8). For Ascott-under-Wychwood, our preferred model suggests that the latest depositions were in the southern passage area and all the individuals in question seem to have died during

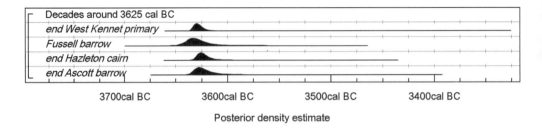

end West Kennet primary

Fussell barrow

end Hazleton cairn

end Ascott barrow

3700cal BC   3600cal BC   3500cal BC   3400cal BC

Posterior density estimate

FIGURE 8 Probability distributions for the end of primary use of four long barrows in southern Britain. Each distribution represents the relative probability that an event occurs at a particular time. The distributions have been taken from the models defined in Bayliss et al. 2007b:Figures 3 and 5–7 (Ascott-under-Wychwood), Meadows et al. 2007:Figures 6–9 (Hazleton), Bayliss et al. 2007c:Figures 4–7 (West Kennet), and Wysocki et al. 2007:Figures 10–11 (Fussell's Lodge).

the third quarter of the thirty-seventh century cal BC: in the 3640s or 3630s (Bayliss et al. 2007b). For Hazleton, the preferred model suggests that the end of the principal Neolithic use of the monument for burial was in *3635–3605 cal BC* (*95 percent probability; end of cairn phase;* Meadows et al. 2007:Figure 8), probably in *3635–3615 cal BC* (*68 percent probability*). And for Fussell's Lodge, all three possible models agree in placing mound construction, which effectively closed the use of the preexisting mortuary structures, probably in the 3630s–3620s cal BC (Wysocki et al. 2007).

We are not suggesting that all long barrows ended at this time; patently, they did not, as shown by the date estimates for Wayland's Smithy I and II (Whittle et al. 2007a). These three examples may also relate in the first instance to local events and sequences: the closure of Fussell's Lodge in south Wiltshire, for example, to the appearance of the enclosure at Robin Hood's Ball (Whittle et al. forthcoming:chapter 4), or those of Ascott-under-Wychwood and Hazleton in the northeast Cotswolds to the appearance of the enclosures at Crickley Hill and Peak Camp, among others (Whittle et al. forthcoming:chapter 9). The models are not precise enough to suggest exact contemporaneity of these events, but are sufficiently precise to suggest a correlation between the continuing appearance and development of causewayed enclosures on the one hand and the ending of some long barrows at least on the other. Given the previous imprecision of informal date estimates, this striking correlation deserves attention.

Are we witnessing a horizon within a horizon? Is there historical connection as well as probable contemporaneity? While we may not be able to get at events as such, we seem to be dealing with accelerated change. In the longer view, the initiation of Neolithic practices probably largely preceded monument construction. Certainly there is better evidence for that from *c.* 3800 cal BC onward. The first monuments involved both construction and placing the dead, and may have been tied into emerging notions of the past, place, small-group identity, and coming to terms with new practices and a new way of life; they may, to some extent, have been inturned and self-conscious (Whittle 2007b). Enclosures appeared—seemingly rapidly—as a very different phenomenon, involving larger assemblies of people, bigger building enterprises, perhaps many more visits from farther afield, some drawing on a different aspect of the past, and above all the deposition of animal bones and other things to do with interaction among the living. Does this reflect simply more people on the ground, and denser social networks? Could it betray emerging tensions in scattered communities, the enclosures emerging as a place where individual kin or clan groupings were resisted or subsumed in wider socialities? The answers are not easy, but only with the kind of time scales we have begun to construct—with or without events—can we hope to see these questions more clearly.

CONCLUSIONS: THE SIGNIFICANCE OF TIME SCALES

Chronological precision for this kind of prehistory is within our grasp, in the form of formal date estimates within a Bayesian statistical framework. That precision extends certainly to a scale of lifetimes, and may regularly extend to generations, and even on occasions to decades (Bayliss et al. 2008; Whittle and Bayliss 2007; Whittle et al. 2007b, 2008). From our most intensively investigated period, from the thirty-eighth to the thirty-sixth centuries cal BC, we can discern a sequence of considerable change, and that probably characterizes both the period from *c.* 4000 cal BC (when new practices first appear) and from the mid-thirty-sixth century cal BC (when new constructions in the form of cursus monuments may appear:Figure 6; Whittle et al. 2008:68). These ramified sequences certainly were full of local events of monument building and modification, and the concentrated appearances of monuments might also have constituted events of a wider significance, but it is the succession of changes over generations and lifetimes that is so far most reliably established and the most significant result so far of the application of the Bayesian approach in the projects on the long barrows and causewayed enclosures of southern Britain.

A final reflection must be to challenge the so far comforting notion that prehistorians can at least, whatever other disadvantages and difficulties they face, deal well with the long term. Even if our grasp on events and our understanding of their potential significance remain undeveloped, we are beginning to move toward the possibility of a much more differentiated prehistory. If blocks of time, the spans of traditional "periods" or "cultures," break down into much more sharply differentiated centuries and parts of centuries, where does that leave the *longue durée*? Is the deep-water image of Braudel sustainable? For the first time in this kind of prehistory, it is becoming possible to separate different time scales, and so our view of the long time scale is now not nearly as simple as previously. We will follow the implications of this in more detail elsewhere (Whittle et al. forthcoming), but can the long time scale remain as dominant as it has been in the past literature? Commenting in 1949—at almost the same date as the radiocarbon technique was first being developed—on both a book by Marc Bloch and the appearance of Braudel's Mediterranean masterpiece in the form of his Sorbonne thesis, the French historian Lucien Febvre reflected:

> We may talk of the general trend of history towards other goals and other achievements. But life itself will have the last word on the details of its successes and failures. (Burke 1973:42)

We are now able to start emphasizing the details of lifetimes and generations in prehistory, and this will change our view of those "general trends," which have so far been our staple.

ACKNOWLEDGMENTS

The long barrows dating project was funded by The Leverhulme Trust and English Heritage, and radiocarbon dating was carried out for us by the Oxford Radiocarbon Accelerator Unit. We are grateful to Michael Wysocki and many others for cooperation. The enclosures dating project was joint-funded by The Arts and Humanities Research Council and English Heritage, and radiocarbon dating was carried out for us by the Oxford Radiocarbon Accelerator Unit, the Centrum voor Isotopen Onderzoek, Rijksuniversiteit Groningen, and the [14]Chrono Centre, Department of Archaeology and Palaeoecology, Queen's University, Belfast. We are grateful to a long list of excavators, museums, and other institutions for cooperation. Thanks are due to Dan Hicks for discussion, and above all to colleagues in SUNY Buffalo for their invitation, hospitality, and stimulating debates.

References Cited

Akins, N. J. 1986 *A Biocultural Approach to Human Burials from Chaco Canyon*. National Park Service, Santa Fe.

Bailey, G. 1981 Concepts, Time Scales, and Explanations in Economic Prehistory. In *Economic Archaeology*, edited by A. Sheridan and G. Bailey, pp. 97–117. British Archaeological Reports, Oxford.

Bailey, G. 2007 Time Perspectives, Palimpsests and the Archaeology of Time. *Journal of Anthropological Archaeology* 26:198–223.

Barclay, A. 2007 Connections and Networks: a Wider World and Other Places. In *Building memories: the Neolithic Cotswold long barrow at Ascott-under-Wychwood, Oxfordshire*, edited by D. Benson and A. Whittle, pp. 331–344. Oxbow, Oxford.

Barclay, A. J., G. Lambrick, J. Moore, and M. Robinson 2003 *Cursus Monuments in the Upper Thames Valley: Excavations at the Drayton and Lechlade Cursuses*. Thames Valley Landscapes Monograph, Oxford.

Bayliss, A. 2007 Bayesian Buildings: An Introduction for the Numerically Challenged. *Vernacular Architect* 38:75–86.

Bayliss, A 2009 Rolling out revolution: Using radiocarbon dating in archaeology. *Radiocarbon* 51:123–47.

Bayliss, A., and C. Bronk Ramsey 2004 Pragmatic Bayesians: A Decade Integrating Radiocarbon Dates into Chronological Models. In *Tools for Constructing Chronologies: Tools for Crossing Disciplinary Boundaries*, edited by C. E. Buck and A. R. Millard, pp. 25–41. Springer, London.

Bayliss, A., and A. Whittle (editors) 2007 Histories of the Dead: Building Chronologies for Five Southern British Long Barrows. *Cambridge Archaeological Journal* 17(1) supplement.

Bayliss, A., C. Bronk Ramsey, J. van der Plicht, J., and A. Whittle 2007a Bradshaw and Bayes: Towards a Timetable for the Neolithic. *Cambridge Journal of Archaeology* 17(1) supplement:1–28.

Bayliss, A., D. Benson, D. Galer, L. Humphrey, L. McFadyen, and A. Whittle 2007b One Thing after Another: The Date of the Ascott-under-Wychwood Long Barrow. *Cambridge Archaeological Journal* 17(1) supplement:29–44.

Bayliss, A., A. Whittle, and M. Wysocki 2007c Talking about My Generation: The Date of the West Kennet Long Barrow. *Cambridge Archaeological Journal* 17(1) supplement:85–101.

Bayliss, A., A. Whittle, A., and F. Healy 2008 Timing, Tempo and Temporalities in the Early Neolithic of Southern Britain. *Analecta Praehistorica Leidensia* 40:25–42.

Benson, D., and A.Whittle (editors) 2007 *Building Memories: The Neolithic Cotswold Long Barrow at Ascott-Under-Wychwood*, Oxfordshire. Oxbow, Oxford.

Bintliff, J. (editor) 1991 *The Annales School and Archaeology*. Leicester University Press, London.

Bradley, R. 2007 *The Prehistory of Britain and Ireland*. Cambridge: Cambridge University Press.

Braudel, F. 1975 *The Mediterranean and the Mediterranean World in the Age of Philip II*. Volume I. Translated by Siân Reynolds. Fontana/Collins, London.

Bronk Ramsey, C. 1995 Radiocarbon Calibration and Analysis of Stratigraphy: the OxCal Program. *Radiocarbon* 36:425–430.

Bronk Ramsey, C. 1998 Probability and Dating. *Radiocarbon* 40:461–474.

Bronk Ramsey, C. 2000 Comment on "The Use of Bayesian Statistics for ^{14}C dates of Chronologically Ordered Samples: a Critical Analysis." *Radiocarbon* 42:199–202.

Bronk Ramsey, C. 2001 Development of the Radiocarbon Calibration Program. *Radiocarbon* 43:355–363.

Bronk Ramsey, C. 2008a Radiocarbon Dating: Revolutions in Understanding. *Archaeometry* 50: 249–275.

Bronk Ramsey, C. 2008b Deposition Models for Chronological Records. *Quaternary Science Reviews* 27:42–60.

Buck, C. E., W. G. Cavanagh, and C. D. Litton 1996 *Bayesian Approach to Interpreting Archaeological Data*. Wiley, Chichester.

Buck, C. E., J. A. Christen, J. B. Kenworthy, and C. D. Litton 1994a Estimating the Duration of Archaeological Activity using ^{14}C Determinations. *Oxford Journal of Archaeology* 13:229–240.

Buck, C. E., J. B. Kenworthy, C. D. Litton, and A. F. M. Smith 1991 Combining Archaeological and Radiocarbon Information: a Bayesian Approach to Calibration. *Antiquity* 65:808–821.

Buck, C. E., C. D. Litton, and E. M. Scott 1994b Making the Most of Radiocarbon Dating: Some Statistical Considerations. *Antiquity* 68:252–263.

Buck, C. E., C. D. Litton, and A. F. M. Smith 1992 Calibration of Radiocarbon Results Pertaining to Related Archaeological Events. *Journal of Archaeological Science* 19:497–512.

Burke, P. (editor) 1973 *A New Kind of Prehistory: from the Writings of Febvre*. Translated by K. Folca. Routledge and Kegan Paul, London.

Christen, J. A. 1994 Summarizing a Set of Radiocarbon Determinations: a Robust Approach. *Applied Statistics* 43:489–503.

Christen, J. A., and C. D. Litton 1995 A Bayesian Approach to Wiggle-Matching. *Journal of Archaeological Science* 22:719–725.

Cleal, R. 2004 The Dating and Diversity of the Earliest Ceramics of Wessex and South-West England. In *Monuments and Material Culture. Papers in Honour of an Avebury Archaeologist: Isobel Smith*, edited by R. Cleal and J. Pollard pp. 164–192. Hobnob Press, East Knoyle.

Coles, B., and J. Coles 1986 *Sweet Track to Glastonbury*. Thames and Hudson, London.

Dixon, P. 1988 The Neolithic Settlements on Crickley Hill. In *Enclosures and Defences in the Neolithic of Western Europe*, edited by C. Burgess, P. Topping, C. Mordant and M. Maddison, pp. 75–88. British Archaeological Reports, Oxford.

Evans, C., and I. Hodder 2006 *A Woodland Archaeology. Neolithic Sites at Haddenham. The Haddenham Project Volume 1*. MacDonald Institute for Archaeological Research, Cambridge.

Figes, O. 1997 *A People's Tragedy: the Russian Revolution 1891–1924*. Pimlico, London.

Galimberti, M., C. Bronk Ramsey, and S. Manning 2004 Wiggle-Match Dating of Tree-Ring Sequences. *Radiocarbon* 46:917–924.

Hamilton, W. D., A. Bayliss, A. Menuge, C. Bronk Ramsey, and G. Cook 2007 "Rev Thomas Bayes: Get Ready to wiggle"—Bayesian Modelling, Radiocarbon Wiggle-Matching, and the North Wing of Baguley Hall. *Vernacular Architect* 38:87–97.

Healy, F. 2004 Hambledon Hill and Its Implications. In *Monuments and Material Culture. Papers in Honour of an Avebury Archaeologist: Isobel Smith*, edited by R. M. J. Cleal and J. Pollard, pp. 15–38. Hobnob Books, East Knoyle.

Hillam, J., C. M. Groves, D. M. Brown, M. G. Baillie, J. M. Coles, and B. J. Coles 1990 Dendrochronology of the English Neolithic. *Antiquity* 64:210–220.

Ingold, T. 1993 The Temporality of the Landscape. *World Archaeology* 25:152–174.

Ingold, T. 2007 Materials Against Materiality. *Archaeological Dialogues* 14:1–16.

Knapp, A. B. 1992 *Archaeology, Annales, and Ethnohistory*. Cambridge University Press, Cambridge.

Liddell, D. M. 1935 Report on the Excavations at Hembury Fort, Devon, 4th and 5th seasons 1934 and 1935. *Proceedings of the Devon Archaeological Society* 2(3):135–175.

Lindley, D. V. 1985 *Making Decisions*. 2nd ed. Wiley, London.

Lucas, G. 2008 Time and the Archaeological Event. *Cambridge Archaeological Journal* 18(1):59–65.

Meadows, J., A. Barclay, and A. Bayliss 2007 A Short Passage of Time: The Dating of the Hazleton Long Cairn Revisited. *Cambridge Archaeological Journal* 17(1) supplement:45–64.

Mercer, R. J. 1981 Excavations at Carn Brea, Illogan, Cornwall, 1970–1973: a Neolithic Fortified Complex of the Third Millennium BC. *Cornish Archaeology* 20:1–204.

Mercer, R. J., and F. Healy 2008 *Hambledon Hill, Dorset. Excavation and Survey of a Neolithic Monument Complex and Its Surrounding Landscape*. English Heritage, Swindon.

Nicholls, G., and M. Jones 2001 Radiocarbon Dating with Temporal Order Constraints. *Applied Statistics* 50:503–521.

Olivier, L.C. 2001 Duration, Memory and the Nature of the Archaeological Record. In *It's about Time: the Concept of Time in Archaeology*, edited by H. Karlsson, pp. 61–70. Bricoleur Press, Göteborg.

Oswald, A., C. Dyer, and M. Barber 2001 *The Creation of Monuments: Neolithic Causewayed Enclosures in the British Isles*. English Heritage, London.

Reimer, P. J., M. G. L. Baillie, E. Bard, A. Bayliss, J. W. Beck, C. J. H. Bertrand, P. G. Blackwell, C. E. Buck, G. S. Burr, K. B. Cutler, P. E. Damon, R. L. Edwards, R. G. Fairbanks, M. Friedrich, T. P. Guilderson, A. G. Hogg, K. A. Hughen, B. Kromer, F. G. McCormac, S. Manning, C. Bronk Ramsey, R. W. Reimer, S. Remmele, J. R. Southon, M. Stuiver, S. Talamo, F. W. Taylor, J. van der Plicht, and C. E. Weyhenmeyer 2004 IntCal04 Terrestrial Radiocarbon Age Calibration, 0–26 cal kyr BP. *Radiocarbon* 46:1029–1058.

Robb, J. 2007 *The Early Mediterranean Village: Agency, Material Culture and Social Change in Neolithic Italy*. Cambridge University Press, Cambridge.

Saville, A. 1990 *Hazleton North: the Excavation of a Neolithic Long Cairn of the Cotswold-Severn Group*. English Heritage, London.

Sewell, W. H. Jr. 2005 *The Logics of History: Social Theory and Social Transformation*. University of Chicago Press, Chicago.

Steier, P., and W. Rom 2000 The Use of Bayesian Statistics for ^{14}C Dates of Chronologically Ordered Samples: a Critical Analysis. *Radiocarbon* 42:183–198.

Stuiver, M., and P. J. Reimer 1993 Extended ^{14}C Data Base and Revised CALIB 3.0 ^{14}C Age Calibration Program. *Radiocarbon* 35:215–230.

Tyers, C., J. Sidell, J. van der Plicht, P. Marshall, G. Cook, C. Bronk Ramsey, and A. Bayliss 2009 Wiggle-Matching Using Known-Age Pine from Jermyn Street, London, UK. *Radiocarbon* 51: 385–396.

Whittle, A. 1988 Contexts, Activities, Events—Aspects of Neolithic and Copper Age Enclosures in Neolithic Central and Western Europe. In *Enclosures and Defences in the Neolithic of Western Europe*, edited by C. Burgess, P. Topping, C. Mordant and M. Maddison, pp. 1–19. British Archaeological Reports, Oxford.

Whittle, A. 2007a The Temporality of Transformation: Dating the Early Development of the Southern British Neolithic. In *Going Over: The Mesolithic-Neolithic Transition in North-West Europe*, edited by A. Whittle and V. Cummings, pp. 377–398. Oxford University Press for the British Academy, Oxford.

Whittle, A. 2007b Building Memories. In *Building Memories: the Neolithic Cotswold Long Barrow at Ascott-under-Wychwood, Oxfordshire*, edited by D. Benson and A. Whittle, pp. 361–364. Oxbow, Oxford.

Whittle, A., and A. Bayliss 2007 The Times of Their Lives: From Chronological Precision to Kinds of History and Change. *Cambridge Archaeological Journal* 17(1):21–28.

Whittle, A., A. Barclay, A. Bayliss, L. McFadyen, R. Schulting, and M. Wysocki 2007b Building for the Dead: Events, Processes and Changing Worldviews from the Thirty-Eighth to the Thirty-Fourth Centuries cal BC in Southern Britain. *Cambridge Archaeological Journal* 17(1) supplement:123–147.

Whittle, A., A. Bayliss, and M. Wysocki 2007a Once in a Lifetime: The Date of the Wayland's Smithy Long Barrow. *Cambridge Archaeological Journal* 17(1) supplement:103–121.

Whittle, A., A. Bayliss, and F. Healy 2008 The Timing and Tempo of Change: Examples from the Fourth Millennium cal BC in Southern England. *Cambridge Archaeological Journal* 18(1):65–70.

Whittle, A., F. Healy, and A. Bayliss forthcoming *Gathering Time: Dating the Early Neolithic Enclosures of Southern Britain and Ireland*. Oxbow, Oxford.

Wysocki, M., A. Bayliss, and A. Whittle 2007 Serious Mortality: The Date of the Fussell's Lodge Long Barrow. *Cambridge Archaeological Journal* 17(1) supplement:65–84.

CHAPTER FIVE

The Neolithic Argonauts of the Western Mediterranean and Other Underdetermined Hypotheses of Colonial Encounters

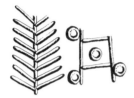

Pedro Díaz-del-Río

Abstract *The more we charge specific historical events with explanatory causality, the more possible alternative pasts we will be able to construct. In this paper I argue that this fact critically affects the interpretations of those of us who rely on an extremely limited and incomplete data set, and no available textual source. This adds up to the fact that prehistorians seldom have the evidence to claim that a particular set of occurrences may in fact be a transformative event in a Sewellian sense, partially—but not only—because of the difficulties in establishing any detailed succession of happenings, and thus have problems arguing that a specific event had a structural effect. Nevertheless, and as Sewell also suggests, we may shift in spatial and temporal scales and confront "eventful" analyses of macrohistorical processes. In order to discuss these issues I have used a characteristically underdetermined hypothesis: the arrival of seafaring Neolithic colonists—Argonauts—on the Iberian coast, a local event that has been said to have a structural effect at a regional scale.*

An event is a significant occurrence, its significance depending on the structure within which it occurs for its existence and effect (Sahlins 1988:142). The elaboration of Sahlins's approach by Sewell (2005) suggests that historians should first define the structural transformation to be explained, followed by the observation of the contingent sequence of occurrences that may have had an effect on the structure in which it had taken place. Events are precisely those sequences that generate structural results. Although his exemplary case studies are bounded in both time and scale, he suggests that eventful analyses should not be limited to short temporal and/or geographical scales. An eventful analysis of large-scale or macrohistorical processes should accept global contingency, path dependency, and the existence of temporally heterogeneous causalities. The temporality of Sewellian events is theoretically constructed in relation to the time scale of the processes being studied (Sewell 2005:121).

The approach, as applied by Beck and others (2007), may be enlightening for those of us that rely exclusively on the archaeological record for our historical interpretations, but I believe that its general applicability can be problematic in at least three different ways. First, the more we charge specific historical events with explanatory causality, the more possible alternative pasts we will be able to construct. It is a matter of the probabilistic nature of our inferences. This issue, important for all historians, becomes critical for those of us that work in our deep prehistory, with an extremely limited and incomplete data set and no available textual source. Our interpretations are most frequently underdetermined and, in the best scenario possible, only Ockham's razor may allow us to decide between competing accounts. Secondly, prehistorians have serious difficulties in establishing any accurate succession of occurrences, something certainly problematic given Sewell's insistence in the critical importance of the sequence of happenings in shaping the possible structural effects of the events. The most common way that prehistorians go about it is by increasing the time scale of the observation, and that may be why we may feel more comfortable focusing on "eventful" macrohistorical processes. Finally, and even if we are ready to assume multiple and equally possible pasts, we seldom have the evidence to persuasively claim that a particular set of occurrences may in fact be a transformative event in its Sewellian sense.

In this paper I explore and critically review a well-known Old World archaeological interpretation that gives a decisive historical role to a hypothetical event, and charges it with transformative significance: the arrival of foreign Neolithic *Argonauts* to the western Mediterranean coast as a set of occurrences triggering a fast short-term cascade of structural transformations throughout Iberia. The structural transformation that this event is supposed to have set off is the demise of hunter-gatherers and the consolidation of the so-called peasant way of life.

There is an increasing consensus that the Mesolithic-Neolithic transition in Iberia was substantially fast. With some few exceptions, as the northern Cantabrian region (see Arias 2007; Straus 2009), most hunter-gatherer groups were substituted by or became agropastoralists in perhaps no more than 200 years. For a good number of scholars, this is the time span between the arrival of the Neolithic Argonauts on the eastern coast (*c.* 5550 cal BC) and the colonization of the interior steppe-like region some time around 5400 cal BC or maybe earlier. In most cases the archaeological record offers no transition. It suggests a sharp change, with a sudden, almost-entire reliance on domestics and an important use of pottery containers, among other material traits. These remains, together with some pits and feeble domestic structures, are considered by some to be the material result of the earliest peasant societies in Iberia. In short, the arrival of the Neolithic Argonauts involved a large-scale landscape transformation of void "islands," triggering a further assimilation, acculturation, or annihilation of hunter-gatherers (García Puchol et al. 2009:237).

The supporters of the wave of advance and its variants assume that all domestic plants (wheat, barley, and legumes), animals (sheep, goats, pigs, and cattle), certain technologies (ceramic, polished stone), and a whole village way of life moved into Europe from Anatolia as components of a package. By the time they arrived at the western Mediterranean, these groups produced the impressed ware called Cardial, and wherever the combination of material remains has been recorded without previous transitional archaeological data, they have been considered an evidence of never-directly-found pure Neolithic colonizers. The exceptionally fast arrival of this package at the Mediterranean coast of Iberia has allowed Zilhão (2001) to propose a maritime colonization of coastal spots void of hunter-gatherers. Early Neolithic evidence recently discovered in the interior areas of Iberia has been interpreted in similar terms, as Neolithic incomers, mainly because of the lack or limited amount of previous Mesolithic evidence.

In the following section, I will present a case study that can be well understood as a Sewellian event. It represents an Early Neolithic distinctive transformation of the built environment and signals the beginning of agro-pastoral ways of life in Iberia. My focus will be regionally based, the spatial pattern of a set of outstanding sites throughout the Serpis Valley, in the western Mediterranean coast of Iberia. I will show how a whole assemblage of new archaeological remains appear as something novel in a specific period of time *c.* 5500 cal BC but, unlike other examples proposed by Beck et al. (2007), recent studies suggest that neither can the direct origin be tracked back, nor the immediate results followed at a local scale. The hypothesis of the arrival of ethnically different seafaring groups as the triggering event—Argonauts with the Neolithic package, knowledge, and knowhow—has been mobilized in order to explain archaeological discontinuities, while the results of these discontinuities have been raised to the level of structural transformations.

My aim is twofold. On the one hand, to show how, although seemingly coherent with the archaeological record, the Argonaut hypothesis is highly underdetermined. Any alternative hypothesis explaining the same evidence without the need to incorporate an eventful colonial encounter would be more parsimonious (Vicent 1997). On the other hand, to call into question the theory that all material discontinuities that archaeologists tend to label as changes between "periods" or "cultures" are in fact structural changes in historical terms. In the final section I highlight the problems of overestimating our capability to archaeologically discriminate events and our need as prehistorians to avoid charging possible events with causality. Nevertheless, although events may be elusive, long-term sequences are frequently accessible. If I have understood correctly the gist of Beck et al.'s arguments, it is not so much about the actual recognition of the event as of recognizing the historical contingency of the order in which the sequences that we analyze take place, whatever the scale we can reasonably access. This would be a truly historically informed Prehistory. In order to do so, we must shift both the time and spatial scales to acknowledge that our prehistory is filled with contingent processes that are by nature, and even if we cannot recognize them, eventful.

The Argonauts Arrive: East Iberia *c.* 5500 cal BC

The Serpis valley (aka Alcoi valley, Alicante, Spain) and its surroundings is one of the most intensely archaeologically researched areas in Iberia, and one with particularly dense Early Neolithic evidence (Bernabeu et al. 2008) (Figure 1). The easiest entrance to this fertile valley of about 800 square kilometers is located less than 15 kilometers away from the Mediterranean coast. The valley bottom is almost completely surrounded by mountains.

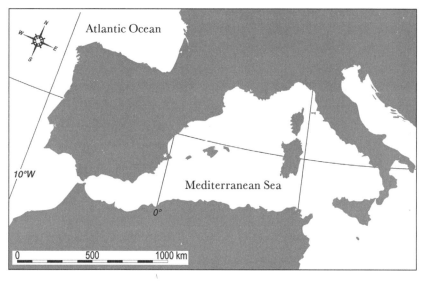

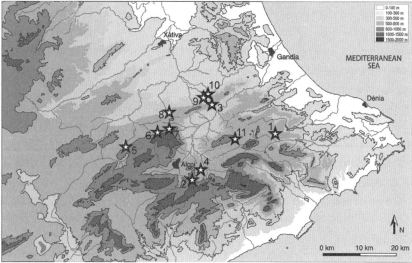

FIGURE 1 Top: The study area (marked with a star) in the Western Mediterranean. Below. Sites from the Serpis Valley mentioned in text. Numbers 5 to 11 are funerary caves. 1. Pla de Petracos; 2. La Sarga; 3. Cova de L'Or; 4. Mas D'Is; 5. La Sarsa; 6.Cova del Moro; 7. Cova dels Pilars; 8. Cova Barranc del Castellet; 9. Cova de L'Almud; 10. Cova Frontó; 11. Cova D'En Pardo (modified from McClure et al. 2008, Figure 1).

Heights vary from 300 to 1300 meters above sea level. These mountains are part of the northern spurs of the Betic chain, running south-southeast, parallel to the coastline and thus leaving small coastal plains. In fact, except for the lowlands of Valencia and Murcia (both known for their agricultural productivity), the next wide coastal plain south is the Guadalquivir valley, on the Atlantic coast. The diversity of elevations, geographical environments, and vegetation communities makes the Serpis valley especially apt for human occupation (Barton 2006:27).

Up to 32 Early Neolithic sites have been recorded in the area, 51 if we include others in the surrounding region of Alicante (García Puchol 2006). They include mainly caves, but also rock shelters and river basin open air sites. The kind of evidence is strikingly diverse: some few timber buildings, a ditch enclosure, burial and habitational caves, and different styles of rock art paintings. When considered as a unified system, the archaeological record of the valley is outstandingly ritualistic in nature, and it may well be conceived as a good case of a ritualized landscape. The area has the oldest radiocarbon dates on short-life domestic samples in all Iberia (5620–5481 cal BC) and has been interpreted by many as one of the clearest evidences of Neolithic colonization of an area void of Mesolithic populations by so-called Cardial groups (for their characteristic impressed shell–decorated ware) or pure Neolithics, both ethnically and culturally foreign.

The highly compartmentalized and typologically detailed sequence, the lack of evidence of Mesolithic-Neolithic interaction, the absence of continuity in all known stratigraphies, and the extremely scarce presence of Late Mesolithic (B phase) in the valley and its vicinity, makes the appearance of the first Neolithic evidence an abrupt change. This change has been explained in the context of the wave of advance model as a clear-cut example of marine pioneer Neolithic colonization (Bernabeu 2006; Zilhao 2001). Whatever its interpretation may be, the archaeological record offers a case of radical change involving schemas and resources that are materialized in several ways: consumption patterns, the built environment, and the increase in ritualized/symbolic materiality.

The rock art sanctuaries at Pla de Petracos and La Sarga are visibly located decorating the rock shelters on the cliffs of two of the entrances to the valley system when approached from the coast. The former site includes 16 panels with macroschematic, Levantine, and schematic styles decorating eight shelters (Hernández et al. 2004), and the latter 26 panels with macroschematic and Levantine styles on three shelters (Hernández et al. 2002). These three rock art styles are significantly different in relation to: (1) the size of their representations, from the almost human-scale figures in the macroschematic to the miniature-like naturalistic Levantine motives; (2) the highly symbolic motives of both schematic styles, which contrast with the naturalistic and narrative hunting-gathering scenes represented in the Levantine style. Overlapping representations in rock art, and formal similarities with elements portrayed on portable objects, suggest that all styles were practiced at least since the Early Neolithic (Cruz-Berrocal and Vicent 2007; McClure et al. 2008). All these strategically located accumulations of symbolic expressions signal the entrance to a valley that includes, among other, the following evidence.

The Cova de L'Or (Martí 1977; Martí et al. 1980), a cavity of about 700 square meters, has one of the best Early Neolithic archaeological collections in Iberia. It is also paradigmatic because of the significant set of materials recovered in a previously unoccupied cave: marine shell ornaments; hair needles; polished axes; bone burins; rings; needles; shell, stone, and fish vertebrae beads; bracelets; bone palette knives and spoons; plaquettes, bones, and drilled teeth; flutes made of bird bones; a bird clay figurine decorated with cardium shell (Martí et al. 2001); an abundant flint industry, some with cereal wear marks; 267 (MNI) domestic sheep and/or goats and 72 pigs among other less consumed animals, out of which more than 70 percent is represented by young specimens; dispersed human bones; and an important set of complete finely elaborated and highly decorated Cardial ware vessels, one of them filled with two kilograms of red pigment powder made out of local hematite and cinnabar obtained from a long distance source (García et al. 2006). These remains were accompanied by one of the highest accumulations of cereal seeds in Neolithic Iberia: a unique deposit of toasted wheat and barley seeds. Two samples obtained from the deposit analyzed by Hopf (1966) included 3,416 seeds of three different kinds of wheat and 2,176 of two kinds of barley seeds. This cave, located well away from the nearest arable land, has been considered a place of social storage (Vicent 1989) and all the evidence suggests certain long-distance connections, the coming together of different small groups, and their probable involvement in ritual activities.

The next set of evidence comes from the only open-air site documented and systematically dug on the valley bottom. The site, known as Mas D'Is, is located right by the source of the river Penàguila (Bernabeu et al. 2002, 2003, 2006). The area has been highly modified by erosion, creating a characteristic landscape of creeks and slightly sloped agricultural lands. As a result of this erosion, the preserved extension of the site is approximately ten hectares. The Cardial Neolithic record has been located in two separated areas. The earliest structures are a set of 28 postholes of around 15 cm width each, ten of which have been interpreted as part of a big apsidal timber longhouse of about ten meters long and four wide. Other similar posthole structures, still quite undefined, are located 250 meters northwest from this. These rather small postholes are somehow related to other structures such as an oven and several concentrations of stones. As happens in many other Early Neolithic sites of Western Europe, the Early Neolithic domestic evidence in Iberia is quite slight, especially when compared to later III millennium BC villages.

Slightly north of these postholes lies a 59 meter long, 12 m wide, and 4 m deep ditch that has been interpreted as a circular causewayed enclosure (Bernabeu et al. 2002, 2003, 2006), but that may well be an isolated ditch. Its early Neolithic radiocarbon date suggests the coming together probably of several dispersed groups, which would invest an important amount of their labor in modifying the built environment in a way unknown in the preceding periods. Again, unlike later Copper Age enclosures, this first monumental ditch was left unfilled and was slowly refilled by natural processes, occasionally interrupted by short-time—maybe seasonal—activities. Contrasting with the richness and variety of items accumulated in caves such as the Cova de L'Or, the ditch at Mas D'Is represents a set of gatherings that left little more evidence than a radically modified space, an earthwork.

Finally, the last set of evidence refers to seven small early Neolithic burial caves, all located on the mountains north of the valley (Bernabeu et al. 2001), that should be added to the already mentioned human remains at the Cova de L'Or and Cova de La Sarsa. These burial caves signify the surrounding landscape, increasing its ritual significance.

By the turn of the fifth millennium the evidence of human activity in the valley seems to disappear. The intensified ritualized landscape deployed at the Serpis valley was abandoned, and its highly symbolic and unique built environment lost its significance. By then, most Iberians were already Neolithic.

The case of the Serpis valley, intensely investigated and especially apt for human occupation, has been used as one of the best examples of colonization. At the center of the interpretation of all the described radical material change of patterns in the archaeological record is the presence of incoming Argonauts of the western Mediterranean.

UNDERDETERMINED EVENTS, CONTINGENT SEQUENCES

The sharp transition, and the fact that domestics appear without previous agriotype, has been explained through the arrival of foreign and ethnically different Neolithic colonizing groups to Iberia. As Martí (2008:23) claims, "The introduction of agriculture and domestic animals requires the need to resort to some kind of demic diffusion, notably where there is no documented prior human substrate." The hypothesis of a colonizing event, mobilized in order to interpret a radical change in the archaeological record, becomes central to the explanation of the earliest Neolithic evidence and the further presence of Neolithic traits throughout Iberia as its cascading effect. In brief, the arrival of the Argonauts is presented as a sine qua non set of transformative occurrences causing a regional structural change.

There are at least two questions that arise from this interpretation. In the first instance, whether the hypothesis would resist the application of Ockham's razor, that is, if any alternative interpretation explaining the same archaeological data would be more parsimonious (Vicent 1997). Secondly, and in a broader temporal and spatial scale, whether the suggested change really exemplifies a structural transformation whose post-event evidence we should seek out in subsequent periods. That is, if we should understand the Early Neolithic as a macrohistorical Sewellian event, accepting that the first period of the three-tier Neolithic reflects a historical-sociological transformation: the introduction of a peasant way of life, as suggested by some authors (e.g. Bernabeu et al. 2003).

The answer to the first question seems to me straightforward. The arrival of Argonauts is a highly underdetermined hypothesis, and the increase of archaeological data throughout Iberia will only multiply the possibility of similar alternative interpretations. As I already suggested, prehistorians have serious difficulties in recognizing events, and even if we did so, the more we charge them with causality, the more possible alternative pasts we will be able to construct. A rapid transformation of hunter-gatherers in some few generations would probably leave no other trace than a radical change in whatever is finally preserved *in* and *of* the archaeological record. It would be somehow naïve to expect that all the detailed steps of short-term transitions in our prehistory would be widely detectable. Some of the most spectacular transformations in the Iberian archaeological record, such as the sharp and transition-less emergence of Los Millares culture, or the abrupt change between the Millarian Copper and Argaric Bronze Age cultures (e.g., Gilman 2002; Chapman 2003), would suggest that building hypotheses reliant on colonial encounters may be a risky business (see Martínez Navarrete 1989 for a critical historiographic review of the colonial model). On the other hand, making hunter-gatherers agents of their own historical change may not be that unreasonable. In fact, as Michael Jochim—unsuspected of being "indigenist"—has recently stated, "If Iberian hunter-gatherers were previously mobile and maintained spatially extensive contacts, then one might expect a much faster rate of agricultural expansion, as the knowledge and crops could be widely distributed over great distances" (Jochim 2009:309). This seems to me more parsimonious, at least considering what we know about the spread of Neolithic traits throughout Iberia. It would probably be more robust in explaining sets of archaeological data that are either increasingly problematic or openly contradictory with the seafaring colonial model. Nevertheless, the colonial hypothesis functions as some kind of normal science, and if it was the case it may possess "a built-in mechanism that ensures the relaxation of the restrictions that bound research whenever the paradigm from which they derive ceases to function effectively" (Kuhn 1973:24).

The second question relates to the existence or not of a structural change, and becomes a matter of the chosen spatial and temporal scale of observation. I believe that by narrowing our analysis to such possible events and their suggested short-term cascade effects, we may be overlooking or underestimating the incredible rate of variability of the archaeological record throughout the Neolithic sequence.

There is the important rate of variability throughout the different Neolithic sites inside Iberia and beyond, including those colonizers that are supposed to be ethnically distinctive. Funerary evidence, architecture, consumption patterns, symbolic expressions, or craft manufacture are highly variable. This variability questions in itself the existence of any kind of colonial encounters, but also the directionality of the Neolithic as a fast and unified structural change.

Certainly, variability can only be observed at a certain spatial scale. For those working in other areas of the world (e.g., North America), it would seem enlightening to observe the overall geographical extension of the object at debate for those that defend the existence of ethnically pure Neolithic colonizers: the western Mediterranean, with its 821,000 square kilometers, could be fitted into the area occupied by the Great Lakes or the Gulf of Mexico. Sicily, Corsica, Sardinia, among 32 other islands, shorten distances between certain coasts. For what we can hint about pre-Neolithic societies, marine fishery may have been a well-developed subsistence strategy in the Iberian Levant since the late Paleolithic (Morales and Roselló 2004:120), and we now know that both Sardinia and Cyprus had recurring seasonal occupations since at least the eleventh and ninth millennia BC respectively (Knapp 2008:21). This suggests that seafaring contacts and exchange networks were probably at work on the Iberian coastlines well before the appearance of the first domestics. The possibility of movement of people and things would have been favored by certain qualities of the western Mediterranean coast: extended visibility and connectivity of the maritime, among others. Horden and Purcell (2000:137) have put forward an example that may be of great usefulness in the present case: the geography of the northwest Mediterranean coast from the Arno to the Ebro valleys can be considered a single maritime façade with small coastal plains and four important corridors leading to the continental interior. One could go on suggesting that the next wide coastal plain is the Valencia region, where some of the finest and earliest Neolithic evidence has been recovered and is the object of my case study.

Although the connectivity of the western Mediterranean coast has been historically variable, it seems that the Neolithic is one such period in history where this connectivity was increasingly materialized in the archaeological record. The example of the distribution of obsidian from the four Mediterranean island sources at Pantelleria, Lipari, Palmarola, and Monte Arci (Robb 2007:194) is a good example of the role of seascapes during this period. We should nevertheless not overestimate this connectivity during the Early Neolithic. Indicators such as the obsidian distribution in Italy suggest that although routes were probably the most common spreading mechanism, obsidian remains are still quite scarce when compared to later periods (Robb 2007:196). We should also not assume that those that inhabited coastal areas were all necessarily seafaring oriented groups, as the magisterial description of the Fijian Rewa by Sahlins (2004) suggests. In any case, it seems that the Neolithic did involve an increase in the materialization of movements, at least of objects, an observation that adds to the increase in materiality in general, as suggested by Hodder (2005:131).

Summing up, a reasonable spatial scale to observe the possible structural transformation of society during the Early Neolithic should involve all Iberia in the context of the western Mediterranean. When observed to this scale, local events such as those described in the previous case study seem to be more occurrences than eventful transformations.

We are thus left with the matter of choosing the temporal scale. By focusing on the Early (Cardial) Neolithic as a coherent short-term transformative event—in Sewell's sense—we lose sight of maybe one of the most important structural transformations produced throughout the Neolithic: the fact that, contrary to what most historians or sociologists would think, all the evidence for a village way of life did not clearly appear in Iberia until approximately two and one-half millennia after those events took place. To put it in Sewell's terms, I would suggest that what we know as the Neolithic (VI–IV millennia BC) has its historical significance in being a long-term period of ruptures in the articulation of resources and schemas, only rearticulated and distinctively materialized by the early third millennia BC.

For all we know, many if not all the resources, knowledge, knowhow, and technologies were in the hands or available to Iberian late sixth millennium BC groups. Nevertheless, when compared to a peninsular scale, these groups seemed to have used, reused, transformed, and invented a whole array of material expressions in their own specific way. It was only by c. 3000 cal BC, at this very specific historical context, that all these adopted and transformed array of materials actually resulted in a novel sociohistorical pattern: the emergence of effective lineages, capable of mobilizing important amounts of population, creating novel patterns of wealth, increasing territoriality, and transforming the landscape as had never been seen previously. It was the combination of traditionally available resources and some later incorporated set of technologies (e.g., the plough) that were displayed and recombined, allowing the historical objective conditions for the closing of the structural change in a specific contingent moment in time and space. I believe that this moment—which we call the Copper Age (Los Millares culture and its contemporaries)—is the one and only termination of the social processes that we know as Neolithic.

The contingencies of history are again surprising when observed at a western Mediterranean scale. These expanding agro-pastoral village lifestyles emerged by the time of the demise of Italian villages (Robb 2007:305). But in order to understand those divergent tendencies of Copper Age societies we should shift again to the regional and local scales.

CONCLUDING REMARKS

I share with other authors (such as Zilhão 2003:220) the view that people must have made their own prehistory. We nevertheless do not need social imperatives, nor Argonauts of the western Mediterranean, to interpret the Neolithic. It seems easier to me not to subsume the agency of those who peopled our prehistory under imperatives that homogenize in a single event what was a clearly diverse array of processes, and to accept that a diversity of groups incorporated, interpreted, and finally invented their own Neolithic.

Throughout this paper I have suggested that events are, of course, important for prehistorians, but that by focusing on them we run the risk of losing the perspective given by long-term history and, as a result, overlooking certain key structural transformations. Events and structures are observation criteria and the scales of observation are critical to any historical analysis. As I have tried to show, by folding all the Neolithic into a short-term eventful structural change we may miss the opportunity to systematically organize contingent occurrences, that is, to scrutinize the structure (Sahlins 1988:135).

ACKNOWLEDGMENTS

All the ideas that I put forward in this paper have been previously developed by Juan M. Vicent, from whom I keep on learning the craft of doing (Pre) History. I would also like to express my deep gratitude to Joan Bernabeu, who reviewed, thoroughly criticized, and counterargued the complete paper. My special thanks to Antonio Gilman and Maribel Martínez Navarrete for their always sharp comments. Maria Cruz Berrocal provided me with some detailed data while working on a similar topic. The paper has been written within the Research Project HAR2009-14360-C03-02, funded by the Spanish Ministry of Science and Innovation.

References Cited

Arias, P. 2007 Neighbours but Diverse: Social Change in North-West Iberia during the Transition from the Mesolithic to the Neolithic (5500–400 cal BC). *Proceedings of the British Academy* 144:53–71.

Barton, M. 2006 El Medio Físico. In *El Abric de La Falguera (Alcoi, Alacant). 8.000 años de ocupación humana en la cabecera del río de Alcoi*, edited by O. García-Puchol and J. E. Aura, pp. 27–42. Ayuntamiento de Alcoi & Caja de Ahorros del Mediterráneo, Alcoi.

Beck, R. A., D. J. Bolender, J. A. Brown, and T. K. Earle 2007 Eventful Archaeology. The Place of Space in Structural Transformation. *Current Anthropology* 48(6):833–860.

Bernabeu, J. 2006 Una visión actual sobre el origen y difusión del Neolítico en la Península Ibérica. Ca. 5600–5000 cal. A.C.. In *El Abric de La Falguera (Alcoi, Alacant). 8.000 años de ocupación humana en la cabecera del río de Alcoi*, edited by O. García-Puchol and J. E. Aura, pp. 189–211. Ayuntamiento de Alcoi & Caja de Ahorros del Mediterráneo, Alcoi.

Bernabeu, J., Ll. Molina, T. Orozco, A. Diez, and M. Barton 2008 Los valles del Serpis (Alicante): 20 años de trabajo de campo. In *IV Congreso del Neolítico Peninsular. Volume I,* edited by M. S. Hernández, J. A. Soler and J. A. López, pp. 50–57. Museo Arqueológico de Alicante, Diputación de Alicante.

Bernabeu, J., T. Orozco, and A. Diez 2002 El poblamiento Neolítico: desarrollo del paisaje agrario en les Valls de L'Alcoi. In *La Sarga. Arte rupestre y territorio*, edited by M. Hernández and J. M. Segura, pp. 171–184. Ayuntamiento de Alcoy & Caja de Ahorros del Mediterráneo, Alcoy.

Bernabeu, J., T. Orozco, A. Diez, M. Gómez, M. and F. J. Molina 2003 Mas D'Is (Penàguila, Alicante): Aldeas y recintos monumentales del Neolítico Inicial en el Valle del Serpis. *Trabajos de Prehistoria* 60(2):39–59.

Bernabeu, J., Ll. Molina, A. Diez, and T. Orozco 2006 Inequalities and Power. Three Millennia of Prehistory in Mediterranean Spain (5600–2000 cal BC). In *Social Inequality in Iberian Late Prehistory*, edited by P. Díaz-del-Río and L. García Sanjuán, pp. 97–116. BAR International Series 651. British Archaeological Reports, Oxford.

Bernabeu, J., Ll. Molina, and O. García Puchol 2001 El mundo funerario en el horizonte cardial valenciano. Un registro oculto. *Saguntum* (P.L.A.V.) 33:27–36.

Chapman, R. 2003 *Archaeologies of Complexity*. Routledge, London.

Cruz-Berrocal, M., and J. Vicent 2007 Rock Art as an Archaeological and Social Indicator: The Neolithisation of the Iberian Peninsula. *Journal of Anthropological Archaeology* 26:676–697.

García, P., I. Domingo, and C. Roldán 2006 Nuevos datos sobre el uso de materia colorante durante el Neolítico Antiguo en las comarcas centrales valencianas. *Saguntum* (P.L.A.V.) 38:49–60.

García Puchol, O. 2006 La lectura del inicio de la secuencia Neolítica en el Abrigo. In *El Abric de La Falguera (Alcoi, Alacant). 8.000 años de ocupación humana en la cabecera del río de Alcoi*, edited by O. García-Puchol and J. E. Aura, pp. 173–180. Ayuntamiento de Alcoi & Caja de Ahorros del Mediterráneo, Alcoi.

García Puchol, O., Ll. Molina, J. E. Aura, and J. Bernabeu 2009 From the Mesolithic to the Neolithic on the Mediterranean Coast of the Iberian Peninsula. *Journal of Anthropological Research* 65(2):237–252.

Gilman, A. 2002 Assessing Political Development in Copper and Bronze Age Southeast Spain. In *From Leaders to Rulers*, edited by Jonathan Haas, pp. 59–81. Kluwer Academic/Plenum Publishers, New York.

Hernández, M., P. Ferrer, and E. Catalá 2002 La Sarga (Alcoy, Alicante). Catálogo de pinturas y horizontes artísticos. In *La Sarga. Arte rupestre y territorio*, edited by M. Hernández and J. M. Segura, pp. 51–100. Ayuntamiento de Alcoy & Caja de Ahorros del Mediterráneo, Alcoy.

Hernández, M., P. Ferrer, E. Catalá, J. Soler, and R. Pérez 2004 *Pla de Petracos. Patrimonio de la Humanidad*. Diputación Provincial de Alicante, Alicante.

Hodder, I. 2005 The Spatio-Temporal Organization of the Early Town at Çatalhöyük. In *(Un)settling the Neolithic*, edited by D. Bailey, A. Whittle and V. Cummings, pp. 126–139. Oxbow. Oxford.

Hopf, M. 1966 Triticum monococcum y Trititum dicoccum en el Neolítico antiguo español. *Archivo de Prehistoria Levantina* XI:53–73.

Horden, P., and N. Purcell 2000 *The Corrupting Sea. A Study of Mediterranean History*. Blackwell, Oxford.

Jochim, M. 2009 The Process of Agricultural Colonization. *Journal of Anthropological Research* 65(2):299–310.

Knapp, A. B. 2008 *Prehistoric and Protohistoric Cyprus. Identity, Insularity, and Connectivity*. Oxford University Press, Oxford.

Kuhn, T. S. 1973 *The Structure of Scientific Revolutions*. International Encyclopedia of Unified Science. Volume II. University of Chicago Press, Chicago.

Martí, B. 1977 *Cova de L'Or (Beniarrés-Alicante) Volumen I .Serie de Trabajos Varios 51*. Servicio de Investigación Prehistórica, Valencia.

Martí, B. 2008 Cuevas, poblados y santuarios neolíticos: una perspectiva mediterránea. IV Congreso del Neolítico Peninsular (I). *Alicante*:17–27.

Martí, B., A. Arias-Gago del Molino, R. Martínez, and J. Juan-Cabanilles 2001 Los tubos de hueso de la Cova de L'Or (Beniarrés, Alicante). Instrumentos musicales en el Neolítico Antiguo de la Península Ibérica. *Trabajos de Prehistoria* 58(2):41–67.

Martí, B., V. Pascual, M. D. Gallart, P. López, M. Pérez-Ripoll, J. D. Acuña, and F. Robles 1980 *Cova de L'Or (Beniarrés-Alicante) Volumen II. Serie de Trabajos Varios 65*. Servicio de Investigación Prehistórica, Valencia.

Martínez Navarrete, Mª. Isabel 1989 Una revisión crítica de la prehistoria española: la Edad del Bronce como paradigma. *Siglo* XXI. Madrid. http://hdl.handle.net/10261/9426.

McClure, S. B., Ll. Molina, and J. Bernabeu 2008 Neolithic Rock Art in Context: Landscape History and the Transition to Agriculture in Mediterranean Spain. *Journal of Anthropological Archaeology* 27(3):326–337.

Morales, A., and E. Roselló 2004 Fishing Down the Food Web in Iberian Prehistory? A New Look at the Fishes from Cueva de Nerja (Málaga, Spain). In *Pettis animaux et sociétés humaines. Du complément alimentaire aux ressources utilitaires. XXIV rencontres internationales darchéologie et dhistoire dAntibes*, edited by J.-P. Brugal and J. Desse, pp. 111–123. Éditions Association pour la promotion et la diffusion des connaissances archéologiques (APDGA), Antibes.

Robb, J. 2007 *The Early Mediterranean Village. Agency, Material Culture, and Social Change in Neolithic Italy.* Cambridge Studies in Archaeology. Cambridge University Press, Cambridge.

Sahlins, M. 1988 *Islas de historia. La muerte del capitán Cook. Metáfora, antropología e historia*. Gedisa, Barcelona.

Sahlins, M. 2004 *Apologies to Thucydides. Understanding History as Culture and Vice Versa*. University of Chicago Press, Chicago.

Sewell, W. H. Jr. 2005 *Logics of History. Social Theory and Social Transformations*. University of Chicago Press, Chicago.

Straus, Lawrence G. 2009 The Late Upper Paleolithic-Mesolithic-Neolithic Transitions in Cantabrian Spain. *Journal of Anthropological Research* 65(2):287–298.

Vicent, J. M. 1989 *Bases teórico-metodológicas para el estudio del comienzo de la metalurgia en la Península Ibérica*. Unpublished Doctoral dissertation. Universidad Autónoma de Madrid, Madrid.

Vicent, J. M.1997 The Island Filter Model Revisited. In *Encounters and transformations. The Archaeology of Iberia in Transition*, edited by M. Balmuth, A. Gilman and L. Prados-Torreira, pp. 1–13. Monographs in Mediterranean Archaeology 7. Sheffield Academic Press, Sheffield..

Zilhão, J. 2001 Radiocarbon Evidence for Maritime Pioneer Colonization at the Origins of Farming in West Mediterranean Europe. *Proceedings of the National Academy of Sciences* 98:14180–14185.

Zilhão, J. 2003 The Neolithic Transition in Portugal and the Role of Demic Diffusion in the Spread of Agriculture across West Mediterranean Europe. In *The Widening Harvest. The Neolithic Transition in Europe: Looking Back, Looking Forward*, edited by A. J. Ammerman and P. Biagi, pp. 207–223. Colloquia and Conference Papers 6. Archaeological Institute of America, Boston.

Chapter Six

Eventful Archaeology, the Heuneburg Mudbrick Wall, and the Early Iron Age of Southwest Germany

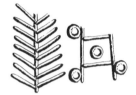

Bettina Arnold

Abstract *The Period IV Heuneburg mudbrick wall, constructed sometime around 600 BC and destroyed by fire some 60 years later, clearly represents a break with the indigenous fortification systems that preceded and succeeded it. Other evidence for Mediterranean contact and influence, particularly in the form of imported pottery, is minimal until after the razing of the mudbrick wall Heuneburg and its associated outer settlement around 540 BC. This suggests that the impact of the initial event represented by the physical alteration of the environment in the form of the mudbrick wall extended to structural transformations within the society over the next two generations. An analysis of the late Hallstatt Heuneburg mortuary landscape from the "eventful archaeology" perspective is particularly appropriate in this case because the transformation of the built environment appears to have preceded and naturalized the social transformations that were to follow. The eventual leveling of the mudbrick wall takes on added significance in view of the fact that by the time of this iconoclastic action, the social rupture and rearticulation wrought by contact with distant power centers were already irreversible. This rearticulation can be seen in the construction of a massive wall and ditch system surrounding the hillfort after 540 BC as well as in the erection of four monumental burial mounds on the remains of the outer settlement, one of which contained four secondary burials with gold neckrings, ordinarily only found in paramount central chamber graves. Traditional archaeological interpretations of the mudbrick wall will be presented in light of the eventful archaeology paradigm, taking into consideration recent evidence from the mortuary and settlement record associated with this early Iron Age hillfort in southwest Germany.*

TRANSITIONS DEFINE TRADITIONS

In a pioneering article on the individual in prehistory, Karl Narr had the following to say about the "mad builder" of the Heuneburg and his mudbrick wall masterpiece:

> A construction that certainly would have been quite revolutionary for its time and place…retains the features of a very dominant personality—a powerful ruler of the citadel, with wide-ranging contacts, open to innovation as long as it could serve as a vehicle for his need for display and the external demonstration of power and wealth.…Here we are face to face—if only in shadowy form—with the lineaments of a personality for whose evaluation as an individual it is relatively immaterial whether or not we can determine in which burial mound he was interred, or which corpse we can assign him to. That takes nothing away from our sense that we are in the presence of a historical personality. (1972:256)

In general, the archaeological record presents itself as a cumulative concatenation of actions, most of which, in the manner of palimpsests, have partly or completely obliterated earlier patterns of behavior. Occasionally, however, a window, or at least an aperture, opens in the mostly undifferentiated mélange of human detritus that constitutes the archaeological record, and a ray of light breaks through to cast some part of the natural or human landscape of the past in high relief. One such momentary illumination occurred around 600 BC at the Heuneburg hillfort, a modest fortified spur of land overlooking the Danube River in the part of the German state of Baden-Württemberg known as Swabia.

Several factors make this particular case study an ideal opportunity to test as well as critique the eventful archaeology paradigm. The Iron Age occupation of the site was relatively short, with major shifts and transformations taking place over a period of 200 plus or minus 20 years. However, by the time the hillfort was abandoned between 450 and 400 BC, the cultural and social structures that had characterized this region since the Bronze Age had been permanently reconfigured, a process that began with the erection of a wholly alien form of fortification system on the plateau that subsisted for at least two generations. Around 600 BC, a person or persons unknown initiated and presumably supervised the construction of a perimeter wall on the plateau made of air-dried mudbrick on a stone foundation, a unique phenomenon in west-central Iron Age Europe. To paraphrase Sewell, the mudbrick wall at the Heuneburg represents a built manifestation of an event that transformed the social and cultural structure of the community (2005:199), and the cumulative impact of that event is reflected in the structure of both the later settlement and its mortuary landscape.

THE EARLY IRON AGE IN SOUTHWEST GERMANY

The founding of Massalia, modern day Marseilles, by Ionian Greeks from Phocaea in 600 BC looms large in any discussion of the Iron Age Heuneburg hillfort because this particular event has traditionally been assumed to have had a major impact on a group of hillforts referred to as *Fürstensitze*, or chiefly seats, that occupy what is known as the West Hallstatt zone between 600 and 400 BC (see Wells 1980, among others). These sites are found in an area extending from southwest Germany and eastern France into parts of Austria and Switzerland north of the Alps. The presence of imports, including Attic pottery and other wares associated with the consumption of alcoholic beverages, including wine, also imported, has generally been considered the principal defining characteristic of these sites (see Fischer 1982, among others).

The burial mounds surrounding these hillforts often include extremely richly outfitted central chamber graves, known as *Fürstengräber*. The primary interments, referred to as central burials, may be surrounded by up to 130 secondary burials and were often looted in antiquity or more recently. Three unlooted primary late Hallstatt/early La Tène interments with Mediterranean imports have been recovered since the 1950s: the male elite burial of Hochdorf near Stuttgart, dated to about 550 BC; the female elite burial of Vix in Burgundy, which has been dated to around 450 BC; and the Glauberg Grave 1, also dated to the fifth century BC. The *Fürstensitz /Fürstengrab* association is problematic both because of the implied parallel drawn between medieval feudalism and early Iron Age social structure and because it presents this burial category as monolithic when it is in fact quite variable. In more recent years the Fürstensitz/Fürstengrab association has also been challenged, as at least three non-hillfort settlements are now known to have yielded Attic pottery (Biel and Krausse 2005).

In addition, the 600 BC date for the founding of Massalia makes it unlikely that the establishment of this colony could have been the catalyst for social changes occurring in temperate Europe at the same time or even earlier. Thucydides is the first classical source to mention this event, followed by Strabo, Pausanias, Livy, and others, with a less reliable account provided by Justin (Hodge 1998:64–65). There is some disagreement regarding the 600 BC date; the sources are split between a founding date around 600 and another around 545 BC. Ceramic evidence from archaeological investigations at Massalia itself supports the earlier date (Hodge 1998:65), but it is unlikely that the Phocaeans who arrived in Massalia at that time had no previous knowledge of the place, or that the local inhabitants had had no previous contact with Greek traders (Hodge 1998:65–66). At what point then did some rumor of these interactions, or entanglements, as Dietler and others have called them (Dietler 1990, 1998, 1999), reach an aspiring elite near the source of the Danube?

THE HEUNEBURG HILLFORT

Hecataeus of Miletus and Herodotus, writing around 500 BC and 450 BC, respectively, both locate the territory of the Keltoi in the interior of temperate Europe, in the hinterland of the Greek colony of Massalia. Herodotus specifically identifies this region as being near the source of the Danube, which he calls the Istros (Gersbach 1982:10, 1995:93). Two major early Iron Age hillfort sites near the sources of the Danube in southwest Germany have produced evidence for contact with the Mediterranean world during the late Hallstatt phase of the early Iron Age: the Hohenasperg near Stuttgart and the Heuneburg near Ulm. The best preserved and most intensively studied of the two is undoubtedly the 3.3 ha Heuneburg, which was excavated for a quarter century, followed by a period of analysis and publication beginning in 1979 (Gersbach 1982, 1989; Kimmig 1983). In the past seven years excavations have begun again in the outer settlement, an extensive area that was at least five times the size of the plateau (Bofinger 2005, 2006; Reim 2003, 2004).

The hillfort was first fortified during the Middle Bronze Age, in the sixteenth and thirteenth centuries BC. Siegfried Kurz's recent settlement survey of the Heuneburg region has confirmed the fact that before the Middle Bronze Age the area within five kilometers of the hillfort seems to have been relatively sparsely occupied (Kurz 2007). By the end of the Middle Bronze Age, the population had apparently increased significantly, based on the appearance in the landscape of numerous hamlets and farmsteads and their associated tumulus cemeteries (Kurz 2007:150). Burial mounds during this period, also known as the Tumulus Bronze Age, were typically less than 10 meters in diameter, usually contained a single central interment, and were organized in clusters assumed to represent some type of kin-based social group.

After a Late Bronze Age hiatus, the hillfort was resettled in the early Iron Age between about 600 and 400 BC, when it suffered a final conflagration and was not intensively occupied again until the sixth to the eleventh centuries AD. Beginning in AD 1323, the abandoned plateau was utilized as arable by the Talhof farmstead just outside its southern ramparts, which significantly disturbed the later Iron Age deposits in the center of the hillfort (Kimmig 1983:85–86).

The site's stratigraphic prehistoric profile reveals eight occupations or periods and 23 separate construction phases marked by repairs to or replacements of successive fortification systems. The Middle Bronze Age hillfort was protected by a log-cabin single-box style fortification of wood and stamped earth that followed the natural contours of the plateau. The Heuneburg at this time was thought to have controlled a considerable part of the surrounding region, although little is known about the burial record of this period (Gersbach 1982:7–9). During the Late Bronze Age the Heuneburg appears to have been largely unoccupied, possibly because of the dominance during this period of the hillfort on the summit of the Bussen, an impressive landscape feature due east across the Danube Plain that is the most prominent topographical reference point in the region.

Egon Gersbach has suggested that during the Iron Age the hillfort may have been the primary central place on the eastern axis of the north-south exchange system that traversed the Hegau and the central Swiss plateau as well as the valleys of the Wutach and the upper Rhine, passing through the Burgundian Gate to the Rhône. In addition, transalpine links through upper Swabia and the Bodensee across the Alps connected the region to upper Italy. The site is strategically located at a natural ford across the Danube, which is navigable at this point but not farther upstream (Gersbach 1982:14).

Significantly, the Iron Age occupation of the hillfort begins not with the mudbrick wall of Period IVb but with the Period IVc indigenous fortification system. Also, as a result of recent adjustments to Reinecke's traditional chronology for the beginning of Hallstatt D, which some would now date to 620 rather than 600 BC, the Iron Age Heuneburg Period IVc could have begun twenty years earlier than originally thought (van den Boom and Pape 2000:58–59). There is also some disagreement as to the precise beginning date of the mudbrick wall occupation, which could have been built at any time between 600 and 550 and may have ended between 540 and 520 BC. Not much has been made of the fact that the transition, whenever it occurred, appears to have been a peaceful one, unlike the end of the mudbrick wall occupation c. 540 BC. The destruction of the final Iron Age occupation of the site is also contested and is given as 480, 440, or even 400 BC (Kurz 2006:3; van den Boom 1989:81–83). The site's chronology is based mainly on time-sensitive material culture such as fibulae and imported ceramics, with some absolute dates derived from dendrochronological evidence, but as all of these have different but serious flaws as temporal markers, the inconsistent results are not surprising.

Imported pottery at the Heuneburg initially was attributed to the mudbrick wall phase, but extensive analyses of the Attic pottery and other Mediterranean imports from the site have shown that the bulk of the imported pottery actually postdates the mudbrick wall period. Fragments of only six classifiable vessels were found in Period IV (mudbrick wall) contexts, and only two of those did not refit with sherds from Period III to I vessels (post-mudbrick wall contexts). By contrast, fragments of 15 imported Mediterranean vessels were found in Period III to I contexts dated to Ha D2/3 (Pape 2000:143–144; Figure 32). The wine transport amphorae of southern Gallic type appear mainly in Periods II and I (van den Boom and Pape 2000:57), ending around the time that Attic pottery at Massalia begins to show signs of declining (Pape 2000:146). By the time imported pottery reached all-time highs at Massalia in the last third of the fifth century BC (Gantès 1992:175; Table 3), the Etruscans had recovered their monopoly on the northern import trade, and after 400 BC the port of Spina at the mouth of the Po River was the principal entry point for Mediterranean luxury goods into temperate Europe. At the Heuneburg this shift can be seen in the appearance of an Etruscan-style handle mold from a Schnabelkanne as well as fragments of ceramic imitations of this Etruscan style of wine pitcher in the latest levels of the site (Pape 2000:146). Clearly the geopolitical situation in the Mediterranean had an impact on developments at various hillforts in the West Hallstatt zone at the end of the late Hallstatt period, but the question of what the elites in this area knew, and when they knew it, is both important and remains obscure.

The Mudbrick Wall Occupation at the Heuneburg

What is clear is that the mudbrick wall was as much of an eventful rupture in contemporary European archaeology as in the temperate European Iron Age world, and the Heuneburg hillfort has dominated the literature for several decades as a result. Dehn, Gersbach, Kimmig, and others have argued that in spite of the relative paucity of mudbrick fortification systems known from excavated contexts in ancient Greece and the hinterland of Massalia before 600 BC, the Mediterranean region must have been the source of the inspiration that led to the construction of the Heuneburg mudbrick wall (Dehn 1958:93; Gersbach 1995:91). Although most ancient Greek public buildings, particularly in later periods, were constructed of stone (Tomlinson 1989:1), the earliest fortification systems of major sites in Greece and its colonies were constructed of mudbrick. Wood was scarce throughout the Mediterranean, and was used in architecture only where absolutely necessary (Tomlinson 1989:1). Stone was abundant in most, but not all areas. At Olynthos, for example, clay was abundant and stone scarce, while at Mantineia in Arcadia, located in an upland plain with an inexhaustible supply of clay, the stone quarries were some distance from the city (Fields 2006:11). Although all-stone fortification systems ultimately became more common than mudbrick walls in Greece, they never replaced mudbrick entirely (Fields 2006:10).

Evidence can be found in written sources as well as a limited number of archaeological examples, including the West Gate of Eretria and structures at sites such as Delphi, Argos, Corinth, Kerameikos, Eleusis, and Olynthos (Fields 2006). Air-dried mudbrick on a stone base had the advantage over stone of being quicker and cheaper as well as fireproof (Tomlinson 1989:1). Bricks could be made rapidly using unskilled labor and did not require complex equipment.

Unfortunately, the earliest levels of occupation at Massalia and other Greek sites in the vicinity of the original Phocaean colony are rarely preserved, and the sixth-century fortifications were in most cases destroyed or replaced by later stone constructions. Fortification systems with square towers and bastions like those from the Period IV Heuneburg also do not appear in the hinterland of the Golfs du Lion and the immediate vicinity of Massalia until after 600 BC, when they replace the indigenous construction techniques that had previously been in use there (Arcelin and Dedet 1985; Gersbach 1995:92). Mudbrick houses from the earliest occupation levels of several of these sites have been found, however, so this building material was clearly in use in southern France during the early Iron Age.

Kimmig has argued for a western Mediterranean source of influence for the Heuneburg mud-brick wall, citing the use of this construction technique at sites such as Gela in southern Sicily in the fourth century BC and the mud-brick wall on a limestone base documented at Saint-Pierre-les-Martigues on the Etang de Berre west of Massalia (1983:Figure 36). However, to date all examples of mud-brick fortifications on stone foundations with towers and bastions from the western Mediterranean postdate the Heuneburg mud-brick wall, so only additional excavation is likely to resolve this question (Kimmig 1983:132).

Who instigated the construction of the mudbrick wall at the Heuneburg and under what conditions could such a radical departure from the indigenous style of fortification have been conceived and successfully carried out? The theories suggested over the years have ranged from the importation by local leaders of Greek or Celtic architects and possibly some workmen with the requisite technical skills to local craftspeople who had acquired the necessary expertise through trade connections or travel (Dehn 1958:96; Fischer 1982:12; Gersbach 1995:92–93; Kimmig 1983). These are questions we are unlikely to be able to answer, even if the remaining two-thirds of the hillfort plateau and all of the preserved portions of the outer settlement are eventually excavated. Whoever the person in charge of initiating this project might have been, had they been alive today they would have had a wildly successful career in sales. Their job was to convince their supporters that it would be a terrific idea to build a fortification system of air-dried mudbricks in an area of Europe with an average annual rainfall of 1000 mm (40 inches). The fact that this apparently lunatic scheme was carried out suggests awareness of the advantages of this type of architecture on the part of more than one member of the decision-making group, however constituted.

The benefits of the new construction type were threefold: First, mudbrick, if properly protected from the elements, has a much longer use-life than the indigenous fortification system of wood and stamped earth, which at the Heuneburg needed to be replaced roughly once each generation (Gersbach 1982:16). Even in inclement conditions, unfired mudbrick is relatively impervious to the weather as long as the surface is properly treated, as the reconstructed wall segment on the Heuneburg hillfort demonstrated when it withstood the winter storm dubbed Lothar that tore through Swabia in December 1999, causing millions of Euros in damage. Second, the indigenous construction technique required a lot of wood, a commodity that pollen and dendrochronological evidence suggests was becoming scarce in the vicinity of the site at this time. Moreover, the indigenous fortification system was especially vulnerable to fire, both from hostile attacks and from industrial accidents such as those associated with the pyrotechnic industries documented on the plateau and outer settlement during the Iron Age occupation (Drescher 1995:255–364).

Finally, and perhaps most significantly, mudbrick, unlike the log-cabin-style wood and earth system, could be whitewashed once a weatherproof coating had been applied to the brick surface. The competitive display advantage of whitewashed mudbrick over local construction techniques of wood and earth is likely to have played a major role in the decision to build this alien form of wall course. The hillfort plateau is not especially imposing today and was barely noticeable when approached across the Danube Plain until a section of the mudbrick wall was reconstructed on top of the original stone foundations several years ago. Now the site advertises its presence in a way that is impossible to overlook, thereby fulfilling one of the requirements of a fortification system as described by Aristotle in his *Politics* (1331a11): the wall course surrounding a city should be both ornament and protection and ought to simultaneously impress visitors and depress enemies (Tomlinson 1989:93). The gleaming wall course with its bastions and towers would have conveyed a clear message of power and exclusivity, and presumably the intended audience included potential enemies as well as members of the local community whose support the elites required to further their interests (Gersbach 1982:17). Even conceiving of such a monument represented a radical departure by local elites on a symbolic and technical level as well as in the mobilization of the resources required to build it, an example of what Sewell calls an unexpected act that sets in motion a comparable logic of cultural transformation (2005:203).

The labor and skill sets needed to erect the mudbrick wall were as unprecedented as the concept itself. The Heuneburg mudbricks were made of at least three different types of clay, some of which were evidently transported from some distance away, presumably as finished bricks rather than as raw material (Gersbach 1995:35). The outer façade of the 756 meter-long wall surrounding the Heuneburg plateau, from the stone base with its mudbrick superstructure to the wooden wall walk, is estimated to have been at least five meters high (Gersbach 1995:90), requiring tens of thousands of mudbricks and a volume of roughly 1,366 square meters of stone to build. Despite the close proximity to the Heuneburg hillfort of sandstone sources, at least five different types of stone from up to 20 kilometers away were used to build the foundation (1995:10–14). The suggestion is that the wall was constructed using a form of corvée labor that symbolized the allegiance of the groups involved to its builder and that surrounding communities provided both strong backs and actual building material in a symbolic as well as functional act of relationship. Given the evidence of the destruction of the Period IV Heuneburg, which was accompanied by the collapse of burning sections of the mudbrick wall on top of the bodies of five children and at least one adult male defender (Gersbach 1995:91), the threat of internecine violence might have been a motivating factor in the organization of this communal labor project. Clearly, however, the stone foundation of the fortification system, with its block and plate facing and its rubble core, is as alien to this region as its mudbrick superstructure. The engineering solutions used to deal with the problem of building the stone foundation on top of an existing earthen bank of varying height and width that sloped steeply inward along the western side of the plateau were conceived and executed by someone with a great deal of expert knowledge (Gersbach 1995:20–21). The crenellated watchtowers along the north face of the site had more than one story and were linked by a covered wall walk made of wood, burned and collapsed portions of which were uncovered during the excavations.

From the eventful archaeology perspective, however, when and where and how the impulse and expertise to build this fortification system at the Heuneburg originated is less significant than the impact of the event on the built environment and, through the physical transformation of space, its effect on the social system. This approach may offer a way to engage with the archaeological evidence from recent excavations in and around the Heuneburg without the stultifying dependence on models drawn from medieval feudalism or studies of the evolution of the archaic state, both of which have dominated the interpretation of the Iron Age Heuneburg for decades (Kimmig 1983:159, 163, 174; Kurz 2007:180–181).

EVENTFUL ARCHAEOLOGY IN AN IRON AGE CONTEXT

The Period IV Heuneburg mudbrick wall clearly represents a break with the indigenous fortification tradition that preceded and succeeded it. It certainly qualifies as an example of what Sewell describes as a happening that significantly transforms, rather than reproducing, social and cultural structures (1996:262). It is also the only period of occupation at the site to have suffered two conflagrations before finally being razed and replaced by an early form of *murus Gallicus* around 540 BC (Table 1). Gersbach has argued that the break between Period IV and Period III, which is marked by a destruction horizon, represented a departure as radical as the one ushered in by the construction of the mudbrick wall (1995:176). Other changes in Period III include the construction of so-called *Herrenhäuser*, or chiefly houses, in the southeastern area of the site. In addition, while the Period IV buildings were typically made of oak beams, the Period III houses were built of white pine, a faster growing but less

TABLE 1
SIMPLIFIED HEUNEBURG HILLFORT CHRONOLOGY (AFTER KURZ 2006)

Period I	Final Iron Age occupation (one destruction horizon at end of period)	Ha D3/LTA	450/400 BC
Period II	Transitional occupation (one destruction horizon)	Ha D3	510–500 BC
Period III	Post-mudbrick wall occupation	Ha D2/D3	540–510 BC
Period Iva–Ivb	Mudbrick wall occupation (two destruction horizons)	Ha D1	600–540 BC
Period Ivc	Earliest Iron Age occupation	Ha C/Ha D1	640–600 BC

durable wood, implying that the hardwood stands in the vicinity had been depleted by this time (Gersbach 1995:176).

The eventual leveling of the mudbrick wall takes on added significance in view of the fact that by the time of this iconoclastic action, the social rupture and transformation it symbolized and initiated had become embedded in the cultural system. One aspect of this rearticulation can be seen in the construction of a massive wall and ditch system with a stone gate of Mediterranean style surrounding the hillfort and part of the outer settlement after 540 BC (Bofinger 2005, 2006). The increase in imports during Period III viewed through the eventful archaeology lens also suggests rearticulation. In effect, the later imports should perhaps be seen as a symptom, rather than the cause, of the social transformation that occurred in the preceding period. Brian Shefton refers to the Period III–I increase in the number of imported vessels as a "full-flow surge" (2000:36), which it certainly seems to have been compared to the earlier and later occupations at the site, and suggests that "powerful Mediterranean impulses had at the Heuneburg preceded the wine trade and the introduction of Attic pottery by a very considerable margin" and that these imports should be detached "from a broader consideration of southern influences" (2000:39). Van den Boom and Pape make very much the same point in coining the term *import horizon* for Periods III–I (2000:59). The import flow, however it was organized, ceased before the Iron Age Heuneburg succumbed to a final conflagration at the end of Period I. In these deposits have been found fragments of several local imitations of Attic kylikes and Etruscan Schnabelkannen, possible evidence of emulation in response to scarcity (Pape 2000:108).

Gersbach and others have postulated that the PIV/PIII rupture was the result of a dynastic takeover (1982:26), possibly motivated by internal social stresses related to the restricted circulation of limited quantities of imported luxury goods (Gersbach 1982:32). Given the small numbers of imports, the rupture and social transformation that are clearly evident should be reexamined from a perspective that does not view the disruption of the imported prestige goods flow as the primary catalyst. The explanation for the violent transition from Period IV to III could be the result of differential reproductive success within two competing lineages, for instance, or of territorial expansion on the part of neighboring groups centered around hillforts such as the Alteburg or the Große Heuneburg, neither of which has been adequately explored to date (Biel 2009:75).

The destruction of the Period IV Heuneburg is marked by the burning of the hillfort and extramural settlements, as well as numerous partial or complete bodies and 16 iron projectile points, all but three of which were found outside the walls in the burned debris of the wall walk (Gersbach 1983:126). The razing of the mudbrick fortification system suggests a desire to annihilate and erase the evidence of this alien technology. At the same time, there is considerable evidence for continuity in the material culture of the site complex, decreasing the likelihood that the Period III people were in fact incomers from another region. Moreover, the presence of Mediterranean imports implies continued connections with the world in which the mudbrick technology had originated.

Other differences between the mudbrick wall occupation and the succeeding periods are also notable. Joachim Wahl, who has examined the human remains from the site, notes that the quantity, type, and demographic profile of the osteological material vary by period.

The smallest number of remains dates to the period before the destruction of the mudbrick wall, with skeletal fragments from five adults and one neonate. The 540 BC destruction horizon included skeletal fragments from one adult, two infant/juveniles, and one neonate and complete skeletons of one adult and two infant/juvenile individuals. The postconflagration occupations of Periods III–I, by contrast, yielded 10 infant/juvenile cranial fragments, 25 infant/juvenile long bones, three adult long bones, and two complete infant/juvenile skeletons (1995:Table 3). The adult cranial fragments include two perforated left parietal bones that appear to have been modified while the bone was still "green" or fresh, one of which was found associated with the mudbrick wall destruction horizon, prompting Wahl to suggest that many of the Period III–I remains could probably be attributed to that event as well, and may have been disturbed by later construction of the new settlement (1995:382).

At the same time that the settlement evidence suggests a rearticulation of the social system in Period III, a rupture is represented by the erection of four monumental burial mounds on the remains of the Period IV outer settlement in the Giessübel-Talhau parcel, one of which contained four secondary burials with gold neckrings, ordinarily only found in paramount central chamber graves. Until recently, elite mortuary activity before 540 BC was thought to have centered on a mound group three kilometers west of the hillfort, with the Hohmichele, the second largest burial mound in Europe, at its heart. In erecting four new 50 meter diameter "megamounds" within a stone's throw of the hillfort, Period III elites were making a spatial as well as structural break with the previous tradition of elite burial in the Hohmichele mound group, in which some mounds appear to have continued to be used as burial places into Period I but which so far have not produced any evidence for new mounds postdating the mudbrick wall Heuneburg. The splendid isolation of the Giessübel-Talhau mounds, all of which are the same size, compared to the Hohmichele embedded in its community of medium-sized and smaller mounds, seems to reflect a changed attitude toward power and its expression in mortuary ritual in the post–mudbrick wall era. The distance of the Giessübel-Talhau mounds from other tumuli and their proximity to the hillfort apparently reflect exclusivity and disassociation from the remaining population, communicating a dynastic sensibility in material form (Kimmig 1983:48).

The resiting of the elite mound activity, as well as the shift in the prescribed symbolic association between gold neckrings and central burials represented by the secondary gold neck ring graves in Tumulus 1, appear to represent the kind of transformation of cultural categories that lies at the heart of Sewell's definition of eventful temporality (1996:263). In this case it is possible that we are also seeing in action what Sahlins refers to as qualitatively disparate collective histories in which the significance, of events and of the transformation of structures, is contingent upon variables such as social status, role, and the mode by which such histories are transmitted (1985:49). The mounds around the Hohmichele are clearly not in the top tier with respect to size or quality of grave goods—no gold neckrings are known from any of them—which may be why Tumulus 18 in this group bridges the ruptures in the settlement record between Periods IV and I (Arnold et al. 2003). Apparently, the individuals buried in the mounds in the Hohmichele group were either not impacted by the same forces as elites buried in the Giessübel-Talhau mounds or experienced those forces differently.

The tyranny of texts has contributed its own confounding influence to the interpretation of the Heuneburg mudbrick wall occupation. The written evidence for the founding of Massalia, and the assumption that it was this event that ushered in the first contact between the Greek world and temperate European peoples, has effectively created a temporal straitjacket that complicates evaluations of the Period IV mudbrick wall. The presumed link between the founding of Massalia and the erection of the mudbrick wall led excavators for decades to engage in special pleading to explain the paucity of imported ceramics in Period IV strata. It was simply inconceivable that imports would appear only *after* the destruction of the mudbrick wall; therefore, post-depositional disturbance must have resulted in the movement of at least some of the Period IV pottery upward. This theory has been rejected since, based on more detailed analysis of the stratigraphic contexts (Kurz 2006:9).

The interpretation of the mortuary landscape surrounding the hillfort has suffered from a similar interpretive hobbling. Sewell's approach to structural transformation suggests that the ruptures represented by the construction and destruction of the mudbrick wall and the rearticulation represented by the Period III–I occupations will be seen in the mortuary context as well but not necessarily in the same way, to the same extent, or at the same time. The Hohmichele mounds are a good illustration of the problem of noncontiguous courses of events that are the result of differential investment in different categories of social practice. The Hohmichele seems to parallel the Heuneburg mudbrick wall occupation in that all the burials in the portion of the mound excavated by Riek in the 1930s date exclusively to HaD1, that is, pre-540 BC. This was the reason scholars assumed for a long time that all the mounds in this mound group had been abandoned when the four Giessübel-Talhau tumuli were erected after 540 BC. While Tumulus 17 in the Hohmichele group also seems to reflect a rupture following the deposition of the HaD1 central cremation and accompanying female inhumation, unlike the Hohmichele it was eventually reused (Arnold et al. 2000, 2001). Graves 1 and 3 in this mound were deposited more than one meter above the central enclosure at least 100 years after the deposition of the central burial, and both of these contained weapon-bearing males with evidence of contact outside the region: possibly the Iberian peninsula in the case of Grave 1; northern Italy (in the form of a miniature *sanguisuga* fibula) in the case of Grave 3.

The possibility of links between the Heuneburg and Iberia is worth exploring further. There is evidence to suggest that contact between the West Hallstatt area and the Iberian Peninsula was limited but continuous. An iron helmet plume holder similar to the helmet crest clamp in the cauldron grave from Tumulus 17 Grave 1 was recently discovered on the Ebro River, where early Iron Age settlements have produced evidence for imported Greek pottery (Yanguas 2007: 295). The Hochdorf gold neckring is another example of contact with Iberia. It was decorated with repoussé horse images quite different from those found on the other gold objects in the grave and, when chemically analyzed, proved to have a signature consistent with Iberian gold sources. An Iberian bronze belt plate was found in one of the burials in the Magdalenenberg at the eastern edge of the Black Forest, whose female grave good assemblages are very similar to those in Tumulus 17, 18, and the intramural woman's grave from the Period IV destruction horizon. Susanne Riekhoff has suggested that the significance of contact between the Iberian Peninsula and the West Hallstatt area has been underestimated to date and would repay closer examination (2001:185–186). Based on our excavations in Tumulus 17 and Tumulus 18 of the Hohmichele mounds, I would agree. The previous focus on Massalia as the primary conduit for Mediterranean impulses at the Heuneburg will require revision as more mortuary data become available.

The case study presented here clearly indicates that even when an event can be identified archaeologically, as in the case of the mudbrick wall, its effects may not be experienced in the same way or be equally visible across the spectrum of social categories or archaeological contexts. Tumulus 18, for example, appears to have been established before the Hohmichele, with a central cremation ceramic assemblage that could date as early as 650 BC (before the Heuneburg mudbrick wall was built), and it remained in continuous use, based on the eleven types of fibulae found in its 18 burials, until the very end of HaD3 and possibly into LTA (Arnold et al. 2003). There is no evidence of rupture, or even discontinuity, in this mound; given its relatively small size, it is remarkable that there is only one incidence of a later grave disturbing an earlier one, suggesting that the same community buried their dead there during the 200 years of its uselife (Table 2). This is a demonstration of Sewell's point that structures must be conceived of as plural rather than singular (2005:206), and it underscores the importance of keeping Sahlins's theory of interest in mind when attempting to evaluate the impact of external contact based on archaeological evidence derived from different structural contexts.

The path dependent model of social process that Sewell proposes (1996:274) provides a more nuanced way to conceptualize the causal link between the mudbrick wall Heuneburg and subsequent occupations than previous models. The initial rupture may have taken the form of a structural change in the built environment, but it could not have occurred without substantive transformations in the social system, which were amplified in some modalities in subsequent periods and had relatively little impact in others. Also significant is the fact that without the evidence from the settlement excavations, there would be no indication that the elites of this region had any access to Attic pottery or other Greek

TABLE 2

TUMULI 17 AND 18 PROVISIONAL BURIAL SEQUENCE COMPARED
TO THE HILLFORT CHRONOLOGY

Hillfort Periods	Tumulus 17 Burials	Tumulus 18 Burials	Cultural Phase	Absolute Dates
Period I	Grs. 1,3	Gr. 3	Ha D3/LTA	450/400 BC
Period II		Gr. 12	Ha D3	510–500 BC
Period III		Grs. 9,13	Ha D2/D3	540–510 BC
Period Iva–Ivb	Central Chamber, Gr. 4	Grs. 4,5,6,9 Grs. 14,19 Grs. 15,16	Ha D1	600–540 BC
Period Ivc		Central Chamber	Ha C/Ha D1	640–600 BC

imports. No imported ceramics have yet been found in any of the burial mounds associated with the hillfort (van den Boom and Pape 2000:59).

This case study demonstrates that an effective eventful archaeology must involve as many categories and scales of evidence as possible, taking into consideration the fact that while spheres of action may have been imbricated in different social categories, focusing on just one of these will generate a distorted and misleading picture. The mudbrick wall may reflect an eventful rupture in this society, but it must be interpreted in the context of the continuity and variable rearticulation reflected in other contexts, such as the Hohmichele mound group, in order to be understood. By focusing on the mudbrick wall as the initial, but not final, defining event, new hypotheses can be generated that are less dependent on the chronocratic strictures of the founding date of Massalia or the seriation of Attic pottery. Indeed, links to Massalia itself appear to have been relatively unimportant in the initial phase of social transformation at the Heuneburg. This realization in turn allows an examination of the mortuary record from an entirely different perspective. Event and structure come together in this case study to produce a sociomental topography of the past (Zerubavel 2003:1) that operates on several temporal and social scales with variable effects. Some 2,600 years after the mudbrick wall builder had his brainwave, perhaps we are beginning to detect some method in his madness.

References Cited

Arcelin, P., and B. Dedet 1985 Les enceintes protohistoriques du Midi méditerranéen des origines à la fin du 2ème s.av.J.-C. In Bernard Dedet and M. Py (eds.) *Les enceintes protohistorique de Gaule Meridionale.* Association pour la Recherche Archéologique en Languedoc Orientale 14:11–37. Caveirac.

Arnold, B., M. L. Murray, and S. A. Schneider 2000 Untersuchungen in einem hallstattzeitlichen Grabhügel der Hohmichele-Gruppe im "Speckhau," Markung Heiligkreuztal, Gemeinde Altheim, Landkreis Biberach. *Archäologische Ausgrabungen in Baden-Württemberg* 1999:64–67.

Arnold, B., M. L. Murray, and S. A. Schneider 2001 Abschließende Untersuchungen in einem hallstattzeitlichen Grabhügel der Hohmichele-Gruppe im "Speckhau," Markung Heiligkreuztal, Gemeinde Altheim, Landkreis Biberach. *Archäologische Ausgrabungen in Baden-Württemberg* 2000:67–70.

Arnold, B., M. L. Murray, and S. A. Schneider 2003 Untersuchungen an einem zweiten hallstattzeitlichen Grabhügel der Hohmichele-Gruppe im "Speckhau," Markung Heiligkreuztal, Gemeinde Altheim, Landkreis Biberach. *Archäologische Ausgrabungen in Baden-Württemberg* 2002:78–81.

Biel, J. 2009 Die Vorburg der Heuneburg bei Herbertingen-Hundersingen, Kreis Sigmaringen: zum Abschluss der Geländearbeiten. *Archäologische Ausgrabungen in Baden-Württemberg* 2008:70–75.

Biel, J., and D. Krausse 2005 *Frühkeltische Fürstensitze: Älteste Städte und Herrschaftszentren nördlich der Alpen?* Keltenmuseum Hochdorf, Hochdorf.

Bofinger, J. 2005 Archäologische Untersuchungen in der Vorburg der Heuneburg: Siedlung und Befestigungssysteme am frühkeltischen Fürstensitz an der oberen Donau, Gde. Herbertingen-Hundersingen, Kreis Sigmaringen. *Archäologische Ausgrabungen in Baden-Württemberg* 2004:82–86.

Bofinger, J. 2006 Stein für Stein. Überraschende Befunde im Bereich der Befestigungssysteme der Heuneburgvorburg, Gde. Herbertingen-Hundersingen, Kreis Sigmaringen. *Archäologische Ausgrabungen in Baden-Württemberg* 2005:73–78.

Dehn, W. 1958 Die Heuneburg an der oberen Donau und ihre Wehranlagen. *Neue Ausgrabungen in Deutschland* 140:127–145.

Dietler, M. 1990 Driven by Drink: The Role of Drinking in the Political Economy and the Case of Early Iron Age France. *Journal of Anthropological Archaeology* 9:352–406.

Dietler, M. 1998 Consumption, Agency and Cultural Entanglement: Theoretical Implications of a Mediterranean Colonial Encounter. In *Studies in Culture Contact: Interaction, Culture Change, and Archaeology*, edited by J. Cusick, pp. 288–315. University of Southern Illinois Press, Carbondale.

Dietler, M. 1999 Rituals of Commensality and the Politics of State Formation in the "Princely" Societies of Early Iron Age Europe. In *Les Princes de la Protohistoire et l'Emergence de l'État*, edited by P. Ruby, pp. 135–152. Naples: Cahiers du Centre Jean Bérard, Institut Français de Naples 17—Collection de l'École Française de Rome 252.

Drescher, H. 1995 Die Verarbeitung von Buntmetall auf der Heuneburg. In *Baubefunde der Perioden Ivc-Iva der Heuneburg*. Heuneburgstudien IX, edited by Egon Gersbach, pp. 255–364. Philipp von Zabern Verlag, Mainz.

Fields, N. 2006 *Ancient Greek Fortifications 500–300 BC*. Osprey, Oxford.

Fischer, F. 1982 Frühkeltische Fürstengräber in Mitteleuropa. *Antike Welt* Special Issue 13 pp. 1–72. Raggi Verlag, Feldmeilen.

Gantès, L-F. 1992 L'apport des fouilles récentes à l'étude quantitative de l'économie massaliètes. In *Marseille grecques et la Gaule*. Actes du Colloque international d'histoire et d'archéologie et du Ve Congrès archéologique de Gaule méridionale (Marseille, 18–23 novembre 1990), edited by Michel Bats, Guy Bertucci, Gaétan Conges, and Henri Tréziny, pp. 171–178. *Etudes Massaliètes* 3.

Gersbach, E. 1982 *Die Heuneburg bei Hundersingen a.d. Donau (Gemeinde Herbertingen, Kreis Sigmaringen): Streiflichter auf die lange Geschichte einer bedeutenden Wehranlage*. Privatdruck Heuneburg-Museumsverein, Hundersingen.

Gersbach, E. 1989 *Ausgrabungsmethodik und Stratigraphie der Heuneburg. Heuneburgstudien VI*. Philipp von Zabern Verlag, Mainz.

Gersbach, E.1995 *Baubefunde der Perioden Ivc-Iva der Heuneburg. Heuneburgstudien IX*. Philipp von Zabern Verlag, Mainz.

Hodge, A. T. 1998 *Ancient Greek France*. University of Pennsylvania Press, Philadelphia.

Kimmig, W. 1983 *Die Heuneburg an der oberen Donau*. 2nd. ed. Führer zu archäologischen Denkmälern in Baden-Württemberg. Konrad Theiss Verlag, Stuttgart.

Kimmig, W. (editor) 2000 *Importe und Mediterrane Einflüsse auf der Heuneburg*. Heuneburgstudien XI. Philipp von Zabern Verlag, Mainz.

Kurz, S. 2006 Relative und absolute Chronologie der Heuneburg. *Frühe Zentralisierungs- und Urbanisierungsprozesse nördlich der Alpen*. Kolloquien und Arbeitsberichte des DFG SPP 1171: Kolloquium Bad Dürkheim April 2005: Chronologische Eckdaten zu den Zentralisierungs- und Urbanisierungsprozessen während der Späthallstatt- und Frühlatènezeit.

Kurz, S. 2007 *Untersuchungen zur Entstehung der Heuneburg in der späten Hallstattzeit.*Forschungen und Berichte zur Vor- und Frühgeschichte in Baden-Württemberg. Konrad Theiss Verlag, Stuttgart.

Narr, K. J. 1972 Das Individuum in der Urgeschichte. Möglichkeiten seiner Erfassung. *Saeculum* 23:252–65.

Pape, J. 2000 Die Attische Keramik der Heuneburg und der Keramische Südimport in der Zone nördlich der Alpen während der Hallstattzeit. In *Importe und Mediterrane Einflüsse auf der Heuneburg.* Heuneburgstudien XI, edited by Wolfgang Kimmig, pp. 71–176. Philipp von Zabern Verlag, Mainz.

Reim, H. 2003 Die Außenbefestigungen der Heuneburg bei Hundersingen, Gde. Herbertingen, Kreis Sigmaringen. *Archäologische Ausgrabungen in Baden-Württemberg* 2002:72–76.

Reim, H. 2004 Eine befestigte Siedlung der jüngeren Späthallstattzeit im Vorfeld der Heuneburg bei Hundersingen, Gde. Herbertingen, Kreis Sigmaringen. *Archäologische Ausgrabungen in Baden-Württemberg 2003*:56–61.

Riekhoff, S. 2001 Die Kelten in Deutschland: Kultur und Geschichte. In *Die Kelten in Deutschland*, edited by Sabine Riekhoff and Jörg Biel, pp. 12–277. Konrad Theiss Verlag, Stuttgart.

Sahlins, M. 1985 *Islands of History.* University of Chicago Press, Chicago.

Sewell, W. H. 1996 Historical Events as Structural Transformations: Inventing Revolution at the Bastille. *Theory and Society* 25:841–881.

Sewell, W. H. 2006 *Logics of History: Social Theory and Social Transformation.* University of Chicago Press, Chicago.

Shefton, B. B. 2000 On the Material in Its Northern Setting. In *Importe und Mediterrane Einflüsse auf der Heuneburg.* Heuneburgstudien XI, edited by Wolfgang Kimmig, pp. 27–41. Philipp von Zabern Verlag, Mainz.

Tomlinson, R. A. 1989 *Greek Architecture.* Duckworth, London.

Van den Boom, H. 1989 *Keramische Sondergruppen der Heuneburg.* Heuneburgstudien VII. Philipp von Zabern Verlag, Mainz.

Van den Boom, H., and J. Pape 2000 Die Massalistischen Amphoren. In *Importe und Mediterrane Einflüsse auf der Heuneburg.* Heuneburgstudien XI, edited by Wolfgang Kimmig, pp. 43–70. Philipp von Zabern Verlag, Mainz.

Wahl, J. 1995 Die Menschenknochen von der Heuneburg bei Hundersingen, Gde. Herbertingen, Kr. Sigmaringen. In *Baubefunde der Perioden Ivc-Iva der Heuneburg.* Heuneburgstudien IX, edited by Egon Gersbach, pp. 365–383. Philipp von Zabern Verlag, Mainz.

Wells, P. S. 1980 *Culture Contact and Culture Change: Early Iron Age Central Europe and the Mediterranean World.* Cambridge University Press, Cambridge.

Yanguas, S. O. 2007 Túmulo del Príncipe Celta de Pañetero. In *El Tesoro del Patrimonio Histórico de Fitero*, edited by Serafín Olcoz Yanguas, p. 295. Tudela: Comunidad Foral del Navarra.

Zerubavel, E. 2002 *Time Maps: Collective Memory and the Social Shape of the Past.* University of Chicago Press, Chicago.

PART II

Eventful Histories and Beyond

CHAPTER SEVEN

The Annales, Events, and the Fate of Cities

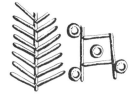

John Bintliff

Abstract *Sewell's emphasis on Events in the historical development of societies is a welcome contribution to the recent debate on Time and Archaeology, stimulating the important application in a cross-cultural perspective by Beck et al. 2007. In many respects, the Annales School of History in France gave us some decades of thoughtful discussion of Time and Process, which largely remain unknown to archaeologists, who tend to reduce the sophistication of its more recent exponents to the "long-term" determinism of Braudel. This paper will review the continued potential of the post-Braudelian synthesis of Annaliste approaches to past societies. I shall illustrate the argument with a consideration of how we might understand the short-, medium-, and long-term history of cities, using the case-study of the ancient and modern city of Argos in Greece.*

Conveying the concept of "eventful" history across disciplines, to create an "eventful" archaeology, enhances our interpretation of the Past by focusing attention on critical moments of change in the archaeological record. It resonates well with Stephen Jay Gould's theory of Punctuated Equilibrium in Evolutionary Biology (1989), which several scholars have argued to be applicable to Archaeology and Anthropology (Bintliff 1999). Here long periods of relative stability in a cultural system could be disrupted by short periods of abrupt and wholesale reorganization of a society. Gould's insistence that the motor for drastic change could be an unpredictable event or chance shift in a vital element in an ecological system led him to argue that "rerunning the tape of History" would quite plausibly lead to very different outcomes than those we now observe. "Prediction" is impossible; rather, the job of a researcher into the Past can only "Postdict" over what has occurred. Likewise, growing archaeological interest in Chaos and Complexity Theory (Bentley and Maschner 2003;

Bintliff 1997, 2004), builds on the repeated observation in the Natural and Physical World, that tiny fluctuations in the behavior of one component in a highly sensitive complex system can lead over time to wildly divergent pathways of development, the so-called Butterfly Effect (Lewin 1993).

However, Sewell's "eventful History" (2005) and its application to Archaeology by Beck et al. (2007), as well as Punctuated Equilibrium and Complexity theories, rightly balance "The Event" against "Structure." Challenging Gould's rejection of any determinism shaping the biological Past, Simon Conway Morris (2003) has argued that disrupted biological systems repeatedly rebuild similar adaptive radiations and ecosystems to those destroyed by contingency. The individual elements in the new ecosystems may be very different, but the structure of life recurs again and again around a limited number of formats. In the same way, Complexity theorists counterpoise unpredictable, chaotic change with the repetitive evidence that complex systems gravitate toward a limited repertoire of structures, or "Attractors."

Actually, the discipline of History has engaged throughout the twentieth century in its theoretical debates with this central issue of the Event and its relationship with persistent, longer-term Structures, whether in the sociopolitical, economic, or cultural sphere. The leading arena for this discussion has been in the books and articles associated with the French *Annales* School of historians (centering on its mouthpiece periodical *Annales, Economies, Sociétés, Civilisations*; cf. Bintliff 1991). Indeed, one of the key stimuli to their creation of a new, "total" History was their attack on the limitations of nineteenth-century history writing and its overemphasis on "Events," where the study of Great Men, Battles, Revolutions, memorable political decisions, and "dates" in general, had been the basis for comprehending historical processes. In a new framework for analyzing the Past (Figure 1), several generations of *Annales* historians, most famously Fernand Braudel, argued that History is always the outcome of multiple processes, but critically these operate in parallel but on different wavelengths of time. To comprehend any specific "event" one must situate it in a wider framework of processes, which might involve the preceding century or even millennium of time. Likewise, a persistent Structure, let us say a type of political system or land use, visible for hundreds of years or more, may have been brought into being, or disappear, as the result of a short-term event, personality, or novel idea.

Some misunderstanding has arisen in Archaeology over the application of the *Annales* model for history. John Barrett (1994) for example, found it wanting, as it did not specify the *precise* way in which the different levels of time process interact with each other. The same error occurs when the *Annales* is dismissed on the grounds that Braudel, in its most famous book, *The Mediterranean and the Mediterranean World in the Age of Philip II* (1949 [1972]), although filling in the various time scales and different subfields of the historical record, argued for the ultimate dominance of the long-term in the course of Mediterranean developments. The *Annales* approach improves over other historical models by exactly *not* specifying in advance how a particular period or event can be explained; it merely asks us to reconstruct the broadest framework for our analysis, so that the precise interplay of time and process can later be allowed to appear for any particular case study. The same method could equally well reach a conclusion that a single person or event or idea was absolutely critical for a radical transformation in the longer-term trajectory of a case-study society.

HISTORY   SHORT TERM—ÉVÉNEMENTS
OF   Narrative, Political History;
EVENTS   Events;
                                Individuals.

STRUCTURAL   MEDIUM TERM—CONJONCTURES
HISTORY   Social, Economic History;
                                Economic, Agrarian,
                                Demographic Cycles;
                                History of eras, regions,
                                societies;
                                Worldviews, ideologies,
                                (*Mentalités*).

                 LONG TERM—STRUCTURES OF THE 'LONGUE DURÉE'
                                Geohistory: 'enabling and
                                constraining';
                                History of civilizations,
                                peoples;
                                Stable technologies,
                                world views (*Mentalités*).

FIGURE 1 Braudel's model of historical time.

The sophistication of the *Annales* is an object lesson for us: in *Carnival at Romans* (1979), Ladurie aims to account for the lack of long-term impact from some striking revolutionary events, in comparison to similar events at a later point of history. In *Montaillou* (1978) he replays how the decisions and mindsets of individuals in a medieval village reacted with broader chronological trends as well as major short-term events operating at a far larger geographical scale. The *Annales* call such case-study investigations *Problème Histoire*, Problem History, reminding us that accounting for what did *not* happen is just as important as what *did*, in our explanations of the Past. Indeed, for me the concept of "eventful history" runs two perpetual risks. Firstly, it can underplay the enabling and constraining factors in the longer term, a useful concept we owe to the French historical geographer Vidal de la Blache (1926), which could make an event significant for the future. Secondly, we could easily ignore the reality, that events that cause dramatic changes on a wide scale are vastly outnumbered by those which merely ripple the surface of more powerful trends (to quote Braudel).

A CASE STUDY: THE FATE OF CITIES

I would like to offer some reflections on how we might begin to understand a major archaeological database—urban settlements with many millennia of occupation, during much of which we dispose of *historical information*, with the deliberate provocative aim of asking how relevant the Event might be in the long-term trajectory of cities.

La Grèce et le bassin égéen

FIGURE 2 The location of the city of Argos on the Greek Mainland.

For archaeologists working in the Mediterranean, there exist at least several thousand long-lived ancient urban sites, a considerable percentage abandoned and thus amenable to scientific analysis. In my study-region of Boeotia, Central Greece, for example, our project has carried out total surface survey of five of the 15 ancient towns, ranging in size from 11 to 100 hectares, and is currently working on a sixth at Koroneia (cf. Bintliff and Snodgrass 1988). The immense period of occupation for all these towns immediately challenges the investigator to manage the problem of time and processes in his explanation. The surface archaeology is the primary source for identifying trends at the *Annales* middle term, phases of several centuries, and the long term, some 500 to several thousands of years. But we also have textual information at much shorter time scale resolution than that typical for surface archaeology, namely that of the world of "events."

I would like to illustrate the potential of a multi-scalar analysis of time frames for such sites through the example of the city of Argos in the Peloponnese, (Figure 2) in Southern Mainland Greece, where we have the advantage of more than 100 years of large-scale excavation and innumerable small rescue projects, as well as much historical source evidence (Piérart and Touchais 1996; Pariente and Touchais 1998). The town arose as a village in Late Neolithic times, but appears to have been continuously occupied till today, mostly as an urban site, thus offers 7,000 years of a settled community.

THE LONG TERM

If we begin with the longest time scale, continuous settlement at this location since the Late Neolithic can be related to favorable ecology. The site sits at the edge of a vast fertile lowland, the Plain of Argos, and further toward the sea it always possessed extensive delta land suitable for grazing. Its mountain-edge position ensured a plentiful supply of springwater, and in cyclical times of militarism a smaller and a larger mountainous acropolis provided secure strongholds. All these lasting factors ensured at least a substantial village over the last 7,000 years, with a resource catchment to nourish a town, if political circumstances favored that. But Argos as an urban site would require more than a suitable subsistence catchment, since other early settlements in the Plain of Argos offered comparable locations for population nucleation.

In fact, Argos's centrality to its region (Figure 3) has always tended to favor it assuming a Central-Place role for surrounding communities, what Complexity Theory would term a strong attractor, while its fertile countryside could nourish exceptional nucleation. In times of cultural climax, dense regional population, and a highly developed settlement hierarchy, we might expect to find that the primate town of the region lay at Argos. Indeed, throughout Greek and Roman antiquity, under the Byzantine Empire, and in the Early Modern period, Argos has been the chief urban center of its region.

THE MEDIUM TERM

However, a strikingly different pattern emerges if we refocus our attention to our evidence for the medium-term processes, phases of several centuries. If we concentrate just on periods of regional complex society, we find that Argos appears (Figure 4) only as cyclically dominant and subordinate in a rotation of central-places around other major centers around the rim of the Plain of Argos. Here we discover that it is the Plain itself, and its coastal advantages, that form what Robert Adams (1981) terms a "Heartland of Cities."

UNDERSTANDING THE CYCLICAL CHANGES IN THE MEDIUM TERM, AND THE ROLE OF THE SHORT TERM OR EVENT

Let us turn firstly to how these major shifts in Argos' status occurred, and secondly ask whether this caused a radical reorganization of the city's communal life. Thirdly, what role did short-term events play in these larger-scale changes? Fourthly, are there important events that do not coincide with these medium-term cycles, and did they have any major significance to the citizens of Argos?

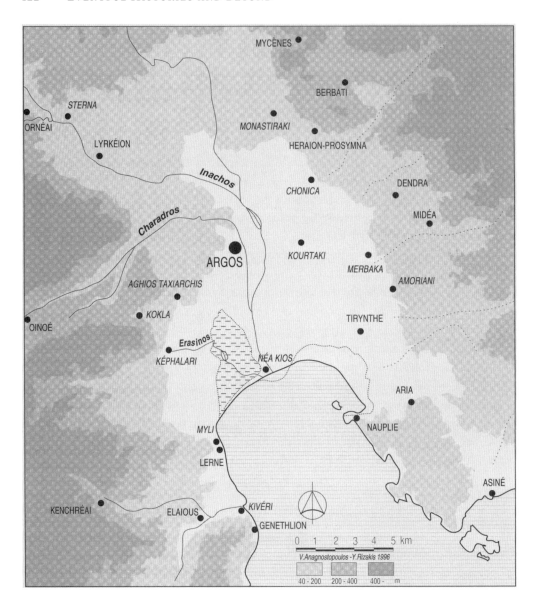

FIGURE 3 The Plain of Argos with major ancient and modern settlements.

The Early Bronze Age central-places at Lerna and Tiryns (Figure 5) appear to arise in response to a maritime network of social and economic interaction, in which these regional foci form the "gateway communities" for the Plain of Argos. As part of a system of contemporary early central-places throughout the Aegean Mainland and Islands, no specific local factors have been identified, nor the intervention of "events" of a short-term historic character. The marginal role of the Argos settlement underlines the centrality of the maritime face of the region. The transition to the Middle Bronze Age (Figure 6) is associated with massive destructions and abandonments, and although similar effects strike the entire

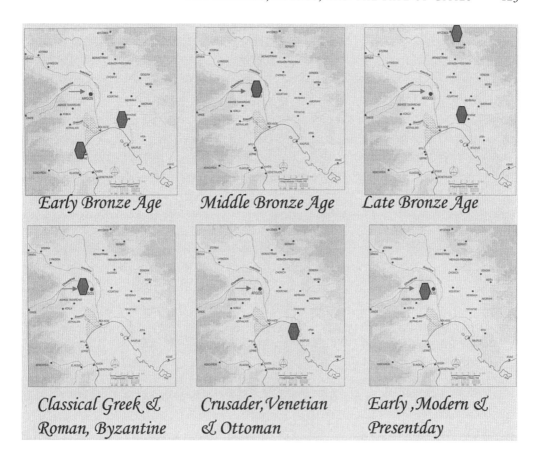

Early Bronze Age   Middle Bronze Age   Late Bronze Age

Classical Greek &   Crusader, Venetian   Early, Modern &
Roman, Byzantine   & Ottoman   Presentday

FIGURE 4 Rotating central-places in the long-term settlement history of the Argos Plain.

Aegean world, it is argued that short-term events probably were vital to the collapse of complex society at the end of the third millennium BC. The reemergence of a settlement system from apparent chaos takes a very different form in the Argos Plain and much of Mainland Greece as a whole, with small villages and occasional town-like clusters of villages lacking any architectural pretensions, while interregional exchanges shrink drastically. In this introverted world of villages, Argos assumes its natural role as a small-scale central-place, larger than other Plain settlements and with the only cluster of rich graves. Then abruptly, in a very short space of time, across the transition from Middle to Late Bronze Age (Figure 7), a very minor peripheral village in the northern Plain fringes, Mycenae, shoots into prominence with the fabulously rich and politically charged Shaft Grave burials. Although subsequently several other Plain settlements respond with elite tholos tombs, Argos is not one, and after several hundred years of apparent competition for power, the mature Mycenaean civilization seems to resolve control of the Argos region into the inland and coastal fortified palace towns of Mycenae and Tiryns. The rise of Mycenae is so abrupt and unpredictable, that one must at present assume that the dynasts buried in the Shaft Graves rose to

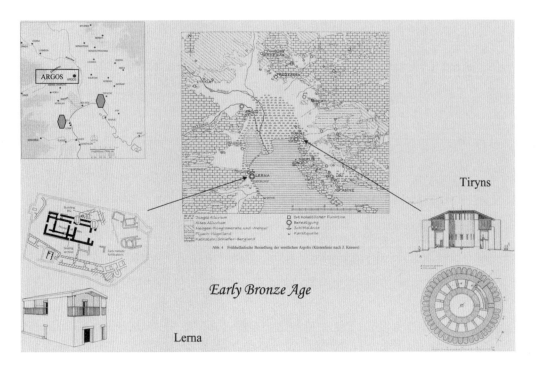

FIGURE 5 Central-places in the Early Bronze Age Argos Plain and the distribution of contemporary settlements.

wealth and power through short-term historical events that we cannot yet trace in the coarse archaeological record of the period. Judging by the prominence of militarism in the Shaft Graves and Mycenaean culture in general, it is likely that aggressive warfare is key, perhaps initially on an interregional level.

The end of the Bronze Age witnesses another short era of events, causing massive settlement destruction, abandonments and migrations. The reemergence (Figure 8) out of renewed chaos of a regional settlement pattern in the Iron Age shows a stripped-down to the bone form of Late Bronze Age society—competing warrior chiefs in each major settlement with their followers. A largely introverted Argos Plain region sees Argos itself once again expanding to become the largest settlement, although made up of a cluster of villages, and with most of the richer status burials. By the end of the first historic or Archaic Era, ca. 500 BC, Argos has expanded its power once again, to incorporate all the other regional settlements into its state (Figure 9). With the emphasis on regional population recovery after the collapse of Mycenaean palace civilization, and a largely internal economic boom, Argos's return to centrality appears to reactivate a long-term trend rather than reflecting contingent events, and the Plain as a whole follows a much wider pattern in South-East Mainland Greece of a gradual rise toward a new cultural florescence. Since this phase of primacy will last for the next 1000 years, we could seem to be entering a simple longue durée—but as I shall show, in reality there is an internal significant wavelength of medium-term cycles.

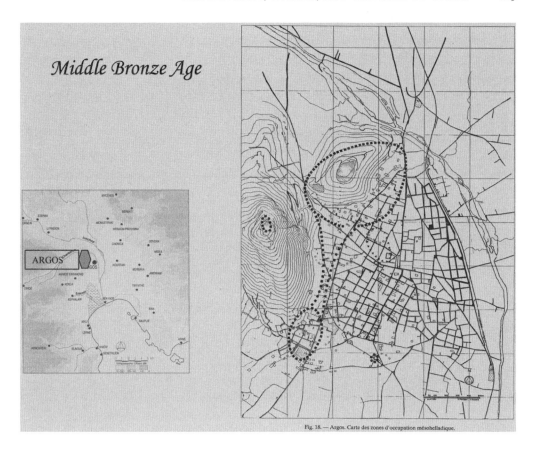

Fig. 18. — Argos. Carte des zones d'occupation mésohelladique.

FIGURE 6 Argos as the central-place in the Middle Bronze Age Argos Plain and the extent of its multifocal settlement.

The culmination of this flourishing in Classical Greek times, moreover, with the construction of a monumental civic center, shows a radical shift in the character of Argive urban life. Aristocracy has been replaced by a moderate democracy, and the city invests in its parliament, law courts, exercise grounds, and theatre. Although this is also part of a very general trend among Classical Greek cities, where some half shifted during this era to democracy, the rest remaining aristocratic or ruled by kings, the decision in each city was significantly affected by events and personalities, as well as the political constitution of allies and enemies in foreign relations.

Archaeologically, this steady medium-term ascendancy to a climax regional power with impressive public buildings shows no trace of at least three historic events, which certainly had a devastating impact on the lives of large numbers of Argive citizens. In 494 BC an unexpected invasion by old border enemies the Spartans, led to the almost complete annihilation of the male citizens in a military massacre (6,000 lost), after which sources claim the city was run for some time by its slaves. In 487 BC another 1,000 male citizens died fighting the Athenians. Yet, one generation later the losses had been made good. Furthermore, the adoption of democracy was clearly not unopposed, and seething beneath the surface was

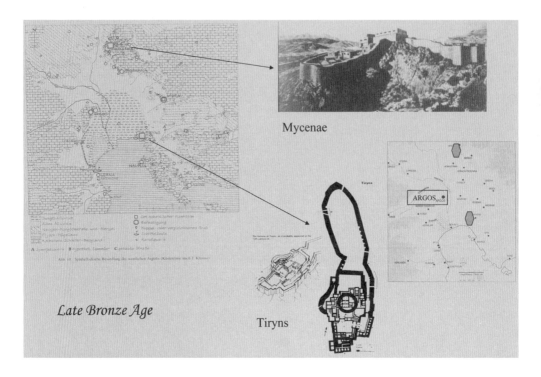

FIGURE 7 Central-places in the Late Bronze Age Argos Plain.

a class conflict, which broke into a reign of terror on two occasions: in 418 an attempted aristocratic coup was followed by 300 executions, and in 370 BC another coup attempt saw 1,200 major landowners publicly tortured to death. It is likely that the entire class was wiped out. But in the following centuries there reemerged a class of wealthy landowners, who dominated the city for the following 800 years till the end of Antiquity.

In Hellenistic and Roman Imperial times, apparent continuity in the flourishing of the city of Argos as the regional central-place is borne out archaeologically by new major investment in monumental civic works. A great aqueduct for the communal water supply and several large public bath complexes, have been uncovered. But inscriptions in stone make clear that all these facilities are paid for by a dominant class of wealthy landowners who now run the town, as well as by outside sponsors such as the Roman Emperor Hadrian, who endows famous Greek cities as an act of heritage management. One especially powerful local benefactor even managed to have his mausoleum erected, contrary to Greco-Roman laws, in the city center, full of expensive gold finery. The trend throughout the Hellenistic and Roman world for rule by rich elites is a general one, thus Argos merely reflects a far wider process on the medium- to long-term timescale. The regional economy is still largely introverted, ensuring Argos's natural centrality.

In Late Antiquity, the city remains the prosperous center of its region. The ruling landowners erect prestigious mansions with rich mosaics in the town and on their rural estates. Once more, though, monumental constructions reflect a changed urban mentality

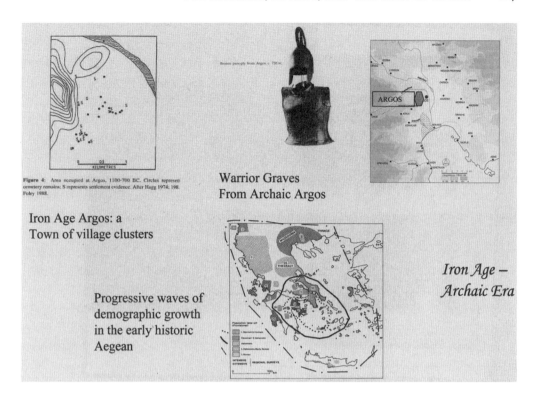

Figure 4: Area occupied at Argos, 1100-700 BC. Circles represent cemetery remains; S represents settlement evidence. After Hagg 1974: 198. Foley 1988.

Warrior Graves
From Archaic Argos

Iron Age Argos: a
Town of village clusters

ARGOS

Iron Age –
Archaic Era

Progressive waves of
demographic growth
in the early historic
Aegean

FIGURE 8 Argos as the central-place in the Iron Age to Archaic eras, its dispersed Iron Age settlement form, a cuirass from an Argive Archaic Warrior Grave, and the expanding waves of population growth in the early historic Aegean.

and focus for public life: the pagan temples are demolished and robbed for private purposes, but especially for the main new public architecture—the Christian churches, which spring up all over the urban fabric. Indeed, historical sources inform us that increasingly the management of this and other cities is shifting toward the Church and the regional army, reflecting both the rise of the new Christian Establishment and the prevalent insecurity in the Roman Empire under Barbarian attack. Over this era the archaeology shows that the traditional public buildings decay and are built over, marking a gradual transformation of the Classical form of town to that typical of the Middle Ages, dominated by castles and churches. In all these respects, Argos merely follows the course of most other towns in the Roman world, pushed by the same large-scale forces of change.

The succeeding Byzantine Empire retains Argos as the regional urban center, dominated by its castle and new forms of church in the city and its region. We might see this as continuity with the transitional form of town we observed in Late Antiquity, but historic sources tell a different story: perhaps the structure of the town is still the same, but the people are probably quite different. Around 585 AD tribes of invading Slavs conquer the whole region, taking it out of the Byzantine Empire for 200 years. Local Slav place names confirm a large-scale repopulation of a devastated countryside. Scanty and localized finds of

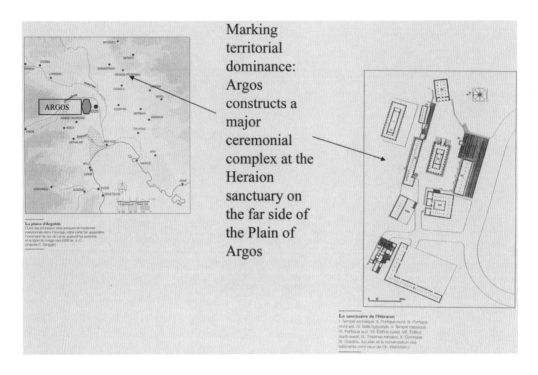

Marking territorial dominance: Argos constructs a major ceremonial complex at the Heraion sanctuary on the far side of the Plain of Argos

FIGURE 9 Argos as the central-place in the Archaic and Classical periods and its associated regional ceremonial centre at the Argive Heraion.

Slav-type ceramics from Argos offer only slight material traces of these revolutionary events in the fate of the town and its region. Here, certainly historic events are crucial at the level of the community and its identity, although the urban structure when it recovers under renewed Byzantine control recapitulates the Late Antique form where the church and army dominate. Imperial ideology enforces the submergence of Slav identity, ultimately making everyone culturally Greek and Orthodox in religion. The broken system of the medium term appears to heal up as if nothing had happened.

With the invasion of Greece by the Western Crusaders (Figure 10) in the thirteenth century AD, however, a lasting disruption occurs. The Plain of Argos passes into the hands of the Republic of Venice. The Venetian colonial empire is based on its powerful fleet and flourishing international trade, and it thus prefers to establish fortified coastal urban strongpoints to rule from. Argos is left to decline in favor of the massively fortified port town of Navplion. This maritime orientation forms the second natural central-place attractor for the region, and the lack of a role for events is shown by the fact that the peripheralization of Argos lasts from the Crusader through the Venetian and into the Ottoman period, a period of some 600 years, dominated by the externally orientated politics of foreign empires on Greek soil. Argos is nonetheless a flourishing village, benefiting from its fertile district and ideal role as rural market.

But within this archaeologically undifferentiated picture, our historic sources tell us that once again, the time scale of events has erupted, leaving no archaeological traces in

FIGURE 10 Navplion as the central-place for the Argos Plain in the Medieval and early Postmedieval eras.

the city, and just strong hints in the countryside. Only archival sources reveal the immense change to the region. In 1397 Argos was captured by Turkish raiders, and its population carried off to slavery. The Venetians repopulated the town and region with Albanian colonists. In the countryside of Southern Greece these immigrants were still using their own language well into the last few decades.

In 1786 the Ottoman rulers, for military reasons, relocate their administration for the Peloponnese and the Argos Plain from Navplion to the distant inland city of Tripolitza. Almost immediately Argos regains its role as the Early Modern regional focus, with now the chief central-place functions reverting to regional economics and provincial administration. Once more local elites erect mansions in Argos, first copying rich house forms from the declining Ottoman Imperial cities, then adopting Westernizing European urban fashions. A renewed spate of public monumental buildings is observed. This revisiting of ancient forms of urban life is certainly the dramatic effect of the "eventful" pulling out of imperial power from the region, reconfiguring the landscape into what we have argued to be its natural central-place attractor at Argos. The next 150 years appears to recapitulate the ancient landowner-centered, regional market town. Then in the Postwar era, wealth from the globalization of Greece transforms the townscape to a form never seen before in its 7000 year development, a high-rise of commercial and apartment blocks. The regional economy is now increasingly embedded in commercial exports and European Community finances, although the dominance of regional agriculture remains, thus ensuring that Argos's supremacy as the leading city of the plain will persist for the foreseeable future.

CONCLUSION

I have tried in this presentation to take apart the 7,000 years of continuous nucleated settlement at the city of Argos, teasing out the interactions of the long, medium, and short term. We have seen that "eventful" archaeology and history is always in dialectic with longer-term trends and processes; that some events are critical to understanding major transformation; other events—however enormous for the lives of contemporaries—seem in a longer perspective to be like Braudel's temporary ripples on the ocean. Some events leave clear archaeological traces, others are invisible but for our historic records. The medium-term cycles of urban rise and decline are in deeper harmony with longer-term structural oscillations between a limited number of shapes or attractors. But independent of these longer trends, we also observed at least two almost complete repopulations by alien incomers. Yet today most Argos citizens will assure you they are the proud descendants of the ancient Argives, identifying with those 7,000 years of genuinely continuous human occupation at this favored location. An appropriate quotation occurs in a modern novel by Italo Calvino:

> Sometimes different cities follow one another on the same site and under the same name, born and dying without knowing one another, without communication among themselves. At times even the names of the inhabitants remain the same, and their voices' accent, and also the features of the faces; but the gods who live beneath names and above places have gone off without a word and outsiders have settled in their place. (Italo Calvino, *Invisible Cities*)

ACKNOWLEDGMENTS

The author wishes to thank Professor G. Touchais, Professor A. Snodgrass and Professor P. Marzolff for permission to use selected images in this paper.

References Cited

Adams, R. M. C. 1981 *Heartland of Cities*. University of Chicago Press, Chicago.

Barrett, J. C. 1994 *Fragments from Antiquity*. Blackwell, Oxford.

Beck Jr., R. A., D. J. Bolender, J. A. Brown, and T. K. Earle 2007 Eventful Archaeology: the Place of Space in Structural Transformation. *Current Anthropology* 48:833–860.

Bentley, R. A., and H. D. G. Maschner (editors) 2003 *Complex Systems and Archaeology*. The University of Utah Press, Salt Lake City.

Bintliff, J. L. 1997 Catastrophe, Chaos and Complexity: the Death, Decay and Rebirth of Towns from Antiquity to Today. *The Journal of European Archaeology* 5:67–90.

Bintliff, J. L. 2004 Time, Structure and Agency: The Annales, Emergent Complexity, and Archaeology. In *A Companion to Archaeology*, edited by. J. Bintliff, pp. 174–194. Blackwell, London.

Bintliff, J. L. (editor) 1991 *The Annales School and Archaeology*. Leicester University Press, Leicester.

Bintliff, J. L. (editor) 1999 Structure and Contingency. Evolutionary Processes in Life and Human Society. Cassell, London.

Bintliff, J. L., and A. M. Snodgrass 1988 Mediterranean Survey and the City. *Antiquity* 62:57–71.

Braudel, F. 1972 The Mediterranean and the Mediterranean World in the Age of Philip II. Fontana/Collins, London.

Calvino, I. 1997 *Invisible Cities*. Random House, London.

Conway Morris, S. 2003 *Life's Solution*. Cambridge University Press, Cambridge.

Gould, S. J. 1989 *Wonderful Life*. Hutchinson, London.

Ladurie, L. R. 1978 *Montaillou. Cathars and Catholics in a French village 1294–1324*. London, Scolar Press, London.

Ladurie, L. R. 1979 *Carnival, a People's Uprising at Romans, 1579–1580*. Braziller, New York,

Lewin, R. 1993 *Complexity. Life at the Edge of Chaos*. J. M.Dent, London.

Pariente, A., and G. Touchais (editors) 1998 *Argos et L'Argolide. Topographie et Urbanisme*. De Boccard, Paris.

Piérart, M., and G. Touchais 1996 *Argos. Une ville grecque de 6000 ans,* Centre National de la Recherche Scientifique Editions.

Sewell, W. H., Jr. 2006 *The Logics of History*. University of Chicago Press, Chicago.

Vidal de la Blache, P. (1923 (1926)) *Principles of Human Geography*. H. Holt, London.

CHAPTER EIGHT

Modeling the "Amazon" Phenomenon

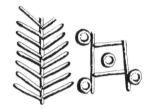

Colonization Events and
Gender Performances

Timothy Taylor

[P]eople don't like change. But make the change happen fast enough and you go from
one type of normal to another.

—Terry Pratchett, *Making Money*

Abstract *Using the so-called Amazons as an example, I will argue that culture contact and rapid economic change may be acutely reflected in the gender subsystems of archaeological cultures. Arising quickly in the fifth century BC on the Russian and Ukrainian steppes, and traceable both historically/mythically and archaeologically through putative gynoid skeletons with "male" weaponry (aka "Amazon burials"), the Amazon phenomenon (or phenomena) is undertheorized. I will try to show that it may best be modeled in terms of inferred changes to elite-level status dynamics that warped gender relations; it therefore may have parallels with ethnographically documented cases of gender- and status shifts in the early period of the North American fur trade. In order to understand how this can be, the widespread underestimation of the scale and reach of the Mediterranean/Aegean classical economy has to be overcome. By referring to recent fieldwork at sites such as Belsk in eastern Ukraine (plausibly Herodotus's "Gelonus"), coupled with quantitative work on the slave trade, I present a picture of females from the higher social strata being progressively cut out of new slavery-generated wealth in the Black Sea region. They may have chosen to gender cross in order more effectively to compete with predominantly male martial nomadic elites among whom wealth differences were becoming increasingly marked through Greek colonial contact. Issues of bias in the historical accounts and in the archaeological funerary record will also be examined.*

INTRODUCTION

This chapter examines ancient, ethnographic, and modern contexts where changes in the expression of gender may be understood to have coincided with changes in the socioeconomic circumstances of, and thus opportunities presented to, the biological sexes in societies undergoing externally driven change. It is argued that the balance of pathways to power that gender typically mediates is easily upset in contact situations, or during periods of otherwise rapid economic change, and that this may be visible in the archaeological record. Rather than interpret evidence for "gender diversity" in past societies as some essentially timeless "way of the Other," the moment at which outside observers record such phenomena is often in the moment at which players within the observed society are moving fastest to realign themselves with an altered balance of opportunities for success.

In particular, this chapter examines the "Amazon" or warrior woman phenomenon, recorded for the fifth century BC in the south Russian steppes by ancient authors associated with the Greek Black Sea colonization, and correlated by several scholars with the identification of biological females given warrior-style burial at around the same time, especially in the Don River basin. Although there is a series of problems with both the textual and archaeological data, it nevertheless seems worthwhile to attempt to model the potential congruence of alterations in gender performance with historical events.

The conventions that govern the performance of gender, which in public spaces typically focus on what is considered sex-appropriate dress, are both fixed and volatile, having at once to follow the dictates of fashion, which by its nature shifts, and to maintain coherence in terms of a cultural grammar generating a consistent meaning through the differentiation of signifiers. For a variety of reasons, including the way in which the socioeconomic roles of women have developed in the past century or so, it seems that the gendered grammar of clothing allows a subversion more in one direction that another. On November 27, 2009, the news site *Japan Today* reported under the headline "Nagoya policemen dress in drag to nab purse snatchers":

> An all-male police squad dressed as women has been deployed in Nagoya with the goal of catching attempted purse snatchers. The policemen, dressed in short skirts, stockings, high heels, wigs and carrying designer bags, have been walking the streets of Nagoya since last month in a bid to lure bag snatchers.
>
> One 26-year-old officer said: "It's cowardly to target women who are weak." Another 25-year-old policeman admitted that he "panicked" when a male driver propositioned him from his car.
>
> The unit consists of four male officers who are at least 160 cm tall. They all have a black belt in judo, karate or some other martial art. The squad works out of Naka police station which is in the center of Nagoya's entertainment district.
>
> A spokesman for the police said that the squad has so far failed to nab any would-be thieves.

The policy described here (whether or not it is judged effective in either arraigning or deterring criminality) is predicated on a series of shared cultural assumptions operative at a time of increased display of gender-coded wealth and power through, essentially, the conspicuous consumption of internationally branded fashion accessories (luxury handbags). The police response might have been to train more policewomen in martial arts and send them undercover but, due to the immediately preexisting perception of gender roles in modern Nagoya society, such women appear unavailable for deployment, while the alternative strategy of altering the outward gender coding of biologically male police officers is almost immediately operationalizable.

Fifth-century BC Athens operated one of the first known police forces, comprising readily identifiable, fox fur-wearing Scythian bowmen—essentially an ethnically distinct mercenary guard force who were deemed to have the freedom to operate outside the complex social interface of the citizen demes, and thus hopefully bring a level of impartiality to the deployment of potentially lethal sanction/summary justice on the city's streets after dark. This was possible because of the developing relations between the Greek state and the Scythian world of the southern Black Sea steppe (Taylor 1994, 2005, 2006). Both Herodotus (the father of ethnography, if not of history) and Hippocrates (his near contemporary and the originator of a scientific, evidence-based approach to disease) described aspects of the Scythian tribes, notably the horse-riding elite groups, in some detail. Both of them record instances that struck them of gendered performance that appeared "unusual," essentially two instances of what might be termed gender-crossing in which behaviors, vocalizations, and dress of the opposite sex had been adopted and were connected with a recognized social status or ethnic identity: the *Amazons* are described as a race of warrior women whom some young Scythians met in battle on equal terms as men, believing them men, only to be shocked by the revelation of their true biological identity when they stripped armour from the dead; the *Enarees* were males, in some way biologically compromised, cross-dressers, with a specialist role as clairvoyant shamans or soothsayers (although not the sole class of religious specialist among the Scythians). The two named identities have something in common and may demand a degree of symmetrical or reciprocal analysis, but there is space in this chapter only for focus on one of these, the former, whose differences both authors present at the level of ethnic difference, and whose descriptions carry such clear mythic overtones that later authors used them as the basis for the creation of an archetype so powerful that it is still with us. Ironically, that very potency has tended to overshadow the fact that there may have been a happening- and event-based historical reality underlying the primary descriptions of these authors.

SAHLINS, SEWELL, AND COLLINGWOOD

Before turning to the issue in detail, we must examine how it is that happenings become events. As in the case of the Japanese policemen in drag we have reports of happenings that may, or may not, have become (or be about to become) part of events. As Marshall Sahlins indicated, *happenings* may, or may not, be *events* (independent of whether any attempt to cause social change occurred): "The event is the happening interpreted—and interpretations vary" (Sahlins 1984:153). When happenings do attain to event status then they do so, according to William Sewell (whose concept of "eventual sociology" was inspired by Sahlins's ethnographic analyses), insofar as they are seen to create meaningful social change. But such classification leaves many questions unanswered: the estimation of meaningful social change being highly context sensitive (Sewell 1992, 2005; Nathanson 2009).

If we begin by asking the question where an event theory of Amazons is to be found, at a disciplinary level, then a series of answers are possible: history, classics, ancient history, prehistory, archaeology, economics, sociocultural anthropology, sociology, gender studies, bioanthropology, medical anthropology, Indo-European studies and comparative mythography, and so on. Beginning with the event-relevant sociology, we may note that Sewell has little to say on gender beyond (1) citing Joan Scott on "gender and the politics of history," in which he accepts her diagnosis of problems concerning "face value" assumptions in positivist agendas—specifically the lack of questions concerning "categories and interpretations"; and (2) using (in some detail) Sahlins's account of changing gender structures on Hawaii in response to Cook's voyage, especially the abolition of the tabu system (which had largely been applied to restrict women's action) following widespread fraternization by Hawaiian women with English sailors (who fed them on interdicted pork and plantain). There is an idea here of one event disrupting an otherwise timeless stable structure, something that Sahlins himself has been criticized for. As Nicholas Thomas wrote, contrasting sociology and anthropology on the one hand with history on the other (1989:118f):

> Codes of meaning or arrays of behavioural rules are not immediately "caused". They are expressive in a circular way, or functional and mutually determining. If events are discussed at all, they lack the singular character of the historical deed or accident. In the notion of a speech act or in some other cultural enactment we find the event much reduced in relation to the generative scheme. What takes place has no life as an intrusion with a loose and partly unfixed causality, but is rather the expression of a structure, the manifestation of a cultural order or a set of notions about behaviour.

Thomas outlines Sahlins's rough contrast between "prescriptive" and "performative" cultural structures. The prescriptive are orientated toward conformity with type, or with established traditions, with circumstances and events assimilated to a prevailing order and their perhaps divergent nature suppressed. Sahlins, by contrast, in *Islands of History* (1985:xii), writes, "Performative orders assimilate themselves to contingent circumstances," extending themselves, renegotiating forms, and inventing political forms. As Thomas puts it, "They accommodate the disjunction between structure and event which prescriptive forms resist"; however, he goes on to complain that Sahlins's theory involves prescriptive categories "endlessly resisting revaluation and events continuing to be received into a prior scheme, even the same prior scheme" (Thomas 1989:105).

Thus, a discrepancy is set up between a very rigorous scheme of cultural reproduction on the one hand and the archaeological record, pocked with major transformations of subsistence and settlement pattern (if not political organization) in Australasian societies. In short, Thomas in 1989 saw precisely archaeology as providing the kind of knowledge of events that could subvert Sahlins's schema (which, judging from Hiscock's major 2008 synthesis, it has impressively achieved). This is rather ironic given that Giddens's structuration was, at that very time that Sahlins was writing, inspiring archaeologists to eschew the importance of such knowledge (e.g., Giddens 1979). It is perhaps useful at this point to examine a historical perspective in rather greater detail, and I want particularly to turn to Robin Collingwood, who (as often) is worth quoting here *in extenso*, from his lectures delivered in the late 1920s and made recently available (1993:213):

> The historian, investigating any event in the past, makes a distinction between what may be called the outside and the inside of the event. By the outside of the event I mean everything belonging to it which can be described in terms of bodies and their movements: the passage of Caesar, accompanied

by certain men, across a river called the Rubicon at one date, or the spilling of his blood on the floor of the senate-house at another. By the inside of the event I mean that in it which can only be described in terms of thought: Caesar's defiance of Republican law, or the clash of constitutional policy between himself and the assassins. The historian is never concerned with either of these to the exclusion of the other. He is investigating not mere events (where by a mere event I mean one which has only an outside and no inside) but actions, and an action is the unity of the outside and inside of the event. He is interested in the crossing of the Rubicon only in its relation to Republican law, and in the spilling of Caesar's blood only in its relation to a constitutional conflict. His work may begin by discovering the outside of an event, but it can never end there; he must always remember that the event was an action, and that his main task is to think himself into this action, to discern the thought of its agent.

We should note in passing that—incidentally anticipating a point that would be made by Alison Wylie in her analysis of the "interpretive dilemma" (Wylie 1989)—Collingwood expanded on this as follows (1999:140f):

Crusoe did not *first* ascertain that this was a human footprint and *then* infer that it had been made by a human visitor. Neither do I *first* discover certain stratified remains (La Graufesenque Samian, Flavian coarse pottery, mint coins of Vespasian) and *then* infer a Flavian occupation. To discover *what* the evidence is, is already to interpret it....One must be careful then not to assert an *inferential relation* between the "evidence" and the "conclusion to which it leads". The relation between the two things is more like the relation between seeing a surface and seeing a body. To see the surface intelligently *is* to see the body: and if *not* seen intelligently the surface doesn't provide data from which a body can be inferred.

HERODOTUS, HIPPOCRATES, AND ARCHAEOLOGY

Conditioned by these considerations, we now turn to the data bearing on the phenomenon/ phenomena labelled "Amazon," and firstly to the account given by Herodotus (Book 4 of *The History*) who tells a sort of "Just So" story about why it is that the Sauromatian tribes, located to the east (mainly) of the Don River in the mid-fifth century BC, speak a dialect that is clearly connected to Scythian (an Indo-Iranian language) but with significant differences. Herodotus uses the Greek "Amazon," with its disputed etymology (an Indo-Iranian root word meaning "war makers" is probable, though the classical tradition related its meaning to lacking a breast or breasts: see below), but he gives it along with the apparently indigenous word *Oior-pata*—a denotation he tells us means "man-slayers" in Scythian. In this tale, a Greek raiding party who are attempting to take three boatloads of Amazons back home as captives (their inferred destination the slave markets) underestimate the women and are wholly massacred on board. The Amazons, lacking seamanship, are brought ashore in the marshlands where the Don River empties into the Sea of Azov, travel inland, appropriate horses, and start an aggressive campaign against the local free Scythian tribes (that is, those not paying allegiance to the Royal Scythian polity centered on the Dnieper bend to the west). As Herodotus puts it:

The Scyths could not tell what to make of the attack upon them—the dress, the language, the nation itself, were alike unknown—whence the enemy had come even, was a marvel. Imagining, however, that they were all men of about the same age, they went out against them, and fought a battle. Some of the bodies of the slain fell into their hands, whereby they discovered the truth.

This truth—the evidence of female warriordom—caused the Scythians to pause, and to attempt to maintain conditions of accommodation and nonconfrontation, "on account of their strong desire to obtain children from so notable a race." In a touching passage, Herodotus describes the toilet routines of the women, and how the young Scythian men, by shadowing them, were eventually successful in gaining a more intimate acquaintance with the Amazons in living form, and this culminates in an offer of communal marriage, then accepted:

> The two camps were then joined in one, the Scythians living with the Amazons as their wives; and the men were unable to learn the tongue of the women, but the women soon caught up the tongue of the men. When they could thus understand one another, the Scyths addressed the Amazons in these words—"We have parents, and properties, let us therefore give up this mode of life, and return to our nation, and live with them. You shall be our wives there no less than here, and we promise you to have no others." But the Amazons said—"We could not live with your women—our customs are quite different from theirs. To draw the bow, to hurl the javelin, to bestride the horse, these are our arts—of womanly employments we know nothing. Your women, on the contrary, do none of these things; but stay at home in their wagons, engaged in womanish tasks, and never go out to hunt, or to do anything. We should never agree together. But if you truly wish to keep us as your wives, and would conduct yourselves with strict justice towards us, go you home to your parents, bid them give you your inheritance, and then come back to us, and let us and you live together by ourselves."

This agreement being made, the interethnic group moved three days ride to the east of the Don River, where they became the nation of the Sauromatae. Thus it is, Herodotus tells us, that

> the women of the Sauromatae have continued from that day to the present to observe their ancient customs, frequently hunting on horseback with their husbands, sometimes even unaccompanied; in war taking the field; and wearing the very same dress as the men. The Sauromatae speak the language of Scythia, but have never talked it correctly, because the Amazons learnt it imperfectly at the first. Their marriage-law lays it down that no girl shall wed till she has killed a man in battle. Sometimes it happens that a woman dies unmarried at an advanced age, having never been able in her whole lifetime to fulfil the condition.

Hippocrates also describes Amazons, in *Airs, Waters, Places*, in similar though not identical terms:

> In Europe there is a Scythian race, called Sauromatae, which inhabits the confines of the Palus Maeotis [Sea of Azov region], and is different from all other races. Their women mount on horseback, use the bow, and throw the javelin from their horses, and fight with their enemies as long as they are virgins; and they do not lay aside their virginity until they kill three of their enemies, nor have any connection with men until they perform the sacrifices according to law. Whoever takes to herself a husband, gives up riding on horseback unless the necessity of a general expedition obliges her. They have no right breast; for while still of a tender age their mothers heat strongly a copper instrument constructed for this very purpose, and apply it to the right breast which is burnt up, and its development being arrested, all the strength and fullness are determined to the right shoulder and arm.

It has been a frequent response to doubt Herodotus almost in his entirety (seeing him as, for example, a mythologist of "The Other": Hartog 1988), and to view the various recipes and descriptions that are collated in the corpus of the Hippocratic writings as of varying provenance and reliability (as indeed they are). However, in the case of the two accounts above, we have to pause and ask ourselves what I call the Mark Twain question.

In the beginning of Huck Finn, the author distances himself from his previous, and less deadly serious book, deploying an engaging device: "You don't know about me without you have read a book by the name of The Adventures of Tom Sawyer; but that ain't no matter. That book was made by Mr. Mark Twain, and he told the truth, mainly. There was things which he stretched, but mainly he told the truth." Thus a truth claim is made in an overtly fictional context: Huck did not exist as a particular person in reality. But as a type, he is real. The real historical context is of happenings like the one in the book (the escape from an unemployed, alcoholic, brutally abusive father; temporary adoption by a family caught up in a violent neighborhood feud), connected more broadly to actual social events unfolding (connected especially to the dynamic of the changing economics and morality of the labor market and issue of black slavery).

Herodotus and the Hippocratic corpus have also to be read in such a spirit; contrary to Hartog's (1988) analysis, if Herodotus were trading in constructed myth only, his audience would have evaporated, because Herodotus's audience must have included many knowledgeable players in the game he describes. The travel that facilitated the writing of the history took him to wealthy commercial family homes around the Black Sea, where his lectures on travel were put to the ferocious redaction that only those with critically engaged interest could have provided. If the Amazons were one big lie—a presentation, alongside the Enarees, of some sexual/genderal alienness, more or less arbitrarily expressed—then his listeners would have found him out. The origin myth for the female warriors may have been wholly confected (albeit in terms of being a folk foundation myth of a sort that Herodotus found fit to record, as he did in many places in *The History*), but the presence of contingents of women warriors among the tribal groups of the steppe, especially among the Sauromatae, seems to have been accepted as fact with little demur. It is also logically inferable that his listeners would have had some corroborative knowledge of their own. Not only had a police force of Scythian archers been installed in Athens, but Scythian slaves (or, at least, slaves out of Scythia, which is not exactly the same thing) were both household goods and exportable commodities (Taylor 2001).

In Sahlins/Sewell terms, Herodotus describes individual, almost random, happenings becoming events, and events then creating meaningful social change: a captives' shipboard massacre leads to geographical displacement, consequent skirmishes, and the attendant revelation of female identity in enemy combatants to a male group who then pursue a conscious strategy of political, social, and reproductive alliance. The social fact that is explained is the predilection of Sauromatian women to go out hunting and also on campaign with their menfolk, and the existence of structured traditions about the age and statuses involved, and the plausibility of the account is strengthened by the reference to these known circumstances having come into existence at a particular point in the past, which serves as a pivot for conceptualizing linguistic differentiation between what to the Greeks appeared almost identical types of martial nomadic groups—Scythians and Sauromatae—out on the grassland steppe. What is not explained is the original emergence of the concept of the female warrior group known as "the Amazons" originally taken captive by the Greek slave raiders. Along with other foundational myths that Herodotus gives, it is perhaps unfair to understand these early phases of his social histories as to be taken entirely literally.

The origin of the change in gender roles is implied to lie back in time, before the century in which Herodotus himself is writing (and as we shall see, this is congruent with archaeological evidence). It would without doubt have occurred to his audience that an exclusively female race could not have existed for long without means to reproduce. That is: although "warrior women" could be a mythically timeless trope, the structure of the story, in which husbands are provided for these women, or, more precisely, for their maternal ancestresses, far away in space and time, may well have implied a backstory behind the backstory to Herodotus's audience, alongside a tacit agreement not to unpick a satisfying tale by unsuccessfully going after it. The essential point stands that the story is about social change, and even if it presents what would later become a fixed archetype—the Amazon—it at the same time educates us about the possibilities of societies, and especially their men and women, constituted as distinct interest groups, negotiating gender roles between themselves and consciously directing social change as active agents.

As for Hippocrates, in a descriptive account plausibly attributed to Hippocrates of Cos himself and thus written independent of Herodotus but also in the fifth century BC, we have a description of a traditional status and attendant practices. Although the cauterization of the right breast as described, seems, medically speaking, unsuited to the purpose given (of channeling strength to the right arm and shoulder), there are nevertheless congruencies with archaeological data of a surprising kind that should cause us to pause before rejecting the account out of hand. True, Hippocrates's other accounts of sexual anatomy, such as sperm being produced in the head and thereby heating it, causing baldness in reproductively functional males but not in eunuchs, or the womb wandering around the female body in search of moisture, appear equally bizarre. Nevertheless, modern explanations can be seen to fit the observed phenomena, though conceptualized in a way that was axiomatically beyond medical knowledge at its point of systematic origin: thus, male (and female) cranial baldness is brought about through action of the androgen, testosterone, while an estimated 70 million women worldwide suffer from endometriosis, where uterine tissue painfully migrates to other parts of the body, such as the neck (though named, the explanation of this disease has not significantly advanced since Hippocrates first described it).

There is a long history of scholarly approach to the issue of the Amazon phenomenon/ phenomena. Rostovtzeff (1918) connected it to a mother goddess cult and an essentially matriarchal society, and a similar but not identical approach has been taken recently by Jeannine Davis-Kimball (Davis-Kimball et al. 1995, Davis-Kimball 2002) who, in the light of her excavations at the fifth-century BC cemetery of Pokrovka, reconstructs central roles for women as priestesses, "hearth women," and warriors in steppe Iron Age societies in general. Along with Rolle (1989) and Guliaev (2003), Davis-Kimball has attempted a fairly straight rationalization of text and archaeology: both have used the term *Amazon burials* as a factual descriptor; neither really theorizes biological sex as a historically particularized crystallization from a gender system rooted in mental categories (a point to return to in relation to some comments made by John Bintliff and, earlier, by R. G. Collingwood). Both ignore the diachronic aspect. Despite pointing out differences with the textual accounts, especially that of Herodotus, which appears to localize the Amazons east of the Don when the archaeological evidence, even for the fifth century BC, extends into the western steppe toward the

Danube (i.e., into Scythia proper: but see below on dating), these authors essentially project Amazons as an archetype—a sort of timeless category—with real existence. This approach is one that Hartog, with his skeptical, hermeneutic approach to Herodotus rejects firmly as merely a construction of non-Greek "Otherness" masquerading as an account of reality to pander to the normative gender presuppositions of the target audience. In this, Amazons are again projected as a timeless category, albeit imagined.

My own past approach (see especially Taylor 1994) was consilient, noting the potential area of intersect of textual and archaeological inferences, but undertheorized and lacking test data; coupled with an enthusiasm for Herodotus as a descriptive commentator, this view of Amazons as several changing yet potentially congruent phenomena perhaps lacked critical plausibility. Better theorized, but facing the same underlying data problems, has been Bryan Hanks (2008), whose critical analytical approach, skeptical of Davis-Kimball's proposed social structure of "hearth women," "warrior women," "priestesses," and "warrior-priestesses," also bemoans inadequacies in data and theory that get in the way. Here we see Amazons as a question (or series of questions) far from resolution: a pending theoretical and methodological problem.

From a literary point of view, the timing of the Amazon phenomenon/phenomena in question are interesting. Despite Greek textual reference to the Dnieper River (the Borysthenes) and the "mare-milking Scythians" from the second half of the eighth century BC (Homer; Hesiod), only individual Amazon warrior women are mentioned in the *Iliad*, most notably Penthesilea, whose home country may have been given by Homer's pupil, Arctinus of Miletus, as Thrace (in the *Aethiopus*, which is not known directly). That is, Homer, with an opportunity to connect Scythia with Amazons, does not, even though his poem is set down at the very time that Greek Black Sea contacts are being rekindled (Taylor 1994). It is only in the mid-fifth century BC, with the accounts of Herodotus and Hippocrates (discussed above) that we have anything like an ethnographic description of Amazon origins, or any locational information that is not personalized. These are also the only accounts that can boast any originality in respect of broad custom and practice. Later writers become ever more trope-bound, dependent on the emergent canonical tradition, right through to Ammianus Marcellinus.

The record of funerary archaeology begins either in the late sixth or the fifth century BC (Guliaev 2003:120), and consists of skeletally female weapons graves of various kinds. The majority tend to be of females in the age range 16–30, buried mainly but not exclusively alone, typically with a combination of "female" and "male" gravegoods. In practice, this means that inhumed skeletons are the primary, or highest status, within their particular burial kurgan (barrow, mound), and are accompanied by personal jewelry, mirrors, and, less often, spindle whorls, alongside the remains of bows and quivers of bronze- and iron-tipped arrows and spears/javelins, but only very rarely swords, and never battleaxes (Fialko 1991:8–11).

Fialko was able to document more than a hundred female warrior graves in the south Russian steppe of Scythia proper (i.e., east of the Danube but west of the Don: Fialko 1991; Guliaev 2003). This contrasts with but does not necessarily completely contradict the locational information of Herodotus, as the majority of these graves are datable to the fourth century, and those attributed to the fifth are often quite generally dated. That is to say, at the time *The History* was formalized (by, perhaps, 450 BC) it is still possible that the phenomenon was more restricted in extent. But this is a more or less tenuous argument. Of greater moment is the archaeological fact that there is no mass phenomenon of female warrior burial recognizable in the preceding Thraco-Cimmerian archaeological horizon (see Sulimirski and Taylor 1990). Indeed, it is unclear if there are, as yet, clearly sixth-century BC examples. Yet the Greek colonization of the rural hinterland (*chora*) of such key strategic sites as Berezan-Olbia, on the Dnieper estuary (and Dnieper-Bug confluence) of the northern Black Sea coast, clearly occurs in the first half of the sixth century BC (Kryzickij 2006); more seasonal or periodic trading contacts may go back well into the seventh century and earlier (Taylor 1994; see Bintliff 2007 for a broader discussion of outstanding issues in characterizing the timing of interrelations and the nature of colonization phases).

Thus, systematic Greek colonization must have occurred at least a full generation in advance of the first emergence of the archaeological Amazon phenomenon, and probably a good century earlier. That Homer knows of Amazons as a phenomenon, but cannot locate them, may, given the potential generic "war maker" etymology, simply indicate a periodic, individual level elite choice—a woman in a particular social milieu picking up arms as a happening. What we see archaeologically, subsequent to the event of colonization, is meaningful social change, and it is this that is reported on, albeit semi-mythically, by later writers.

Furthermore, the surveys provided by Rolle, Guliaev, Davis-Kimball, and Hanks all demonstrate or explicitly note general increases from the fifth to fourth centuries BC (e.g., at Elizavetovskoe in the lower Don region where seven female weapon burials are dated to the fifth and 24 to the fourth century BC respectively: Guliaev 2003:116). Numbers of these burials demonstrate wounds consonant with battle injury, including cranial injuries and lodged arrowheads. Some few, such as that from Ordzhonikidze (kurgan 13) in the Ukraine, seem to have been buried with what appear symbolically to be their own children. Whether the warrior status thus continued past a point of motherhood for some of these individuals, or whether status persisted in death after it had lapsed in life, are questions that require further investigation.

The Amazons are shown from time to time in Greek iconography, too, most of it dating to the fourth century BC, and including images on pottery and images on goldwork that may have been produced for elite indigenous Scythian (or Greco-Scythian) consumption. They often have conical hats of a sort also known from the warrior women burials; swords are used, but not axes; and they may be associated with funerary horse sacrifice. So, in terms of weaponry, it seems that, both pictorially and archaeologically, Hippocrates' description of the mode of warfare (mounted use of bows and spears) more or less fits. The images do not have any explicitly depicted cauterized breast, but the right breast is nevertheless symbolically draped. One explanation may be that there was indeed a procedure, if not on the soft tissue then at least in terms of the battle dress, that brought the right breast closer to the body to better facilitate the safe operation of the classic Scythian composite reflex bow from the saddle; this would be a binding on the opposite side to the breast protectors worn by right-handed female longbow archers today, consequent on the shorter draw length and the different release position (cf. Taylor 1996:200, where I confused sides, to unintentionally give a left-hander explanation).

The way is perhaps open for Hippocrates' account of breast cauterization to be considered seriously (as has already been done for the related issue of Herodotus's claim of mass blinding of Scythian slaves: Taylor 2001). Cauterization may not have increased the muscular strength of the right arm as claimed, but it might to some degree have arrested development of the right breast, which could have had a beneficial outcome in the martial context depicted. Why indeed should we not free ourselves from the imposition of structuralist and postmodern semioticism and ask, simply, why would Hippocrates have made it up? After all, stranger, more brutal, and biologically even more compromising forms of mutilation, practised by women on their daughters, have been recorded anthropologically, and persist in the modern world.

MATERIAL RESOURCES, SLAVES, AND THE SCALE OF THE ANCIENT ECONOMY

It is possible to move on at this stage from the cultural schema part of Sewell's reformulation of structure to consider the *material resources* element he is so keen to stress, in this case looking at the way in which trade operated from the Greek colonies into the steppe. Products that show up archaeologically en masse from the sixth century BC onward include: finished luxury durables, especially figural toreutic art; luxury consumables such as wine; ceramic containers, such as amphorae in which the wine was transported, and painted fictile vessels, seen as symbolic exotica in a way they would not have been back in Greece (*pace* Vickers and Gill 1996). The trade from the steppe to Greek colonies probably included agricultural primary products including grain and, probably, hemp-cloth (undercutting Egyptian linen); pastoral secondary products, especially horses; silvicultural secondary products/mineral primary products, especially iron; finally, and, I would argue, most critically, slaves.

There is no space here to mount a fully detailed argument on the scale of the ancient economy in Eurasia in the first millennium BC. Quantitative aspects of that have been covered in some detail elsewhere (Taylor 2001), and a brief focus on a single site, the fortification of Belsk, on the Vorskla tributary of the Dnieper, on the boundary of steppe and forest steppe, can serve to give a brief impression of scale. As noted elsewhere, this site, which may be termed a "super-oppidum," measures 12 km from north to south; it has 33 km of c.10 m high earth rampart enclosing 40 square km of territory. Although there are other sites of similar type along the steppe–forest-steppe boundary, this is perhaps the largest, and may plausibly be identified with the wood-palisaded "Gelonus."

Gelonus—the interethnic citadel inhabited by Geloni in the land of the Budini, as described by Herodotus, is said by him to have been 30 stades on a side. As one stade equals c.180 m, we have 5.4 km on a side, giving an area just under 30 km², so that Herodotus slightly underestimates its size by around 25 percent. We cannot blame him, for this archaeological site, massive enough to silence any critics tempted to accuse the ancient author of exaggeration in this connection, is truly awesome (Figures 1–3). The timing of the construction for the ramparts and period of occupation of the site are complex questions, which an ongoing international excavation program will, hopefully, be able to resolve (Murzin, Rolle,

FIGURE 1 Ramparts at Belsk (1).

FIGURE 2 Ramparts at Belsk (2).

FIGURE 3 Ramparts at Belsk (3).

and Skory 2000; Taylor 2003; Murzin and Rolle 2007; Zöllner et al. 2008; interim reports such as Murzin and Rolle 2000 and years following). The associated barrow cemetery begins in the late seventh-century BC, with the high point of activity in the fifth century BC, to which period the majority of the extensive Greek imports date (although they range from the sixth to the fourth centuries BC). Indeed, it seems possible that the northernmost of the three subforts set into the enclosing perimeter rampart (each the size of a western European oppidum in itself), was an ethnic Greek trade entrepôt mediating trade up from the coastal Black Sea colonies (Herodotus notes that the Geloni were, anciently, Greek traders who had strategically settled far up the Dnieper River system, and it may be significant that, with a classic vowel shift from g to h, Geloni may have signalled Hellenes).

Questions about the function of Belsk are legion. Clearly the 40 square km area is too large to be a unitary defensive complex, and the three subforts are as heavily defended on their inner as well as outer sides. Thus, a serious possibility is that the complex represents some kind of secure area, which, at various times, combined functions such as specialized production, warehousing, slaveholding compound, and interethnic market/free trade zone.

Physical anthropological work on material from the Belsk kurgan fields has been hampered by poor preservation, partly as a result of soil thinning and a lack of consistent past analysis (although significant work is more recently underway); at the same time, extensive robbing in antiquity (much of it in the successive Sarmatian period of the third century BC) has removed many diagnostic grave goods. Thus, although no warrior women burials have been identified there, it is also true to say that many, if not the majority of graves cannot be adequately sex or gender "typed," either by grave goods, or biometric indicators, or any combination of the two, whether conventional or "discordant" (and Bryan Hanks rightly bemoans a situation that affects many steppe sites: 2008:19).

However, from the adequate skeletal sexing that has been conducted elsewhere, we do have a significant corpus of warrior women burials and, of those published and listed by Fialko, Guliaev (Guliaev 2002:116f), and others, many have the usual high-status inclusion of an imported Greek wine amphora. Of course, these objects must be placed in the grave by mourners or those conducting the ceremony and do not necessarily represent the property of the deceased at the time of death. Nevertheless, here is prima facie evidence to connect the Amazon phenomena, *sensu lato,* with intensified trade relations with the Greek world during the fifth century BC. But, so far, what we describe here, in Collingwood's terminology, is the "outside" of an event. To understand the inside, the event as action, we have to become aware of its content. Symbolically, it seems clear that these amphorae must indicate that these women needed wine for their feasting in any afterlife, and that they were within the social circle that could command this expensive import. Further, perhaps, social status was constituted *through the ability to have* such an item placed in the grave.

It is by now well documented that contact situations produced events in which new items of trade appear, and new production, transportation and military technologies are deployed, and these, in turn, cause significant, meaningful social change. The introduction of the horse to North America was particularly potent: as Pekka Hämäläinen remarks, "Horses helped Indians do virtually everything—move, hunt, trade, and wage war—more effectively, but they also disrupted subsistence economies, wrecked grassland and bison ecologies, created new social inequalities, unhinged gender relations, undermined traditional political hierarchies, and intensified resource competition and warfare" (Hämäläinen 2008:53).

The issue of gender relations among native American Indian tribal groups has produced an extensive and controversial literature, with disagreement about whether "third" and "fourth" genders of so-called man-woman and woman-man *berdaches* were constructed (Williams 1986; Lang 1998; Roscoe 1998) or whether a more conventional understanding of swapped sex roles between biological men and women suffices to capture an apparent complexity generated by problems in the translation of indigenous category terms, and a highly directed academic agenda (e.g., Murray 1984; cf. also Klein 1983). The former position (currently in the ascendant) typically projects native gender diversity as a form of timeless difference (or, at least, as having had very long-term traditional stability), until contact, when a prudish suppression of diversity was pursued. Nevertheless, archaeological evidence to support such a conjecture is inadequate, and careful readings of early contact narratives might lead one to assume that the frequency in which, especially, biological women took over previously near-exclusively male gender roles increased sharply in the early phase of contact, that is, prior to the unquestionable imposition of European genderal norms. Indigenous women, whose pre-contact paths to power and status typically focused more on basketry and other domestic production, in contrast to the classic male hunting role (e.g., Kehoe 1995:114ff discussing the Blackfoot), finding themselves systematically excluded from beneficial post-contact trade relations that focused on exchange of hides and furs, and trade in horses and guns, became more likely to position themselves as "men," with female wives and families. This is not to say that such gender crossing had not previously occurred: in Alaska especially, where big game hunting was essential to survival long before the fur trade, Kaska and Ingalik families without sons would select a daughter to "be like a man," learn to hunt and participate in otherwise male sweat lodge ceremonies (Taylor 1996:204, with further references). The advent of European trade relations (as well, perhaps, as differential loss of warrior males in warfare) would simply have promoted something that ordinarily was a happening to the level of an event horizon, where significant numbers of women took over male roles and therefore began to have a form of specific corporate identity.

Arguing along similar lines, Bettina Arnold (1995) has discussed the effect that the outmigration of booty-hungry all-male war groups might have had on women's roles in Iron Age societies in central and western Europe, and Hanks has indicated that such possibilities require investigation farther east (Hanks 2008:31). It is indeed possible to model the Amazon phenomenon/phenomena as an event with economic underpinnings, in which, in particular, the ability to raid and thus benefit from the supply of slaves to the Greek colonies, stimulated processes by which biological women, at least for a time, took on "male" roles. The ability to switch roles, traditionally perhaps available at an individual level, may have become an increasingly strategic choice at family, clan, or tribal level, and have thus led to the sort of female-only training camps that could so easily have given birth to the myth of a female nation. We should keep faith with our ancient authors (we are obliged to, as they lived close to the times and places under discussion while we, heavily theoretically armed as we are, do not). Perhaps then we can discern that Herodotus's description of a multiship raid capturing a group of exclusively female warriors could plausibly be unalloyed fact. If there was such a happening, or one like it, then it could have catalyzed events farther west on the steppe, as this "Amazon" group, having escaped their captors, integrated with a martial nomadic Scythian group where women warriors had not previously existed in corporate form. Whether Amazons should be seen as constituting a third (or a fourth) gender is questionable. The time-factored aspect of the phenomenon at the level of individual lives is clearly revealed in the ancient texts: for Herodotus and Hippocrates, Amazon "gender" is starkly performative, as Amazon women pass through status rites (killing enemy combatants) to access motherhood (in like fashion, the effeminate Enarees may, in early life, have played out "male" roles: Taylor 2006).

Returning to Sahlins, and his account of the catalytic effect of Captain Cook's arrival in the South Seas, we may note that Jonathan Friedman suggests that Cook's arrival and doings are the only events that structure fails to encompass, as they are externally produced. They therefore do not in themselves amount to any kind of structured history (Friedman 1985). Sewell sees the same weakness(es) in Sahlins, but tends to revise him, allowing that structures should be "plural rather than singular and as being composed not just of cultural schemes but mutually reinforcing sets of cultural schemes *and material resources*" (my emphasis). A real economy (even, in Marxist terms, perhaps "concrete history") is thus allowed in under a variety of possible conceptions.

If we followed Sahlins/Giddens in respect of the complex issues raised by "Amazons" and Scythia, we could say that Greek colonization and the slave trade is the critical event-sparking change. But this would downplay the importance of preexisting hierarchiza-tion and the widespread "relations of dependence" in Scythia *pace* Herodotus. Herodotus, significantly, says that Scythian nobility operated without "bought slaves," with the implica-tion that slavery was a common, preexistent institution that objectified and utilized human bodies/subjects without there being a disembedded, that is deritualized, commodity trade in such (one might think of the later contrast between serfdom and chattel slavery—although serfs were indeed sometimes sold: Taylor 2005). The appearance of Amazon women—dressed "as men"—thus manifests itself against a prior background of heavy outward cod-ing, extending far beyond straightforward gender, and critical to creating and maintaining distinction in a slave-owning, slave-trading, significantly hierarchized social formation.

Following Sewell's urge to respect the materiality of resources, not just their cognitive-symbolic value (*sensu* Giddens), allows us to approach the nexus of resources and conceptions about resources in ancient Scythia differently. Not only is "the subject" available through multiple lenses: archaeology, textual exegesis, comparative anthropology, direct historical approaches, Indo-European studies of language and mythography, and so on, but it also bears on a remarkably wide range of putative subjects above the individual level: hierarchies among Greeks and Scythians of different social and ethnic identity and status, gender differ-ences, gross economic differences between *oikonomia* and *krematistike* and, underlying and cross-cutting all, the mobilization of people as material things or items—the primary labor resource in the slave trade (and thus pointing the way toward a more *symmetric* analysis, *pace* Gell and materiality theory: Taylor 2008, 2010).

CONCLUSION

John Bintliff rightly pointed out a key irony in gender archaeology: "I want to know why men have continually assumed physical, social, economic and intellectual dominance in human societies," he wrote, not unreasonably, going on to say that if gender is viewed, as it is in much postprocessual archaeology and gender theory, as a *purely* cultural phenomenon then "the entire point of privileging the topic at the present time is…removed" (Bintliff 1995:30). Bintliff concludes that we need a plural approach, and Collingwood makes this same point (albeit unfortunately deploying the standard latent linguistic androcentrism of his day): "Man as body is *whatever the sciences of body say that he is*….Man as mind is *whatever he is conscious of being*" (Collingwood 1992:7). Collingwood's distinction between the inside and outside of events has already been noted: "[H]istory consists of actions, and actions have an inside and an outside; on the outside they are mere events, related in space and time but not otherwise; on the inside they are thoughts, bound to each other by logical connexions" (Collingwood 1993:118).

Amazons were not just surface (i.e., really "women underneath") but can be inferred as a series of events (*sensu* Collingwood) emerging (1) at a societal level, seen in "their" archae-ological emergence and coterminous description by Greek others (I suspect this represents a quite rapid and destabilizing change) and (2) at an individual, recurring level, as one sex in a particular stratum of society, over a period spanning a couple of centuries, considered gen-dered choices, options, and constraints in order to become something different. In Sahlins's terms we have a preexistent prescriptive cultural structure, (2), and performative orders, (1), which renegotiate and invent new political forms, accommodating the disjunction between prescriptive structure and event. Combining (1) and (2) above in a manner Sewell suggests, we might be able eventually, and with the correct agendas for field research and postexcavation analysis, to trace spatial and diachronic change in such a way as to test the material economic drivers proposed in the model outlined here.

Acknowledgments

For support in relation to the fieldwork aspect of this paper I should like to thank the following projects and institutions: the British Academy Black Sea Initiative, the Academy of Sciences of the Ukraine (Kiev), the Belsk field team, and the Kharkiv Young Archaeologists; individually I would like to thank David Braund, Slava Murzin, Renate Rolle, Sergey Makhortykh, and Evgeny Chernenko; for broader discussion over the years I particularly thank Michael Vickers. I am grateful to Peter Biehl and Doug Bolender for the invitation to participate at their inaugural event; and, as always, grateful to my editor wife, Sarah Wright, for saving me from the usual grammatical mistakes. Errors of fact and judgment (as well as lapses of taste) are my own.

References Cited

Alekseev, A. Yu. 2008 Some Chronological Problems of European Scythia. In *Impact of the Environment on Human Migration in Eurasia*, edited by E. M. Scott, A. Ya. Alekseev, and G. Zaitseva, pp. 9–20. NATO Science Series: IV: Earth and Environmental Sciences. Kluwer, Amsterdam.

Arnold, B. 1995 "Honorary Males" or "Women of Substance"? Gender, Status, and Power in Iron-Age Europe. *Journal of European Archaeology* 3(2):155–168.

Bintliff, J. 1995 Whither Archaeology? Revisited. In *Whither Archaeology? Papers in Honour of Evžen Neustupný*, edited by M. Kuna and N. Venclová, pp. 24–35. Institute of Archaeology, Prague.

Bintliff, J. 2007 Issues in the Economic and Ecological Understanding of the *Chora* of the Classical *Polis* in Its Social Context: A View from the Intensive Survey Tradition of the Greek Homeland. In *Surveying the Greek Chora: The Black Sea Region in a Comparative Perspective*, edited by P. G. Bilde and V. F. Stolba, pp. 13–26. Black Sea Studies 4. Aarhus University Press, Aarhus.

Collingwood, R. G. 1992 *The New Leviathan; or Man, Society, Civilization, and Barbarism; Revised Edition, with "Goodness, Rightness, and Utility" and "What Civilization Means,"* edited by D. Boucher. Oxford University Press, Oxford.

Collingwood, R. G. 1993 *The Idea of History: Revised Edition, with Lectures 1926–1928*. Edited by J. van der Dussen. Oxford University Press, Oxford.

Collingwood, R. G. 1999 *The Principles of History; and other Writings in the Philosophy of History*. Edited by W. H. Dray and W. J. van der Dussen. Oxford University Press, Oxford.

Friedman, J. 1985 Captain Cook, Culture and the World System. *Journal of Pacific History* 20: 91–201.

Giddens, A. 1979 *Central Problems of Social Theory: Action, Structure and Contradiction in Social Analysis*. Macmillan, London.

Guliaev, V. I. 2003 Amazons in the Scythia: New Finds at the Middle Don, Southern Russia. *World Archaeology* 35(1):112–125.

Fialko, E. E. 1991 Zhenskiye pogrebeniya s oruzhiem v skyfskikh kurganakh stepnoi Skyfii. *Naukova Dumka* (Kiev):4–18.

Hämäläinen, P. 2003 The Rise and Fall of Plains Indian Horse Cultures. In *The American Indian: Past and Present*, edited by R. L. Nichols, pp. 53–77. Oklahoma University Press, Norman.

Hanks, B. 2008 Reconsidering Warfare, Status and Gender in the Eurasian Steppe Iron Age. In *Are All Warriors Male? Gender Roles on the Ancient Eurasian Steppe,* edited by K. M.Linduff and K. S.Rubinson, pp. 15–34. AltaMira, Lanham.

Hartog, F. 1988 *The Mirror of Herodotus: The Representation of the Other in the Writing of History.* Translated by J. Lloyd. University of California Press, Berkeley.

Hiscock, P. 2008 *The Archaeology of Ancient Australia.* Routledge, London.

Klein, A. M. 1983 The Political Economy of Gender: A Nineteenth-Century Plains Indian Case Study. In *The Hidden Half: Studies of Plains Indian Women*, edited by P. Albers and B. Medicine, pp. 143–174. University Press of America, Washington, DC.

Kryzickij, S. D. 2006 The Rural Environs of Olbia: Some Problems of Current Importance. In *Surveying the Greek Chora: The Black Sea Region in a Comparative Perspective,* edited by P. G. Bilde and V. F. Stolba, pp. 99–114. Black Sea Studies 4. Aarhus University Press, Aarhus.

Lang, S. 1998 *Men as Women, Women as Men: Changing Gender in Native American Cultures.* University of Texas Press, Austin.

Murray, S. O. 1994 On Subordinating Native American Cosmologies to the Empire of Gender. *Current Anthropology* 35(1):59–61.

Murzin, V. J., and R. Rolle (editors) 2000 *Issledovaniya sovmestnoi Ukrainsko-Nemetskoi arkheologicheskoi ekspeditsii* v 2000g. Kiev.

Murzin, V. J. and R. Rolle 2007 *Bolshie gorodishcha lesostepnoi Skifii.* [http://www.kurgan.kiev.ua/Skiftown.html].

Murzin, V. J., R. Rolle, and S. A. Skory 2000 Arkheologichni doslidzhenniya spilnoi ukrainsko-nimetskoi ekspeditsii "Bilsk" v1994 potsi. *Vostochnoevropeiskiy arkheologicheskiy zhurnal* 4(5) [http://archaeology.kiev.ua/journal].

Nathanson, C. A. 2009 Problems, Crises, Events, and Social Change: Theory and Illustrations. *Sociological Research Online* 14(5) [http://www.socresonline.org.uk/14/5/11.html].

Rolle, R. 1989 *The World of the Scythians.* Batsford, London.

Roscoe, W. 1998 *Changing Ones: Third and Fourth Genders in Native North America.* St. Martin's Press, New York.

Rostovtzeff, M. I. 1922 *Iranians and Greeks in South Russia.* Clarendon, Oxford.

Sahlins, M. 1984. *Islands of History.* University of Chicago Press, Chicago.

Sewell, W. H. 1992 A Theory of Structure: Duality, Agency, and Transformation. *American Journal of Sociology* 98(1):1–29.

Sewell, W. H. 2005 *Logics of History: Social Theory and Social Transformation.* University of Chicago Press, Chicago.

Sulimirski, T., and T. Taylor 1990 The Scythians. In *The Cambridge Ancient History* Vol. III, part 2 (2nd ed.), edited by Boardman et al., pp. 547–590. Cambridge University Press, Cambridge.

Taylor, T. 1994 Thracians, Scythians, and Dacians, 800 BC-AD 300. In *The Oxford Illustrated Prehistory of Europe*, edited by B. W.Cunliffe, pp. 373–410. Oxford University Press, Oxford.

Taylor, T. 1996 *The Prehistory of Sex.* Bantam, New York.

Taylor, T. 2001 Believing the Ancients: Quantitative and Qualitative Dimensions of Slavery and the Slave Trade in Later Prehistoric Eurasia. *World Archaeology* 33(1):27–43.

Taylor, T. 2003 A Platform for Studying the Scythians. *Antiquity* 77(296):413–415.

Taylor, T. 2005 Ambushed by a Grotesque: Archaeology, Slavery and the Third Paradigm. In *Warfare, Violence and Slavery in Prehistory*, edited by M. Parker Pearson and I. J. N. Thorpe, pp. 225–233. BAR International Series 1374. British Archaeological Reports, Oxford.

Taylor, T. 2006 The Origins of Human Sexual Culture: Sex, Gender and Social Control. *Journal of Psychology and Human Sexuality* 18(2/3 and 4):69–105.

Taylor, T. 2008 Materiality. In *Handbook of Archaeological Theories*, edited by R. A. Bentley, H. Maschner, and C. Chippindale, pp. 297–320. AltaMira, Lanham.

Taylor, T. 2010 *The Artificial Ape: How Technology Changed the Course of Human Evolution*. Palgrave Macmillan, New York.

Thomas, N. 1989 *Out of Time*. Cambridge University Press, Cambridge.

Vickers, M., and D. Gill 1996 (new ed.) *Artful Crafts: Ancient Greek Silverware and Pottery*. Clarendon, Oxford.

Williams, W. L. 1986 *The Spirit and the Flesh: Sexual Diversity in American Indian Cultures*. Beacon Press, Boston.

Wylie, A. 1989 The Interpretive Dilemma. In *Critical Traditions in Contemporary Archaeology*, edited by V. Pinsky and A. Wylie, pp. 18–27. Cambridge University Press, Cambridge.

Zöllner, H., B. Ullrich, R. Rolle, S. Makhortykh, and M. Orlyuk 2008 Results of Geophysical Prospection in the Scythian Settlement of Belsk (Bol'šoe Belskoe Gorodišce). In *Layers of Perception*, edited by A. Posluschny, K. Lambers, and I. Herzog, p. 25. *Proceedings of the 35th International Conference on Computer Applications and Quantitative Methods in Archaeology* (CAA) (Kolloquien zur Vor- und Frühgeschichte 10). Habelt, Bonn.

CHAPTER NINE

The Allure of the Event in Roman Provincial Archaeology

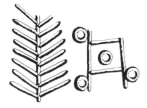

Louise Revell

Abstract *The relationship between historical narrative and archaeological data has been problematic in the study of the Roman provinces, with archaeology used to plug the gaps in the narratives drawn from textual sources. Since the nineteenth century, the central question within provincial archaeology has been the formation and administration of provincial societies, with named historical actors as key players. In the last twenty years, attention has instead focused on longer term processes of cultural change, such as the development of urbanism and the economy. At the same time, calls for a more socially based archaeology have only been partially met, and topics such as gender are still largely marginalized.*

This paper explores the ideas of an eventful archaeology from the perspective of the archaeology of the Roman provinces, and in particular, those of the Roman west. It explores three themes in particular: (1) the definition and identification of the event; (2) the relationship between event and process; and (3) the consequences for how we might write an eventful archaeology.

When Sewell (2005) posited the idea of an eventful sociology, the challenge for archaeologists was whether we could use this theory as a way to interpret the past, and if so, what the problems might be (Beck et al. 2007). Sewell constructed this theory within the sphere of early modern history, for which there is a sequence of documented events. The aim of his thesis was to assert the importance of these as a driver of change in contrast to a contemporary historiography, which stressed agency, practice, and social structures, concentrating on slowly changing processes and cultural ideas. We can compare the changes in historical theory to the development of archaeological thought from culture-history through processual to post-processual archaeology (Johnson 1999; Trigger 1989). With a similar dominance of agency-based social archaeology influenced by the work of Anthony Giddens (1984), the question of change has become problematic within a theoretical framework stressing continuity. The idea of an eventful archaeology raises the question to what extent contingent events played a role within the changes apparent in the archaeological record.

The archaeology of the western provinces of the Roman empire has long been, and still is, dominated by the narrative of cultural change from pre-Roman or Iron Age to Roman. This change is very visible within the archaeological record, with increased urbanization, the expansion of the economy, the worshipping of new gods through new rituals in new types of buildings, and the adoption of Latin and writing. This has been broadly termed Romanization, which tends to be used as both a description and an explanation (Woolf 1998:7). While many Roman archaeologists are now uncomfortable with this term (Mattingly 1997), as a coverall shorthand for the changes evident within the archaeological record, it still holds some value. At first view, the narrative of the western provinces of the Roman empire would seem to accord with Sewell's view of an eventful past: the changes in the archaeology can be attributed to a series of events of invasion and conquest by the Roman army. However, this is a relationship which has been undertheorized. Leaving aside the question of bias within the textual evidence, there has been surprisingly little explicit discussion of the relationship between event and process.

The western provinces of the Roman empire provide a useful case study for how we think about an eventful archaeology. We have clear evidence of archaeological change, which can be more closely dated than in many other archaeological periods thanks to the coinage, epigraphy, and a relatively precise ceramic sequence. We also have a broad-based narrative of events, but which has annoying lacunae for certain places and periods, and which lacks the detail of later historical periods. Roman archaeologists have adopted this narrative of events as a framework and at times an explanation for change, but they have not thought about the consequences of this adoption or its limitations. Within the ideas of social evolution, this was not a problem. The Greco-Roman world was a necessary and important step on the progression to nineteenth-century modernity. In the last 30 years, we have rejected this view of the past, and deconstructed the modern imperialist context, which led to a privileging of Roman culture and Roman imperialism (Freeman 1997; Hingley 2000). However, this has left the problem of exploring how we deal with the change in material culture and its relationship to events. In this paper, I want to problematize this relationship between events and Romanization in three ways. The first is how we identify which events are important in the process of change; the second is how far they might cause a complete change in the nature of society; and the final problem I want to raise is how the events then go on to shape the archaeological narrative we might write.

THE IDENTIFICATION OF THE EVENT

For the Roman period, it is tempting to assume that military action, whether conquest or rebellion, led to changes within the archaeological record. Therefore, the conquest and incorporation of an area into rule by Rome would seem an important moment to interrogate the relationship between event and change. However, recent work has de-centered the conquest as the stimulus for change, and instead created a somewhat fuzzier process (Creighton 2006; van Dommelen and Terrenato 2007; Ward-Perkins 1970; Woolf 1995). Central to this questioning of the relationship between conquest and change has been the realization that in areas of the western empire which were conquered during the third and second centuries BC, there is remarkably little change until the end of the first century BC/early first century AD. In political terms this relates to the end of the Republic, and the advent of the emperors under Augustus and his successors. This is clearest in areas which were conquered during the late third and second centuries BC, particularly the Iberian peninsula and southern France, and in the development of towns and the adoption of monumental public buildings (Ward-Perkins 1970). Rather than an immediate change in the second and first centuries BC, many of the changes in material culture date to the end of the first century BC and first half of the first century AD. Although a small number of Romanized buildings were constructed before this, the large-scale replanning of towns and the increase in their number only occurs later.

This temporal mismatch is evident in the Iberian peninsula. As part of the treaty in 206 BC at the end of the Second Punic War, certain areas in the south and east of the peninsula were transferred from Carthaginian to Roman control, and, after a period of rebellion, were formally constituted as the two provinces of Hispania Citerior and Ulterior by a provincial law, probably in 197 BC. During the second and early first centuries BC, we see very little development of Roman style towns. Very few new towns were founded (Keay 1995): the only certain official foundation was Carteia in 171 BC, although it has been suggested that there were others at Emporion and Valentia (Keay 1995:296–298). Even in these, the only monumental buildings appear to have been Capitolia, the distinctive triple-shrined temple to Jupiter, Juno and Minerva. Elsewhere, there was continuity of use of the preexisting settlements and architectural styles. At Tarraco and Cordoba, which later developed into the provincial capitals of Tarraconensis and Baetica, there is little evidence for the construction of monumental Roman-style architecture during the second century BC. At Saguntum, the town was reconstructed following its destruction by the Carthaginians. It seems to have largely followed the preexisting layout, and the only evidence for Romanized architecture is a new temple, again with three chambers suggestive of a Capitolium (Aranegui Gascó 2006).

It is only from the second half of the first century BC onward that we begin to see substantial changes in the forms of architecture. At Saguntum, the Republican forum was largely demolished and replaced with a monumental complex, which incorporated a basilica and possible shrine to the imperial family. It was decorated with marble and statues of Augustus and his family, and was probably paid for by a member of the local elite, Cnaeus Baebius Geminus (Keay 1995:317 and Figure 7). This is repeated at other towns, such as at Italica. The Iberian settlement became the home to wounded Roman soldiers in the late third century BC during the Second Punic War, but the only trace of monumental structures dating to the Republican period are at Cerro de los Palacios and again, may have been a Capitolium (Bendala Galán 1982). The first securely dateable Roman architecture is the possible forum, which was Augustan, and the temple, which dates to the reign of his successor, Tiberius. Again, at the neighboring town of Munigua, evidence of settlement dates back to the fifth century BC, but the first Roman-style architecture is the monumental temple complex, which dates to the first century AD.

A similar pattern can be seen in southern Gaul, which was conquered slightly later in the second century BC to provide a land bridge from Italy to the Spanish provinces (King 1990). There was a small number of deliberate ex novo urban foundations, such as Narbo in 118 BC, but it is only during the end of the first century BC that there is a large-scale foundation of Roman constituted towns. One example of this is modern Arles, which has evidence of occupation from the sixth century BC, but was re-founded as a colony for veteran soldiers by Caesar (Rivet 1988:190–196). The earliest traces of the forum contain Augustan monuments, and the theatre also dates to the Augustan period. The nearby site of Glanum has evidence for settlement pre-dating its conquest in the second century BC, and the agora and peristyle houses show the impact of the nearby Greek colony of Marseille (King 1990: 68; Rivet 1988:198–200). Again, it is only during the Augustan period that we see the construction of a substantial forum and basilica, and a temple dedicated by Agrippa.

This contrasts with the tempo of change in provinces conquered at a later period, such as central and northern Gaul, subjugated in the middle of the first century BC, and Britain, from the mid-first century AD onward. In these cases, the evidence demonstrates that the process of Romanization was more accelerated. The town of Samarobriva Ambianorum (modern Amiens) has produced no traces of pre-conquest occupation (Bayard and Massy 1983). The earliest evidence dates to the Augustan period, with the laying out of the street grid, followed by the proto-forum toward the middle of the first century. This is relatively short-lived and was replaced with a more monumental structure, probably AD 60–80, and before the end of the century, this was joined by a substantial amphitheatre. In Britain, within twenty to thirty years of conquest towns such as London, St. Albans, and Colchester were founded and have evidence for street plans and monumental architecture. Colchester was a very early foundation, probably around AD 50, and within a decade the street grid was laid out and the monumental temple to deified Claudius constructed, as well as up to a possible four other public buildings (Crummy 1993). At London, there is evidence for the layout of the town in the 50s AD, and substantial growth in the second half of the first century (Bateman 1998). Similarly, at Verulamium, the Late Iron Age oppidum was transformed into a small urban settlement with some Roman style buildings prior to the Boudiccan destruction of AD 61, and although there was an initial hiatus, a range of public buildings such as the forum and the temple-theatre complex dates to the 70s and 80s AD (Niblett 2001).

It is clear that the lengthy hiatus we see in eastern and southern Spain and southern France is not replicated in areas that were conquered at a later date, so this delay is not a product of the time it might take to effect the construction of the provincial administrative structures. Instead, it calls into question the role of conquest as the pivotal event in the process of cultural change. If we want to write an eventful account of Romanization, we need to look for alternative contenders. This can be seen in more agency-driven models of Romanization, and in particular, to the integration of the archaeology of cultural change with the text-based examination of imperialism at Rome. One current model of Romanization was proposed by Martin Millett in *Romanization of Britain* (Millett 1990). This moves away from the idea that the cultural change was inevitable, the product of the barbarous western provinces desiring civilization, or that it was purely imposed by the imperial authorities of Rome. Instead, it places center stage the role of the local people, and as importantly, the way they were incorporated into the political and administrative structures of the empire. Key to this was the methods through which the imperial authorities administered the provinces, and the role of provincial towns within this.

The imperial authorities at Rome, principally the emperor, relied on a very small bureaucracy based at or sent out from Rome. Instead, daily administrative duties were handed back to the local elites in the form of urban magistrates (Garnsey and Saller 1987:20–40; Lintott 1993:129–153). In this way, the local population became part of the Roman state machinery, with the ability to gain citizenship and rise through the social ranks to become part of a super-provincial elite at Rome. By the end of the second century AD, approximately half of the known consuls and senators were from the provinces (Alföldy 1976; Hammond 1957), and the emperors were increasingly from provincial families. This incorporation of the local elites provided them with a social and political context for adopting Roman habits and Roman material culture. Within the changing political context, it became a way for them to retain their elite rank by remodeling themselves from warriors to magistrates. Similarly, the importance of the towns as the focus for local political activity and imperial administration became a context for their monumentalization, with buildings and architectural iconography connected with the emperor as a means of expressing loyalty to Rome. Thus, the elites adopted Roman forms of housing, dining practices, and symbols of power. This provides the explanation for the temporality of the cultural change noted earlier. This model of towns as the central point of the administration system, and the importance of the urban magistrates seems to be the product of a series of legal and administrative reforms begun by Augustus (Lintott 1993; Nicolet 1991). Therefore, in one sense, a sequence of law reforms provided the stimulus for cultural change. However, even these have a context, in the reshaping of Roman political structures that was already underway, and was the consequence of the events of the Civil Wars, with the provinces coming into increasing focus as a power-base for the rival senators.

This is not the end of the narrative: the chartering of new towns and the formulation of provincial laws set in place a further chain of more localized events. The tribal elites, in order to maintain their position, adopted these new urban magistracies, the citizenship that came with it, and the new modes of demonstrating status: they paid for public buildings, they commemorated the event with Latin inscriptions, and they set up statues of themselves and each other in togas. We can see this in Gaul, with the family of Epotsorovidos (King 1990: 66). The genealogy of the family is given in an inscription set up by his great-grandson Caius Iulius Rufus (CIL 13.1036), and from this we can trace the process of cultural change. He describes himself as great-grandson of Epotsorovidus, presumably a member of one of the Gallic tribes. His son was granted citizenship by Julius Caesar, and adopted the *tria nomina* of Caius Iulius Otuaneunos, mixing the Roman name structure with his Gallic surname. This was continued by his son Caius Iulius Gedomonicus (about whom we know no more than his name), and it was only with Rufus that we see a fully Romanized name. Rufus served within the Roman administration, and is recorded as holding both the post of *praefectus fabrorum*, an army position, and the priesthood of Rome and Augustus, a priest of the imperial cult at the provincial capital of Lugdunensis (modern Lyon). He had also learned how to act as a magistrate and to pay for the construction of pieces of monumental architecture for the wider community to enhance his own prestige. In AD 19 he paid for the construction of the amphitheatre attached to the cult center at Lugdunensis (ILTG 216), as well as a triumphal arch to Germanicus at his home town of Saintes (CIL 13.1036). This can then be taken a stage farther, drawing in the wider community. As they came to use the facilities and resources of the town as part of their daily lives, they increasingly began to adopt a Roman identity, whether consciously or not (Revell 2009). Their ability to adapt to this new physical and social environment was part of the process of cultural change, and part of the increased Romanization we see in wider aspects of the archaeological record.

In other towns we do not have the epigraphic evidence to show the process in the same detail, but the archaeological evidence suggests that similar processes were occurring. Some of this was required through the stipulations of the charters given to these new towns. Political organization involved popular elections (González 1986:chapters 51–59), with the assumption of a forum within which political activity would take place. There was also a requirement for communal religious festivals and spectacles in the Roman fashion (Crawford 1996:393–454, chapters 54, 70, 71). However, these were all to be organized and in some cases paid for by the elite, and required the participation of the citizen body of the town, thus relying upon the local peoples adopting and carrying out these new practices. Thus, we are left with a picture of cultural change that is the product of a sequence of events, both at Rome and in the western provinces. However, the events which are here important are not the battles and victories that brought these areas into the empire, but instead events we might think of as political or legalistic. This is not to downplay the importance of the warfare, but it was not the direct stimulus to the changes we see in the archaeological record. Thus, we have an eventful narrative, but of a sequence or cascade of seemingly mundane events, occurring both at Rome and within the provinces themselves.

A FEMINIST CRITIQUE

This change in Roman forms of material culture provides a broad corroboration with the idea of an eventful archaeology. However, the nature of this cultural shift also provides two caveats about how we then apply the idea of an eventful archaeology to the way in which we construct narratives of the past, and it is these which I want to explore in the rest of this paper. The first is the extent of the cultural shift. Millett's model of Romanization, described above, is based upon changes within quite specific social structures, in particular, new ways of expressing rank and social status. This is usually assumed to extend to other aspects of society, producing a complete structural disjuncture. This is something that accords with the male-driven ancient textual sources and modern archaeological agendas; however, it is an assumption that needs to be questioned. The idea that our view of the past and its narrative have been constructed by male-dominated agendas was explicitly raised by Joan Kelly in her article "Did Women Have a Renaissance?" when she wrote: "One of the tasks of women's history is to call into question accepted schemes of periodization" (Kelly 1984:19). She argued that whereas the Renaissance is generally viewed as a time of positive social and cultural change, for women this was a time when the power and authority they could wield during the Medieval period was removed due to a new division between personal and public life and new ideas of relationships between men and women.

The same question can be asked for women within the provinces: What, if any, were the consequences of Romanization for ideologies of gender? Gender is a question that has largely been ignored within Roman archaeology, particularly the archaeology of the western provinces (Scott 1995, 1997). This is in spite of the importance of gender in Ancient History, and the growth of post-processual agendas within Roman archaeology in Britain, with a concentration on ideas of identity (Hill 2001). However, there are some suggestions of continuity in family structures and the life course, although there has been little work systematically collecting the evidence (Revell in press). However, my own work on the gendered life course and the regional variability apparent within it has demonstrated that there is a danger in assuming that all aspects of life underwent fundamental structural changes prompted by Romanization (Revell 2005).

When we look at the commemoration of the deceased within the Roman west, there is a fundamental mismatch between the Romanization of the means of commemoration, and the continuity in the underlying social structures, which influence patterns of commemoration. There was widespread adoption of stone grave markers written in Latin as a form of commemorative material culture. Among the information given about the deceased within the epitaph may be the age at death, although this is not found on all Roman epitaphs, and the proportion of epitaphs with age-statements varies from one community to the next. The patterning of the ages commemorated does not follow expected patterns of mortality, which suggests that age-statements are subject to cultural patterning, and can be used to reconstruct ideologies of gender and age. For example, the epitaphs from *regiones* 4–6 in central Italy show a marked emphasis on the commemoration of children and young adults, with more than 80 percent of age-statements corresponding to those aged 30 and under (Revell 2005; Revell in press) (Figure 1). This profile reflects an ideology of gender where the transition to adulthood was marked by taking up the roles of wife for women, usually in the late teens (Shaw 1987) and citizen/magistrate for men at age of 25. Death is seen as more poignant

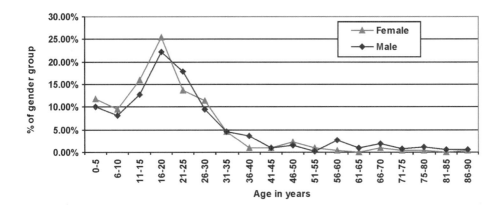

FIGURE 1 Age distribution on epitaphs from regiones 4, 5 and 6 (Italy), n = 634.

when the deceased has not yet made this transition, as articulated in inscriptions that lament the brief passing of life as being especially poignant. This can be see in the inscription to a 13-year-old girl, which exhorts the passer-by to look upon her tomb "for you do not know the brief span of my life" (CIL 9.4810). Age-statements for those whose deaths occurred in childhood and the years through to the early 20s are included because they point to this unfulfilled promise of the deceased. This echoes the forms of life-course which we see in the Roman textual sources (Harlow and Laurence 2002; Laurence 2000), and suggests that that in these areas, we are seeing a Romanization of family and gender structures.

In contrast, when we look at the evidence from other areas we see a different pattern of commemoration, which reflects a non-Roman ideology of age. The evidence from the Etruscan city of Tarquinia, approximately 75 km north of Rome, is particularly striking, as we might expect a city relatively close to Rome to undergo a more complete change in social structures. However, here there is less concentration on childhood, and a more pronounced concentration on those in their 40s to 70s (Figure 2). The percentage of epitaphs commemorating those aged 30 years and under is much lower, at just over 30 percent, and we see a much higher proportion of age-statements referring to those is their 60s and above. This echoes the pattern found in the Etruscan-language inscriptions from South Etruria, which date to the fourth century BC (Nielsen 1989). Here there is a dual emphasis on those dying in early adulthood and old age. It has been argued that this shows a respect for the older generations, and grandparents in particular. Whether this is the case or not, it demonstrates a certain level of continuity on age structures from the Etruscan to the Roman period in this area. It suggests that come the first-third centuries AD, the period to which the majority of the Latin inscriptions date, there is a difference between *regiones* 4–6 and the city of Tarquinia in how the various age groups are judged, and consequently, how age and gender are conceptualized. This regional variability continues when we look outside of Italy, to southern Spain and Britain (Figure 3). Even more marked is the difference with Thugga in North Africa, where commemoration of the elderly shows that it was considered a significant stage within the life-course for both men and women.

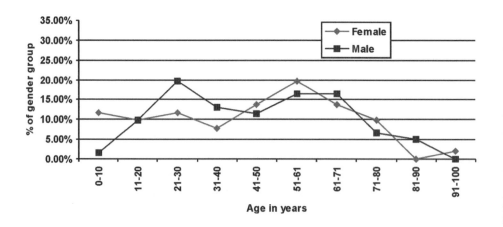

FIGURE 2 Age distribution on epitaphs from Tarquinia, n = 112.

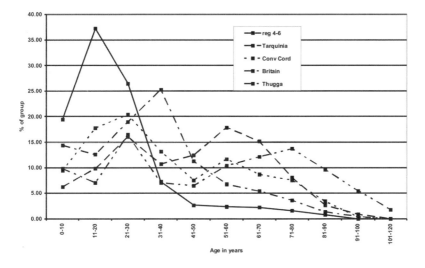

FIGURE 3 Age distribution on epitaphs from regiones 4–6, Tarquinia, Conventus Corubensis (Spain), Britain, Thugga (Afrcia), n = 1110.

Overall, this evidence shows a change in the means of commemoration, with the adoption of Roman-style epitaphs in Latin. In contrast, the underlying categories of infant, child, adult, old adult, and elderly, and how these were understood for each gender, do not adhere to the norms at Rome, suggesting the continuity of pre-Roman ideologies. It brings into question the criteria we use for identifying the event, and the importance we attach to it in terms of complete social transformation. If the research questions focus on settlement patterns, or development of political structures, for example, will the same events be significant as a research question about religious change, or the changing role of women? The challenge then becomes that rather than a return to a single narrative of events with uniform outcomes, we need to allow for a more complex interweaving of event and change, with the explicit assumption that different events may impact upon different social structures.

THE CONSEQUENCES OF THE NATURE OF THE TEXTUAL SOURCES IN THE WRITING OF ARCHAEOLOGY

The second caveat I want to raise is the question of how we integrate events and processes to actually write an eventful archaeology. There has been a difficult relationship between historical narrative and archaeological evidence (Laurence 2001; Sauer 2004). At its extreme, archaeology has been stereotyped as the handmaiden of history, filling out the detail of a narrative driven by historical accounts. The culture-history approach of Childe similarly tried to replicate a historical narrative from the archaeological evidence. In light of this problematic relationship between archaeological evidence and the construction of a narrative, how do we write an eventful archaeology as opposed to an event-driven archaeology? This is a question that is particularly apposite for Roman archaeology, where we have the simulacrum of an event-filled narrative, but in reality, the nature of the historical record is such that when we come to apply it to the provinces, we are left with a number of methodological problems.

The textual sources, both literary and epigraphic, are on the whole centered on Rome and political power, whether held by the kings, the senatorial elite, or the emperors. Whether writing in Latin or Greek, the historians from the Republican and early and mid-imperial periods (i.e., up to about the 3rd century AD) were based in Rome (Braund 1996; Stewart 1995). The provinces are only mentioned when they were drawn into events that had an impact on Rome, or involved actors from Rome. This in reality produces a meager narrative for any specific town or region as it only features when connected with people or events that were important for Rome. We are left with some important lacunae in our overall knowledge of provincial events, and in certain cases we do not even know precisely when a community was formally brought into Roman control.

This has had a problematic effect on the way these events are related to the archaeological record. At its most basic level, there is a danger of relating poorly dated archaeological trends to attested events, with the consequence that the evidence is sucked toward these points. Keith Branigan's account of the development of the town of Verulamium (modern St. Albans) and the surrounding villas is tied into political events at Rome, with the assumption that they would have had a direct influence on the fortunes of a relatively insignificant community in Britain (Branigan 1973). The villas around the town go into decline or are abandoned or destroyed in the second half of the fourth century AD, and Branigan attributes this to events following the attempted usurpation of the Emperor Constans by the Magnetius, with troops and assistance from Britain (Branigan 1973:126–8). The historian Ammianus Marcellinus (14.5.6–8) recounts how reprisals were exacted in AD 353–54 by the imperial agent Paulus: "[L]ike a flood he suddenly overwhelmed the fortunes of many, casting freeborn men into prison and degrading some with fetters, all this by fabricating charges that were far removed from the truth" (14.5.6). Branigan ties the abandonment and demolition of the villa at Gadebridge into these events: "Clearly the owner of Gadebridge had supported Magnentius and had now seen his property confiscated and his buildings demolished as a result" (Branigan 1973:127), viewing it as part of the wider reprisals. However, it has been argued that Ammianus' historical method is underpinned by a contrast between moderation and excess, part of the Roman view that history should provide examples (*exempla*) of correct behavior (for example, Livy *preface* 9–11). The actions of men such as Paulus represent the excesses which undermined the just and civilized rule of the good emperor (Seager 1986). If we accept this argument, it brings with it the possibility that the destruction of the period was exaggerated for literary (and moralizing) effect, and that we should not be looking for a widespread archaeological manifestation of his actions.

In a similar way, documentary evidence attests that Hadrian visited the province of Britain in AD 121/22 (SHA *Hadrian* 11.2). Consequently, any public building constructed in Britain in the first half of the second century AD is tentatively associated with Hadrian's visit in AD 121/22 until proven otherwise. In the case of the forum at Wroxeter, the inscription dedicating the building to the emperor (RIB 228) has led archaeologists to attribute the construction of the building to patronage of the emperor (for example, Potter and Johns 1992:82). In reality, the dedication can be dated to AD 130, making it likely that the construction began before his visit. This magnetic attraction of the presence of an emperor in the province has led to other building projects being dated on very flimsy evidence, and has led to the construction of a grand narrative for the province, such as a deliberate development of the urban centers as part of a wider plan for the stabilization of the frontier areas of the empire (Webster 1988:140–143). These individual narratives then feed into wider discussions of long-term processes, such as Wacher's construction of a grand narrative of the adoption of urbanism in Britain, which he sees as culminating under Hadrian (Wacher 1995).

While it is easy to reject this approach to writing archaeological narrative as one that would today be considered theoretically naïve, there are more subtle ways in which the presence or absence of a textual narrative can impact upon the way in which we tell the story of cultural change. This can be seen in the case of Gaul, and a pair of papers published in *Archaeological Dialogues* in 2002 by Greg Woolf and Jan Slofstra (Slofstra 2002; Woolf 2002). These explored the nature of the cultural changes in central Gaul and Batavia respectively, and both offered important perspectives on the process of Romanization. While the presence or absence of texts did not necessarily dictate the interpretation of either author, the consequences can be seen in the different forms of narrative structure within each paper (Revell 2002). In telling the story of the Batavians on the Rhine frontier, Slostra has a reasonable narrative framework with some central actors; in contrast, Woolf has a few hints and then silence. Slofstra sets his account of Romanization within a framework of the early treaties, battles, and revolts, with recognizable Roman commanders and Batavian kings. The product is a narrative of cultural changes with a tempo based around these recognizable events, with named key individuals and short periods of analysis. In contrast, although Woolf also deals with equivalent political events, he does not have the same detail and so they stand less prominently. Instead, the narrative is one of group elites and long-term trends, with a different focus and a different tempo. His main focus is internal social changes: although his setting, like that of Slofstra, is one of Roman imperial mechanisms, in the absence of identifiable people and moments of action, the relationship is more anonymous and continuous.

These two different forms of narrative exemplify how the constraints of the different scales of time can have an impact upon the way in which we write and interpret the past. This indirectly raises the question of how much importance we should attach to these moments in history. Was the revolt by Civilis and the Batavians, for example, important to the process of cultural change, or was it a temporary moment, which may have had some consequences, but which ultimately did not drastically impact upon the process of change? Slofstra and Woolf's papers suggest that this relationship between known events and writing of these cultural change is not as unproblematic as Romanists, and archaeologists more generally, have assumed. If we are to write an eventful account of the past, we need to be more attuned to the slippery nature of the historical narrative, and the ways in which it intersects with the processes and changes we see in the archaeological evidence. We also need to be more critical about how we write the narrative, not only in terms of the preciseness (or not) of the events, but also in the process of selection and presentation.

CONCLUSIONS

To return to the ideas of an eventful archaeology, for Roman archaeologists, one of the important elements of Sewell's proposition and the approach posited in Beck et al. (2007)

is that it allows for the messiness of structural reproduction and so provides a framework to explain social change. Sewell stressed that structural systems were not bounded but involved a substantial element of contingency, which could then be changed through sequences of events or ruptures. The case study of Romanization demonstrates that we need to problematize the nature of the event. There is a difference between event and eventful, and while I have tended to use the term *event* in this paper, in fact I am referring to a sequence or cascade of events. However, the events that at first appearance seem the most important, such as battles and conquest, were in reality not the only factors. The large-scale cultural changes within the provinces were to a large extent the reaction to a sequence of administrative changes. This suggests that in exploring the relationship between event and structural change, we may need to look for the events in multiple locations, and involve multiple actors with different constraints and motivations, possibly not even working to the same end. The attraction of an eventful Romanization is that it places the changes within a context, and rather than a teleological inevitability, makes it the product of specific historical contingencies. It also places people at the heart of the event. They were making the adjustments and enacting the changes through their ability to adapt to the new social and political structures: to move and use the spaces of the new forms of buildings to get through their localized lives, but at the same time, to reproduce the structures of Roman cultural norms and ideologies on a wider scale. In some ways, I am less dismissive of the everyday occurrences than Sewell, as it is these which take the large-scale decisions about administering provinces and building monumental temples, baths, fora, amphitheatres, and bring about their impact on the more localized experience of social structures.

ACKNOWLEDGMENTS

I would like to thank Douglas Bolender for his invitation to take part in the conference at Buffalo, and the other participants for their comments on the paper, as well as more informal discussion. Over the years, my ideas on the relationship between Archaeology and Ancient History have been formulated through discussions with Tim Champion, Matthew Johnson, Ray Laurence, and Martin Millett. Jon Adams and Vedia Izzet kindly read drafts of the paper. None should be held responsible for the ideas expressed here.

References Cited

Alföldy, G. 1976 Consuls and Consulars under the Antonines. *Ancient Society* 7:263–299.

Aranegui Gascó, C. 2006 From Arse to Saguntum. In *Early Roman towns in Hispania Tarraconensis*, edited by L. Abad Casal, S. J. Keay and S. Ramallo Asensio, pp. 63–74. Journal of Roman Archaeology Supplementary Series 62, Portsmouth, RI.

Bateman, N. C. W. 1998 Public Buildings in Roman London: Some Contrasts. In *Roman London: Recent Archaeological Work*, edited by B. Watson, pp. 47–57. Journal of Roman Archaeology Supplementary Series 24, Portsmouth, RI.

Bayard, D., and J. L. Massy 1983 *Amiens Romain: Samarobriva Ambianorum*. Revue Archéologique de Picardie, Heilly.

Beck, R. A., D. J. Bolender, J. A. Brown, and T. K. Earle 2007 Eventful Archaeology: The Place of Space in Structural Transformation. *Current Anthropology* 48(6):833–860.

Bendala Galán, M. 1982 Excavaciones en el Cerro de los Palacios. In *Italica (Santiponce, Sevilla): Actas de las Primeras Jornadas Sobre Excavaciones Arqueológicas en Itálica*, edited by AA.VV, pp. 234–240. Ministerio de Cultura, Madrid.

Branigan, K. 1973 *Town and Country: Verulamium and the Roman Chilterns*. Spurbooks, Bourne End.

Braund, D. 1996 *Ruling Roman Britain: Kings, Queens, Governors and Emperors from Julius Caesar to Agricola*. Routledge, London.

Crawford, M. 1996 *Roman Statutes*. Bulletin of the Institute of Classical Studies Supplement 64, London.

Creighton, J. 2006 *Britannia: the Creation of a Roman Province*. Routledge, London.

Crummy, P. 1993 The Development of Roman Colchester. In *Roman Towns: The Wheeler Inheritance. A Review of 50 years' Research*, edited by S. J. Greep, pp. 34–45. Council for British Archaeology Research Report 93, York.

Freeman, P. W. M. 1997 Mommsen through to Haverfield: The Origins of Romanization in Late 19th-Century Britain. In *Dialogues in Roman Imperialism: Power, Discourse and Discrepant Experience in the Roman Empire*, edited by D. Mattingly, pp. 27–50. Journal of Roman Archaeology Supplementary Series 23, Portsmouth.

Garnsey, P. and R. P. Saller 1987 *The Roman Empire: Economy, Society and Culture*. Duckworth, London.

Giddens, A. 1984 *The Constitution of Society. Outline of a Theory of Structuration*. Blackwells, Oxford.

González, J. 1986 The *lex Irnitana*: a New Copy of the Flavian Municipal Law. *Journal of Roman Studies* 76:147–243.

Hammond, M. 1957 Composition of the Senate, AD 68–225. *Journal of Roman Studies* 47:74–81.

Harlow, M., and R. Laurence 2002 *Growing Up and Growing Old in Ancient Rome*. Routledge, London.

Hill, J. D. 2001 Romanisation, Gender and Class: Recent Approaches to Identity in Britain and their Possible Consequences. In *Britons and Romans: Advancing an Archaeological Agenda*, edited by S. James and M. Millett, pp. 12–18. Council; for British Archaeology Research Report 125, York.

Hingley, R. 2000 *Roman Officers and English Gentlemen*. Routledge, London.

Johnson, M. 1999 *Archaeological Theory: An Introduction*. Blackwell Publishers, Oxford.

Keay, S. J. 1995 Innovation and Adaptation: The Contribution of Rome to Urbanism in Iberia. In *Social Complexity and the Development of Towns in Iberia*, edited by B. W. Cunliffe and S. J. Keay, pp. 291–337. Proceedings of the British Academy vol. 86, London.

Kelly, J. 1984 Did Women Have a Renaissance? In *Women, History and Theory: the Essays of Joan Kelly*, edited by J. Kelly, pp. 19–50. University of Chicago Press, Chicago.

King, A. C. 1990 *Roman Gaul and Germany*. British Museum Press, London.

Laurence, R. 2000 Metaphors, Monuments and Texts: the Life Course in Roman Culture. *World Archaeology* 31(3):442–455.

Laurence, R. 2001 Roman Narratives: The Writing of Archaeological Discourse—The View from Britain. *Archaeological Dialogues* 8:90–123.

Lintott, A. 1993 *Imperium Romanum: Politics and Administration*. Routledge, London.

Mattingly, D. 1997 Dialogues of Power and Experience in the Roman Empire. In *Dialogues in Roman Imperialism: Power, Discourse and Discrepant Experience in the Roman Empire*, edited by D. Mattingly, pp. 7–24. Journal of Roman Archaeology Supplementary Series 23, Portsmouth, RI.

Millett, M. 1990 *The Romanization of Britain: an Essay in Archaeological Interpretation*. Cambridge University Press, Cambridge.

Niblett, R. 2001 *Verulamium. The Roman City of St. Albans*. Tempus, Stroud.

Nicolet, C. 1991 *Space, Geography and Politics in the Early Roman Empire*. University of Michigan Press, Ann Arbor.

Nielsen, M. 1989 Women and Family in a Changing Society: a Quantitative Approach to Late Etruscan Burials. *Analecta Romana Instituti Danici* 17–18:53–98.

Potter, T. W., and C. Johns 1992 *Roman Britain*. British Museum Press, London.

Revell, L. 2002 Story-Telling in Roman Archaeology. *Archaeological Dialogues* 9(1):44–47.

Revell, L. 2005 The Roman Life-Course: A View from the Inscriptions. *European Journal of Archaeology* 8(1):43–63.

Revell, L. 2009 *Roman Imperialism and Local Identities*. Cambridge University Press, Cambridge.

Revell, L. in press Geography and Environment. In *The History of Children and the Family Volume 1: Antiquity (500 BCE–800 CE)*, edited by M. Harlow and R. Laurence. Berg, Oxford.

Rivet, A. L. F. 1988 *Gallia Narbonensis: Southern Gaul in Roman Times*. Batsford, London.

Sauer, E. W. (editor) 2004 *Archaeology and Ancient History: Breaking Down the Boundaries*. Routledge, London.

Scott, E. 1995 Women and Gender Relations in the Roman Empire. In *Theoretical Roman Archaeology: Second Conference Proceedings*, edited by P. Rush, pp. 174–189. Avebury, Aldershot.

Scott, E. 1997 Introduction: On the Incompleteness of Archaeological Narratives. In *Invisible People and Processes. Writing Gender and Childhood in European Archaeology*, edited by J. Moore and E. Scott, pp. 1–12. Leicester University Press, Leicester.

Seager, R. 1986 *Ammianus Marcellinus: Seven Studies in his Language and Thought*. University of Missouri Press, Columbia.

Sewell, W. H. 2005 *Logics of History: Social Theory and Social Transformation*. University of Chicago Press, Chicago.

Shaw, B. D. 1987 The Age of Roman Girls at Marriage: Some Reconsiderations. *Journal of Roman Studies* 77:30–46.

Slofstra, J. 2002 Batavians and Romans on the Lower Rhine: The Romanisation of a Frontier Area. *Archaeological Dialogues* 9(1):16–38.

Stewart, P. 1995 Inventing Britain: The Roman Creation and Adaptation of an Image. *Britannia* 26:1–10.

Trigger, B. 1989 *A History of Archaeological Thought*. Cambridge University Press, Cambridge.

van Dommelen, P., and N. Terrenato (editors) 2007 *Articulating Local Cultures: Power and Identity under the Expanding Roman Republic*. Journal of Roman Archaeology Supplementary Series 64.

Wacher, J. S. 1995 *The Towns of Roman Britain*. Second edition. Batsford, London.

Ward-Perkins, J. B. 1970 From Republic to Empire: Reflections on the Early Provincial Architecture of the Roman West. *Journal of Roman Studies* 60:1–19.

Webster, G.1988 Wroxeter. In *Fortress into City*, edited by Graham Webster, pp. 120–144. Batsford, London.

Woolf, G. 1995 The Formation of Roman Provincial Cultures. In *Integration in the Early Roman West. The Role of Culture and Ideology*, edited by J. Metzler, M. Millett, N. Roymans and J. Slofstra, pp. 9–18. Dossiers d'Archéologie du Musée National d'Histoire et d'Art IV, Luxembourg.

Woolf, G. 1998 *Becoming Roman: the Origins of Provincial Civilization in Gaul*. Cambridge University Press, Cambridge.

Woolf, G. 2002 Generations of Aristocracy: Continuities and Discontinuities in the Societies of Interior Gaul. *Archaeological Dialogues* 9(1):2–15.

Chapter Ten

The AD 79 Eruption of Mt. Vesuvius

A Significant or Insignificant Event?

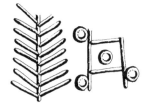

Penelope M. Allison

Abstract *The AD 79 eruption of Mt. Vesuvius was a catastrophic event for the Roman towns of Pompeii and Herculaneum. While scholarly focus on this, natural, event has assured Pompeii a place in the history of Roman daily life, it has downplayed Pompeii's place in the history of the region. How much has this focus misrepresented Pompeii's true role in the archaeology and history of southern Italy?*

This chapter will briefly review Pompeian scholarship and discuss Pompeii's archaeological and historical significance in the political, economic, and social history of the Campanian region. It will use examples from the material and epigraphical record at Pompeii to illustrate the misappropriation of these remains to epitomize a universality of Roman urban life. I will argue, conversely, that much can be learned from the Pompeian remains about south Italian urban living before and during the Roman period.

THE EVENT

Pliny the Younger was 17 years old and staying with his uncle, the elder Pliny, at his naval base in Misenum (Figure 1), when, on August 24, or conceivably on November 23 (see Pappalardo 1990:209–210), AD 79, that notorious relative and natural scientist set off to investigate the unusual cloud forming over Mt. Vesuvius—an investigation that led to his death some 20 km from the erupting mountain. The younger Pliny had preferred to stay with his head in his books and so lived to report to his friend Tacitus, not only the circumstances of his uncle's death (Pliny *Ep.*:6.16) but also the process of this eruption (Pliny *Ep.*:6.20). These now famous letters are considered the first ever "eyewitness" account of a volcanic eruption, which also left two Roman towns, Pompeii and Herculaneum, so completely devastated that

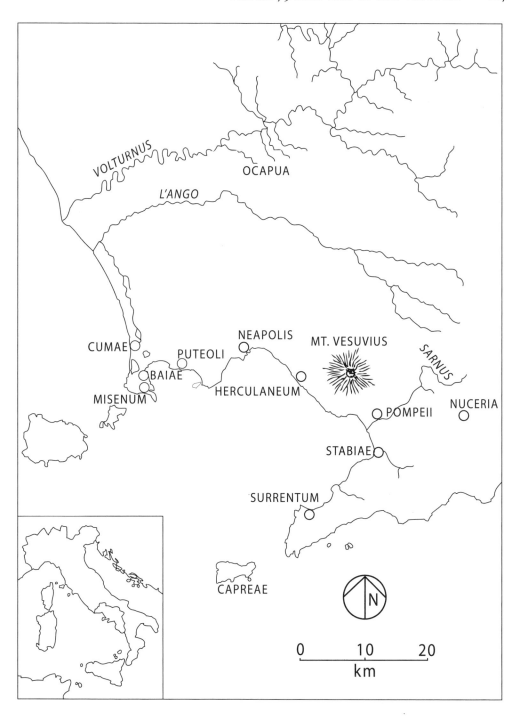

FIGURE 1 Map of the Bay of Naples (adapted from J. B. Ward-Perkins and A. Claridge, *Pompeii AD 79* [Sydney, 1980]).

they remained largely unknown to the intellectual world for nearly 2,000 years. However, their subsequent discovery, and particularly that of the more completely excavated Pompeii, has had a huge impact on both the scholarly world and the public imagination.

This chapter briefly discusses the significance of this eruption for the Campanian region and how investigations into the Pompeii remains from that event have structured our knowledge on this town's place in Campania's social history.

THE LITERARY RECORD

How interested were contemporary Roman writers in this eruption and in the devastation of these two towns?

The two letters written by Pliny the Younger, sometime after AD 107, provide our best documentation of the actual eruption. However, they do not mention the towns of Pompeii or Herculaneum. Tacitus, writing between AD 104 and AD 109 made brief reference to this eruption as one of the disasters to affect Italy during the early years of the reign of the emperor Titus (*Histories*:1.2), the other disaster being a fire that devastated Rome. Suetonius (*Titus*:8.3), also writing in the early second century, commented on three disasters that occurred in Titus's reign: the third being outbreaks of plague, which were reportedly the worst of these three. Eusebius (*Chronicle* AD 79), and Josephus (*Jewish Antiquities*:20.7.2), made passing reference to the eruption's consumption of the surrounding countryside, and to the deaths of certain individuals (sources cited by Cooley 2004:39). Our other main source of evidence is Dio Cassius's rather dramatic and fanciful report (66:21–23), written probably in the late second or early third century. This report, preserved through a summary by Xiphilinos (see Cooley 2004:38; contra Allison 2004:23) is the only one to name Herculaneum and Pompeii as the two entire cities buried by this eruption.

And there is little written about the impact of this eruption. Suetonius commented that Titus sent aid, and Dio Cassius (66.24.1,3–4) described how this emperor was rather preoccupied with the fire that consumed a large part of Rome, and so sent a delegation of two ex-consuls to Campania to re-found settlements and to give the money and possessions of those who had no heirs to those who had lost their property as a result of this catastrophe. Pliny (*Ep.*:6.16) tells us that the eruption destroyed one of the loveliest regions on earth.

Otherwise, this event was remembered mainly in poetry and religious superstition. Statius, a local poet writing in the AD 90s, wrote about the towns that *recovered* from Vesuvius's fiery storm and continued to thrive (*Silvae*:3.5.72–75, 4.4.78–85), while Martial (*Epigram*:4.44), in c. AD 88 (Cooley 2004:41–42), described the green vine-covered hills now buried under flames and ash. The Jewish Sibylline oracle of AD 80 (4.130–136; cited in Cooley 2004:42) blamed the eruption and destruction of many towns on the wrath of the Jewish God, while Tertullian, about a century later (*Apology* 40.8), argued that the eruption could not be considered as a sign of the wrath of the pagan gods against Christians because Campania was not complaining of Christians at this time.

Thus, the historical records for the aftermath of the eruption are somewhat contradicting about its impact on the region's beauty and prosperity. The poetic representation indicates a land that was devastated, but that—with enriched volcanic soils—was quickly repopulated and revitalized. This eruption brought the town of Pompeii to the attention of Rome, but only fleetingly. The region continued to prosper without it.

Neither the archaeology nor the history shows that Campania's contributions to the Roman economy and society were impacted on by the eruption of Mt. Vesuvius (Allison 2002a:114–116). On the contrary, towns such as Capua, in northern Campania (Figure 1), continued to flourish, and the port of Puteoli, near Naples, grew dramatically to become an important gateway for Mediterranean trade to the Italian peninsula (Frederiksen 1984: 285–293, 319–337). Amphorae bearing wine from the Campanian region continued to be exported around the Roman world (Tchernia 1981).

Seneca (*Natural Questions*:6.1.1–3), writing shortly before his suicide in AD 65, and Tacitus, in his *Annals* (*Ann.*:15.22), both indicated that Pompeii had been a busy Campanian town. But Pompeii was not, nor ever had been, an important Roman town, politically or economically. According to Alison Cooley (2004:1):

> It was not large and important like Naples or Puteoli, and not fashionable like Stabiae or Baiae. No Pompeian ever made his or her name in Roman literature or politics, and no crucial moments in history hinged on events in Pompeii.

So the eruption of Mt. Vesuvius put the Campanian market town of Pompeii and the seaside resort of Herculaneum out of action but the rest of the Roman world remembered the event in poetry, and with superstition, and continued undeterred along its prosperous economic and political trajectories.

ARCHAEOLOGICAL AND ANTIQUARIAN INTEREST IN POMPEII

Lack of political interest in Pompeii, by the center of Roman power, meant lack of a need to explore and recover this town, which in turn has meant that there has been much more to recover and record during its modern exploration. The AD 79 eruption played a significant part in bringing Pompeii to the attention of the modern world, where it has had a major impact on the artistic and intellectual life of the eighteenth, nineteenth, twentieth, and now twenty-first centuries (Allison 2002a).

From the mid-eighteenth century, the excavations of Pompeii and Herculaneum have brought forth a wealth of art that has been removed to embellish, not only the Bourbon palaces (see painting by Louis Jean Desprez: Trevelyan 1976:Figure 46; Gordon 2007:Figure 5), but also the houses of the European élite. The neoclassicism of the Renaissance world of Palladio, with its marble statues and colonnades, was now surpassed by all manner of portable antiquities, or "bric a brac," that could be installed in the grand houses of Europe, or indeed replicated (e.g., see Sir William Hamilton's portrait by David Allen—Trevelyan 1976:Figure 40).

Scholars such as Heinrich Schliemann and the British architect Sir John Soane (Amery and Curran 2002:157–160) imitated Pompeian wall-painting in their houses, signifying their social, cultural, and intellectual status. Indeed, Schliemann's entire house in Athens was painted with replicas to resemble a Pompeian house, using William Zahn's watercolors of Pompeian wall-paintings as his models (Zahn 1829–1859). Other followers of fashion also decorated parts of their dwellings in the Pompeian style (e.g., Pompeian Room in the Garden Pavilion, Buckingham Palace: Trevelyan 1976:Figure 64). Even in the farthest reaches of European influence, *Pompeiana* abounded. In Ballarat, one of the gold-rich towns in the State of Victoria in Australia, the center piece in the Pavilion of the History Museum, unveiled on August 3, 1888, was a sculptural group titled the "Flight from Pompeii" (http://www.ballarathistory.org/gardpavl.html). Its base is decorated with scenes from Bulwer Lytton's novel, *The Last Days of Pompeii* (1850), with the blind girl Nydia, unaffected by the darkness from the eruption, leading her friends to safety. The event was here being commemorated through its romantic reinterpretation in modern fiction.

Luckily for us, a more intellectual interest was taken by scholars such as Johannes Winckelmann who deplored the looting, secrecy, and incompetence that surrounded the early excavations of the Bourbon kings of Naples (see Leppmann 1971:175–185; Gordon 2007:43). During the nineteenth century, scholars such as Thomas Dyer (1867) and August Mau (1899) saw in these remains Roman life "frozen in time." Pompeii became a symbol of Roman urban life. It was seen as a provincial version of Rome—a typical Roman town that can give us detailed insights into Roman urban and domestic life in the first century AD. What we read about in the ancient literature is materialized in the remains from this Campanian market town.

If the material remains did not quite fit with the written, then they were made to do so. For example, Varro (*de Ling. Lat.*:V, 125) remembered that the so-called *cartibulum*, an oblong marble table stood near the *compluvium*, the opening in the roof in the *atrium*, when he was a young boy at the end of the second century BC. So the excavators at Pompeii moved the remains of a marble table, inscribed with the name "*P. Casca Longus,*" from its findspot in the back garden of what appears to have been both a shop and residence, House I 10,8–9 ([Figure 2]; see also Allison 2004:www.stoa.org/projects/ph/rooms?houseid=2), to the front hall of the neighboring grander house and renamed the latter the House of *P. Casca Longus,* now more commonly called the *Casa dei Quadretti teatrali* ([Figure 3]; see Allison 1992:52). In other words, if the original provenances of these artifacts did not fit the ideal of Roman domestic behavior, as evidenced in the written texts, then they were quickly made to do so.

The epigraphy, and particularly the electoral *programmata*, on the walls of the houses provide us with the names of the people who lived and worked in Pompeii. Many of these names were in the Latin format—*praenomen, nomen,* and *cognomen*—and some seemed to have tentative links with politically important families, such as Julius Polybius, a town magistrate, whose Greek *cognomen*, Polybius, is thought to signal his freed status, and his *nomen,* Julius, his status as an ex-slave of the imperial Julia family (e.g., de Franciscis 1988:30; compare Allison 2001:esp. 65–66).

So the eruption of Mt. Vesuvius has given us the best replica of daily life in Rome that we are ever likely to have. But how much has the focus on Pompeii for understanding Roman daily life misrepresented Pompeii's true place in the archaeology and history of Campania? The wealth of remains that were extant in AD 79, thanks to Mt. Vesuvius's eruption, have obscured investigation of Pompeii's development until that point, and investigations into these remains has destroyed any archaeological evidence of any later occupation of the immediate area. For some 200 years the exploration of Pompeii has concentrated on the evidence this event provides for Roman daily life in the first century AD. Here we have

FIGURE 2 Marble table legs in the garden of House I 10, 8–9 (A. Maiuri, *Notizie degli Scavi* [1929], Figure 22).

FIGURE 3 Front hall of the *Casa dei Quadretti teatrali*, with puteal moved from the garden and table legs moved from neighboring house (photo P. M. Allison).

a snapshot so rich that there seems no need to discover, or interest in, how this town had developed to this point, what were the factors that made it how it was, and what happened to this region after this eruption.

In the 1860s Giuseppi Fiorelli, who is credited with bringing scientific archaeology to Pompeii (see Trigger 2006:62–63, 290; Dwyer 2007), had carried out "standing buildings analyses" and isolated three phases of building at Pompeii (Fiorelli 1873: 78–84), which he identified as primitive (Tyrrhenian, i.e., Etruscan, and Pelagasian, according to Strabo, *Geog.*:5,4,8), Samnite, and Roman. August Mau (1882) and Robert Carrington (1933) refined these chronologies for both Pompeian architecture and wall-painting, also using "standing buildings analyses." In other words, these scholars developed artistic and architectural histories for Pompeii but did not investigate below the AD 79 ground level.

In the 1930s and '40s some excavations were carried out below this level, directed by the then Superintendent of the Naples region, Amedeo Maiuri (Maiuri 1942). However, Maiuri's excavations were largely to establish the "*Ultima fase edilizia di Pompei,*" the last building phase after the reported earthquake of AD 62. Maiuri aimed to establish what building had been carried out between these two major catastrophes—the AD 62 earthquake and the AD 79 eruption.

During 1960s and '70s when the archaeological systematics of the New Archaeologists provided the predominant paradigm (Trigger 2006:392–418) and Levi-Strauss's structuralism was in its ascendancy (Trigger 2006:463–464), Pompeian scholarship stagnated and was considered moribund. In 1977 the then Superintendent, Fausto Zevi, placed an embargo on any further excavation in Pompeii and called for restoration and documentation programs (Descoeudres et al. 1994:50). A major earthquake in 1980 awoke a widespread awareness of the urgency for such programs, leading Zevi's successor Giuseppina Cerulli Irelli to mount an international effort to record the extant excavated remains before they were damaged any further by earthquakes, eruptions, or general degradation. Grahame Barker had referred to my own tentative beginnings into Pompeian research at this time (see Allison 2002b) as "[my] study of a *wall* in Pompeii" (Barker personal communication 1984).

During the 1980s some excavation was indeed carried out but this was mainly limited either to outside the city or to rescue archaeology within it. The former led Stefano De Caro to conclude that the peripheral wall, thought to have been built by Roman colonists after 80 BC, had actually been built in the first half of the sixth century BC (for references see Geertman 2007:84–85). This indicated that the city, which was extant in AD 79, had already taken this form some 600 years earlier when this region was under Greek, or possibly Etruscan, domination (Arthur 1986:39).

Excavations carried out between 1980 and 1981 by Paul Arthur, from the Temple of Venus through the forum to the *Casa di Bacco*, to install new electrical cables to modern offices in the latter, revealed Greek-type architectural terracottas from the Temple of Apollo, and other sixth-century BC finds, that led Arthur to suggest Pompeii had been a trading port at the threshold of three cultural systems—Etruscan, Greek, and native (Arthur 1986). Arthur's excavations confirmed that this Sanctuary of Apollo dated back to the sixth century BC. Previous explorations (De Caro 2007:73) had also revealed votive offerings of early-sixth-century BC Middle Corinthian craters, imported from Greece. These finds point to the central place of the Greek god Apollo in the archaic city of Pompeii, and thus to strong Greek connections. However, De Caro also noted inscriptions on local Bucchero pottery that imply an Etruscan presence.

Since the late 1980s there has been a revival in Pompeian interests, both public and academic, and a burgeoning of Pompeian studies and excavation. Baldasarre Conticello resumed the excavations of Pompeian houses (see e.g., Varone 1988:147–151). He also granted excavation permits to a team from the University of Rome, La Sapienza (see Carafa 1997: esp. 15–20), and to foreign teams, such as an Anglo-American team, led by Rick Jones from Bradford University and Sara Bon from the University of North Carolina (see Bon et al. 1997), and a team from Reading University and the British School at Rome, led by Michael Fulford and Andrew Wallace-Hadrill (see Fulford and Wallace-Hadrill 1998).

John Dobbins from the University of Virginia, has also excavated around the forum, particularly in the Sanctuary of Apollo (Dobbins et al. 1998), and continued to refine the chronology of this early sanctuary and of Pompeii's principal public space. The Reading University team's excavations in Insula I, 8 revealed stone-built houses dating to the period 420–275 BC in the so-called *Neustadt* (Fulford and Wallace-Hadrill 1998:133); houses whose orientation followed the alignment of the final city layout. This part of the town was previously thought to have been laid out by the Romans, notably the colonists in 80 BC (see Laurence 1994:12–19; Gertmann 2007).

Thus, in the last decade or so concerted excavation efforts below the AD 79 level are starting to build up a history of Pompeii and its urban development, which had essentially been obscured by past interest in Pompeii as a resource and a time capsule for understanding Roman urban life in AD 79. Rather, they are producing a picture of a long-established pre-Roman urban system.

GREEKS IN POMPEII

But, as noted by Fiorelli and Mau, the extant remains of AD 79, without digging any deeper, can give us insights into a Pompeii that should not, even in the first century AD, be viewed as "typically Roman" but rather as part of the sociocultural network that had grown out of what is generally known as Magna Graecia—the area colonized by Greek city-states as early as the eighth century BC (Frederiksen 1984: esp. 54, 85–88).

Jos de Waele, from the University of Nijmegen, carried out largely above-ground investigations of the structure and decoration of Doric temple in the so-called Forum Triangolare (de Waele 2001). These investigations led him to argue that this was a Greek temple to the deities Athena and Heracles that, like the Temple of Apollo, was also built at the end of the sixth century BC (see also de Waele 1993).

The Latin epigraphy which has been used to demonstrate the "Romanness" of this town also gives insights into a "Greekness" that continued to play a significant role in Pompeii's social and political organization. The names of some of Pompeii's leading citizens during its last years suggest that these citizens had Greek ancestry, and that the supremacy of Greek families—which may well have predated the arrival of Sulla and the transposition of this town into a Roman colony (Cicero, *Pro Sulla*:60–62)—continued into its final phase of occupation. Despite the new Roman colonists, and the introduction of Latin, the descendents of the former inhabitants continued to play a leading role in the religious, political, and economic life of the town.

Greek family names (*nomina*) are found to be prominent in the Pompeii of AD 79. An example is the Eumachii (see Cooley 2004: esp. 98–101). The grandiose building on the east side of forum was dedicated by Eumachia and her son to Augustan Concord and Piety and, therefore, dates to the early first century AD (Cooley 2004:98–101). This Eumachia was a public priestess—for whom it is not clear—but the fullers (*fullones*) dedicated a statue to her (CIL X, 813; see Cooley 2004:100–101)) and a large and impressive tomb was built for her outside the Nocerian gate (see Cooley 2004:141–142). The Eumachia family also produced bricks, roof tiles, and amphorae (Allison 2006:cat. no. 310), some of which have reportedly been found in the south of France (Cooley 2004:172). This was a seemingly wealthy family who were influential in a number of spheres in Pompeii at the time of the eruption, but who could no doubt trace their ancestry back to the pre-Roman, Greek, occupants of Pompeii.

The *cognomina* of other leading citizens may also have been of Greek origin, but not necessarily as freed slaves, as is often argued (Andreau 1976:150; Mouritsen 1988:62). The aedile Julius Polybius, who possibly owned and lived in the large house that bore his electoral *programmata* and also graffiti referring to a Julius Phillipus, was very possibly not an imperial freedman, as has been concluded from his *nomen* and *cognomen* (de Franciscis 1988:30), but rather an enfranchised Greek whose family status in this Roman colony put him among the town's elite who could stand for and acquire high political office, and which also may have given him a connection with the Julia family (Allison 2001:67).

And why can we still see what has been considered a Hellenistic house, the House of the Faun (see Zanker 1993:41–52), which was extant at the time of the eruption? Its first-style wall-decoration, its famous Alexander mosaic, its peristyled gardens, and its dancing faun, in the center of the front hall, all date to the second century BC, before the establishment of the Roman colony. Why was the antique décor of this large and elegant house preserved and not modernized in the latest fashions? Was it still occupied by a wealthy and important pre-Roman family, possibly a Greek family judging by these decorative details, whose affluence and importance in Pompeii continued until the eruption?

Thus, even without further excavation into the earlier levels, it is possible to investigate the non-Roman aspects of Pompeian life and culture in the first century AD, if we stop looking at this town as a Roman city frozen in time.

Summary and Conclusions

It is often assumed that Pompeii's hellenization was a result of the Roman expansion in the Mediterranean and the hellenization process of Rome (e.g., Zanker 1993:40; Cooley 2004:5)—that Pompeii was a provincial version of things going on in Rome, rather than that the Pompeians and their neighbors were among the Hellenes who were instrumental in introducing Greek culture to Rome. Such assumptions are implicit in Laurence's perspective of a "Roman Pompeii" (Laurence 1994).

Scholarly focus on the eruption, on the city that it preserved, and on the limited historical information on Pompeii, has obscured the true nature of this town and its population in the first century AD. Pompeii was not "a little Rome." It certainly had an administrative system that reflected that at Rome, but there is evidence that this system predated the Roman colonization of the town (Cooley 2004:5, 8–11).

Pompeii in AD 79 had a long history of being part of Magna Graecia. If Mt. Vesuvius had not erupted would we understand this better? Focus of scholarship on the event—"the frozen moment" of popular mythology (e.g. Augusti 1967:15; Binford 1981:205; compare Allison 2004:202)—has long obscured information on structural change that can be found both in the remains left by the eruption and in the layers now being excavated beneath.

Effects of the eruption on the productivity of region today (not least in tourism) far outweigh any negative effects of this event may have had on the productivity of Campania in the first century AD (Allison 2002a:119–121). And the effects of the eruption on scholarship into Roman urban and domestic life in the first century AD have submerged investigations into Pompeii's place in the history of the region and also Pompeii's place in our investigations of that history.

So the eruption of Mt. Vesuvius had little impact on the society and economy of the Bay of Naples. The importance of this eruption is what it has done for the disciplines of archaeology and art history. However, the material record has so overwhelmed Pompeian scholars that they have been slow to look beyond the event to its impact on the history of the region, and to our abilities to explore it. In the last decade, Pompeian scholarship has started to catch up with events in other historical disciplines, using the material remains at Pompeii to investigate the "*longue durée*" and moving away from an event-centered history.

Thus, this catastrophic event did not change history, but rather it has constricted our understanding of that history. Pompeian research has been concerned with using primary sources but, until the last decade or so, it has not really actually shown much interest in the historical narrative or given much thought to what Sewell calls the "temporalities of social life" (Sewell 2005:4). To take a small, but pertinent, example, if Varro remembered (*de Ling. Lat.*:V, 125) that the *cartibulum* had stood near the *compluvium* at the end of the second century BC, why would such tables still be standing in this position in this South Italian town toward the end of the first century AD? Surely this signals that Pompeii is not a "little Rome"? Why have Pompeian scholars shown little interest in such temporalities of domestic and social life, but have preferred to concertina all extant remains to investigate Roman domestic life in the early Empire? They too have been devastated by the eruption.

In summary, the eruption of Mt. Vesuvius had little impact on Roman society in the first century AD, and affected only a small proportion of Campanian society. In contrast, it has had a huge impact on approaches to Roman society across the modern world—both scholarly approaches and wider public interest. But, the concentration of scholarship on this event has created a "micro-history" (Sewell 2005:74–78) that has misrepresented Pompeii's place in Roman, and pre-Roman, Campania and has also misrepresented the role of its remains in helping us to investigate the impact of the Greek cities of South Italy on the emerging center of Rome—its social and cultural behaviors. Only very recently have Pompeian, and Roman, scholars looked more critically at large-scale processes beyond the event that so caught everyone's imagination—and still does.

So, the eruption of Mt Vesuvius was a significant natural event which continues to have a significant impact on archaeology, but it was not a significant historical event.

ACKNOWLEDGMENTS

I am grateful to the *Soprintendenza archeologica di Pompei* and particularly to Prof. Pietro Giovanni Guzzo and Dr Antonio Varone, for permission to carry out my research in Pompeii. I would like to thank Doug Bolander and the Institute for European and Mediterranean Archaeology at the University of Buffalo for their invitation to take part in this conference and for their kind hospitality. I wish the Institute a prosperous and eventful future.

References Cited

ABBREVIATIONS

CIL = *Corpus Inscriptionum Latinarum*

ANCIENT SOURCES

Cicero *Pro Sulla*. Translated by C. MacDonald, 1997. Loeb Classical Library. William Heinemann, London and Harvard University Press, Cambridge.

Dio Cassius *Roman History*. Translated by E. Cary, 1974. Loeb Classical Library. William Heinemann, London and Harvard University Press, Cambridge.

Martial *Epigrams*. Translated by W. C. A. Ker, 1919. Loeb Classical Library. William Heinemann, London and Harvard University Press, Cambridge.

Pliny *Epistulae: The Letters of the Younger Pliny*. Translated by B. Radice, 1963. Penguin Books, Harmondsworth.

Seneca *Natural Questions*. Translated by T. H. Corcoran, 1972. Loeb Classical Library. William Heinemann, London and Harvard University Press, Cambridge.

Suetonius *De Vita Caesarum*. Translated by J. C. Rolfe, 1951. Loeb Classical Library. William Heinemann, London and Harvard University Press, Cambridge.

Statius *Silvae*. Translated by D. R. Shackleton Bailey, 2003. Loeb Classical Library. William Heinemann, London and Harvard University Press, Cambridge.

Strabo *Geography*. Translated by J. L. Jones, 1949. Loeb Classical Library. William Heinemann, London and Harvard University Press, Cambridge.

Tacitus *Annals*. Translated by J. Jackson, 1962. Loeb Classical Library. William Heinemann, London and Harvard University Press, Cambridge.

Tacitus *Histories*. Translated by J. Jackson, 1962. Loeb Classical Library. William Heinemann, London and Harvard University Press, Cambridge.

Tertullian *Apology*. Translated by T. R. Glover, 1953. Loeb Classical Library. William Heinemann, London and Harvard University Press, Cambridge.

Vellieus Paterculus *History of Rome*. Translated by F. W. Shipley, 1924. Loeb Classical Library. William Heinemann, London and Harvard University Press, Cambridge.

Varro *De Lingua Latina*. Translated by R. G. Kent, 1958. Loeb Classical Library. William Heinemann, London and Harvard University Press, Cambridge.

MODERN SOURCES

Allison, P. M. 1992 Artefact Assemblages: Not the Pompeii Premise. In *Papers of the Fourth Conference of Italian Archaeology, London 1990* 3, pt I, edited by E. Herring, R. Whitehouse, and J. Wilkins, pp. 49–56. Accordia Research Centre, London.

Allison, P. M. 2001 Placing Individuals: Pompeian Epigraphy in Context, *Journal of Mediterranean Archaeology* 14(1):54–75.

Allison, P. M. 2002a Recurring Tremors: The Continuing Impact of the AD 79 Eruption of Mt Vesuvius. In *Natural Disasters and Cultural Change*, edited by R. Torrence and J. Grattan, pp. 107–125. One World Archaeology series, Routledge, London and New York.

Allison, P. M. 2002b *Casa della Caccia Antica*. Hirmer, Munich.2004 (reprinted 2005)*Pompeian Household: An Analysis of the Material Culture*. Monograph 42, Cotsen Institute for Archaeology, UCLA, Los Angeles (online companion www.stoa.org/pompeianhouseholds/).

Allison, P. M. 2006 *The Insula of the Menander in Pompeii volume iii: The Finds, a Contextual Study*. Oxford University Press, Oxford.

Amery, C. and B. Curran Jr. 2002 *The Lost World of Pompeii*. With an Introduction by Andrew Wallace-Hadrill. Francis Lincoln Ltd, London.

Andreau, J. 1974 *Les affaires de Monsieur Jucundus*. École française de Rome, Rome.

Arthur, P. 1986 Problems of the Urbanization of Pompeii: Excavations 1980–1981. *The Antiquaries Journal* 66:29–44.

Augusti, S. 1967 *I colori pompeiani*. De Luca, Roma.

Binford, L. R. 1981 Behavioral Archaeology and the "Pompeii Premise." *Journal of Anthropological Research* 37:195–208.

Bon, S. E., R. Jones, B. Kurchin, and D. J. Robinson 1997 The Context of the House of the Surgeon: Investigations in Insula VI, 1 at Pompeii. In *Sequence and Space in Pompeii*, edited by S. E. Bon and R. Jones, pp. 32–49. Oxbow, Oxford.

Bulwer Lytton, Baron E. G. 1850 *The Last Days of Pompeii: Lucretia, or, the Children of the Night* (first published 1834)**.** Chapman and Hall, London.

Carafa, P. 1997 What Was Pompeii before 200 B.C.? Excavations of the House of Joseph II, in the Triangular Forum and in the House of the Wedding of Hercules. In *Sequence and Space in Pompeii*, edited by S. E. Bon and R. Jones, pp. 13–31. Oxbow, Oxford.

Carrington, R. C. 1933 Notes on the Building Materials of Pompeii. *Journal of Roman Studies* 23:125–138.

Cooley, A. 2004 *Pompeii: A Sourcebook*. Routledge, London.

De Caro, S. 2007 The First Sanctuaries. In *The World of Pompeii*, edited by J. J. Dobbins and P. W. Foss, pp. 73–81. Routledge, London.

De Franciscis, A. 1988 La Casa di C. Julius Polybius. *Rivista di Studi Pompeiani* 2:15–36.

Descoeudres, J.-P., P. Allison, R. Carson, P. Connor et al. 1994 *Pompeii Rediscovered: The Life and Death of a Roman Town*. Meditarch, Sydney.

De Waele, J. A. K. E. 1993 The "Doric" Temple on the Forum Triangulare in Pompeii. *Opuscula Romana* 3: 105–118.

De Waele, J. A. K. E. 2001 *Il tempio dorico del Foro triangolare di Pompei*. Erma di Bretschneider, Rome.

Dobbins, J. J., L. F. Ball, J. C. Cooper, S. L. Gavel, and S. Hay 1998 Excavations in the Sanctuary of Apollo at Pompeii, 1997. *American Journal of Archaeology* 102(4):739–756.

Dwyer, E. 2007 Science or Morbid Curiosity? The Casts of Giuseppe Fiorelli and the Last Days of Romantic Pompeii. In *Antiquity Recovered: The Legacy of Pompeii and Herculaneum*, edited by V. C. Gardener Coates and J. L. Seydl, pp. 171–188. The J. Paul Getty Museum, Los Angeles.

Dyer Thomas H. 1867 *Pompeii: Its History, Buildings and Antiquities*. Bell and Daldy, London.

Fiorelli, G. 1873 *Gli Scavi di Pompei dal 1861 al 1872*. Relazione al Ministro della Istruzione Pubblica. Tipografia del Regno nel Liceo. V. Emanuele, Naples.

Frederiksen, M. 1985 *Campania*. British School at Rome, London.

Fulford, M., and A. F. Wallace-Hadrill 1998 Unpeeling Pompeii. *Antiquity* 72:128–145.

Gertmann, H. 2007 The Urban Development of the Pre-Roman City. In *The World of Pompeii*, edited by J. J. Dobbins and P. W. Foss, pp. 82–97. Routledge, London.

Gordon, A. R. 2007 Subverting the Secret of Herculaneum: Archaeological Espionage in the Kingdom of Naples. In *Antiquity Recovered: The Legacy of Pompeii and Herculaneum*, edited by V. C. Gardener Coates and J. L. Seydl, pp. 37–57. The J. Paul Getty Museum, Los Angeles.

Laurence, R. 1994 *Roman Pompeii: Space and Society*. Routledge, London.

Leppmann, W. 1971 *Winckelmann*. Victor Gollancz, London.

Maiuri, A. 1942 *L'Ultima Fase Edilizia di Pompei*. Istituto di Studi Romani, Rome.

Mau, A. 1882 *Geschichte der decorativen Wandmalerei in Pompeji*. Reimer, Berlin.

Mau, A. 1899 *Pompei: Its Life and Art*. Translated by Francis W. Kelsey. Macmillan Company, New York and London.

Mouritsen, H. 1988 *Elections, Magistrates and Municipal Élite: Studies in Pompeian Epigraphy*. L'Erma di Bretschneider, Roma.

Pappalardo, U. 1990 L'eruzione pliniana del Vesuvio nel 79 d.C: Ercolano. In *Volcanology and Archaeology: Proceedings of the European Workshops of Ravello, November 19–27, 1987 and March 30–31, 1989*, edited by C. A. Livadie, F. Widemann, pp. 197–215. Council of Europe, Strasbourg.

Sewell, W. H. Jr. 2005 *Logics of History: Social Theory and Social Transformation*. University of Chicago Press, Chicago.

Tchernia, A. 1981 Quelques remarques sur le commerce du vin et le amphores. In *The Seaborne Commerce of Ancient Rome: Studies in Archaeology and History*, edited by J. H. D'Arms and E. C. Kopff, pp. 301–312. Memoires of the American Academy in Rome 36, Rome.

Trevelyan, R. 1976 *The Shadow of Vesuvius: Pompeii AD 79*. The Folio Society, London.

Trigger, B. G. 2006 *A History of Archaeological Thought*. 2nd edition. Cambridge University Press, Cambridge.

Varone, A. 1988 Attività dell'Ufficio Scavi. *Rivista di Studi Pompeiani* II:143–154.

Zahn, W. 1828–1859 *Die schönsten Ornamente und merkwürdigsten Gemälden aus Pompeji, Herculaneum und Stabiae I–III*. G. Reimer, Berlin.

Zanker, P. 1993 *Pompei: società, immagini urbane e forme dell'abitare*. Translated by Andrea Zambrini. Giulio Einaudi, Torino.

Chapter Eleven

Testing Eventful Archaeologies

Eventful Archaeology and Volcanic "Disasters"

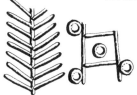

John P. Grattan

Abstract *There has been a boom in archaeological research focused on the effects of ancient catastrophes on cultural change. A great deal of the literature examining the role of natural disasters in human history is sensationalist and based on unproven correlation and impact. A more useful approach utilizes sound analyses that clearly demonstrate causation. Well researched, balanced case studies make the most important contribution to our understanding of how human societies have lived and coped with environmental perturbations. One of the aims of this paper, therefore, is to present studies that take a penetrating and critical view of whether and how disasters have shaped the past. Sewell rightly argues that "A single isolated rupture rarely has the effect of transforming structures because standard procedures and sanctions can usually repair the torn fabric of social practice." In the case of natural disasters, as the examples presented here will demonstrate, the event is incidental; it is context which is king.*

In general, popularist treatments of ancient disasters and their obsession for death, destruction, and flight have been grossly overstated. In contrast, many of the case studies showed that human societies have been incredibly resilient and have recovered remarkably well despite having experienced wide-scale destruction and/or significant mortality. The case studies presented here show that by adopting wider perspectives social scientists can mobilize historical studies together with the information contained in oral history and ideologies to achieve a rich understanding of how human societies have experienced, coped with and used volcanic events. The new picture that is emerging is colored not only by death, destruction, and collapse, but also by recovery, regeneration, and creation of new environments and cultural patterns.

Events in the Archaeological Record: A Useful Concept?

The proposal by Beck et al. (2007) that Sewell's concept of an event offers a theoretical vocabulary by which change in the archaeological record may be explained creates a useful opportunity to discuss the processes by which structural transformations may come about and be recognized in the archaeological record. We should note that Sewell was concerned with historical rather than archaeological events; the drafting of the Magna Carta, Luther nailing his complaint to the door of Worms Cathedral, the American Declaration of Independence, are but a few of the many examples that could be cited in support of Sewell's thesis. In respect of the archaeological record, however, it is the contention of this chapter that key events are seldom clearly identified and that the pursuit of them in archaeological research may tempt the researcher into adopting a monocausal and narrowly deterministic research paradigm. Archaeological research is easily corrupted by determinism and the adoption of a research focus on the "event" may really be thinly disguised "eventful determinism." This paper contends that structural change in the archaeological record can rarely be ascribed with confidence to the operation of a single mechanism but rather that archaeological research may seek to identify crucial vulnerabilities that may influence critical thresholds.

A further potential problem in the adoption of this paradigm is the issue of scale and how it is recognized; a structural transformation in the life of one individual or the organization of one archaeological site may not be seen as at all significant by the overarching culture, while equally the reverse may also be true. Surely, there is a continuum of event, response, and transformation operating from the scale of the individual to the culture. Why maintain a research focus on change at all? Should we be surprised that change takes place? Decision making at any scale is likely to lead to change, as will fluctuation in a myriad of environmental factors. Therefore, the variability of natural environmental processes and the pressures they apply on all human scales from the individual to the civilization need to be acknowledged as normal, not as unusual. The structural transformation paradigm, rather, implies that stasis is the norm and that its disturbance or transformation is significant. This paper will propose the contrary viewpoint, that change and transformation are actually the constants in human culture and that it is stasis which is unusual and needs to be explained by social theory.

Testing the Paradigm

This chapter now explores the impact of unchallengeable events in the archaeological record; there can be no more powerful potentially transformative event than a volcanic eruption; it is therefore useful to consider their impact and subsequent cultural responses in the light of Beck et al.'s proposal.

There has been a recent boom in archaeological research focused on the effects of large-scale geophysical processes on cultural change (Bawden and Reycraft 2001; Grattan and Torrence 2007; Hoffman and Oliver-Smith 2002; Oliver-Smith and Hoffman 1999; McCoy and Heiken 2000; McGuire et al. 2000; Torrence and Grattan 2002a). However, a great deal of the literature examining the role of natural disasters as significant events in human history is based on unproven correlation and uncertain detail as to the specific mechanisms by which the culture was affected.

A more useful approach utilizes sound analyses that clearly and unambiguously demonstrate causation. Well-researched, balanced case studies make the most important contribution to our understanding of how human societies have lived and coped with environmental perturbations (Torrence and Grattan 2002b). One of the aims of this chapter, therefore, is to present studies that take a penetrating and critical view of whether and how disasters have shaped the past. Sewell (2005) rightly argues that "[a] single isolated rupture rarely has the effect of transforming structures because standard procedures and sanctions can usually repair the torn fabric of social practice." If we use natural disasters as "isolated ruptures" many of the examples presented below will demonstrate that the event is incidental; it is context which is king.

Already, studies along these lines have produced some surprises, as illustrated in Torrence and Grattan (2002a). The book demonstrated that, in general, popularist treatments of ancient disasters and their obsession with death, destruction, and flight have been grossly overstated. In contrast, many of the case studies showed that human societies have been incredibly resilient and have recovered remarkably well despite having experienced wide-scale destruction and/or significant mortality (Moseley 2002:194, 211). The few examples of collapse were limited to disasters with very high-magnitude environmental agents or involved societies that were unstable or already in decline (Siebe et al. 1996; Mastrolorenzo et al. 2006; Leroy 2006). A second way that modern approaches to natural disasters have influenced scholarship is through shifting the primary focus away from the strength of the environmental forcing mechanism as the primary agent of change to the vulnerability of past societies (Torrence and Grattan 2002b). Disasters are now seen as social rather than simply environmental phenomena (Whittell 2009; Shimoyama 2002; Oliver-Smith 2002). Although current thinking is clearly an improvement over the previous separation of environmental and social science approaches to disasters, the new emphasis on vulnerability has meant that people are mainly conceived of as helpless "victims," which detailed archaeological research clearly shows to be wrong. Here again it is clear that it is the social context of the event, at scales ranging from the individual to the culture, that is important, rather than the event itself. In the next section of this chapter, volcanic events will be considered, moving forward in time from 75,000 years BP to the present day and in scale from the rare planet-chilling Super Eruption to the more mundane city-threatening volcanic eruption.

Volcanic Events

The Toba Super Eruption: Genetic Bottlenecks and Volcanic Winters

The debates surrounding the impact of the last eruption of the Toba Supervolcano neatly encapsulate the concerns expressed above. By any empirical measure a significant volcanic event, the debate surrounding its impact on climate and human evolution illustrates the problems inherent in adopting an event-biased research paradigm and the determinist approach this encourages. This eruption occurred shortly before a period of intense glaciation and coincided with an apparent profound genetic bottleneck in human mitochondrial DNA, and has been blamed in the academic literature for causing both (Ambrose 1998; Rampino and Ambrose 2000; Rampino and Self 1993a and b). Recent research discounts the climatic influence of the Toba event, the magnitude of the eruption and even the nature of the genetic bottleneck (Gathorne-Hardy and Harcourt-Smith, 2003; Oppenheimer 2002).

This example encapsulates the problem with the adoption of an eventful research paradigm. Here several apparent events in the Quaternary and biological record are identified and associated on the assumption that the eruption must have been the cause. Later research can be seen to challenge the basis for this. The search for ruptures and transformations will inevitably lead to erroneous association and assertion and stifle hypothesis-driven research.

SANTORINI AND THE COLLAPSE OF MINOAN CIVILIZATION

The ongoing debate as to the impact of the Bronze Age eruption of the volcano Santorini on Minoan civilization Crete illustrates the pitfalls of an eventful approach. As a significant physical event the eruption has been associated temporally, though vaguely, with a cultural event, the demise of Minoan civilization; in effect, much research seeks to prove that the structural transformation is explained by the eruptive event. However, it is clear from careful reading of the published archaeological research that the case for a catastrophic environmental impact capable of critically weakening Minoan culture is simply not proven; indeed, there is no volcanic mechanism identified that is unequivocally capable of doing so (Driessen 2002; Manning and Sewell 2002; McCoy and Heiken 2000).

HEKLA 3 AND "THE TIME OF DARKNESS"

A further problem inherent in the adoption of an eventful approach to archaeological research is that it may lead to the development and reinforcement of circular arguments. The production of a an ice core chronology of volcanic sulphate (Hammer 1984) and a tree ring chronology (Baillie 1989) was coupled with one interpretation of the archaeological record (Burgess 1985) and developed into a hypothesis that argued that a relatively modest volcanic event, the c. 1100 BC eruption of the Icelandic volcano Hekla was responsible for a worldwide volcano-climate crisis (Burgess 1989), a crisis that grew in the telling into a 20-year-long volcanic winter "a time of darkness" (BBC TV broadcast March 23, 1992). Subsequent dispassionate paleoenvironmental research undermined the whole edifice of related events and structural transformations, the precision of the ice core chronology was called into question, the date of the eruption was moved, the archaeological abandonment was disproved and the climatic impact of the eruption was shown to be extremely minor, not catastrophic (Buckland et al. 1997; Charman et al. 1992; Grattan 1998; Grattan et al. 1999; Sadler and Grattan 1999). It is worth noting that despite the weight of academic research, which has completely disproved the giant eruption = catastrophic weather = cultural collapse hypothesis, the Bronze Age volcanic catastrophic event has become so insidiously embedded in Scottish archaeology that it has so far proved impossible to dislodge, and the "time of darkness" remains an article of faith. Thus, what was clearly an event-driven research paradigm linked together disparate trains of environmental research and combined them to explain a cultural transformation. Baillie (1991) described this approach as "suck in and smear," where he showed how imprecisely dated and unrelated events could easily become associated through the murky imprecision of most archaeological dating methods.

VOLCANO WEATHER AND MARGINAL ENVIRONMENTS

A further test of the eventful paradigm can be made by considering the relationship between volcanic eruptions, poor climate, harvest failure, and famine in marginal environments. Climatically marginal environments are sensitive to slight fluctuations in climate, so even modest volcanogenic modification of weather might be expected to induce stress and cause a cultural response. Indeed, if one considers an agriculturally marginal environment such as the highlands of Scotland, it is possible to identify severe famines coincident with Icelandic volcanic eruptions. The focus on the volcanic event is however misplaced. If one simply considers the incidence of famine in the Scottish highlands throughout the medieval and into the modern period it is clear that famine occurred in one out of three years, regardless of any distant volcanic process. Thus, in this context the famine event is actually normal, not unusual, and any link with a volcanic event fortuitous at best (Dodgshon et al. 2000). Here again the eventful paradigm is seen to be next to useless; certainly it would not identify the social and economic factors deeply embedded in Highland society that actually were the root cause of most of the famines throughout Scottish history.

MEGA EVENTS AND HISTORY: THE LAKI FISSURE ERUPTION

Focusing on a massive volcanic event can be equally misleading. Within a typical window of opportunity afforded by archaeological dating methods, the huge eruption of Laki Fissure in 1783 could be held responsible for destruction layers and oral histories associated with the American War of Independence, the French Revolution and the Napoleonic Wars, and, even if dating was poor, with the Wars of the Spanish Succession and the Franco Prussian War. Of course it was responsible for none of these and though the impacts of the eruption at the time were extreme it had no lasting impact and, outside Iceland, was swiftly forgotten (Brayshay and Grattan 1999; Grattan and Brayshay 1995). A research paradigm grounded in events and looking for transformation in the archaeological record could easily be misled by a volcanic event of this magnitude.

THE CONTEXT IS THE KEY: VOLCANO WEATHER AND THE TAMBORA ERUPTION

A further pitfall for the eventful paradigm is the inherent assumption that we can see the past clearly and understand mechanisms and events. We cannot. A very clear illustration of this problem can be seen in the eruption of the Indonesian volcano Tambora and European weather in 1816. The Tambora eruption was huge, the biggest known eruption of the past 12,000 years. Modification of the weather was severe, with 1816 being recorded in Europe and North America as "Eighteen hundred and froze to death" and "the year without a summer" (Post 1977; Stommel and Stommel 1979). In Europe the disruption of atmospheric circulation patterns led to catastrophic rainfall, low temperatures, and famine (Harington 1992). One might therefore assume that volcano weather was bad news for everyone in Europe. In fact, the very circulation disruption that brought rainfall and famine to the Netherlands, France, and Germany (Lamb 1992), brought beneficial climatic conditions and a bumper harvest to Denmark (Kington 1992). Perhaps more significantly, the induced famine in the countries to the south meant that Danish farmers enjoyed high prices for their grain (Neumann 1990). Famine and plenty, occurring within a few hundred miles of each other caused by the disruption of global weather by a volcanic eruption half the world away and a year earlier!

The work of Houle et al. (2007) also illustrates very clearly that we cannot always anticipate the nuances inherent in events. This work noted the severity and longevity of winters associated with volcanic events as indicated by the extent of the winter ice bridge on the St Lawrence River, Canada. They noted that major volcanic events, in particular the Tambora eruption, led to severe freezing and the formation of massive ice bridges. But they also noted that the size and longevity of the ice bridge actually facilitated and encouraged economic development and trade between areas otherwise isolated from each other; the weather was severe but the economic impact was positive. Within the archaeological record such a nuanced consequence would be impossible to identify. We could date the eruption and note the severe temperatures, but we would assume entirely negative consequences from such an event.

DISCUSSION

When a much wider range of potential outcomes are considered, one discovers a complex mix of responses to extreme events. Most significantly, even with a focus on extreme events, unanticipated creative as well as destructive effects on human societies are commonly observed. The key to this approach is the consideration of vulnerability, disaster, and recovery as a process that unfolds over a reasonably long period of time (Oliver-Smith and Hoffman 2002) and not event-driven. Scholars who have examined disasters over the long term have often found that their effects can linger on for a long time and/or be used and reinterpreted by subsequent societies (Blong 1982; Elson et al. 2002; Galipaud 2002; Lowe et al. 2002; Plunket and Uruñuela 1998). Humans have not just responded to their environment, even when coping with the consequences of catastrophic events. Instead, people often move beyond the devastating initial impacts and respond in a myriad of creative and fascinating ways.

Focusing on the evidence provided by a single devastated site can be misleading. Pompeii was destroyed but the wider Roman world was unaffected (Allison 2002), numerous structures have been destroyed by volcanic activity in Mexico but the cultures affected responded vigorously to the pressure. In Japan reconstruction of destroyed villages depended more on the will and energy of the controlling authority than on the magnitude of the event (Shimoyama 2002).

An archaeology of events need also take account of what we do not know! The ice core record suggests that there have been many more significant eruptions in human history than we currently know of. Indeed, the greatest of these, in AD 1258, was unknown until recently and inevitably would have had an impact on vulnerable communities around the world.

The case studies presented here show that the eventful paradigm limits archaeological research and that it is only by adopting wider perspectives and flexible hypotheses that archaeologists and environmental and social scientists can hope to achieve a rich understanding of how human societies have experienced, coped with, and used volcanic events. An eventful paradigm with a volcanic focus would emphasis the narrow negative when in reality the picture is colored by recovery, regeneration, and creation of new environments and cultural patterns. Extreme events have been very powerful factors in human history, but the consequences have not all been negative (Grattan and Torrence 2007).

References Cited

Allison, P. 2002 Recurring Tremors: The Continuing Impact of the AD79 Eruption of Mt. Vesuvius. In *Natural Disasters and Cultural Change*, edited by R. Torrence and J. Grattan, pp. 107–125. Routledge, London.

Ambrose, S.H. 1998 Late Pleistocene Human Bottlenecks, Volcanic Winter, and Differentiation of Modern Humans. *Journal of Human Evolution* 34:623–651.

Baillie, M. G. L. 1989 Hekla 3: How Big Was It? *Endeavour, New Series* 13:78–81.

Baillie, M. G. L. 1991 Suck In and Smear, Two Related Chronological Problems for the 90's. *Journal of Theoretical Archaeology* 2:12–16.

Bawden, G., and R. M. Reycraft 2001 *Environmental Disaster and the Archaeology of Human Response*. Maxwell Museum of Anthropology, University of New Mexico Albuquerque.

Beck, R. A., D. J. Bolender, J. A. Brown, and T. K. Earle 2007 Eventful Archaeology. *Current Archaeology* 48(6):833–860.

Blong, R. 1982 *The Time of Darkness: Local Legends and Volcanic Reality in Papua New Guinea*. University of Washington Press, Seattle.

Brayshay, M., and J. Grattan 1999 Environmental and Social Responses in Europe to the 1783 Eruption of the Laki Fissure Volcano in Iceland: A Consideration of Contemporary Documentary Evidence. In *Volcanoes in the Quaternary*, edited by C. Firth and W. McGuire, pp. 173–188. Geological Society, London.

Buckland, P. C., A. J. Dugmore, and K. J. Edwards 1997 Bronze Age Myths? Volcanic Activity and Human Response in the Mediterranean and North Atlantic Regions. *Antiquity* 71:581–593.

Burgess, C. 1985 Population, Climate and Upland Settlement. In *Upland settlement in Northern Britain*, edited by Colin Burgess, pp. 195–229. B.A.R. British Series 143, Oxford.

Burgess, C. 1989 Volcanoes, Catastrophe and the Global Crisis of the Late Second Millennium BC. *Current Archaeology* 117:325–329.

Charman, D. J., J. P. Grattan, S. West, and A. Kelly 1995 Environmental Response to Tephra Deposition in the Strath of Kildonan, Northern Scotland. *Journal of Archaeological Science* 22(6):799–809.

Dodgshon, R. A, D. D. Gilbertson, and J. P. Grattan 2000 Endemic Stress, Farming Communities and the Influence of Volcanic Eruptions in the Scottish Highlands In *The Archaeology of*

Geological Catastrophes, edited by W. McGuire, D. R. Griffiths, P. L. Hancock, and I. S. Stewart, pp. 267–280. Geological Society, London.

Driessen, J. 2002 Towards an Archaeology of Crisis: Defining the Long Term Impact of the Bronze Age Santorini Eruption. In *Natural Disasters and Cultural Change,* edited by R. Torrence and J. Grattan, pp. 250–263. Routledge, London.

Elson, M, M. Ort, J. Hesse, and W. Duffield 2002 Lava, Corn, and Ritual in the Northern Southwest. *American Antiquity* 67: 119–135.

Gathorne-Hardy, F. J., and W. E. H. Harcourt-Smith 2003 The Super Eruption of Toba, Did It Cause a Genetic Bottleneck? *Journal of Human Evolution,* 45: 227–230.

Galipaud, J.-C. 2002 Under the Volcano: Ni-Vanuatu and Their Environment. In *Natural Disasters and Cultural Change,* edited by R. Torrence and J. Grattan, pp. 162–171. Routledge, London.

Grattan. J. 1998 The Response of Marginal Societies and Ecosystems in Britain to Icelandic Volcanic Eruptions. In *Life on the Edge: Human Settlement and Marginality,* edited by C. Mills and G. Coles, pp. 21–30. Oxbow Books, Oxford.

Grattan, J. P., and M. B. Brayshay 1995 An Amazing and Portentous Summer: Environmental and Social Responses in Britain to the 1783 Eruption of an Iceland Volcano. *The Geographical Journal* 161(2): 125–134.

Grattan J. P., D. D. Gilbertson, and D. J. Charman 1999 Modelling the Impact of Icelandic Volcanic Eruptions upon the Prehistoric Societies and Environment of Northern and Western Britain. In *Volcanoes in the Quaternary*, edited by C. Firth and W. McGuire, pp. 109–124. Geological Society, London.

Grattan, J. P., and R. Torrence 2007 Beyond Doom and Gloom: The Long Term Consequences of Volcanic Disasters. In *Living under the Shadow: The Cultural Impacts of Volcanic Eruptions,* edited by J. Grattan and R. Torrence, pp. 1–19. Left Coast Press, Walnut Creek, CA.

Grattan, J. P., and R. Torrence (editors) 2007 *Living under the Shadow: The Cultural Impacts of Volcanic Eruptions*. Left Coast Press, Walnut Creek, CA.

Hammer, C. U. 1984 Traces of Icelandic Eruptions in the Greenland Ice Sheet. *Jökull* 34: 51–65.

Harington, C. R. (editor) 1992 *The Year without a Summer.* Canadian Museum of Nature, Ottawa.

Hoffman, S. M., and A. Oliver-Smith 2002 *Catastrophe and Culture: The Anthropology of Disaster.* School of American Research Press, Santa Fe.

Houle, D., J. D. Moore, and J. Provencher 2007 Ice Bridges on the St Lawrence as an Index of Winter Severity from 1620–1920. *Journal of Climate* 20: 757–764.

Kington, J. A. 1992 Weather Patterns over Europe in 1816. In *The Year without a Summer* edited by C. R. Harington, pp. 358–371. Canadian Museum of Nature, Ottawa.

Lamb, H. H. 1992 First Essay at Reconstructing the General Atmospheric Circulation in 1816 and the Early Nineteenth Century. In *The Year without a Summer* edited by C. R. Harington, pp. 355–357. Canadian Museum of Nature, Ottawa.

Leroy, S. A. G., H. Jousee, and M. Cremaschi 2006 Dark Nature: Responses of Humans and Ecosystems to Rapid Environmental Change. *Quaternary International* 151: 1–3.

Lowe, D, R. Newnham, and J. McCraw 2002 Volcanism and Early Maori Society in New Zealand. In *Natural Disasters and Cultural Change,* edited by R. Torrence and J. Grattan, pp. 126–161. Routledge, London.

Manning, S., and D. A. Sewell 2002 Volcanoes and History: A Significant Relationship? In *Natural Disasters and Cultural Change,* edited by R. Torrence and J. Grattan, pp. 264–291. Routledge, London.

Mastrolorenzo, G., L. Pappalardo, C. Troise, A. Panizza, and G. Natale 2006 Volcanic Hazard Assessment at the Campi Flegrei Caldera. In *Geological Society, London, Special Publications*, 269: 159–171.

McCoy, F. W., and G. W. Heiken 2000 The Late Bronze Age Explosive Eruption of Thera (Santorini), Greece: Regional and Local Effects. In *Volcanic Hazards and Disasters in Human Antiquity,* edited by F. McCoy and G. Heiken, pp. 43–70. Geological Society of America, Boulder.

McCoy, F., and G. Heiken (editors) 2000 *Volcanic Hazards and Disasters in Human Antiquity.* Geological Society of America, Boulder.

McGuire, W. J., D. R. Griffiths, P. L. Hancock, and I. S. Stewart (editors) 2000 *The Archaeology of Geological Catastrophes.* The Geological Society, London.

Moseley, M. 2002 Modelling Protracted Drought, Collateral Natural Disaster, and Human Responses in the Andes. In *Catastrophe and Culture*, edited by S. Hoffman and A. Oliver-Smith, pp. 187–212. School of American Research, Santa Fe.

Neumann, J. 1990 The 1810s in the Baltic Region, 1816 in Particular: Air Temperatures, Grain Supply and Mortality. *Climatic Change* 17(1): 97–120.

Oliver-Smith, A. 2002 Theorizing Disasters: Nature, Power, and Culture. In *Catastrophe and Culture*, edited by S. Hoffman and A. Oliver-Smith, pp. 23–48. School of American Research, Santa Fe.

Oliver-Smith, A., and S. M. Hoffman 1999 *The Angry Earth: Disaster in Anthropological Perspective.* Routledge, London and New York.

Oppenheimer, C. 2002 Limited Global Change Due to the Largest Known Quaternary Eruption, Toba ~74Kyr BP? *Quaternary Science Reviews* 21: 1593–1609.

Post, J. D. 1977 *The Last Great Subsistence Crisis of the Western World.* John Hopkins University Press, Baltimore.

Plunket, P., and G. Uruñuela 1998 The Impact of Popocatépetl Volcano on Preclassic Settlement in Central Mexico. *Quaternaire* 9: 53–59.

Rampino, M., and S. Ambrose 2000 Volcanic Winter in the Garden of Eden. In *Volcanic Hazards and Disasters in Human Antiquity,* edited by F. McCoy and G. Heiken, pp. 71–82. Geological Society of America, Boulder.

Rampino, R., and S. Self 1993a Bottleneck in Human Evolution and the Toba Eruption. *Science*, 262:1955.

Rampino, R., and S. Self 1993b Climate-Volcanism Feedback and the Toba Eruption of ~74,000 Years Ago. *Quaternary Research* 40: 269–280.

Sewell, W. H. 2005 *The Logics of History: Social Theory and Social Transformation.* University of Chicago Press, Chicago.

Shimoyama, S. 2002 Volcanic Disasters and Archaeological Sites in Southern Kyushu, Japan. In *Natural Disasters and Cultural Change,* edited by R. Torrence and J. Grattan, pp. 326–342. Routledge, London.

Siebe, C, M. Abrams, J. Macías, and J. Obenholzner 1996 Repeated Volcanic Disasters in Prehispanic Time at Popocatépetl, Central Mexico: Past Key to the Future? *Geology* 24:399–402.

Stommel, H., and E. Stommel 1979 The Year without a Summer. *Scientific American* 240(6): 134–140.

Torrence, R., and J. P. Grattan(editors) 2002a *Natural Disasters and Cultural Change*. Routledge, London.

Torrence, R., and J. P. Grattan 2002a The Archaeology of Disasters: Past and Future Trends. In *Natural Disasters and Cultural Change,* edited by R. Torrence and J. Grattan, pp. 1–18. Routledge, London.

Whittell, G. 2009 Katrina Disaster Was Man Made. *The Times*, November 20, p. 55. London.

CHAPTER TWELVE

Events, Temporalities, and Landscapes in Iceland

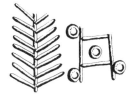

Oscar Aldred and Gavin Lucas

Abstract *Events are only events when they have happened; they have tense. Considering then the links between temporality and the event is one way to tease out the importance in understanding "durable ruptures": the structures that remain resilient to change and have high degrees of residuality. This paper considers long-term structures in the Icelandic landscape by considering them as assemblage-like: composed of elements with variable degrees of reversibility and residuality, but which collectively form coherent structures. The resilience then of the landscape's elements, such as boundaries and routes, to change by events is dependent on their ability to adapt outside their configured contexts and to act as structural anchors. In doing so the connections between temporality, events, and landscape are explored in one valley, in Þegjandadalur, in northeast Iceland.*

EVENTS, OBJECTS, AND ASSEMBLAGES

In what sense do archaeologists deal with events? And what do we mean by an event anyway? The concept of event is by no means straightforward and there are a plethora of philosophical issues and positions that we cannot address here. Archaeologically, the concept of event has received little attention and tends to be considered in terms of a more privileged opposite, such as process or structure (see Lucas 2008). At a very general level one might define an event as "something that happens"; it is thus a truism to say that archaeologists deal primarily with things not events. Nonetheless, we frequently interpret these things as the residue of events. We excavate a grave and from it infer the act of inhumation, the death of an individual, funerary rites, even larger phenomena such as religious conversion and so on. We survey and excavate landscape features such as sites and boundaries, and from them infer the planning and arrangement, individual and group participation (chiefly-will), acts of enforcement, and larger phenomena such as political and economic influences and so on. But what is implied when we make these inferences? In this chapter, we would like to problematize the nature of this inferential process—but not in terms of formation processes or middle range theory, but rather in terms of the ontological relationship between objects and events.

In many ways, we should be wary of dichotomizing object and event—or between social and historical disciplines, which are object-oriented (e.g., archaeology, material culture studies), versus those that are event-oriented (history, ethnography, sociology). Events, of course, only exist through material contexts while one might describe material culture as eventful in the sense that it only functions or signifies in the context of events. From such a perspective, the term *eventful archaeology* might be more appropriate than the archaeology of events. Nonetheless, stressing such overlap between the two entities "object" and "event," does not necessarily get us any farther in understanding what we are dealing with or how it might effect the nature of our interpretations. Thus, does this overlap mean archaeologists are in fact digging up events not objects, or rather eventful objects? And if so, what is an eventful object? Moreover, if we are dealing with eventful objects, then our inferential process is surely not about *reconstructing* past events from object residues, but rather about *understanding the relationship* between one eventful object and another. And how does this differ from an approach that merely considers the relationship between one object and another?

This last point can be clarified through an example. Consider a landscape; one can explore its internal configuration—the boundaries, the farm place and its respective locations—and compare the arrangement to another landscape to look at differences and similarities. From this, we might infer aspects of status or function connected to topography, resources, population, social structure, and so on. Or consider a grave as an object; one can also explore its internal configuration—the skeleton, grave goods, pit—and then compare this to other graves to determine similarities and differences. On this basis, we might infer aspects of identity such as gender or status, which might be interpreted as a material manifestation of social structures or ideology, as enacted through the specific event of the funerary rite resulting in the grave before us. But what role does the event play in such interpretations? If we consider it carefully, it is nothing more than a shorthand for the particularity that is *this* grave or landscape—as opposed to any other grave and landscape. Which is to say, in both of these examples, it is merely a *particular* manifestation of an inferred social structure, ideology, etc. The event is reduced solely to its function as a particular and in that case, it is synonymous with the particularity of the object (i.e., *this* landscape or *this* grave).

However, in the movement from the particular object to the general pattern back to the particular event, we have also switched ontologies—or ontological entities. In this middle ground of the generalization, something has happened, which obscures the relationship between object and event—a supra-entity (call it what you want—practice, structure, ideology, society, or even culture) intervenes, which masks the ontological switch, the consequences of which are suppressed insofar as both object and event seem to share the same conceptual movement between the general and particular (Figure 1). In order to avoid this, we need to keep the object and event on the same plane at all times—to look at their relationship without this movement of generalization (Figure 2). In this way, we can get much closer to an understanding of the eventful object.

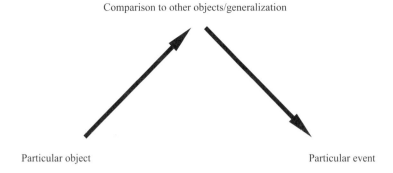

FIGURE 1 Comparison to other objects/generalization.

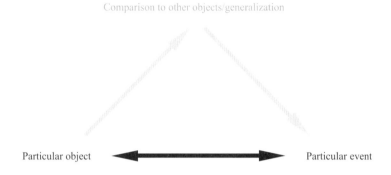

FIGURE 2 Assemblage as event.

By considering the relations between an object and event in this way the issue of time becomes central; what role do objects play in defining the limits of an event, and conversely, what role do events play in defining the limits of an object? In other words, any event needs to be seen as an assemblage of objects while every object needs to be seen as the product of an event(s). Linking these two together creates a circular relation but one that also dissolves the difference. A funerary rite involves a collection of objects (bodies, grave goods, a coffin, etc.) that during most of the rite are variously mobile, as in orbit around a virtual center (Figure 3). At the end of the rite, some but not necessarily all of these elements converge and stabilize at this center point (the grave) while the others disperse to conjoin other mobile assemblages. The pottery vessel in the grave is the product of a similar event, but one that happened long before—an assemblage of clay, water, potter's hands. In this view, objects are simply stabilized, compacted events, while events are simply assemblages of objects. Thinking about events as material and objects as temporal highlights the central issue here: the temporality of materiality; or, how to do an archaeology of *becoming* rather than of *being*. In this way, a material event or eventful object are symmetrical and refer to the same thing. If one thinks of events in material terms, it is about how objects come together and disperse at specific times and places; if one thinks of objects in eventful terms, it is about how an object persists before it becomes something else—or part of something else.

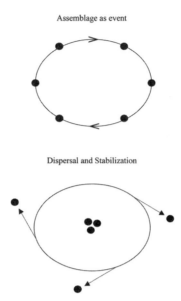

Assemblage as event

Dispersal and Stabilization

FIGURE 3 Dispersal and stabilization.

We want to suggest that the way forward thus lies in moving the terminology away from the concept of event or object toward that of the assemblage, where the critical point is to understand the temporality of any assemblage in terms of its formation and dispersion. An assemblage is neither an object nor an event but something in between, an eventful object if you will, but we prefer to use the concept of assemblage because *it stresses the relationality inherent to a temporalized materiality*. However, on the one hand, we are aware that the notion of the assemblage carries connotations within archaeology, which differ somewhat from our meaning, so we need to clarify this. On the other, it is precisely our intention to theorize the archaeological concept of assemblage, which is usually not discussed.

What do we mean by an assemblage? If we return to our example of the grave, it is of course a fine example of an assemblage, an eventful gathering of material objects. In this case, the traditional notion of assemblage coincides quite neatly with our theorized one. However, most assemblages do not remain as stable as graves—indeed, graves are quite special assemblages insofar as they are (usually) constructed in such a way that they should not be deconstructed. In most cases, however, materials come together in much more temporary arrangements, to be dispersed after shorter or greater intervals—think of food preparation or dining. Archaeologists rarely unearth such assemblages; and though of course we unearth the components of such assemblages (pottery fragments, animal bones, etc.), this is not the same as unearthing the assemblage itself in the same way as we do in a grave. Yet often, we speak of pottery or bone collections from a layer or site as assemblages; in this sense, our theoretical notion of the assemblage diverges from the traditional one. To understand the pottery and bone as parts of assemblages, we must be able to situate these elements within *an archaeologically discernible set of relations*, which might not necessarily be the ones we typically think of.

The point is, few assemblages leave an archaeological trace, but those that do tend to do so precisely because either they exhibit a certain resilience to dispersion or they are removed from the effect of dispersive forces—i.e., taken out of social circulation (like some graves). In one sense, the archaeological record is defined precisely by this latter cause. Most, if not all, archaeological sites are archaeological because they have been abandoned. Sometimes this abandonment is rapid (e.g., Pompeii); usually it is much more drawn out. Sometimes sites are never fully abandoned but remain quarantined from disruption (e.g., Stonehenge). In all these cases however, this views the archaeological record solely from the perspective of external forces, making the record itself a passive recipient of entropy. However, the record also carries a more active facet of entropy, a resilience to disruption. This is only partly about physical resilience; chiefly what we are talking about is social resilience, a keeping together of its internal cohesion even after physical dispersal. But this is more about external versus internal forces for disruption and resilience. This resilience is largely what defines those assemblages, which are more likely to be perceptible in the archaeological record. To illustrate the arguments we have used, we want to use an example of a landscape study from Iceland.

Þegjandadalur

The valley of Þegjandadalur is located in northeast Iceland, in the county of Suður-Þinge-yarsýsla. It is one valley among hundreds in Iceland, which have similar levels of preservation. This one was chosen here because a relatively large number of archaeological investigations have taken place (Figure 4). Consequently, the archaeological practices that have been used to understand landscape formation have some interest, but here we limit ourselves to a descriptive narrative only and its implications for assessing the issues of resilience and dispersion in "landscape" assemblages. The boundaries in Þegjandadalur have been mapped using vertical and oblique aerial photographs, with some ground survey and small-scale excavations to ascertain date, form, and preservation. The boundary system forms part of a much wider process of dividing the landscape, which in general probably began in the tenth century AD and which stopped being maintained in the late tenth or early eleventh century (Árni Einarsson et al. 2002; Aldred 2009). An archaeological ground survey has also been conducted of all visible ruins and the identification of other sites made, based on historical sources, oral testimonies, and place-name records from the early twentieth century.

There are fifteen farms in Þegjandadalur, distributed on both sides of the stream that runs down the center of the valley; on its sides are two relatively tall and steep ridges. As one moves farther south into the valley the land rises gradually. At the northern end, there are two farms, called Grenjaðarstaður and Múli, both of which have had a long-term presence in the landscape—they are what we would call primary farms, with probable pre-tenth-century origins and have probably never been fully abandoned, though only Múli is a working farm today. In the valley proper there are eight farms with boundaries around them that were probably established in the late tenth to early eleventh century. These eight farms were abandoned sometime between the late thirteenth and fifteenth century, indicated by both the 1262 and 1477 volcanic tephras (see below) and the lack of mention of these farms in documentary sources dating to 1525. Around the early eighteenth century several new farms were established in the northern part of the valley, adjacent to Grenjaðarstaður and Múli.

The commonest form of dating from our work in Þegjandadalur, and in Iceland as a whole, is derived from tephras—volcanic ash—which is used to construct temporal profiles.

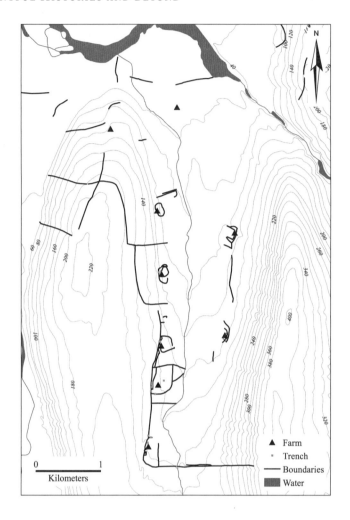

FIGURE 4 Þegjandadalur: farm sites, boundaries, and archaeological investigations.

Most historic tephras can be dated to within a year, if not the time of year that volcanic eruptions took place; these are chronologically sequenced according to various visible descriptive
and chemical characteristics. We are therefore able to accurately date the *terminus post/ante
quem* of explanatory sites using tephrochronology. However, regional diversity is dependent
on a number of factors such as wind direction, quantity, and the resilient quality of ash
emissions, amounts of soil erosion and accumulation, which affect the reliability of the
chronologies we use. Nonetheless, in the absence of artifacts and other ecofacts to date with,
tephras are an incredibly useful source with which to measure time.

Bringing it back to the theoretical issues we have raised, what we want to look at
here is not the before and after of volcanic events, but rather the *becoming* perspective
in which eventful objects disperse and gather according to different landscape assemblage
configurations. To help form this perspective we first identify in the archaeological record
several resilient features: things we commonly use in landscape archaeologies; settlements

and boundaries. What we want to emphasize is not the similarities or differences to other landscapes, but rather to look at the properties in the dispersal and gathering of assemblages in this particular landscape, in Þegjandadalur.

Landscapes are in a constant state of becoming. What we mean by this is, in theorizing landscape what we see are the forces of before and after pulling away the ground from under the feet of landscape's present by rendering it in a constant "flux"; an unfolding series of presents—a constant becoming*ness*. While we tend to focus on the completed element—the boundary, the farm—as a unit in constructing chronologies (an individual event, if you like), our aim is to unpack such a straightforward chronology as a reconstruction of a sequence of events, like a palimpsest, to consider the landscape as an assemblage of dispersed and gathered eventful objects. By this, we mean to ask: How do we characterize the resilience of landscape features in an active, rather than passive way, that is, not simply in being there because of the absence of dispersive forces, but because they *resist* dispersion through their material form? We are not simply trying to understand the materiality of motivation and the circumstances under which elements continue to be used, but rather we aim to explore the material characteristics of this resilience through their continued use, sometimes under different forms than their originally intended production.

It is no easy matter to dismantle the earth- and turf-built boundaries in Þegjandadalur (until the advent of machinery in the twentieth century), and this could be seen as the only property of resilience and one could simply stop the examination there. However, their survival is not only because of their physicality, it is also a combination of the absence of dispersive forces (erosion, machinery) and their inherent entropy, that is, the amount of energy required to dismantle them. But this does not really solve anything. After all, a massive amount of human energy went into their construction, so, equally, there should be no reason why similar human energy was not available for their destruction. We could perhaps understand this further by examining why their presence provided no obstacle to subsequent uses of the valley. There are perhaps two approaches to this. The first is to explore an indifference to keep them, the second, and perhaps more explanatory, is to assess their continued practical and meaningful uses as markers in the landscape.

Why were they not removed from the landscape? The answer is surely either because they continued to function in the same way or else new meanings and uses were attached to them. The boundaries were probably intended to define and demarcate farmland in the valley, and were thus inextricably linked to settlement and occupancy of the land. Much later, however, after the abandonment of the valley, they took on other roles by becoming walking routes as well as in some cases continuing as farm or district boundaries. Even later they become of interest to archaeologists.

But even this only takes us so far—what we want to understand is how the temporal development of the landscape reveals an increasing inertia to change as expressed through its durable elements, such as these boundaries. In purely sequential terms, there are obvious links between boundary elements of different date: we can see new configurations being created as a direct consequence of a later boundary element incorporating an earlier one (Figure 5). But what is interesting is how this sequentiality can be interpreted as an accumulation, which limits or constrains subsequent possibilities for the landscape

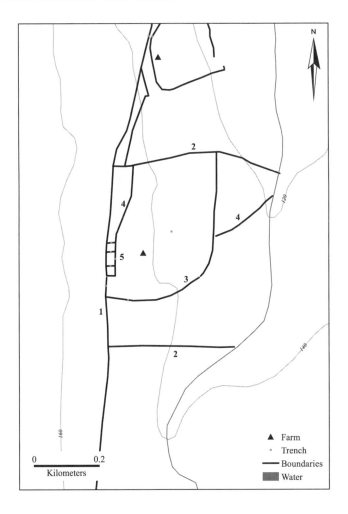

FIGURE 5 New assemblages indicated by later boundaries joining onto earlier ones and reconfiguring the assemblage around the farm of Ingiríðarstaðir (stratigraphic sequence 1-5).

without a massive input of energy to reverse this process. If one places the initial boundary formation as part of the seasonal activities in the landscape by the farms at the mouth of the valley, namely, summer grazing and tending to animals, then at certain times of year the boundaries around the farm would have been inert, even though present. Disruption occurred when the seasonal practices were altered by new occupations and boundary reconfigurations, such as constraining movement through the enclosure of space. In Þegjandadalur, a disruption took place as new occupancies established themselves in the valley, altering seasonal practices of mobility and land uses in a dramatic way: we see a gradual reduction in the land available for use due to the creation of new spatial constraints in the form of boundaries and settlements. Consequently, land that was once only active at certain times of the year became active all year round. In later periods, when the settlements were abandoned, the constraints were removed and the land reverted as it did in the earliest phases.

What we see happening then are episodes of expansion and contraction in settlement that were inversely related to the availability of land for dwelling in the valley. The landscape assemblage (both the things that are materially evident in the archaeological record today, but also the practices that left few material traces) in Þegjandadalur constantly changed with the establishment and abandonment of occupancies. All of these examples, however, were more or less contemporary with the creation of the boundaries and settlements in the valley. What is also revealed and equally as important is what happened after this time, and how the boundaries were incorporated into other assemblages. Tracks through the valley continued to be drawn toward the farms (which act as visible but abandoned markers). Some of the boundaries were used as walkways, while others were incorporated into later farm and administrative divisions. As such, some of the boundaries continued to have a presence that was beyond their original landscape assemblage. The fact that they remained as physical features in the landscape meant that they continued to have presence in the creation of new assemblages.

An eventful archaeology in this study hinges around several factors. Firstly, that it is the archaeological record—in its present-day state—that we are interested in. After all, this is what we engage with, and even though it is fragmentary, this nonetheless tells us something about the how objects were utilized in the past and what degrees of permanence remained, such as levels of investment in construction. In other words, what survives as part of the archaeological record is not simply a product of chance or external forces, but equally and more importantly, the resilience of the material system to dispersion. And this resilience has historical consequences. Secondly, the coalescence of eventful objects into assemblages allows us to view the practices that operated within a landscape, not as a "completed" article but as a work-in-progress—prone to changes of one sort or another (and that resilience in this dynamic is an important consideration). And thirdly, relations between eventful objects are embedded in a kind of "ecosystem" in which relatively small changes have a profound effect on land practices and subsequent assemblages. Here we choose to examine the land available for grazing practices, but it might just as well have been to determine what effect settlement expansion and land occupation had on the way people walked and traveled through the valley. As such, the gathering of objects into new assemblages is dependent on how resilient they are, not only in terms of their durability as physical entities, but also to what extent they are able to function and take on alternative meanings within new assemblages—ones for which they were not originally intended.

Finale

What we hope to have added to this discussion toward an eventful archaeology is that the ontology of the event should be rethought with respect to archaeology. Archaeology needs to define the event in terms of materiality, and not draw solely on events constituted by social or historical processes. By studying eventful objects as gatherings and dispersions, the coalescence and reconfiguration of objects between different assemblages will reveal something to us about how the event is constituted in the archaeological record.

References Cited

Aldred, O. 2009 Unfamiliar Landscapes: Infields, Outfields, Boundaries and Landscapes in Iceland. In *Recent Approaches to the Archaeology of Land Allotment*, edited by A. Chadwick, pp. 299–321. BAR International series 1875.

Einarsson, Á., O. Vésteinsson, and O. Hansson 2002 An Extensive System of Medieval Earthworks in North East Iceland. *Archaeologia Islandica* 2, 61–71.

Lucas, G. 2008 Time and Archaeological Event. *Cambridge Archaeological Journal* 18(1):59–65.

CHAPTER THIRTEEN

Freedom as a Negotiated History, or an Alternative Sort of Event

The Transformation of Home, Work, and Self in Early New York

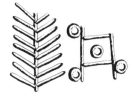

Christopher N. Matthews

Abstract *During the early American period in New York the labor force shifted from one that included a large number of enslaved persons to one consisting entirely of persons who were free. This transformation was formalized through a Gradual Emancipation Act passed in 1799 that allowed slavery to continue legally in the state until 1827. This movement toward freedom may be tied to a political economic shift recorded by both historians and archaeologists that redesignated the basis of social standing from work to the possession of the self illustrated by the demands of the labor market and in the creation of the home as a space apart from work. While colonial and early postcolonial labor was largely controlled by masters who both employed and housed workers, with freedom, laborers and masters alike were removed from the workplace to informally class-segregated residential sections of the city. From these homes masters and laborers then convened in the new public space of the labor market, which materialized their equivalence as persons and potential citizens of the American democracy. Using data from archaeological studies of the New York metropolitan region, this chapter identifies how the expectations of freedom smoothed the ruptures caused by the dispossession of workers from the control of their labor and the introduction of the home as a possession that defines the "real" self.*

Freedom's just another word for nothin' left to lose.

—Janis Joplin, "Me and Bobby McGhee"

What is the difference between slavery and freedom? In twenty-first century culture, these concepts are so ingrained in our thinking—the first imagined as an absolute evil and the other as a self-evident good—that we view this question as only an abstract philosophical dilemma. We rarely stop to wonder what *slavery* and *freedom* mean in concrete terms.

—Sue Peabody and Keila Grinberg, *Slavery, Freedom, and the Law in the Atlantic World*

Embodied in William Sewell's (2005) theoretical proposal for an "eventful sociology" is the relatively simple idea that history matters in part because history has matter, or consequences that contribute to the qualities, meanings, and textures of material life. As Beck et al. (2007:834) suggest, archaeologists should be attracted to this idea because of its applications to the study of material culture, such that, as Sewell describes, "schemas can be inferred from…material form." Schemas, or generalizable social principles, are mechanisms by which agents come to learn and, more important, to validate their experiences. Appealing in this approach is an appreciation that much of social life is under consistent negotiation, that people act as much from positions of security and knowledge as they do from fear, distrust, and uncertainty. Validation sustains negotiated arrangements, which is another way of describing a functioning society. The lack of validation generates crisis and, for some, if not most or all, the desire for social reconstruction. But are there not many forms of validation?

Negotiations have a way of bringing assumptions about persons, groups, objects, resources, and relationships to the surface of social discourse, where they can be uncovered, validated, and/or challenged. This is one way to describe what Sewell calls an "event." However, negotiation is neither a cause nor a result of history, in the sense of a force that has the power to bring about change. It is something quite different. History enables negotiation, for making and writing histories is the basis of the constructions that put people in positions requiring negotiation. What people say about themselves and others; what they believe to be likely or true about themselves and others; and what they hope may come to be likely or true about themselves and others derive from the histories people construct about themselves and others (Roseberry, 1989; Sider and Smith 1997). Negotiation and history, that is, cohabitate. In fact, the experience of negotiation may serve as the basis for many forms of validation for participants may consider themselves agents in the making of history. Yet, are such *constructed* considerations always valid?

This requires looking more carefully at what an event is. For Sewell, it is "sequences of occurrences that result in transformations of structures" (in Beck et al. 2007:835). I suggest this overlooks one of the more profound forms of events: those moments in which transformation appears possible or even inevitable, but does *not* occur. In this sense something "eventful" may come to pass, it may even be recorded and experienced as an event, yet structural change does not come about. I suggest we call this process a *non-event*. In such cases, history overwhelms agency, for history produced the event and the expressions in material and other forms of discourse record the event *as* history.

My language here is perhaps unnecessarily difficult. On the one hand, I am distinguishing between dominant grand narratives known as History and the multiple and conflicting narratives considered to be histories of places, people, relationships, etc. However, I am also rejecting this distinction by putting History and histories together saying that History is a construct of given social histories that effectively produce events, and non-events, to mask their persistence. In this chapter I help to explain this understanding through a study of the history and archaeology of captivity and freedom in early New York. In this case, freedom, proposed and still largely accepted as the basis of a vast structural transformation associated with the creation of modern democracies, is examined as a non-event.

This approach is novel in one sense because it considers freedom in relation to and alongside slavery such that they are considered as integrated rather than opposed social and productive systems (see esp. Fields 1985). Second, in archaeological and material culture research, freedom typically assumes a *material* form that is usually stripped from it in standard usage, which emphasizes instead freedom's symbolic and spiritual qualities. I believe these reconfigurations not only sustain interesting analyses, but allow for necessary reflection on the construction of events *as* events through practices such as building and demolishing cities, homes, monuments, and other sites; engaging in violence or war; or recording these occurrences now and in the past as events in history, archaeology, philosophy, and related disciplines. To illustrate this approach I look at the archaeology of New York City during the early American era, roughly 1787–1840. I consider cases that speak to the process of class formation after the end of slavery, which illustrate how freedom produced new ways of life that impeded the development of a critical class consciousness. Freedom became an ideology, a standard foundational belief about human beings on which Americans built a new society, but in the process freedom also became an ideal used to restrict citizenship only to those who could demonstrate the capacity for free living constrained by the capitalist labor market.

A New Archaeology of the City as a Capitalist Metropolis

The archaeology of early American cities has recovered a wealth of valuable data recording the details associated with the urbanization, industrialization, and modernization of material life in recent centuries. Patterns in material culture from the largest aspects of the landscape to minute details gleaned from crockery and food remains show that the development of American cities entailed a revolution in social life. This revolution transformed basic characteristics of daily life, notably introducing an urban commercial district and the commute to work; and the normalization of consumption so that urban residents purchased rather than produced virtually everything they required. These aspects may be aligned as the root of the modern metropolitan experience, which enacts a subjectivity based on the physical, social, and cultural *distance* between productive life and individuals as citizens.

Aspects of the metropolitan revolution are revealed in material patterns that show that combined homes and workshops common in the eighteenth century were replaced by separate locations designated for work and the home (Wall 1994). Additionally, the emergence of the modern city was realized through specialization where generalized and integrated commercial operations were replaced by persons and organizations focused on specific activities such as wholesale, retail, transport, accounting, marketing, raw materials acquisition, or the production of finished consumer goods. Specialization, however, influenced aspects of social life beyond the business world.

Archaeologists Diana Wall (1991, 1994, 1999) and Rebecca Yamin (2001a, 2001b) in particular have shown how the urban revolution reconstructed gender roles, class and ethnic identities, and even childhood. Diana Wall tracks changes in material culture associated with the creation of the middle-class home as a separate female-dominated sphere within the city. With the separation of home from the workplace, the male head of household commuted to work, leaving his wife and children, and by extension his moral authority over the family, behind. A "cult of domesticity" or "true womanhood" emerged during the nineteenth century in which women assumed the mantle of instilling and protecting the family's morality and social standing (Spencer-Wood 1996, 1999). Focusing on ceramics purchased by middle-class women and used in family meals, Wall shows that material culture played an important role in defining the woman's sphere, as matched sets of dishes enabled the practice of the proper etiquette representative of moral individuals. The family dinner especially became a "constant and familiar reunion" (Olmstead in Wall 1994) of persons who spent most of the day separated from one another and through the meal might (re)construct their familial ties. Dinner became a ritual event that followed a prescribed set of routines involving multiple courses which called for specific actions from key role players such as the service of soup by the mother and the carving and service of meat by the father. Children were to recognize these adult roles, but also to practice their individual etiquette by learning the proper use of the various implements that constituted a place setting such as multiple utensils, dishes, and drinking vessels (Shackel 1993; Leone and Shackel 1987).

Analyzing ceramics recovered from early-nineteenth-century domestic sites, Wall shows that middle-class families regularly subscribed to this behavior. Ceramic assemblages consisted largely of at least one if not more sets of matched dishes including dinner plates, salad plates, muffin plates, cups, saucers, mugs, and service platters. Tracing these patterns through time, she shows that material culture associated with the ritual played an increasingly important role. While early deposits contain predominantly undecorated white ceramics, which did not compete with the food they contained, through time dishes became more decorated and notably more expensive. Later deposits also included remains of specialized covered service platters indicating that the food itself became invisible and thus seemingly secondary to the proper use of the materials required for its consumption. In other words, the performance of the social ritual took precedence over the basic purpose of eating. Wall interprets these finds as evidence of the normalization of domestic rituals as part of city life, and she argues that by the 1830s the marketplace in New York was already considered a dangerous, amoral sphere. Thus, the home became a specialized retreat where security and morality could be found and practiced under the caring and watchful eye of modern wives and mothers.

The households Wall studied were largely middle-class professionals, who lived in new sections built on the edges of the city, such as Greenwich Village. By contrast Rebecca Yamin and her colleagues (Yamin 2001c) have investigated the domestic remains of the immigrant working class who lived in a neighborhood known as Five Points. Just as the separation of home from work led middle-class merchants, artisans, and their specialized middle-level employees to seek new housing, laborers were also removed from the workplace and had to establish homes of their own. Having fewer resources, working-class people settled closer to the commercial and manufacturing districts where they worked and which had lower rents. Five Points was one of these neighborhoods.

The archaeological investigation of Five Points made many important discoveries revealing the material conditions of working-class life such as crowded lots built over with tenement structures, but the artifacts recovered suggest that working-class immigrants quickly adopted the domestic habits prescribed by middle-class etiquette and reform literature (Fitts 2001; Brighton 2001; Reckner and Brighton 1999). Domestic remains included "matching sets of Gothic-shaped ceramics, porcelain tea sets, and Staffordshire figurines" (Fitts 2001:123) that varied little from those found in more prosperous sections of the city. This finding contrasts with the negative stereotypes surrounding working-class immigrant neighborhoods that were commonly recorded in popular accounts that labeled neighborhoods like Five Points as dangerous and notorious (Reckner 2002). Middle-class visitors, including luminaries such as Charles Dickens, in fact took police-escorted "tours" of Five points to witness the spectacle of the slum. The fact that working-class immigrants "owned an extensive variety of goods, including many of the items used by the middle class as symbols of respectability" (Fitts 2001:123) is thus unexpected and worth some consideration.

I think the most telling aspect of these finds is their association with the notion of *respect*, a keyword in nineteenth-century reformist messages including those professed by groups who worked in Five Points, such as the Ladies' Home Missionary Society and the Five Points House of Industry (Fitts 2001; Yamin 2001a). Respect is a relative social value for it involves the evaluation of your actions by others, and, depending on whom the "other" is, the value of different behaviors will vary. Respect, though, is more powerful than just this. Respectable behavior legitimizes and socializes *individual* action, an important process that presumes the individual stands apart from his or her society and must be formally instructed on how to appropriately behave within it. In other words, seeking respect disciplines persons as individuals in the sense that each evaluates themself in comparison with others in a way that establishes the equivalence of people and their segregation from each other. The role that material culture played in producing and disciplining individuals is underdeveloped in the archaeology of the modern city. I believe this is in large part because it calls for an approach that relaxes Wall's and Yamin's focus on gendered and class identities to examine instead the cultural construction of the subject who may claim an identity at all.

Over the course of the nineteenth century New York City emerged as the center of capitalism in the United States (Burrows 1999). No city was more committed or more developed by the forces of commodity production and market exchange. Furthermore, no other place demanded its inhabitants conform to the cultural norms and expectations of individualism as completely. These norms produced the matched sets of dishes and other individualizing artifacts that Wall and Yamin found in the domestic remains of the city's *newly* formed nineteenth-century middle- and working classes. These finds illustrate adherence by people of varied standings to the prescriptions for etiquette, morality, thrift, cleanliness, sobriety, and discipline, all of which describe the behavior of individuals. They formalize, moreover, an understanding that the individual is *free* to earn respect through their independent adherence to social norms, an implication that they are also free to break these norms because they are individually responsible for their own failings (Katz 1990; Goode and Maskovsky 2001). Ultimately, the archaeological record of the city shows how the individual emerged as the core of modern social life since persons were trained in the home and at work to regard themselves as free, an enactment of the basic principle of capitalism.

Max Weber (1970, also see Sayer 1991:134), following Karl Marx (1967) and complemented by Georg Simmel (1969), Walter Benjamin (1986), and others, encapsulates this process in the phrase: "without regard for persons." In capitalism the market is free because it operates without regard for persons, or the qualities that make each individual unique, most especially their unique relationships with kin and community. Following Weber, to account for personhood allows what amounts to an irrational personal interest to play a role in public life. Rather, capitalism considers and demands only the rational, impersonal, quantitative aspects of individuals, especially those aspects that promote the notion of equivalence or the idea that at root all individuals are comparable and capable of being exchanged. The basis of this understanding is the root of capitalism, the abstraction of labor, "considered solely as the mere expenditure of human labor power, measured in its duration, irrespective of the concrete character of the work done" (Sayer 1991:26). Only with this notion in place, as Marx (1967) argues, can human labor be commodified, or regarded qualitatively the same as the machinery and other costs involved in production.

Therefore, the analysis of material culture from the modern city needs to contextualize artifacts not solely as commodities but as the material aspects of commodification, or the processes by which rational individuals were constructed in and for the market. Capitalism itself is described as a state of permanent revolution and we need to relate this feature to the urban revolution thus far described by archaeologists (Marx and Engels 1848). The idea of an unending revolution describes modernity nicely, in that everything is new all the time. The capitalist revolution, however, is less involved with the production of something new but the revolutionary destruction of the concrete social relations that define persons: kin, community, and culture. As all persons are born into the world in such concrete (though not necessarily unchanging) social networks, it is mandatory for capitalism to constantly produce an individual subjectivity anew. Everyone must become an individual by segregating from their public and productive life their irrational, unequal, and natural bonds with other persons, and they must practice this separation consistently throughout their life. This is the revolution that we see in the modern American city, and it is extremely personal, for the abstract urban individual classically described Simmel (1969), Wirth (1964), and others is constructed by each person on their own.

Placing emphasis on the creation of modern individuals through everyday material practice calls for a new sort of archaeology of the city. I describe one such approach in the following description of the archaeology at the King Manor site in Jamaica, Queens, which I want to turn to now as an illustration. Although before the twentieth century the village of Jamaica was located outside the city in rural Queens County, the principle figure associated with the site, Rufus King, embodied the metropolitan spirit. His actions at the site define in important ways the origins of the metropolitan subjectivity as they may be tied to a key basis of modernization, specifically the manner in which King explicitly established his Jamaica property as a site of freedom during the time of slavery in New York.

Federalism, Citizenship, and the Meaning of Modern Freedom

The governing philosophy of the United States changed radically between 1776 and 1787 as the natural republic imagined by Thomas Jefferson in the Declaration of Independence became a modern nation with the U.S. Constitution. Two interwoven factors lie at the heart of this substantial change: the meanings of slavery and freedom and the relations of private and public life. The Jeffersonian ideal highlighted the stability, balance, and symmetry of natural law. It envisioned a society based on the *private* household whose order in part was realized in the balanced relationship between parents and children and masters and slaves (Dain 2003). However, the demands of nation building, democracy, and the independent postcolonial economy led to change with the Constitution and its creation of a Federalist governing system. The new federal government established a modern American *public* culture by forging a novel relationship between citizen and nation. American citizens were simultaneously of their place (i.e., their state, community, kin-groups) *and* the nation, and with the assistance of the strong center able to navigate freely between. This public culture identified and aimed to challenge social inequalities in production, politics, and power that were concealed by private traditions such as slavery. Nevertheless, the construction of a public culture in the Federalist scheme rationalized in a new way the difference between master and laborer. As public citizens, masters and workers were theoretically equal, a factor taken to be independent of the inequalities of their everyday private relations.

While the Constitution did not outlaw slavery, and in fact created the three-fifths rule and fugitive slave provisions that led to later sectional crises, it is nevertheless a document of freedom. Research at the King Manor site examines the everyday practice of the freedom crafted through federalism, public culture, and modern citizenship. In particular, I examine changes in the archaeological record as the labor force at the site shifted from enslaved to free. I argue that changes particularly in the organization of space, redefined the relationship between master and laborer in a way that emphasized the equality of citizens in a "free" society while simultaneously establishing the elevated social status of the patrician King family.

King Manor (Figure 1) is well suited for this investigation because of its association with Rufus King, a stalwart federalist. King was born in 1754 in Scarborough, Massachusetts to a well-to-do merchant family. He attended Harvard College and rose rapidly to prominence in Massachusetts politics during the Revolutionary era. As a delegate to the Constitutional Convention, he was a leading voice in favor of a strong central government emphasizing the need for a unified and free United States for the sake of national security and economic prosperity. In 1786 King married the wealthy heiress Mary Alsop, of New York, and they settled in New York City in 1788. He was then selected to be a senator from New York, a position he held four times into the 1820s. He also served as minister to England twice and was a nominee for the presidency in 1816. He was, in fact, the last Federalist to run for the White House (Ernst 1968).

Beyond politics, life at King Manor also epitomized Federalism. The Kings moved there in 1805 intending to withdraw from public service and adopt the life of a progressive country gentleman farmer. The 90 acre property in rural Queens County was adjacent to

FIGURE 1 Front view of King Manor Museum located in Jamaica, Queens, New York. Note the unbalanced façade reflecting the 1805–10 alterations made to the right half of the house by Rufus and Mary King. These renovations provided a dining/ballroom under two separate bed chambers for the new household's heads. The left side of the house dates to the late 18th century and was built as a formal "Long Island half house" that embodied the symmetry of other Georgian style architecture of the era.

Jamaica village. As a farmer, King focused both on planting and agricultural science, striving to improve American agriculture to better serve the fledgling nation. To this end, he founded the Queens County Society for the Promotion of Agriculture and Domestic Manufactures in 1819. The most pronounced evidence of his political commitment, however, was the use of free labor. While his family, predecessors, and neighbors were slave owners, King employed only free laborers as he expanded and intensified production. Notably, King's political career was marked by a long history of antislavery activities. He was instrumental in banning slavery from the Northwest Territories, and his antislavery speeches during the Missouri debates are regarded as some of the most powerful statements against slavery made by that date. King died in 1827, the same year New York's gradual emancipation program completed.

The history of King Manor before Rufus King also speaks to the potential for realizing the materiality of modern freedom. While the specific date of the earliest occupation is uncertain, documentary evidence suggests Mary Colgan settled there around 1765 (Evans 2002). Colgan's daughter Mary later wed Christopher Smith who in the 1790 and

1800 federal censuses is listed as owning 9 and 10 slaves respectively, a substantial number of African captives that he used for agricultural and household labor. Thus, from c. 1765 to 1805 King Manor was a site of slavery. The arrival of the Kings thus caused a sharp shift from slavery to freedom. As transfers of ownership often create new patterns in artifact types and distributions, this transition should be visible archaeologically.

ARCHAEOLOGICAL FINDINGS

The investigation of slavery and freedom has involved three seasons of fieldwork by Hofstra University students and community volunteers and draws on previous archaeological and cultural landscape research (Grossman 1991; Stone 1997, 1998; Evans 2002). The excavation strategy has been to identify and collect data from primary deposits and undisturbed secondary/midden deposits associated with work areas. This research has also involved an analysis of the standing structure for evidence of labor in the architectural details.

Excavation has focused on two areas of the site, the northwest yard and the east kitchen yard. In the northwest yard *in situ* stones and primary artifact deposits define the location of a privy, last filled in the mid-twentieth century and thus not directly relevant to this discussion. The east kitchen yard lies east of a kitchen wing built by Rufus King in 1806. The first kitchen was located in the section of the house to which King's kitchen was attached. As it essentially creates a second kitchen, King's has been identified as a "summer" kitchen, however, this finding is disputed (Stone 1998). It may be that King desired a separate and larger kitchen than was available in the existing space so building a new kitchen was the best solution. The east kitchen yard area also lies immediately north of a former outbuilding, known as Building K (Cotz 1984), that was removed in the 1930s. This 30' × 10' stone-walled structure may have been a dairy, smokehouse, and/or perhaps a slave quarter. The kitchen area excavations were placed in the area north and thus behind the former location of Building K, a location out of the line of site of the main house that may have served as a place for "unsightly" and possibly illicit activities. The location of Building K was defined archaeologically by a robbed foundation trench dating to its demolition. While this trench disturbed some deposits surrounding the foundation, separating the disturbance from the adjacent historical artifact accumulations has been straightforward.

Results of these excavations suggest a few patterns relevant to reconstruction the landscape and labor routines at the site in the eighteenth century. First, a large number of eighteenth-century wine/liquor bottle fragments have been recovered from the undisturbed areas adjacent to Building K as well as the backfill of the robber's trench (Figure 2). If the backfill from the trench was solely sediments excavated to rob foundation stones then artifacts from the fill might be associated with those from adjacent undisturbed deposits. Doing so shows that this area was a location where wine/liquor bottle refuse accumulated. This supports the idea that in this hidden location laborers found a space to commune and socialize while consuming perhaps illicitly acquired alcohol.

Notably, one bottle base fragment stands out among this set. Recovered from the robber's trench deposit, it has an incised "X" similar to marks found on ceramic vessels at sites with documented resident slaves. While it is unusual to find this mark on a glass vessel, it is

FIGURE 2 Large fragments of 18th-century dark olive green wine bottles recovered at King Manor. These bottles were found in an area behind a small outbuilding. They are interpreted as evidence of a cache of refuse associated with illicit drinking during the period of slavery at the King Manor site.

typical that it would be on the base of a round vessel and thus this may represent the mark of a captive African depicting a Bakongo-inspired or derived cosmogram symbol (Ferguson 1992, 1999; Brown 1994, 2001; Leone 2005).

From adjacent undisturbed deposits additional evidence comes from refined ceramics. While there were few ceramics recovered from the robber's trench backfill, excavation of undisturbed deposits to the north recovered a large quantity of small sherds typical of trampled surface accumulations associated with areas of high activity. These ceramics include a mix of coarse and refined earthenwares representing a cross-section of ceramic types and vessel forms associated with food preparation and service that are expected, given their proximity to the kitchen.

The ceramic types provide the most revealing pattern. Among the refined earthenwares the earliest type is Creamware, a popular ceramic first produced in Staffordshire in 1763. The paucity of delft, white salt-glazed stoneware or other early-eighteenth-century ceramic types in this collection supports the theory that there was no occupation of the site before 1760s. However, following this logic there should also have been abandonment in the early nineteenth century. While there a large number of Creamware (TPQ 1762) and undecorated Pearlware (TPQ 1779) sherds, there are few decorated Pearlware and Whiteware types more typical of the early nineteenth century. This finding stands out because the Kings' new kitchen would have been in the height of activity after 1806. One possible interpretation is that as they organized a new household the Kings redesigned the working landscape by relocating activity spaces for household labor.

My hypothesis is that they brought some of the work that had been previously performed outside into the new larger kitchen and removed other work farther back on the property where they are known to have constructed new barns and service buildings. I suggest they created a domestic space, or a "home," immediately surrounding the house that emphasized its separation from the work spaces of the farm. This finding reproduces the separation of home from work found in the city at the time but in a sense it does so in the reverse (Wall 1994; Blackmar 1989). It did not create a specialized space for work, such as a counting house or a factory, as much as it separated the home out from within an existing space for work. My argument is that we need to see this pattern of specialization more clearly from the perspective of the experience of individualism and social distance, and at King Manor we may do so by tying the Kings' home to the use of free labor.

ARCHITECTURAL EVIDENCE

Turning to consider architectural evidence associated with the transition from the Smith to the King household is illustrative. Two features in particular stand out: the façade and dwelling plan and evidence of labor in the buildings' construction. By 1810 the Kings altered the east side of the front of the house to be the same height as the west side, creating the uniform façade seen today (Figure 1). The west side was previously a formal three-bay Georgian-style Long Island Half house built by Smith. Enlarging the smaller east wing, King produced a level roof line and created on the first floor a formal dining and ballroom with a characteristically Federal-style elliptical curve along its east wall. The second floor had chambers for him and his wife with additional chambers on the floor above for their children. Servants quarters were in the remaining section of the original west wing and on the upper floor of the ell farther to the north.

A notable feature of the new addition is the way it organizes the interior spatial flow. Maintaining part of the original east wing, there is a three-step drop from the second floor level of the Kings' chambers to the servant's section. On the first floor the level between the old and new west wings is even, however, the flow between the pantry, which connected the front sections of the house to the productive areas, is only through a single door off the hallway behind the dining room. These features are a likely legacy of the eighteenth-century Smith family design of the Half-house, which was built when the laborers were enslaved. Different levels and restricted access emphasize the separation of master and slave. I think that this also demonstrates Smith's desire to stay true to the demands of the Georgian style, specifically symmetry, proportion, and harmony (Deetz 1996; Leone 1988; Matthews 2002). To provide a properly formal façade Smith built a higher and proportionally correct front section to produce a stylistically harmonious façade typical of high-style Georgian houses. The premise of this design is that harmonious proportions revealed the natural basis of beauty and order, an order also revealed in the balanced patriarchal relationship between master and slave as a productive unit (Dain 2003). An interesting aspect of King's addition is that it destroys this balance by eliminating the presumed symmetry of the façade. The question is whether this was done to illustrate a different social philosophy.

Embedded in the architecture is suggestive evidence (Figure 3). The chimney stacks on the two sides of the house are related to the Smith and King-era constructions, and

FIGURE 3 The chimneys at King Manor reflect the house's two major construction phases. On the right, the first chimney built by the Colgan-Smith family household in the late 18th century, shows a more massive construction effort compared to the one on the left built by the Kings in c. 1810. The varied levels of effort are interpreted to reflect the different systems of slavery and freedom embodied by the practices of the two families who owned the site.

they differ in an important way. The Smith-era stack is more massive than that built later by the Kings. While meeting a functional need in that the Half-house has back-to-back hearths, the wider stack extends the symmetry of the plan through the roof. This decision also formed a chimney that required larger number of bricks, and thus labor, than did the erection of the narrower stack built by the Kings. For the Kings, a smaller stack was likely more expedient and cost effective, a priority when the laborers are working for wages. A similar example of the difference between the two constructions is found in some interior details. In the formal front parlor of the Smith Half-house there is an elaborate dental molding at the top of the walls, while in the Kings' dining room the molding is by contrast very plain. This distinction is also found in the joinery of a doorway connecting the King dining room to the Smith hallway. On the Smith-era side, the door jamb was built using mitre joints that required a degree of skill to cut and join. On the reverse King-era side of the door, there is instead a simple butt joint that required virtually no skill at all to form.

These varied emphases on style, skill, and labor illustrate the difference between the systems of slavery and freedom. For the slaveowner it was an imperative to demonstrate a mastery over their laborers, for the slaves' work truly was by definition the master's property, while for the master of free laborers, such work was owned by both master and worker. In one sense, the work is property of the laborer until they take payment for it, at which point the product is transferred to a new owner. Additionally, the reputation of a craftsman remains in their work despite who owns their products as it represent their qualities to potential future employers. These aspects of ownership do not apply to the work of slaves who may not claim the work as theirs despite the use of their labor in the making.

The way the Kings built provides a model explaining the patterns identified in the excavated materials. If the productive and perhaps illicit activities that occurred immediately outside of the kitchen were removed to a location farther from the house itself, we see an effort to emphasize the separation of the King family, as a domestic unit, from those who worked for them. Freed from the responsibility and performance of slave ownership, which demanded slaves and the product of enslaved labor be visible if not ostentatious, the Kings were newly burdened by the responsibility to the implied equality of their laborers with their family, while at the same time expressing the high social status expected of a leading political family. Creating a physical distance between work and home, between production and domesticity, between public and private life, helped to make this sort of site possible. At home, it seems King was trying to say, all men are equal even if at work, and in social power they are not. To make this point the Kings carved out a "home" at King Manor in which the work that made living there possible was minimized, hidden, and put at a distance.

CONCLUSION: CITIZENSHIP AND SELF-POSSESSION

The only known thoughts about the building of his family's house in Jamaica, Queens, from among the expansive records of Rufus King at the New York Historical Society are contained in a single sentence from 1810: "A citizen's dignity should be adorned by his house, not derived from it" (Ernest 1968:63). King's thought describes an ideological construction of personhood true to the belief of a federalist and antislavery advocate from the early American era. According to King, persons preexist their materiality, and therefore their spirit or dignity will influence their presence in the world. This positioning of the self outside of and prior to the intersubjective material spaces normally identified in constructivist approaches declares that the world is indeed a product of men in that it may be constructed exactly how they theorize it *ought* to be. King's philosophy resides at one end of a continuum of thinking: that any house *he* lived in would carry his dignity by virtue of association. Thus, no contingency such as the size of the house, the quality of its construction, its location on the landscape, nor even the occupation of its occupant is relevant to the status of the house, which bears only that of its head. His philosophy is that all persons, as citizens, can attain his level of material and social status if they agree that the basis of one's dignity comes not from material and social status but personal value as an individual, as someone conscious of himself as a discrete and self-possessed person.

This observation expands for one on the meaning of American domesticity. The creation of the modern home was not just a class and gendered process (Wall 1994; Yamin 2001a), but one by which the relationship of the modern subject with their labor was conceived. The modern home represented its master as it had during slavery, but it was a home that was materially and symbolically separate from the hard work that made living there possible. The home, that is, was the basis of the private citizen's freedom. With the construction of the home as private, modern Americans created a social space that formed the basis of individual equivalence. As all persons live somewhere, removing laborers from the home of masters sets them free to establish their own home, and build an equivalence with even their masters. The home is thus a positive resource for creating freedom. However, as I described the distinctions that emerged between Greenwich Village and Five Points as neighborhoods in New York City, the resources for realizing freedom were not equally shared. Nevertheless, with the normalization of the modern individual this distinction was made a private matter, and thus irrelevant to the public cultural spaces where laborers and capitalists met. Equivalence is not equality, but the Kings and their peers would have argued that no one ever said it was.

Finally, this understanding of equivalence and self-possession describes the main thesis of this chapter: that freedom was a non-event since the premise of modern freedom was solely the segregation of persons from their labor. This process was not a radical overturning of slavery or an emancipatory event, but the broad application of the core principle of slavery to all working people—that labor and personhood are not entangled. The survival of this contradiction is why freedom as we know it in modern America is a non-event, and therefore something that absolutely requires substantial criticism when we see it deployed, for example, as the basis for engaging in preemptive war and similar assaults that really are the basis for structurally transformative events.

ACKNOWLEDGMENTS

I wish to thank Douglas Bolender and the IEMA Staff at the University of Buffalo for the invitation to participate in the 2008 conference on Eventful Archaeology. Versions of this paper have benefited from the comments of several readers including Mary Anne Mrozinski, Roy Fox, and Kathy Forestall and King Manor Museum as well as Zoë Burkholder, Douglas Bolender, Dan Hicks, Kurt Jordan, Jenna Coplin, Nan Rothschild, Barb Voss, Gerry Sawyer, and Paul Mullins. I thank these colleagues and friends for their input. Any shortcoming or mistakes this paper contains, however, remain my own responsibility.

References Cited

Beck, R. A. Jr., D. J. Bolender, J. A. Brown, and T. K. Earle 2007 Eventful Archaeology: The Place of Space in Structural Transformation. *Current Anthropology* 48(6):833–860.

Benjamin, W. 1986 *Illuminations*. Edited by H. Arendt. Schocken Books, New York.

Blackmar, E. 1989 *Manhattan For Rent, 1785–1850*. Cornell University Press, Ithaca.

Brighton, S. A. 2001 Prices That Suit the Times: Shopping for Ceramics at Five Points. *Historical Archaeology* 35(3):16–30.

Brown, K. L. 1994 Material Culture and Community Structure: The Slave and Tenant Community at Levi Jordan's Plantation, 1848–1892. In *Working Toward Freedom: Slave Society and Domestic Economy in the American South*, edited by L. E. Hudson Jr., pp. 95–118. University of Rochester Press, Rochester.

Brown, K. L. 2001 Interwoven Traditions: Archaeology of the Conjurers Cabins and the African American Cemetery at the Jordan and Frogmore Manor Plantations. In *Places of Cultural Memory: Africans Reflections on the American Landscape*, pp. 99–114. Conference Proceedings. U.S. Department of the Interior, National Park Service.

Burrows, E. G. 1999 *Gotham: A History of New York to 1898*. Oxford University Press, New York.

Cotz, J. A. E. 1984 *Draft Archaeological Sensitivity Model for the Rufus King Manor and Park, Jamaica, Borough of Queens, NYC*. For Gibson Bauer Associates.

Dain, B. R. 2002 *"A Hideous Monster of the Mind": American Race Theory in the Early Republic*. Harvard University Press, Cambridge.

Deetz, J. F. 1996 *In Small Things Forgotten: Archaeology and Early American Life*, Revised and Expanded Edition. Anchor Books, New York.

Ernst, R. 1968 *Rufus King: American Federalist*. University of North Carolina Press, Chapel Hill.

Evans, J. 2002 *Rufus King Manor, King Park, Jamaica, Queens, Cultural Landscape Inventory*. Prepared for Historic House Trust, New York City. On file, King Manor Museum.

Ferguson, L. 1992 *Uncommon Ground: Archaeology and Early African America, 1650–1800*. Smithsonian Institution Press, Washington, DC.

Ferguson, L. 1999 "The Cross Is a Magic Sign": Marks on Eighteenth-Century Bowls from South Carolina. In *I, Too am America: Archaeological Studies of African-American Life*, edited by T. A. Singleton, pp. 116–131. University Press of Virginia, Charlottesville.

Fields, B. J. 1985 *Slavery and Freedom in the Middle Ground: Maryland During the Nineteenth Century*. Yale University Press, New Haven.

Fitts, R. K. 2001 The Rhetoric of Reform: The Five Points Missions and the Cult of Domesticity. *Historical Archaeology* 35(3):115–132.

Goode, J., and J. Maskovsky (editors) 2001 *The New Poverty Studies: The Ethnography of Power, Politics, and Impoverished People in the United States*. New York University Press, New York.

Grossman, J. W. 1991 *Archaeological Tests and Artifact Analysis Results from Rufus King Park, Jamaica, Queens, New York*. Prepared for Land-Site Contracting Corp. On File, King Manor Museum.

Katz, M. B. 1990 *The Undeserving Poor: From the War on Poverty to the War on Welfare*. Pantheon, New York.

Leone, M. P. 1988 The Georgian Order as the Order of Merchant Capitalism. In *The Recovery of Meaning: Historical Archaeology in the Eastern United States*, by M. P. Leone and P. B. Potter Jr., pp. 235–261. Smithsonian Institution Press, Washington, DC.

Leone, M. P. 2005 *The Archaeology of Liberty in an American Capital: Excavations in Annapolis*. University of California Press, Berkeley.

Leone, M. P. and P. A. Shackel 1987 Forks, Clocks, and Power. In *Mirror and Metaphor*, edited by D. Ingersoll and G. Brontisky, pp. 45–61. University Press of America, Lanham, MD.

Marx, K. 1967 *Capital: A Critique of Political Economy*. International Publishers, New York.

Marx, K., and F. Engels 1967a *The Communist Manifesto*. Pantheon, New York.

Matthews, C. N. 2002 *An Archaeology of History and Tradition: Moments of Danger in the Annapolis Landscape*. Kluwer Academic/Plenum, New York.

Peabody, S., and K. Grinberg 2007 *Slavery, Freedom, and the Law in the Atlantic World: A Brief History with Documents*. Bedford/St. Martin's, Boston and New York.

Reckner, P. 2002 Remembering Gotham: Urban Legends, Public History, and Representations of Poverty, Crime, and Race in New York City. *International Journal of Historical Archaeology* 6(2):95–112.

Reckner, P. E., and S. A. Brighton 1999 Free From All Vicious Habits: Archaeological Perspectives on Class Conflict and the Rhetoric of Temperance. *Historical Archaeology* 33(1): 63–86.

Roseberry, W. 1989 *Anthropologies and Histories: Essays in Culture, History, and Political Economy*. Rutgers University Press, New Brunswick.

Sayer, D. 1991 *Capitalism and Modernity: An Excursus on Marx and Weber*. Routledge, New York.

Sewell, W. H. Jr. 2005 *The Logics of History: Social Theory and Social Transformation*. University of Chicago Press, Chicago.

Shackel, P. A. 1993 *Personal Discipline and Material Culture: An Archaeology of Annapolis, Maryland, 1695–1870*. University of Tennessee Press, Knoxville.

Simmel, G. 1969 *The Metropolis and Mental Life. Classic Essays in the Culture of Cities*, edited by R. Sennett. Appleton-Century-Crofts, New York.

Spencer-Wood, S. M. 1996 Feminist Historical Archaeology and the Transformation of American Culture by Domestic Reform Movements, 1840–1924. In *Historical Archaeology and the Study of American Culture*, edited by L. A. de Cunzo and B. L. Herman, pp. 397–445. University of Tennessee Press, Knoxville.

Spencer-Wood, S. M. 1999 The World Their Household: Changing Meanings of the Domestic Sphere in the Nineteenth Century. In *The Archaeology of Household Activities: Gender Ideologies, Domestic Spaces and Material Culture*, edited by P. M. Allison, pp. 162–189. Routledge, London.

Stone, L. 1997 *Report on Archaeological Testing in Advance of Improvements Associated with the Fence Project at Rufus King Park, Jamaica Avenue and 150–153 Streets, Jamaica, Queens, New York*. Prepared for Gazebo Contracting Inc. On File, King Manor Museum.

Stone, L. 1998 *Report of Archaeological Testing in Advance of Improvements Associated with the Drainage and Termite Project at Rufus King Park, Jamaica Avenue and 150–153 Streets, Jamaica, Queens, New York*. Prepared for Fredante Construction Corporation. On File, King Manor Museum.

Wall, D. diZ. 1991 Sacred Dinners and Secular Teas: Constructing Domesticity in mid-19th Century New York. *Historical Archaeology* 25(4): 69–81.

Wall, D. diZ. 1994 *The Archaeology of Gender: Separating the Spheres in Early America*. Plenum Press, New York.

Wall, D. diZ. 1999 Examining Gender, Class, and Ethnicity in 19th century New York City. *Historical Archaeology* 33(1):102–117.

Wall, D. diZ. 2001 Family Meals and Evening Parties: Constructing Domesticity n Nineteenth-Century Middle-Class New York. In *Lines that Divide: Historical Archaeologies of Race, Class, and Gender*, edited by J. A. Delle, S. A. Mrozwoski, and R. Paynter, pp. 109–141. University of Tennessee Press, Knoxville.

Weber, M. 1970 *From Max Weber*, edited by H. Gerth and C. W. Mills. Routledge, London.

Wirth, L. 1964 *On Cities and Social Life: Selected Papers*. University of Chicago Press, Chicago.

Yamin, R. 2001a Alternative Narratives: Respectability at New York's Five Points. In *The Archaeology of Urban Landscapes: Explorations in Slumland*, edited by A. Mayne and T. Murray, pp. 154–170. Cambridge University Press, Cambridge.

Yamin, R. 2001c From Tanning to Tea: The Evolution of a Neighborhood. *Historical Archaeology* 35(3):6–15.

Yamin, R. (editor) 2001b Becoming New York: The Five Points Neighborhood. Special Issue of *Historical Archaeology* 35(3).

Epilogue

CHAPTER FOURTEEN

Archaeology and the Human Career

Revolutions, Transformations, Events

Graeme Barker

INTRODUCTION

It is an enormous privilege, and a daunting challenge, to give the opening address marking the launch of the Institute for European and Mediterranean Archaeology. Archaeology is traditionally defined as the study of the past through its material culture, to distinguish it from history, defined as the study of the past through written records. The bad old view of the relationship between archaeology and history was that archaeology was an expensive way of telling history a few banalities about past societies: that they lived in houses, made pots, ate meat, and so on. The more mature view then developed that archaeology and history were different but complementary ways of investigating the past, with mutually overlapping and equally valuable sets of data. For many of us today, the division is increasingly unhelpful (Moreland 2001); we are all archaeologists in our use of the complicated and partial sources of evidence that are the material remains of the past, whether fragments of animal bone or microscopic pollen grains, potsherds or coins, inscriptions or documents. We are all historians, in that we are trying to use that material culture to write the history of the human past. And we are all anthropologists, trying to understand societies, structures, and behaviors very different from our own.

Yet in all universities, archaeologists, anthropologists, and historians are invariably divided for teaching purposes into a bizarre arrangement of institutional sets and subsets, the reasons for which are lost in time. At my own university, archaeologists practice their trade variously in the Department of Archaeology, the Department of Bioanthropology, the Faculty of Classics, the Faculty of Continuing Education, the Faculty of Oriental Studies until a year ago, the Fitzwilliam Museum, the McDonald Institute for Archaeological Research, and the Museum of Archaeology and Anthropology. Or most of them do. The role of the McDonald Institute, founded about 15 years ago by a generous benefaction from Dr. D. W. McDonald, supports the research of the entire archaeological community through laboratories, project space, seminar facilities, research grants, and publications. Our overarching strategy is to promote archaeology at Cambridge as a discipline concerned with the entirety of the human career from early prehistory to the most recent past, by combining innovative theory and practice across the humanities-science spectrum in inter-disciplinary endeavor, drawing on active field programs throughout the world, and building national and international collaborations, in order to develop new research directions. The vision of the Institute of European and Mediterranean Archaeology is of the same order: "Established to create international and interdisciplinary dialogue between anthropologists, archaeologists, classicists, and those in related disciplines on both sides of the Atlantic, we hope to create a platform and venue for the exchange of ideas, building of networks, and the development of current and future theoretical directions." It is a wonderful vision, and we celebrate its happening.

The conference on "Eventful Archaeology" that follows the inauguration of the Institute has rightfully focused on a topic at the heart of the discipline: How do we explain change in past societies? As Douglas Bolender noted in his conference preamble, many archaeologists in recent decades aligned their view of the past with that of the French historian Fernand Braudel (Braudel 1972): that history consists of an interweaving of different temporalities or processes operating at different time scales: in his terms, *événéments*, or short-term events; medium-scale *conjunctures*, for Braudel the kind of process that operates at the scale of a generation, but for archaeologists often identified as shifts in behavior taking more than a century or several centuries; the *longue durée*, the influences and constraints of environment and technology on what people could do; and cross-cutting all these, *mentalités*, or the way people thought about their world and their place within it. Many archaeologists, prehistorians especially, have argued that our data are best suited to history as—very—*longue durée* (Bintliff 1991; Knapp 1991). The particular suitability of archaeology for investigating medium and long-term processes was certainly at the heart of the processual theoretical agenda in the 1960s and 1970s. Processualist archaeologists tended to scorn the use of archaeology to get at short-term "events" as the stuff of the "culture historical"—or pseudo-historical—model of the past that they were attacking, even though in their ethnographic work processual archaeologists were comfortable with observing short-term events, such as the activities of a group of Inuit at a hunting stand one afternoon, and using those observations to interpret the deep archaeological record (Binford 1978, 1983). The post-processual agenda focused at first on the role of underlying structure shaping behavior, but over time the concern with agency has led to an increasing focus on the short-term, the event, the individual (Johnson 2010).

One of the main criticisms of Braudel was that he failed to demonstrate how his three different temporalities and fourth dimension (ideology) actually interacted with and affected each other to create history. In many ways the same criticism can be leveled at archaeology, in the failure of the processual agenda to engage with individual actors and their role in maintaining or changing the social order, and its reliance on functional efficiency as a prime motor of change; and the failure of the post-processual agenda to lift its gaze from the machinations of the individual actors and notice the *longue durée*'s big shadow falling over them from time to time. We need both perspectives if we are to have a subtle and reflective archaeology that says important things about the past. The "eventful archaeology" conference is an exciting attempt to try to bridge that divide: When, how, and why do small-scale actions combine to create significant social transformations? I can't begin to answer that question, but it has helped me reflect on some of the big social transformations in human history that I have engaged with in my own work that are the theme of my talk today: the origins of our species, the change from hunting to farming, the development of metallurgy, and impact of empire. Perhaps the main single theme is that we are trying to write history from tiny fragments, the fragments that we know are missing are bad enough, but every time we ask new questions of the past and challenge orthodoxy, we realize we are in Donald Rumsfeld country. The second theme is that we need beware of orthodoxies that, though more subtly expressed, are not so very different from the Victorian notion of a ladder of cultural progress as an innate human virtue. The past was another country, they did things differently then, and they knew as little about what it would all lead to as we do today.

THE HUMAN REVOLUTION

There is an emerging consensus that our species originated in Africa and was present in the Levant by 150,000 years ago, but that the major phase of expansion out of Africa was about 70 to 60,000 years ago (Mellars 2006, 2007). These were stone-using people living by hunting and gathering in the often extreme and hostile environments of the Pleistocene or Ice Ages, and in small bands of a few extended families. From that perspective, the process of colonization appears to have been impressively rapid. On the evidence of dated archaeological sites with human skeletal remains, anatomically modern humans were in Australia by perhaps 50,000 years ago, Europe by 45,000 years ago, and, probably crossing by a land bridge between Siberia and Alaska, had spread the length and breadth of the Americas within a few thousand years from around 15,000 years ago. In the Levant, modern humans at first coexisted with, and then replaced, Neanderthals. In Europe, the arrival of modern humans is equated with the appearance of a suite of artifacts and activities assigned to the initial ("Aurignacian") phase of the Upper Palaeolithic (Mellars 1989). This material culture, which includes complex hafted stone tools, bone tools, body ornaments, and cave art, none of which has been convincingly found in the Middle Palaeolithic material culture that is associated with Neanderthals, is assumed to be evidence for what my Cambridge colleague Paul Mellars has called the "Human Revolution," the emergence of a new cognitive and social complexity—"behavioral modernity"—associated with anatomically modern *Homo sapiens* and lacked by Neanderthals (Mellars 1996). In short, modern humans were smarter than Neanderthals, the argument runs, and outcompeted them (with or without violence is debated) in Europe over a few thousand years.

The last decade, though, has brought into question the Eurocentric assumption that has dominated debates for more than a century, of a simple and exclusive linkage between anatomical and behavioral modernity (Henshilwood and Marean 2003; McBreaty and Brooks 2000). In Africa, it now seems that *Homo sapiens* may have evolved as early as

500,000 years ago, following a genetic split from other human stock. The earliest fossil remains of anatomically modern humans in Africa date to about 200,000 years ago. Early indicators of cognitive "modernity" include shell beads at Taforalt in Morocco dated to 82,000 years ago and a decorated piece of ochre and shell beads at Blombos Cave in the Cape dated to c. 75,000 years ago. This sequence of events raises profound questions about why behavioral modernity developed so late compared with anatomical modernity. Meanwhile in Europe, recent re-dating of fossil human remains from several key Aurignacian sites has shown many of them to be intrusive, much later than the layers they were thought to belong to, casting doubt on the assumed direct correlation between this industry and exclusively modern human progenitors (Conaard et al. 2004; Trinkhaus 2005). They have raised the possibility that late Neanderthals may not after all have been exclusively archaic in their behavior. To advance debates about who behaved how, and when, and avoid circular arguments about how a particular species must imply a way of behaving, or a particular set of material culture must imply a particular species made it, we clearly need well-dated archaeological sites with *both* fossil remains *and* material evidence for behavior.

New discoveries in Southeast Asia help move the debate forward, and yet also add to its ambiguities. The evidence comes from Niah Cave on the island of Borneo, and Luang Bua cave on the island of Flores.

At Niah Cave, excavations by Tom and Barbara Harrisson discovered in 1958 an anatomically modern human skull, the so-called Deep Skull, near the bottom of their deepest sounding, the so-called Hell Trench, at the entrance to the West Mouth (Harrisson 1958). A date of 40,000 years ago was obtained from the charcoal collected nearby, at that time the earliest date for anatomically modern human remains anywhere in the world. However, there have always been uncertainties about the Niah discoveries, because the work was never fully published, and one suspicion was that the Deep Skull was intrusive, from one of the hundreds of later (Neolithic) burials discovered in the same part of the cave, dating from about 4,000 to about 1,000 years ago. This was the context for a reinvestigation of the site that I have been coordinating since 2000, funded especially by the UK's Arts and Humanities Research Council. The work has involved more than 40 researchers from half a dozen countries.

We have calculated the likely location of the Deep Skull in the Hell Trench (Barker et al. 2007). Laboratories at Canberra and Oxford have dated charcoal samples we collected from the exposed faces of the Hell Trench at about the same height, to 43,000 and 42,000 years ago (Higham et al. 2008). Charcoal we found in the Harrisson Excavation Archive in Sarawak Musem labeled in Tom Harrisson's handwriting "charcoal by Deep Skull" has been dated to 35,000 years ago, and Bristol University has obtained two uranium-series dates of about 37,000 and 35,000 years ago from fragments of the skull preserved in the Natural History Museum (the main fossil is in Sarawak Museum). It is difficult to compare radiocarbon and uranium-series dates in this period, and bioturbation or soil movement means that radiocarbon dating of charcoal in sediments can only provide a general guide as to the absolute age of the individual. However, it looks as if the original 1958 dating of the Deep Skull to around 40,000 BP was largely correct, making it still the earliest secure evidence for anatomically modern humans in Southeast Asia, indeed among the earliest outside Africa and the Near East. It belonged, by the way, to a teenage girl, and there are fragmentary remains of other bones probably from of the same individual in the Harrisson Archive.

Our excavation of one of the surviving Harrisson baulks or walls, HP6 in their system, revealed a series of organic-rich sediments containing much ash, charcoal lumps, butchered fragments of animal bone, and occasional stone tools, evidence for people making repeated episodic visits to camp at the cave entrance. A series of radiocarbon dates obtained by the Oxford Radiocarbon Laboratory indicate the accumulation of these sediments, and of the human activity associated within them, in the period c. 50,000–40,000 BP.

The human remains found by the Harrissons were in deposits rich in ash, charcoal, and animal bone that they termed the "bone under ash layer," which we equate with the organic-rich layers we found in the HP6 baulk. The study of the more than 10,000 fragments of food refuse bone in the Harrisson Excavation Archive deriving from this "bone under ash" layer has revealed clusters of burnt bone indicating either the residues of hearths or dumps of burnt material from hearths; fragments of bone with cut marks and chop marks; and several examples of semiarticulated animals, implying *in situ* butchery. The people using the cave were clearly killing animals in the locality, bringing them back to the cave entrance, and butchering and processing them there.

Borneo c. 50–45,000 years ago was part of "Sundaland," an enormous land mass created by the lowered sea levels of the late Pleistocene connecting the major islands of present-day Island Southeast Asia to the mainland. Niah may have been up to 100 km from the sea. Today the caves are surrounded by primary rainforest (the Niah National Park), but the pollen from the cave sediments and the ecologies of the animals brought back to Niah by the Pleistocene foragers indicate a mosaic landscape around the cave that included rainforest, open woodland, scrub, savannah, mangrove swamp, and large rivers. The main animal hunted by the people camping at Niah was the bearded pig, followed by orangutan, porcupine, monitor lizard, and turtle, along with an array of smaller species such as langurs and macaques, snakes, lizards, birds, and bats. Hunting and fishing technologies included spears, traps, and snares.

Botanical remains—parenchyma or plant tissues and starch granules—demonstrate the exploitation of rainforest for a variety of roots and tubers, fruit, nuts, and the pith of sago palms. Sago is the key plant staple of the Penan foragers of the Bornean rainforest today, critical for their survival. We have found these microscopic plant remains both in the sediments and on the surfaces of stone tools. Many of these plants are highly toxic, and in Australia, traditional Aboriginal methods for leaching out toxins in nuts, fruits, and seeds included burying them in pits full of ash for a month or so. A series of intercutting pits dated to c. 38–32,000 years ago full of ash and plant remains is likely to be evidence of this method of plant detoxification. Also, on the evidence of high incidences of *Justicia* pollen, our palynologist Chris Hunt concludes that the foragers using Niah 50,000 years ago were deliberately burning the forest, presumably to enhance open or disturbed areas that would have provided good habitats for tubers and other food plants and for hunting and trapping animals attracted to these clearings.

The anatomically modern humans at Niah do not exhibit the classic indicators of "modern" human behavior as defined in the European Aurignacian, but their subsistence practices and engagement with the landscape were of demonstrable socioeconomic complexity (Barker et al. 2007; Rabett and Barker 2007). The levels of resource use, forward planning, and ingenuity underpinning their subsistence strategies, directed specifically toward exploiting the structure and diversity of lowland tropical environments such as the present-day Penan, well illustrate what Chris Stringer has called the "adaptive plasticity" of modern humans. One important implication of the Niah work, the context of a new project that I am directing that is investigating the history of foraging and farming in the highlands of Borneo, is that people have been shaping and changing rainforest from the moment they encountered it.

But behavioral modernity may not have been the exclusive preserve of modern humans in Southeast Asia, just as it may not have been exclusive to modern humans in Europe. The diminutive *H. floresiensis* found a few years ago by Mike Morwood's team on the island of Flores appears to have been associated with blade-like stone tools that contrast favorably with the crude flakes used by modern humans at Niah (Morwood and van Oosterzee 2007). The brain of *H. floresiensis* was small, but had uniquely enlarged frontal and temporal lobes, the areas concerned with higher cognition activities such as initiative and planning. As Mike Morwood commented, "Her brain may have been small, but it was normal, and the front part was restructured in a way that meant she was probably smart, had language, and could plan ahead"—just like modern humans. Yet modern humans clearly outcompeted hobbits, colonizing the whole of Australasia by the end of the Pleistocene.

The increasingly intriguing questions about how different species learned to deal with the challenges of the new environments they encountered, and how these experiences impacted on their ways of living, socializing, and thinking, are at the heart of a new field project I embarked on in 2007, a reinvestigation of the deep stratigraphy of the Haua Fteah cave in Cyrenaica, in northwest Libya, sponsored by the Society for Libyan Studies. Given its position between Sub-Saharan Africa and Europe, North Africa is likely to have been one of the critical routeways by which modern humans arrived in Europe. The Sahara would clearly have posed a significant barrier to humans, but in periods of wetter climate it was broken up by a series of major lake systems when, far from being a barrier, it could have been an attractive route for human movement. So when did anatomically modern humans first arrive on Africa's northern shores? Was behavioral modernity critical to their successful colonization of North Africa? Were they—and they alone—behaviorally modern?

Excavations in the 1950s by Dr Charles McBurney of the University of Cambridge revealed a succession of sediments that he believed spanned a continuous sequence from the present day back to at least 80,000 years ago (McBurney 1967). The latter date was achieved by calculations based on rates of sediment accumulation below the lowest radiocarbon dates he obtained, of c. 40,000 BC. That date coincided approximately with the appearance in the stratigraphy of a European-style Upper Palaeolithic blade industry, the Dabban, which McBurney regarded as evidence for the arrival of behaviorally modern humans at the cave. However, the earliest culture he defined, the Pre-Aurignacian, also contained a significant number of blades and burins, so behavioral modernity at the site may be of much greater antiquity than he supposed—and one recent calculation of the basal sediments is that they are probably more like 200,000 years old, not 80,000 years old as McBurney supposed

(Moyer 2003). Similarly, shellfish were found well below the Dabban, and in southern Africa the ability to exploit coastal resources has been identified as another potential signature of modern human behavior. Two human mandibles found in the Middle Paleolithic sediments were originally categorized as "Neanderthaloid," but scholars now variously identify them as either ancient humans (*Homo sapiens rhodensiensis*), or a component of new "modern humans," or a contemporary but different population, *Homo helmei*. New fossils from the Haua Fteah, associated securely with material culture, will clearly contribute critically to the arguments about who is making what, and who is behaving how. The Haua Fteah has the potential to provide a 200,000-year sequence of human activity and behavior, and its environmental contexts, unrivalled in North Africa. Did significant climatic and environmental shifts coincide with behavioral shifts? Did behavioral shifts coincide with new physical forms? In 2007 we emptied the first four meters of the McBurney trench, down to about 20,000 years ago, but McBurney got down to 14 metres without reaching the bottom, so we have big challenges ahead of us. (Since this lecture was given, the team has reached a depth of 10 meters, with significant results already emerging on the paleoenvironmental and cultural sequences: Barker et al. 2009.)

The study of the emergence of "modernity" has suffered from archaeologists having a kind of checklist of what we think it means to be "behaviorally modern," and looking in the archaeological record from our perspective and with our modern mindset for items to tick off on the list. The increasing complexity and depth of the evidence in Africa, Asia, and Europe may ultimately point not to some kind of emerging and incomplete sense of behavioral modernity, but to several modes of "being human." As our knowledge of early human behavior continues to expand, the challenge will be not to look for earlier versions of ourselves, in effect, but rather to learn what those other paleocultures, lying on the other side of our looking glass, were actually like.

THE AGRICULTURAL REVOLUTION

The origins of agriculture have been debated by archaeologists for most of the discipline's history. Current orthodoxy is that early ("Neolithic") farmers spread out from a few centers of domestication, taking a package of new technologies and domestic animals and/or plants, and using them to colonize new lands (Bellwood 2004; Diamond 1997). For the Victorians, the beginnings of farming represented the critical rung on the Ladder of Progress that lifted humankind out of a life of primeval savagery (hunting and gathering) on its journey upward to urbanism and, eventually, the glories of nineteenth-century industrialization. Writing between the 1920s and 1950s, and focusing mostly on the Near East (Southwest Asia) and Europe, Gordon Childe emphasised the advantages of farming over foraging in terms of the opportunities it provided for sedentary life, population growth, and surplus production, arguing that climatic change at the beginning of the Holocene (the modern climatic era, beginning c.10,000 years ago) encouraged people to develop new relationships of control over plants and animals (e.g., Childe 1936, 1942).

The study of the origins of agriculture was revolutionized in the late 1950s and 1960s by a series of archaeological expeditions, mainly led by North American archaeologists, in search of the origins of agriculture. The teams represented a new kind of interdisciplinary archaeology, with archaeozoologists, and archaeobotanists working alongside the excavators. In the Near East, the focus of the projects was not the Tigris and Euphrates plains but the surrounding hills—what came to be termed the "hilly flanks of the Fertile Crescent." Their work at early village sites such as Jarmo in Iraq, Jericho in Israel, Beidha in Jordan, Çayönü Tepe and Haçilar in Turkey, and Tepe Guran and Ali Kosh in Iran, sites now assigned to the Pre-Pottery Neolithic B culture, provided the basis for a model that continues to be current orthodoxy: that cereals such as einkorn, emmer, and barley began to be domesticated in the southern Levant, in the Jordan valley especially, by "PPNA" hunter-gatherers in the first 1,000 years of the Holocene, from the mid-tenth millennium BC; that sheep and goats began to be herded about the same time in the Zagros mountains; and that the separate components then came together around 8500 BC as the mixed farming system that supported the first sedentary village life (the PPNB villages), along with the emergence of complex ideologies related to fertility and the agricultural cycle.

This coherent sequence of change, however, is only a small part of the story. Some PPNA communities, for example, such as at Netiv Hagdud, were fully sedentary communities, based on hunting and gathering. Jerf el Ahmar, another substantial settlement sustained by hunting and gathering, had a ritual building with bulls' skulls attached to it. Even more remarkable is the site of Göbekli Tepe in southeastern Turkey, apparently a ritual center where PPNA foragers (there is no evidence for domesticated crops or animals) carved massive T-shaped pillars out of the limestone bedrock and decorated them with carvings of aurochs, birds, foxes, gazelle, snakes, and wild boar (Schmidt 2001).

The period from the Last Glacial Maximum 20,000 years ago to the transition to the Holocene 9500 BC was characterized by major climatic fluctuations, with a shift first to a warmer climate and then a sudden return to cold and aridity before the final and rapid shift to the Holocene climatic warming (Sherratt 1997). In the first climatic warming c.13,000–11,000 BC, Early Natufian communities such as at Abu Hureyra on the Syrian steppe were able to develop sedentary settlement on what had formerly been desert but was now well-grassed steppeland, practising systems of foraging that verged on husbandry and, in terms of plant exploitation, were effectively horticulture. The climatic stresses of the ensuing Younger Dryas (c. 11,000–9500 BC), returning the steppe to desert, forced people to abandon Abu Hureyra, to which they didn't return until the PPNB (Moore et al. 2000).

Sedentism was in fact much earlier than the Abu Hureyra settlement, though. Around the Last Glacial Maximum 20,000 years ago Ohalo, by the Sea of Galilee in the Jordan valley, was a more or less all-year-round encampment, used for fishing, fowling, collecting forest foods such as acorns and almonds around the lake, and gathering wild cereals and other grass seeds and hunting on the steppeland above (Nadel et al. 2004). There were thousands of grains and other ear fragments of barley, their brittle rachises indicating that they were morphologically wild, together with emmer wheat, almond, olive, pistachio and grapes (all wild forms), and acorns.

The Southwest Asian evidence emphasizes that, in contrast with Gordon Childe's model of a sudden development of a "Neolithic Package," the transition from hunting and gathering to agriculture here was not a sudden event but a long-drawn-out process stretching back at least 20,000 years, with intensive plant use (without any morphological changes) quite probably of greater antiquity still (Barker 2006). From c. 8500 BC PPNB villages were certainly practising mixed farming, using crops and animals that were more or less the same as their modern counterparts, and employing them together in ways that are recognizably the basis of the modern Eurasian farming system, yet the beginnings of husbandry-like behaviors can be detected far earlier. Importantly, though, the transition from foraging to farming was not a simple linear process, but a fluctuating story of systems of greater and lesser intensiveness, greater and lesser sedentism, greater and lesser reliance on plants and/or animals, reflecting countless decisions by individual communities about how to deal with the challenges and opportunities they were faced with—the climatic and ecological ones that we can see, and the many social, economic, and ideological ones that we can't.

There is similar complexity in Island Southeast Asia. The dominant model for agricultural transitions here has been that farming began first in mainland China at the beginning of the Holocene; and that Neolithic farmers with pottery, polished stone tools, rice, and pigs then spread south through Island Southeast Asia, between about 4,500 and 2,000 years ago, from Taiwan to the Philippines to Borneo, the Indonesian islands, and thence via coastal New Guinea to the Pacific islands, speaking a language that is the origin of the Austronesian languages spoken across much of the region today (Bellwood 1988, 2001). The model implies a clear cultural break in the regional archaeological record between an indigenous population of foragers and the incoming Austronesian farmers.

The evidence at Niah Cave for the complexity of foraging behaviors 50–45,000 years ago is clearly not "Pleistocene agriculture," but it parallels evidence elsewhere in Island Southeast Asia for the sophistication of the forest management strategies practised by Pleistocene foragers, which were further developed and intensified through the Holocene, emerging recognizably as formalized agriculture long before the putative Austronesian expansion. At Kuk in the highlands of New Guinea, pits, stake-holes, post-holes, and runnels on the levees of palaeochannels are interpreted as evidence for taro, sago, and pandanus cultivation (their starch survives on the edges of stone tools, along with phytoliths of banana) as early as 8000 BC (Bayliss-Smith and Golson 1992; Denham et al. 2003). By 5000 BC people were using well-drained mounds to grow these crops. At Niah, Chris Hunt has found pollen and phytolith evidence for rice being grown near the cave c. 4000 BC, almost 2,000 years before, theoretically, the Austronesians brought it to Borneo (Hunt and Rushworth 2005). Isotope studies by John Krigbaum of the bone chemistry of pre-Neolithic and Neolithic and later burials in the West Mouth indicate not a switch from foraging to farming but a diet vacillating between the two, with foraging dominant until historical times (Krigbaum 2005). It is conceivable that the brief and precocious episode of rice growing at Niah is an example of Brian Hayden's theory that many domesticates may have been acquired first by foragers because they valued them as luxury foods or prestige goods, rather than as the dietary staples that they became later on (Hayden 1990, 2003).

My PhD student Lindsay Lloyd-Smith has also found that the burial archaeology, likewise, does not divide neatly into pre-Neolithic and Neolithic practices (Lloyd-Smith 2008). Pre-Neolithic burial forms continued into the Neolithic. Clusters of "pre-Neolithic" graves provided the focus for the "Neolithic" graves. The preservation of memory was clearly important: many burials were marked by wooden grave markers, the tops of some jar burials were left exposed, some graves were reopened for later burials, and some jars containing family groups were carefully placed exactly on top of earlier jar burials. Another PhD student, Franca Cole, is showing that people at Niah shared in a set of Neolithic material culture that was widely distributed across Island Southeast Asia, but the practices they used to engage with it reflected local concepts of meaning and ethnicities, embedded in the past.

At the same time, we should not minimize the profound nature of the transformations in ways of thinking as well as being, as people committed to becoming farmers however rapidly or slowly. A good example of this is exemplified by some Mesolithic and Neolithic burials at Dragsholm in Denmark (Brinch Petersen 1974). One burial was of two women of the Mesolithic Ertebølle culture: they were buried accompanied by a decorated bone dagger, a bone awl, pendants made from wild boar and red deer teeth, beads of teeth of wild cattle and elk, and red ochre. Isotope analysis shows that they had a marine-dominated diet. Some three centuries later, a man was buried nearby accompanied by items of Neolithic material culture: a TRB pot, a stone axe, a stone battleaxe, ten flint arrowheads, and amber pendants. His diet was based on terrestrial foods. The objects in the women's grave are all of organic materials from the animal kingdom, slightly transformed so as to serve as body ornaments but embedded nonetheless in notions of continuity between humans and animals. The man's artifacts are all of materials quarried from the earth, transformed by technologies so as to be unrecognizable compared with the parent material, their forms redolent of male-focused status tied to aggression. As Richard Bradley (1993:35) remarked, "[T]hey were two metres apart in space and less than three centuries apart in time, but the people who were buried there had lived in quite different worlds." Graves as different as this could once be explained simply in terms of population replacement: Mesolithic foragers were replaced by Neolithic farmers, who brought with them new technologies, lifeways, language, and ideologies. The realization that the man at Dragsholm was almost certainly a descendant of the women buried beside him emphasizes the profound transformations in *mentalités* that took place in prehistoric Europe as communities beginning to combine plant and/or animal husbandry with foraging were drawn into profoundly different ties to the land, to their collective past (whether real or imagined), and to one other (Whittle 1996).

In arguing against the notion of agriculture spreading out from a few hearths of domestication in some kind of simple process of population movement, the last thing I would want to imply is that prehistoric societies, foragers or farmers, were somehow fixed in place. Far from it: it is quite clear that prehistoric foragers were capable of moving considerable distances fast, including crossing challenging physical barriers (the Pacific, Atlantic, and Mediterranean seas, for example). Current genetic work by my colleague Martin Jones and his research group is suggesting that the millet used by early farmers in the Ukraine in eastern Europe may have been derived not from the Near East as usually assumed, but from China (Hunt et al. 2008). The forager and farmer worlds were equally open to the rapid exchange of information and material goods. Genetic studies of present-day human, animal, and plant populations in Island Southeast Asia demonstrate complicated and ambiguous demographic histories and pathways of movement across the region from the Last Glacial

Maximum 20,000 years ago to recent millennia that are totally at variance with the ortho-dox Neolithic expansion model (Barker et al. in press).

THE METAL REVOLUTION

As in the case of transitions to farming, evolutionary thinking has characterized much of the theorizing about why prehistoric societies adopted metallurgy, in this case, "as a milestone on the road to urbanism and statehood," but the same kinds of complexities and ambigui-ties are emerging in the evidence. The traditional argument for why metal was adopted was usually technological: as farming was to foraging, so metal was clearly superior to stone, in this case in terms of its malleability, workability, and effectiveness; copper and copper-alloy objects could be reworked several times; raw materials could be recycled into new artifacts (Childe 1957). The second argument has stressed the economic value of metal: the wide-spread appearance of hoarding, the establishment of long-distance trade networks especially for the procurement of tin, the production of standardized metal forms with fixed contents of tin, and the later introduction of weight systems are often interpreted as steps toward the rise of commercial trade and the commoditisation of objects, which eventually became a universally accepted currency in prehistoric Europe (Bradley 1998). Another view has been that metal was adopted because it carried a prestige value and was appropriated by emerging elites to produce objects for ritual display and conspicuous consumption, a pursuit that was in itself a (or the?) major stimulus to the rise of complex ranked societies (Kristiansen and Rowlands 1998).

In this context, the pattern of the adoption of metallurgy by prehistoric societies in Europe is emerging to be as curiously unpatterned as the adoption of farming. The radio-carbon revolution showed that Gordon Childe's *ex oriente lux* model of metallurgy diffusing steadily across Europe from the Near East is not tenable. Metallurgy was being practised as early as the later sixth millennium BC in the Balkans (southeast Europe), but not until the later third millennium BC in northwest Europe. Furthermore, the patchy and often contra-dictory pattern of the earliest metalwork production in Europe demonstrates that, during these three millennia, societies that used metal had neighboring communities who, despite being in close contact with the novel artifacts, did not adopt them. (Shades of how Euro-pean foragers engaged with farming.) Although earlier prehistorians tended to assume an evolutionary sequence from objects of pure copper to objects of arsenical copper, to objects of true tin bronze, compositional analyses demonstrate that in many regions these technolo-gies were often in fact contemporary.

So how did the new technology come to be valued, made sense of, accepted, and incorporated into the social milieu? It is in the context of this complexity that one of my PhD students, Andrea Dolfini, researched how copper metallurgy evolved in Etruria, the western side of central Italy, a region that witnessed the precocious development of metal-lurgical activities in the second half of the fifth millennium BC, the Later Neolithic (Dolfini 2008). A flourishing tradition of metalworking developed during the subsequent Copper Age (3600–2200 BC), based on the smelting, melting, and casting of pure copper, arsenical copper, silver, and antimony. The ores were hewed out of galleries and shafts (up to 30 m deep) in the mountains using wedges, picks, hammers, and fire settings, and then graded and sorted nearby. Smelting took place at the settlements. Most artifacts have been found in graves, mostly with the articulated bodies of adult males (the rest of the population was buried mixed together, with few gravegoods). The metal composition of the artifacts suggests that Copper Age smiths were deliberately selecting particular ores of particular colors (each with particular symbolic associations perhaps) and with particular properties for particular artifacts, rather than for ease of working or efficiency. Bright red easy-to-process malachite and axurite were selected for making axes; silvery grey sulphide ores containing copper, arsenic, and antimony, much more difficult to process, were selected for daggers and halberds (a dagger hafted at right angles to a shaft); ornaments were made of either silver or antimony ores, both silvery white.

The first copper objects made in the later fourth millennium, axes, were copies or skeuomorphs of groundstone axes. There was then a lot of experimenting with shapes in the first half of the third millennium, before the development of fixed shapes that were quite different from stone. Wear damage studies show that the axes in the graves had been used beforehand for activities such as tree felling, whereas the daggers and halberds—made of the most difficult to smelt ores—were buried in mint condition. There was a definite grammar or set of rules regarding what could be buried with what: never copper axes with stone axes or stone daggers, never copper halberds with stone battleaxes, but stone maceheads, flint arrowheads, and pottery could be buried with any other object. Particular artifacts were closely associated with particular parts of the body: stone battleaxes or copper halberds with the top of the head; stone daggers and copper daggers with the back of the head; stone axes and maceheads and copper axes with the chest; flint arrowheads with the upper or lower limbs; a pottery vessel with the whole body (even perhaps representing the body in some cases).

This study is a good example of how the introduction of metallurgy into prehistoric Europe was a socially embedded phenomenon, the outcome of which was neither preordained nor inevitable (Lemmonier 1993); it was the result of a process of learning and negotiation, until social agreement was reached over the meaning and form of objects, over the appropriate arenas and circumstances for their consumption, and over the agents who were meant to manufacture and use them (Sofaer Derevenski 2000). Dolfini's study chimes with anthropologists' studies of nonindustrial societies demonstrating that technology participates fully in social discourse, and embodies culturally specific sets of worldviews, strategies, beliefs, and social actions; and that technological innovation does not simply happen in a society but is brought about as part of the social practices and conventions that define people and their positioning in the material world (Lemmonier 1992; Pfaffenberger 1992).

BECOMING ROMAN

Moving forward another 2,000 years, my final case study considers the impact on the peoples of the desert margins of the Mediterranean basin of the expansion of the Roman Empire. Over the past 25 years I and a series of collaborators in archaeology and environmental science have been involved in investigations of arid-zone archaeology in

North Africa and the Levant, specifically in the Tripolitanian pre-desert of northwest Libya (Barker et al. 1996) and the Wadi Faynan in southern Jordan (Barker et al. 2007). Both regions are arid and degraded landscapes at the junction between a better-watered zone and hyper-arid desert. Before the impacts of oil on the Libyan economy, and of tourism on the Jordanian economy, the two study areas both supported mobile pastoral populations of goat- and camel-herders, mostly seasonal visitors who spent the summer months in better-watered zones and moved out into the true desert in the winter if the rains were good. They also practised patch cultivation, sowing crops on wadi floors after the autumn rains. The Tripolitanian pre-desert was incorporated into the Roman Empire in the late first century AD, the Wadi Faynan, along with the rest of what became Roman Arabia (focused on modern Israel, Jordan, and Syria), a few decades later. Both landscapes were then rapidly transformed by intensive sedentary farming, but there the comparisons cease (Barker 2002).

Pre-Roman settlement in the Libyan pre-desert was in essence like traditional lifestyles, but in the late first century AD there was an extraordinary transformation in settlement forms, with the appearance of hundreds of villa-style farms built in recognizably Roman style, though inscriptions showed that their owners were indigenous Libyans (so we used the term *Romano-Libyan*). During the course of the third century the villas were fortified. Over the next few centuries the pre-desert then gradually reverted to traditional settlement forms, beginning first in the southernmost, most arid, sector. Our detailed palaeoenvironmental studies established that the climate in the Tripolitanian pre-desert throughout the centuries of Romano-Libyan settlement was essentially the same as today, so climatic change cannot be cited as the primary reason either for the sudden appearance of villa settlement or its piecemeal abandonment.

These desert farmers built extensive systems of drystone walls to trap surface runoff after seasonal storms and divert it into fields laid out on the wadi floors. Their simple but effective technologies based on local knowledge of floodwater behavior enabled people to grow a wide range of crops that needed much more water than was available in terms of annual rainfall levels. (Studied by archaeobotanist Marijke van der Veen, these included three cereals, three pulses, four oil plants, and a variety of Mediterranean and African fruits.) Many farms have stone-pressing structures for making oil and wine, and vat capacities show that most farms were producing a surplus well beyond the needs of their inhabitants. It appears that, for a few centuries, the desert populations living on the fringe of the Roman Empire here switched from subsistence to cash-crop farming to take advantage of the new urban markets on the coast. We detected signs of small-scale landscape erosion likely to reflect grazing pressures and fuelwood collection, but nothing to suggest that environmental degradation was on such a scale as to have been a significant factor in the decline of the system and the return to traditional lifestyles. In fact, farmers took positive measures to protect their landscape from erosion by cultivating tree and ground crops, improving animal forage, controlling animal movements and waterflows, and manuring the land.

The key difference between the Tripolitanian pre-desert and Wadi Faynan is that the latter was rich in copper and lead ores. In the pre-Roman Nabataean period, mining was on a small scale and there was a series of small farms in the Wadi Faynan practising irrigation systems much as in Roman Tripolitania. With the incorporation of the region into the

Roman state, however, mining developed on an industrial scale and agriculture was hugely intensified to feed the burgeoning population. The whole operation was closely managed by imperial officials based at the major settlement of Khirbat Faynan, which is securely identified as the ancient city of *Phaino* recorded in literary sources of the day as the center of an imperial mining operation to which Christians and other prisoners were sent to work in awful conditions as punishment. The fields of the Nabataean farms were reorganized into a single irrigation system stretching several kilometers west of Khirbat Faynan. Floodwaters were collected in the surrounding hills and then carefully channeled down the system along low-gradient slopes by an elaborate system of channels, with sluices being opened or closed to control the flow of water into individual fields. The crop and animal regime sustained by this sophisticated hydraulic system was essentially the same as that in the Tripolitanian pre-desert.

There is compelling evidence, though, that after a couple of centuries the landscape was severely compromised by the scale of industrial and agricultural activity. The production of copper required large quantities of charcoal and timber, and by the Roman period these had to be brought in from elsewhere because the local environment had been totally stripped of suitable vegetation. The intense smelting activity around Khirbat Faynan produced a dense pall of airborne pollution from which many particles of toxins—copper, lead, cadmium, zinc, thallium—entered the ecosystem by falling on crops, bare fields, and uncultivated land, where they were taken up by plants, animals, and humans; manuring the land with polluted materials further exacerbated the situation. The extent of Roman pollution can be gauged from: the dramatically high levels of pollutants in buried soil horizons close to the smelters; the presence of massive doses of toxins in bodies buried in Roman-period cemeteries; and the continuing significant levels of heavy metals in the present-day vegetation, crops, and herds. The Roman mining system and its agricultural support system collapsed and the landscape reverted to pastoralism, with the hotspots of Roman metallurgical activity remaining polluted brownfield sites today, their effects visible in the present-day foodchain.

Hence, these two frontier regions, with similar climatic and environmental regimes two thousand years ago, display remarkably contrasting trajectories of landscape transformation within the same context of the encounter with Roman imperialism (Barker 2002). Without seeing the consequences, people made wise and foolish decisions; and they embarked on activities that had minor environmental impacts from which, with their assistance, the landscape recovered, and on activities with devastating impacts both for themselves and for generations to come. Environment, structure, and agency collided in complicated ways, in historically contingent circumstances.

POSTSCRIPT

As an archaeologist I have no sentimental attachment to the past, but a passionate belief that its study matters for the present and future. Our species appears to be unique among living organisms in fashioning its self-image in terms especially of its imagined past. Archaeology can be a frustrating business, part humanities, part social science, part science, though as an intellectual project a shared endeavor par excellence. We have a central role to play in trying to understand the complexity of the human past and a responsibility to convey that complexity to wider audiences, whether or not it suits comfortable or politically convenient notions of identity, nationhood, and all the rest. In closing his inaugural lecture as the newly appointed Disney Professor at Cambridge in 1952, Grahame Clark said that "we [in Cambridge] well know that archaeology appeals to the whole man, rather than merely to the researcher, to the emotions as well as to the intellect. The veneration of antiquity is surely an emotion worthy of cultivation both for its influence on individuals and as making for the closer cohesion of society....Is it altogether too fanciful to suggest that the study of world prehistory [which I would change to "the study of world archaeology"] may even help to nourish the solidarity of mankind on which our well-being, if not our very existence, depends?" That statement is even truer today than it was 50 years ago. The Institute of European and Mediterranean Archaeology has a challenging agenda ahead, it's a wonderful initiative, I look forward to those of us on the other side of the Atlantic being part of its dialogues and deliberations, and I wish it every success.

Notes

This chapter originally was delivered as the inaugural lecture, Institute for European and Mediterranean Archaeology, Buffalo, and has deliberately been kept more or less as delivered, with some updating of detail where necessary.

References Cited

Barker, G. 2002 A Tale of Two Deserts: Contrasting Desertification Histories on Rome's Desert Frontiers. *World Archaeology* 33:488–507.

Barker, G. 2006 *The Agricultural Revolution in Prehistory: Why Did Foragers Become Farmers?* Oxford University Press, Oxford.

Barker, G., D. Gilbertson, and D. Mattingly (editors) *Archaeology and Desertification: the Wadi Faynan Landscape Survey, Southern Jordan.* Council for British Research in the Levant, London.

Barker, G., C. Hunt, and J. Carlos In press. Transitions to Farming in Island Southeast Asia: Archaeological, Biomolecular, and Palaeoecological Perspectives. In *Why Cultivate? Archaeological and Anthropological Approaches to Foraging-Farming Transitions in Island Southeast Asia*, edited by G. Barker and M. Janowski. KITLV Press, Leiden.

Barker, G., H. Barton, M. Bird, P. Daly, I. Datan, A. Dykes, L. Farr, D. Gilbertson, B. Harrisson, C. Hunt, T. Higham, J. Krigbaum, H. Lewis, S. McLaren, V. Paz, A. Pike, P. Piper, B. Pyatt, R. Rabett, T. Reynolds, J. Rose, G. Rushworth, M. Stephens, C. Stringer, and G. Thompson 2007 The "Human Revolution" in Tropical Southeast Asia: the Antiquity of Anatomically Modern Humans, and of Behavioral Modernity, at Niah Cave (Sarawak, Borneo). *Journal of Human Evolution* 52: 243–261.

Barker, G., A. Antoniadou, H. Barton, I. Brooks, I. Candy, N. Drake, L. Farr, H. Hunt, A. Ibrahim, R. Inglis, S. Jones, J. Morales, I. Morley, G. Mutri, R. Rabett, T. Reynolds, D. Simpson, M. Twati, and K. White 2009 The Cyrenaican Prehistory Project 2009: The Third Season of Investigations of the Haua Fteah Cave and its Landscape, and Further Results from the 2007–2008 Fieldwork. *Libyan Studies* 40:1–41.

Bayliss-Smith, T., and J. Golson 1992 Wetland Agriculture in New Guinea Highlands Prehistory. In *The Wetland Revolution in Prehistory*, edited by B. Coles, pp. 15–27. The Prehistoric Society and the Wetland Archaeology Research Project, Exeter.

Bellwood, P. 1988 A Hypothesis for Austronesian Origins. *Asian Perspectives* 26:107–17.

Bellwood, P. 2001 Early Agriculturalist Population Diasporas? Farming, Languages, and Genes. *Annual Review of Anthropology* 30, 181–207.

Bellwood, P. 2004 *First Farmers: the Origins of Agricultural Societies*. Blackwell, Oxford.

Binford, L. 1978 *Nunamiut Ethnoarchaeology*. Academic Press, New York.

Binford, L. 1983 *In Pursuit of the Past*. Thames and Hudson, London.

Bintliff, J. (editor) 1991 *The* Annales *School and Archaeology*. Leicester University Press, Leicester.

Bradley, R. 1993 *Altering the Earth*. Edinburgh University Press, Edinburgh.

Bradley, R. 1998 *The Passage of Arms: an Archaeological Analysis of Prehistoric Hoards and Votive Deposits*. Routledge, London.

Braudel, F. 1972 *The Mediterranean and the Mediterranean World in the Age of Phillip II*. Fontana, London.

Brinch Petersen, E. 1974 Gravene ved Dragsholm. *Nationamuseets Arbeidsmark* (1974):112–130.

Childe, V. G. 1936 *Man Makes Himself*. Watts, London.

Childe, V. G. 1942 *What Happened in History*. Penguin, London.

Childe, V. G. 1957 *The Dawn of European Civilization*. Routledge and Kegan Paul, London.

Conard, N., P. Grootes, and F. Smith 2004 Unexpectedly Recent Dates for Human Remains from Vogelherd. *Nature* 430:199–201.

Denham, T., J. Golson, and P. Hughes 2004 Reading Early Agriculture at Kuk Swamp, Wahgi Valley, Papua New Guinea: the Archaeological Features (Phases 1–3). *Proceedings of the Prehistoric Society* 70:259–297.

Diamond, J. 1997 *Guns, Germs, and Steel*. Jonathan Cape, London.

Dolfini, A. 2008 *Making Sense of Technological Innovation: the Adoption of Metallurgy in Prehistoric Central Italy*. Unpublished PhD dissertation, University of Cambridge.

Harrisson, T. 1958 The Caves of Niah: a History of Prehistory. *Sarawak Museum Journal* 8 (n.s. 12): 549–595.

Hayden, B. 1990 Nimrods, Pescators, Pluckers, and Planters: the Emergence of Food Production. *Journal of Anthropological Archaeology* 9:31-69.

Hayden, B. 2003 Were Luxury Foods the First Domesticates? Ethnoarchaeological Perspectives from Southeast Asia. *World Archaeology* 34:458–469.

Henshilwood, C., and C. Marean 2003 The Origin of Modern Human Behavior. *Current Anthropology* 44(5): 627–651.

Higham, T., H. Barton, C. Turney, G., C. Bronk Ramsey, and F. Brock 2008 Radiocarbon Dating of Charcoal from Tropical Sequences: Results from the Niah Great Cave, Sarawak, and Their Broader Implications. *Journal of Quaternary Science* 24, 189–197.

Hunt, C., and G. Rushworth 2005 Cultivation and Human Impact at 6000 cal yr BP in Tropical Lowland Forest at Niah, Sarawak, Malaysian Borneo. *Quaternary Research* 64 (3):460–468.

Hunt, H., M. vander Linden, X. Liu, G. Motuzaite-Matuzviciute, S. Colledge, and M. Jones 2008 Millets across Eurasia: Chronology and Context of Early Records of the Genera *Panicum* and *Setaria* from Archaeological Sites in the Old World. *Vegetation History and Archaeobotany* 17: s5–s18.

Knapp, A. B. (editor) 1992 *Archaeology,* Annales*, and Ethnohistory*. Cambridge University Press, Cambridge.

Johnson, M. 2010 *Archaeological Theory: an Introduction*. Second edition, Wiley-Blackwell, Chichester.

Krigbaum, J. 2005 Reconstructing Human Subsistence in the West Mouth (Niah Cave, Sarawak) Burial Series using Stable Isotopes of Carbon. *Asian Perspectives* 44 (1):73–89.

Kristiansen, K., and M. Rowlands 1998 *Social Transformations in Archaeology: Global and Local Perspectives*. Routledge, London.

Lemmonier, P. 1992 *Elements for an Anthropology of Technology*. Museum of Anthropology Anthropological Papers, University of Michigan, Ann Arbor.

Lemmonier, P. 1993 *Technological Choices: Transformations in Material Culture Since the Neolithic*. Routledge, London.

Lloyd-Smith, L. 2008 *Chronologies of the Dead: Later Prehistoric Burial Practice at the Niah Caves, Sarawak*. Unpublished PhD dissertation, University of Cambridge.

Lucas, G. 2008 Time and the Archaeological Event. *Cambridge Archaeological Journal* 18(1):59–65.

McBrearty S., and A. Brooks 2000 The Revolution That Wasn't: A New Interpretation of the Origins of Modern Human Behavior. *Journal of Human Evolution* 39:453–563.

McBurney, C. 1967 *The Haua Fteah in Cyrenaica and the Stone Age of the South-East Mediterranean*. Cambridge University Press, Cambridge.

Mellars, P. 1989 Technological Changes and the Middle-Upper Palaeolithic Transition: Economic, Social and Cognitive Perspectives. In *The Human Revolution*, edited by P. Mellars and C. Stringer, pp. 338–365. Edinburgh University Press, Edinburgh.

Mellars, P. 1996 Symbolism, Language, and the Neanderthal Mind. In *Modelling the Human Mind*, edited by P. Mellars and K. Gibson, pp. 15–32. McDonald Institute for Archaeological Research, Cambridge.

Mellars, P. 2006 A New Radiocarbon Revolution and the Dispersal of Modern Humans in Eurasia. *Nature* 439:931–935.

Mellars, P. 2007 Rethinking the Human Revolution: Eurasian and African Perspectives. In *Rethinking the Human Revolution: New Behavioral and Biological Perspectives on the Origin and Dispersal of Modern Humans*, edited by P. Mellars, K. Boyle, O. Bar-Yosef, and C. Stringer, pp. 1–11. McDonald Institute of Archaeological Research, Cambridge.

Moore, A., G. Hillman, and A. Legge 2000 *Village on the Euphrates: from Foraging to Farming at Abu Hureyra*. Oxford University Press, Oxford.

Moreland, J. 2001 *Archaeology and Text*. Duckworth, London.

Morwood, M., and P. van Oosterzee 2007 *The Discovery of the Hobbit*. Random House Australia, Milsons Point.

Moyer, C. 2003 *The Organisation of Lithic Technology in the Middle and Early Upper Palaeolithic Industries at the Haua Fteah, Libya*. Unpublished PhD thesis, University of Cambridge.

Nadel, D., E. Weiss, O. Simchoni, A. Tsatskin, A. Danin, and M. Kislev 2004 Stone Age Hut in Israel Yields World's Oldest Remains of Bedding. *Proceedings of the National Academy of Sciences* 101 (17):6821–6826.

Pfaffenberger, B. 1992 Social Anthropology of Technology. *Annual Review of Anthropology* 21: 491–516.

Rabett, R., and G. Barker 2007 Through the Looking Glass: New Evidence on the Presence and Behavior of Late Pleistocene Humans at Niah Cave, Sarawak, Borneo. In *Rethinking the Human Revolution: New Behavioral and Biological Perspectives on the Origins and Dispersal of Modern Humans*, edited by P. Mellars, C. Stringer, O. Bar-Yosef, and K. Boyle, pp. 411–424. McDonald Institute for Archaeological Research, Cambridge.

Schmidt, K. 2001 Göbekli Tepe, Southeastern Turkey. A Preliminary Report. *Paléorient* 26:45–54.

Sherratt, A. 1997 Climatic Cycles and Behavioral Revolutions: The Emergence of Modern Humans and the Beginning of Farming. *Antiquity* 71:271–287.

Sofaer Derevenski, J. 2000 Rings of Life: the Role of Early Metalwork in Mediating the Gendered Life Course. *World Archaeology* 31:389–406.

Trinkaus, E. 2005 Early Modern Humans. *Annual Review of Anthropology* 34:207–230.

Whittle, A. 1996 *Europe in the Neolithic: the Creation of New Worlds*. Cambridge University Press, Cambridge.

Index

Abingdon (site) 79
Abu Hureya (site) 226
Acheulean 32
Adams, Robert 121
Aegean 122–123
Africa 221–222, 224–225
agency: historical process and 3–4, 9, 151, 154,
    200; history overwhelming 200; prehistoric
    61, 70–71, 97; short-term and 220; social
    continuity and 152; structural practices and
    4, 7, 9
agriculture, origins of 94, 225–226
agropastoralist 89
alcohol 102, 207; *see also* wine
Alicante region 90, 92
Amazons 12, 133–141, 145–148
America era (1787–1840) 201, 211
Americans 201, 205, 212
Amiens 154
amphorae 104, 145, 169, 174
anatomically modern humans 221–224
ancestors 34, 139, 173–174
Annales: emphasis on the long-term 3, 5; events
    3, 51, 118; mentalities 51; problem history 119
Antarctica 34
Antiquity 102, 121, 126, 127, 144, 224,
    227, 233
aquatic resources 57
aqueduct 126
Archaic Era 124

architecture 62, 95, 104, 105, 127, 153–154, 156,
    172, 209
argonaut 89, 90, 94, 96
Argos: city of 105, 120–121, 123–124, 126–130;
    Plain 121–124, 128–129
Aristocracy 125–126
Aristotle 50, 106
Arnold, Bettina 146
Aron, Raymond 61–62
Arthur, Paul 171
Ascott-under-Wychwood (site) 78, 81–82
assemblages: ceramic 202; as events 69,
    191–193; faunal 40; grave goods 110;
    landscape 193–195, 197; lithic 37, 39; mobile
    191; of objects 191;
    temporal-spatial 10
Atlantic 31, 91, 220, 228, 233
Aurignacian 222–223
aurochs 55, 57, 58, 226
Australasia 135, 224
Azilian 32, 37–41, 43

Bailey, Geoff 69
Balkans 49, 54, 55, 58, 59, 229
Barrett, John 118
Bastille, taking of 8, 10
Bataille, George 62
Bayesian statistics 71, 75, 79, 81, 83
becoming 49, 191
behavioral modernity 221–222, 224–225

Belsk (site) 142, 144, 148

berdaches 145

Bergson, Henri 62

Bintliff, John 139, 147

Black Sea steppe 134

Bloch, Marc 51, 83

Blombos cave (site) 222

Boëda, Eric 32

Boeotia 120

Bolshevik 69

Borneo 222–224, 227

boundaries 27, 190, 193–197

Bradley, Richard 228

Branigan, Keith 160

Braudel, Fernand 3, 35, 43, 50–51, 69, 130, 220

Britain: Roman 154, 157, 160–161; southern 70–71, 78–80

Bronze Age: Greek 122; Heuneburg 103; Millarian 94; volcanic eruptions 182

bucrania 55

built environment 90, 92–93, 107, 111

burials: Amazon 139 (141, 145); animal remains and 55; cave 93; central 109–110; child 31; dating of 73, 82; disarticulated 55, 57; elite 102, 124; group 55, 58; kurgans 140–141, 144; as material narratives 61; monumental 109; mounds 102–103, 112; pre-Neolithic/ Neolithic practices 227–228; position 58; rites 55, 58; secondary 109; single 59; warrior 133, 141, 145; *see also* graves

butterfly effect 118

Byzantine Empire 121, 127–128

Caesar 135–136, 154–155

calibration curve 74–75

Calvino, Italo 130

Campania 168–169, 175

Cantabrian region 89

capitalism 12, 203–204

Casa dei Quadretti teatrali 170

causewayed enclosures 71, 78–83, 93

cauterization 139, 141–142

cave art 31, 221

Celtic architects 105

cemetery 139, 144, 232

central places: Argos as 121–122, 126, 128–129; Heuneburg as 103

ceramics: Attic 101–102, 104, 108, 111–112; Cardial ware 90, 92–93, 96; Creamware 208; Pearlware 208; Whiteware 208

chaîne opératoire 36–37, 39, 42

chaos theory 117

charcoal 33, 222, 223, 232

Childe, Gordon 159, 225–226, 229

childhood 158, 202

Christians 127, 168, 232

chronicle history 50

citizenship: America 201, 205; Roman 155

civic works 126

Clark, Grahame 233

class conflict 126

class consciousness 201

climate change 32–34, 42, 225, 231

Collingwood, Robin 61, 135–136, 145, 147

colonial encounters 90, 94–95

colonization: Greek 133, 141; maritime 90; Neolithic 90, 92, 95; Pleistocene 221; Roman 175; Spain 89

commodification 204, 229

complex society 121, 123

complexity theory 117, 118, 121

conjuncture, structural 32, 35, 42–43, 51–52, 69, 220

conspicuous consumption 133, 229

Cook, James (Captain) 8, 52, 135, 146

Copper Age 93, 96, 229–230

Cotswold long cairn (site) 75

Cotswolds region 80, 82

Cova de la Sarsa (site) 93

Cova de L'Or (site) 92–93

Crickley Hill (site) 71, 82

cross-dressing 69, 134

Danube Gorges 54–55, 57–58

Danube Plain 103, 106

dating methods, accuracy of 34, 43, 183

Davis-Kimball, Jeannine 139, 141

de Waele, Jos 173

Delueze, Gilles 49, 62–63

Democracy: Greek 125; modern 201, 205

dendrochronology 70, 75, 79, 104, 106, 182
Denmark 184, 228
determinism 52, 118, 180
Dickens, Charles 203
Dietler, Michael 102
division of labor 37
Dnieper River 136, 140–142, 144
Dolfini, Andrea 229–230
domesticates, introduction of 54, 71
domestication: 225, 228
Don River 133, 136, 137
Dragsholm (site) 228
Durkheim, Émile 51

Ebro River 110
El Kowm Basin 32
Elizavetovskoe (site) 141
emplotment 50
English Heritage 78, 84
Epicurean atomism 62
epigraphy 170, 173, 152,
    156, 160
epitaph 157–159
Ertebølle culture 228
Etruscans 104, 158, 172–173
events: accidental basis of 3, 135; archaeology
    of 6, 8, 18, 27, 111, 197; boundaries of 6–8;
    causation of 180; contingency of x, 5, 50,
    53, 61, 152; criticism of Sewellian 9, 49, 52,
    134–135, 162, 180, 200; defined 4–6, 18, 49,
    68–69, 189–190, 200; historical process and
    6, 152; inside/outside of 63, 135–136, 145,
    147; long-term change and 5; memory and
    10; microhistory and 53; narrative and 54;
    phenomenal change and 62; premodern 12;
    probability distribution of, 23; relation to
    objects 191; representation of 19–21, 51–52;
    reversibility of 10; scale of 63; sequence
    of 79, 90, 162; as singularity 50, 63; social
    context of, 30, 181; structures and 10–11, 51,
    89, 118, 135; temporality of 6, 8–11, 22, 70;
    unpredictable nature of 53, 117; unique 52,
    61; versus happenings/occurrences 50, 68,
    89, 134
event aversive behavior 23, 27
event contagious behavior 23, 27

event driven research 61, 159, 181,
    183–184, 190
event neutral behavior 23, 27
event plot 24–25
event space 19
event standardized behavior 23, 27
eventful analysis 6–9, 88
eventful objects 190, 194–195, 197
eventful sociology 4, 200
everyday life 31, 156, 162, 170, 204–205
exchange, long distance 31–32, 41–42

facies 32–33
Farges, Arlette 30–31
fatalism 52, 62
Febve, Lucien 51, 83
Federalist system 205
Federal-style 209
feudalism 102, 107
fibulae 104, 110–111
Figes, Orlando 69
Fiorelli, Giuseppi 172–173
Five Points (site) 202–203, 212
formal modeling 71, 73
fortifications 101–108, 123, 128, 142, 231
Foucault, Michel 7, 62
France 101, 105, 153–154
freedom 134, 199–201, 204–207, 211–212
Friedman, Jonathan 146
Furet, François 35
Fürstengräber 102
Fürstensitze 101–102
Fussell's Lodge (site) 78, 82

Gaul 154, 155, 161
Geertz, Clifford 52
Gela (site) 105
Gelonus (site) 142
gender: performance of 133–134;
    relations among American Indians 145; roles
    139, 145, 157, 201; structures 135, 158
genetic bottleneck 182
Germany, sites in southwest 32, 101–102
Gersbach, Egon 103–104, 107–108
Giddens, Anthony: regionalism 9–10; theory of
    structuration 4, 135

Giessübel-Talhau (site) 109–110
Ginzburg, Carlo 53
Glanum (site) 154
Göbekli Tepe (site) 226
Gould, Stephen Jay 117–118
graves: chambered 102, 109; continuity in 228;
    as event 69, 190–192; gender in 140, 144;
    goods 109–110, 140, 144–145, 190, 228, 230;
    markers 157, 228; as object 190; rich 123;
    shaft 123–124; see also burials
Greek colonies 102, 142, 146, 154
Greenland 34
Greenwich Village 202, 212
Grenjaðarstaður (site) 193
Grotte Chavet 31, 33
Grotte Cosquer 31
Guattari, Felix 49, 62–63

Habermas, Jürgen 60
Hadrian, Roman Emperor 126, 160–161
Hallstatt 101–104, 110
Hambledon Hill (site) 71, 79
Hangest, archaeological site 38–40
Hanks, Bryan 140, 141, 145–146
Harrison, Tom & Barbara 222–223
Hartog, François 140
Hastings, Battle of 18
Haua Fteah cave (site) 224–225
Hawai'i 8, 52, 135
Hay Hollow Valley 20
Hecataeus of Miletus 102
Hell Trench, Niah cave 222
Hellenistic 126, 174
Herculaneum 12, 166, 168–169
heretics 53
Herodotus 102, 134, 136–140, 142, 146
Herrenhäuser 107
Heuneburg hillfort (site) 101–112
Hippocrates 134, 137–142
historical analysis 6–7, 50
historical determinism 52, 61
historical memory 4, 10, 34, 62
historical intentionality 50
historiography 7, 51, 53, 151
historizication 34
history, uncertainty in 52–53, 62

Hodder, Ian 50
Hohmichele (site) 109–112
Homo floresiensis 224
horncore 58
House of the Faun 174
hunter-gather 30, 32, 40, 89–90, 94, 226

Iberia 89–90, 92–96, 110, 153
ice core 34, 182, 185
Iceland 183, 193
ideal types (Weberian) 53
identity: agency and 63; Amazonian 134; ethnic
    147, 201; gendered 201, 203; group 82, 146;
    object 22; Roman 156
imports 102, 104, 108, 110, 112
Ingold, Tim 70–71
inhumations: 54, 57–59, 110, 189
interments: 55, 102–103
Ireland 78, 80
Iron Age 101–107, 110, 124, 139, 146, 152, 154
irrigation 231–232
Island Southeast Asia 223, 227–228
Italy 32, 95, 103, 110, 154, 157–158, 168, 175, 229

Jamaica, Queens 204, 206, 211
Japan 69, 133, 184
Jeffersonian ideal 205
Jurdejevic, Velimer 18

Kafka, Franz 62–63
Kelly, Joan 156
Khirbat Faynan (site) 232
Kimmig, Wolfgang 104–105
King Manor, Queens (site) 204–212
King, Rufus 204–207, 211
Knap Hill (site) 80
knapping process 38, 40, 42
Kuk (site) 227
Kurz, Siegfried 103
Kwinter, Sanford 62
l'histoire événementielle 10–11, 69
La Sarga (site) 92
La Tène 102
labor: commodification of 204, 212; communal
    106; corvée 106; division of 37; free 205–206,
    209; household 207; markets 138, 201;

relations 9; routines 207; systems of 211;
    unskilled 105
laborers 202, 205–207, 209–212
Ladder of Progress 221, 225
Ladurie, Emmanuel Le Roy 119
landowner 126
landscape: as assemblage 193–195, 197;
    becoming of 196; erosion 231; features
    189–190; mortuary 101, 110; mosaic
    223; resilience of 195; ritualized 92–93;
    transformation of 89, 96, 232; tundra 40;
    working 208
Last Glacial Maximum 226, 228
le Closeau (Azilian site) 40–41
Le Goff, Jacques 51
Lenin, Vladimir death of, 69
Lepenski Vir (site) 54–59
Lerna (site) 122
Levant 221, 226, 231
Lévi-Strauss, Claude 53
lithics: Azilian 38; Bellosian 41–42; Dabban
    blade industry 224–225; Flores 224;
    Magdalenian 37–39, 42; production of 32, 35
lithic analysis 36
Lloyd, Geoffery 51
London 154
long barrow 72, 75, 80–81
long-term, constraints of 119
long-term processes 3, 50, 161, 220
longue durée 5, 11, 35, 69, 83, 124, 175, 220–221
Los Millares culture 94, 96
Luang Bua cave (site) 222
Lucas, Gavin 10, 70
luxury goods 104, 108, 142, 227

macrohistory 41, 88–89
Magdalenenberg, burials in 110
Magdalenian 32–33, 37–42
Maiuri, Amedeo 172
mammoth ivory 31
marginal environment 183
Marx, Karl 12, 35, 146, 204
Mas D'Is (site) 93
Massacre: Argos 125; Amazons 136, 138;
    Wayland's Smithy 78
Massalia 101–102, 104–105, 110–112

McBurney, Charles 224–225
McDonald Institute for Archaeological
    Research 219–220
McTaggart, John 70
medium-term 34, 41, 121, 124–126, 128, 220
mentality (mentalité): Annales notion of 49, 51,
    220; criticism of 51–52; representation
    versus 61,
Mesolithic 22, 49, 54–55, 57–59, 61, 89–90,
    92, 228
metallurgy 221, 229–230
Mexico 184
microhistory 13, 49, 52–53, 62–63, 175
migration: frequency of 23; herd 22; routes 32;
    reindeer 32, 40; sturgeon 58
Millett, Martin 154, 156
Minoan civilization 182
modernity 152, 204
Morris, Simon Conway 118
mortuary: domain 54; landscape 101, 110 ritual
    109; structures 82
Morwood, Mike 224
Mt. Vesuvius 166
mudbrick construction technique 101, 104–107
Múli (site) 193
multi-scalar analysis 120
Munigua (site) 153
Mycenae (site) 123
Mycenaean civilization 123–124
myths, foundational 138, 146

Narr, Karl 101
narratives: archaeological 49, 51, 152, 161;
    contact 145; event and 17; grand 61, 161, 200;
    historical 11–12, 35, 49, 63, 159, 161, 175;
    theory 52
natural disasters 12, 181
natural selection 62
Neanderthals 221–222
Near East 223, 225–226, 228–229
neckring 109–110
neo-Darwinian 61
neolithic: argonauts 89; burials 57–58;
    colonization 90, 92, 95; communities 54;
    cultural repertoire 54, 58; evidence of 93–95;
    farmers 225–228; Greek 121; mentalities

58; Mesolithic- 49, 54–55, 58–59, 61, 92;
metallurgy 229; Pre-Pottery Neolithic A 55,
226; Pre-Pottery Neolithic B 32, 226–227;
in southern Britain 78–79; spread of 58;
transition 70, 79, 89–90, 96; way of life 54
New York City 201–205, 212
Niah cave (site) 222–224, 227–228
non-event 9, 48, 200–201, 212
North Africa 224–225, 231

Ockham's razor 89, 94
Ohalo (site) 226
optimal foraging theory 40
Ordzhonikidze (site) 141
Ottoman period 128
Ottoman rulers 129

pagan temple 127
Paleolithic: events 31; Late 33, 95; Middle 32–33,
225; temporality in 34; Upper 13, 21, 32–34,
40–41;
palimpsest 61, 69, 101, 195
Paris Basin 32, 33, 36–38, 40–41
patchiness, representation of 20
path dependent 88, 111
Peak Camp (site) 82
Penàguila river 93
Penthesilea 140
Phocaeans 102
Pincevent (site) 32, 40–41
Pla de Petracos (site) 92
Pliny the Younger 166, 168
pollution 232
Pompeii 12, 166–175, 184, 193
portable art 40
postprocessual archaeology 3, 147, 151,
157, 220
processual archaeology 151, 220
public buildings 104, 125–127, 129,
153–155, 160
punctuated equilibrium 117–118

radiocarbon dating 70, 73, 222
ramparts: at Belsk 142–144; at Heuneburg 103
red deer 55–60, 228
reindeer 22, 31–32, 40

religious specialists 134
resources: in Giddens 4; materiality of 4, 142,
146–147
respectability 203
revolution, metropolitan 201
Rhine Valley 32, 41, 103, 161
Ricoeur, Paul 49–53, 61–63
Robb, John 70
Robin Hood's Ball (site) 82
rock art 92
Roman provinces 152–157
romanization 152, 154, 156–158, 161–162
Rome 155, 160, 168–170, 173–175
Rostovtzeff, Mikhail 139
ruptures: historical 7; isolated 181; search
for 182; sequence of 162; social 108–109;
structural 5, 8–10, 96
Russian Revolution 68–69
Russian steppes 133, 140

sacrifice, horse 137, 141
sago 223, 227
Saguntum (site) 153
Sahlins, Marshall: description of Captain Cook
8, 52, 135, 146; events and 109, 134
Saint Petersburg 69
Saint-Pierre-les-Martigues (site) 105
Sauromatian tribes 136–138
schemas: ephemeral 9; role in structure 4–5;
Sahlins and 135, 146
Schliemann, Heinrich 169
Scythia 140
Second Punic War 153
Serpis valley 90–91, 93
service network 21
shaman 134
shamanistic transformations 55
Shefton, Brian 108
shells 31–32, 41, 59, 92, 222
skeletal sexing 140, 145
skeleton 75, 109, 190, 221
slave trade 146–147
slaveowner 211
slavery 129, 147, 201, 207, 211–212
slaves, emancipation of 138, 142, 205, 207, 209
Slaves, emancipation of 205

Slofstra, Jan 161

smelting 229–230, 232

social evolution 62, 107, 152

social group, kin-based 83, 103

social inequality 31, 145, 205

social networks 41, 83, 204

Southeast Asia 222–224, 227–228

spatial representation: grid-based 20; vector-based 21

specialization 144, 201

St. Lawrence River 184

Star Carr (site) 55

structures: analysis of 6; as attractors 118; defined 4–5; disruption of 5–6, 10, 12; durability of 6, 10; gendered 134, 158; as ideology 7, 190; innovation of 8–9; maintenance of 10; materiality of 4–5, 9, 142; narrative 161; networks of 5; plurality of 4–5, 111; political 155, 159, 162; super- 12; transformation of 4–6, 9–10, 31, 34, 36–37, 50, 109, 181

structuration 4, 41, 135

subsistence strategy 20, 35, 95, 135, 145, 223

subsistence catchment 121

Suður-Þingeyarsýsla 193

Swabia 101, 103, 106

symbolic system 31

symmetrical analysis 134

Syria 32, 226, 231

Taforalt (site) 222

Tardiglacial 34, 37, 43

Tarquinia (site) 158

temporalities: *Annales* 5, 35, 50–51, 220; climatic 34; duration and 49, 51, 62–63; of change 5, 43; of events 6, 9–11, 21, 88–89, 109; human 34; integration of 7–8, 35, 118, 220; marking 104; materiality and 9–11, 62, 64, 191–192; representation of 19; resolution of 8, 11; as sequence 70; of sites 34; of social life 175

tephrochronology 70, 194

texts: archaeology and 139, 154, 170; historical 11; individual in 146; literary 50; as sources 89, 156, 158, 160–161; tyranny of 110

Þegjendadalur 193, 195–197

Thomas, Nicholas 135

Thugga (site) 158

time: capsule 173; change through, 20, 202; different scales, 161, 220; frozen in, 170, 174; measurement of, 8, 19, 194; modeling of, 22; moment in, 96, 172; period of 5, 7, 184; scale of event 10–11, 24–25, 27, 128, 191; scale of individual 146;

Tiryns (site) 122–123

Titus, Roman Emperor, disasters during reign 168

Tripolitian pre-desert 231–232

Tsarist autocracy 68–69

tumulus 103, 109–111

Twain, Mark 137–138

Valencia 91, 95

Venice, Republic of 128

Verberie (site) 21–22

Verulamium (site) 154, 160

Veynes, Paul 31

Vidal de la Blache, Paul 119

Vlasac (site) 54, 58

volcanic eruptions: Hekla 182; Laki fissure 183; Mt. Vesuvius 12, 169–170, 175–176; Santorini 182; Tambora 183–184 Toba supervolcano 181–182

volcanic winter 181–182

vulnerability to disruptive events 181, 184

Wadi Faynan 231

Wahl, Joachim 108–109

Wall, Diana 201–202

Wayland's Smithy (site) 78, 82

Weber, Max 53, 204

West Kennet (site) 78, 80–82

Wiltshire region 78, 80, 82

Windmill Hill (site) 80–81

wine (*see also* alcohol) 102, 104, 108, 142, 145, 169, 207, 231

Woolf, Greg 161

working class 202–203

workshops, flint 41

Yamin, Rebecca 201–203

Younger Dryas 34, 41, 226